COCKNEY GIRL

To Judy.

with warmest regards

Enda Haber

Cockney Girl

2/23/ 2014

First published in Great Britain in 2012 by The Derby Books Publishing Company Limited, 3 The Parker Centre, Derby, DE21 4SZ.

ISBN 978-1-78091-003-1
Printed and bound by CPI Antony Rowe, Chippenham.

COCKNEY GIRL
GILDA MOSS HABER, PHD

To the memory of Anne Frank, my contemporary.

For my children Yael Ash, Elisheva Shira and Jonathan Haber,
and to my grandchildren

CONTENTS
*Published and or honourable mention

8th June, 1946

To-day, as we celebrate victory, I send this personal message to you and all other boys and girls at school. For you have shared in the hardships and dangers of a total war and you have shared no less in the triumph of the Allied Nations.

I know you will always feel proud to belong to a country which was capable of such supreme effort; proud, too, of parents and elder brothers and sisters who by their courage, endurance and enterprise brought victory. May these qualities be yours as you grow up and join in the common effort to establish among the nations of the world unity and peace.

George R.I.

THE RT. HON. SIR MARTIN GILBERT, C.B.E., DLITT.

9 LYSANDER GROVE
LONDON N19 3QY

Dear Sir:

I have recently had the opportunity to read Gilda Haber's delightful and thoughtful memoir *Cockney Girl*. Written in the voice of an adult looking back over many decades to a way of life that is now part of history, she has brought to life with vivid evocations a remarkable 'lost' world.

I do hope that you will be able to find the time to read what she has written, and consider it for publication. I am sure that a wide readership will be as entranced as I was.

yours sincerely,

Martin Gilbert

PART 1
PRE-WAR ENGLAND
1934-1939

CHAPTER 1
5 NOVEMBER 1934 AUNT MITZI

Monday 5 November 1934

As Daddy burst through the downstairs door, a blast of East London November wind and fog whistled up the staircase like a white, evil genie. 'Minnie,' Daddy shouted. 'Where are you? I've brought you a present!'

'In the living room,' Mummy muttered, knowing he couldn't hear.

In our living room, Mummy and I sat on our used blue Persian carpet before a crackling red fire, our faces flushed with heat. Squinting through the eye of a glittering needle, Mummy sucked the wool's end flat, poised, and then pushed the wool through the needle's empty eye. She stretched Daddy's sock and its hole over a wooden 'mushroom', her darns as taut as the French tapestries hanging in the museum where Daddy had taken me last Sunday.

Daddy's footsteps grew louder.

I ran from the hot living room to our cold third floor landing and now shivering, pressed my face through the banister bars as my young father bounded up the stairs two at a time.

Daddy didn't notice me. I was five, but a part-ghost child, visible only when my parents chose to see or speak to me. 'Children should be seen and not heard.' 'Children may not ask questions. Just do as you're told.' 'Children should not ask for food.' 'Children may not shout,' Mummy often said. Since Daddy was deaf, and children must not shout, I couldn't speak to him. A barber, Daddy spoke to me only on the few occasions he took me to The Museum of Natural History or to Houndsditch hairdressers' wholesalers to buy a new open razor, cigarettes or condoms for sale in our shop. Beneath the twirling red, white and blue barber pole a sign read 'Alf's Ladies and Gents Hairdressers.'

'Minnie,' Daddy shouted again as he drew near our third floor flat.

As the sound of his voice grew closer, Mummy muttered, 'Why does a deaf man shout?'

I thought that since Daddy couldn't hear himself speak, he never knew when he was speaking loudly. Was his a world as silent as when thick, white snow blanketed our grimy East London streets, smothering all sound?

Daddy's head grew larger until he sprang onto our yellowed, linoleum landing. We rented our flat: a kitchen, living room and bedroom, all left of a skinny corridor, from the Michaels' family. Three floors below us the Michaels' narrow, corner grocery shop and kitchen squatted. Whenever I passed their kitchen on the way upstairs, I saw her three big boys, dressed in black, hunched over fat Hebrew books. The Michaels' crooked grocery shop reminded me of the witch's hut in Hansel and Gretel, and fitted snugly like a jigsaw puzzle into the corner of East London's Vallance Road and Cheshire Street. I imagined that we lived, not in a forest of trees, like Hansel and Gretel, but in a forest of dank, skinny East End houses, some of them like the Michaels' tall, three-story house, at the bottom, their tiny, witch-like shop.

A shout from below drew me to the window.

Through our sooty third-floor window, I saw on the dark, corner street pavement, dancers black-silhouetted against red flames, prancing around a straw-stuffed Guy Fawkes' effigy. They'd dressed the dummy in a tramp's clothes and hat. We'd learned in school about the traitor Guy Fawkes' plot to overthrow the King. I ran back to the living room expecting Daddy.

Daddy strode into the living room. Hugging Mumfie, my grey velvet elephant doll, I smiled shyly at my father, but he didn't notice me. Unable to shout at home, I was a silent, but watchful child, and unlike Daddy, I could hear; so I listened to and hoarded every sound, in case like him, when I became eight, I'd also become deaf.

'Black Magic chocolates for our sixth anniversary,' Daddy said triumphantly, offering Mummy the silky black box.

Mummy dropped her needle onto the old, Persian blue carpet, a cast-off from her own mother, the arch-matriarch, my grandmother, Booba. The needle glinted wickedly, brown wool streaming from it like a string of hard words. A skillful darner, Mummy didn't, like most women, knot the end of her wool. But no knot at the end of the wool in her needle made me think there was no end to her anger with Daddy.

'Chocolates!' she again shouted at him, as though he'd committed some crime.

She was allowed to shout.

She turned to me as if he weren't there. 'For six years, I told him I like Jordan Almonds, and he still brings me chocolates. I could scream myself purple in the face, and he wouldn't bring me sugared almonds. Sugared almonds even cost less!'

Even though she said she liked sugared almonds better, Mummy snatched the box of Black Magic from him and ripped open its black, cardboard lid. Inside the lid were drawn the shape of each chocolate and under each shape, was written the filling. Black Magic Chocolates held two of every filling except there was only one diamond-shaped and that was filled with marzipan. Did she know that one was *my* favourite?

I stared longingly at the diamond marzipan. But children must not ask for anything.

'I won three quid on the dogs,' Daddy grinned, snapping three green, crackly King George V pounds in the air.

Mummy dropped the box of chocolates to the floor. I watched the diamond-shaped marzipan sitting snug in its little crinkled paper. Legs tucked beneath her on the frayed carpet, she went back to darning Daddy's sock. Hot coals danced with red, blue and purple flames like those outside devouring Guy Fawkes' clothes and straw hair. Daddy warmed his hands at our fire and then threw off his jacket and unbuttoned his tight little satin-backed waistcoat. Y-shaped suspenders stretched across his strong shoulders. Daddy and his brother-in-law, Izzy, were both amateur boxers. They'd taken lessons at the local Jewish Boys' Club.

'This time you won; how many times have you lost?' Mummy shouted, shaking her forefinger at his black satin back as he left the living room and strutted down the yellowed linoleum to our bedroom. I followed him, smoothing Mumfie's schoolboy shirt, tie and short trousers, and his velvet trunk. I'd adored the children's book, *Mumfie,* and blonde Aunt Mitzi, Mummy's younger sister, whom I also adored, had given me Mumfie, the doll, as a present.

Daddy's little black moustache twitched up with his mouth like Errol Flynn's; a thick, glossy lock of Brylcreemed hair fell into his dark eyes. His father, Hyman Moscovitch, gunsmith, had escaped Russian pogroms and the 25-year – Daddy said – Russian army conscription. Daddy, Mummy and I had all been born in East London. Mummy told me I'd been born in Stepney

Green Hospital and had torn her womb, whatever that was. I stared at Daddy, wishing he'd talk to me, but he almost never spoke to me at home. Still, I could look, couldn't I?

Like many children of Russian Jews, Daddy's dark eyes set in pale skin were full with silent feelings. I had his dark hair and pale skin. Mummy often said that because I was so pale, I ought to be in country air, and sent me away 'for my health,' but I was strong and loved London: the fogs, every step of London's cobbles and open air markets and my elementary Wood Close School. I adored my teacher Mr Kent, my best friend Joycey Kennel, daytime, the clop of cart horses, night-time alone while my parents worked in the shop opposite, the hoot of nearby trains, the docks' crooning foghorns. I enjoyed visits to my steely Booba, loving Zada, teasing uncles and glamorous Aunt Mitzi. It was a shame that Mummy hated her younger sister, Aunt Mitzi. I could not cuddle my aunt in front of Mummy. If Aunt Mitzi hugged and kissed me, I couldn't help it, could I? I stood behind Daddy in our bedroom. I liked watching him.

Daddy dropped a silver shilling into the metal gas meter on the floor, not hearing the clang as it hit bottom. He struck a match on the wall, lit a long taper, and held it to the two gas lights, one at each end above the carved rosewood mantelpiece. A cheery small fire burned in the bedroom fireplace grate. As he turned the gaslights' little handles, I waited for a whiff and small rush of gas. Then 'Pop!' gaslight shone softly through our bedroom. Daddy tucked his winning pound notes into his pocket, sighed happily, and opened his library book, *King Solomon's Mines.* Leaning book and elbows on our mantlepiece, he immediately escaped into his world of adventure. I stared at his back.

Daddy stood only about five foot eight, a common height for an East Londoner, but every morning he tugged straight heavy, round, metal springs nailed to the bedroom wall. His arm muscles swelled into tight balls and then, when he let go, the straight metal springs twanged back into flat circles against the wall. I admired the way he sprang up our steps and when he ran swift as a greyhound after Fascist children who shoved open our barbershop door jangling the shop bell screaming so he would hear, 'Dirty Jew!' I'd peek out of the shop door, watching the soles of Daddy's shoes flip in the air behind him until the ruffians disappeared into their slum council tenements like rats into holes. Daddy returned to his customer lying nearly flat, face slathered with shaving cream awaiting his shave.

Blissfully, now, without taking his eyes off the book, Daddy warmed his cold hands at the bedroom fire. I returned to the living room to see if the diamond-shaped marzipan was still there, imagining licking its chocolate cover and biting deep into its sweet nuttiness.

Binkie, curled in a black ball of fur, slept in front of the fire. I'd found the stray kitten with a pointy tail wobbling on tiny legs, hungry, mewling helplessly in the street for its mother. I'd broken my usual silence to beg Mummy, 'Please, please let's take her home.'

Children must wait to be offered. 'Oh, all right,' she'd grumbled.

Three red sparks flew out of the fire. Binkie leapt into the air, landed, and licked the singed spots with her tiny pink tongue, sighed, tucked her head into her body and curled back into a sleeping fur ball. Mummy threw down her darning and ran to our bedroom I always knew where Mummy was from her clacking high heels. But Daddy did not hear her.

In the bedroom I heard her shouting at Daddy, 'Did you forget we're in a depression, starving men in soup lines, and you blow money on chocolates and dog races?'

Secretly, I loved to watch leashed greyhounds prancing in the street. Their owners looked round proudly to be sure others noticed their fancy prize dogs. I imagined those slender hounds streaking around the track, lean muzzles jutting, ears flattened, four feet bunched in the centre then whipping far out, tails flying, my deaf father at the track, heart thumping with excitement and at the risk of losing and facing Mummy. But now he'd won, and Mummy was still angry with him. If only I could put my hand into his large, rough, barber's hand, and together, watch those dogs fly; if only I could tell him I admired him going to dog races, chasing Fascist ruffians and bringing Mummy chocolates.

From our coal-grimy, third-floor window, I watched old men lamplighters in grey, floor-length back-belted winter coats shuffling through swirling fog at dusk, 4 o'clock in the afternoon. They carried long sticks that they stretched up to street lampposts, feeding them gas that as at home, popped and lit night-time East London. Now lamps glowed soft yellow over narrow, cobbled streets. Some streets, Daddy had once said on the way to the museum, had been built by Romans.

Mummy came back, picked up her needle, ignoring the black box of chocolates and sank down again onto our delft blue carpet. She muttered as she swiftly thrust the needle into the sock, 'My *mazel*, my luck, I had to marry a deaf man'. 'Get married, you're 23 already, an old maid,' Mummy mimicked Booba, her own mother's harsh sarcastic voice. 'And besides, your younger sister, Mitzi, can't get married until you do.' 'But Mama,' I told her, 'I don't love him.' 'Love, shmuv, he's a barber, he's got a good trade, you'll never go hungry,' Mummy copied her own mother's hard voice. 'Well, I'll admit,' Mummy said, 'he does work, when there are customers. Many go hungry these days.'

Children must listen but say silent. Adults talked, but didn't listen, I thought.

'So I've been married for six years so that Mitzi could marry, and you think that sister of mine married? No. You know why? She's still waiting to marry her boss's son, Raphael.'

I had seen Raphael once, when Mummy and I had visited his family's posh West End lace shop on Bond Street where Aunt Mitzi was a secretary. Raphael reminded me of Claude Raines, short, dressed in a silky double-breasted suit with white cuffs and gold cufflinks. 'Very suave,' I heard Mummy say. I was surprised Aunt Mitzi loved a short man: a short, rich man.

'She can wait till *meshiach*, the messiah comes riding in on his white ass. This is one time her good looks won't help her. Raphael's family wants *nadn*; we're just a poor, East End Jewish family and only two generations British. He comes from a snobbish four-generation-British-Jewish West-End family. They can be in love from *heint bis morgen*, forever, and it won't do her any good. The only tragedy is,' Mummy said wistfully, now looking at me, 'Mitzi and Raphael really are in love. But if he marries her, his family will cut him out of the business. Both of them like money. But no money, no Raphael. Mitzi thinks her blue eyes will get her anything!'

Another secret hugged to my skinny chest was that besides admiring Daddy's love of adventure, I longed to grow up like my glamorous Aunt Mitzi: tall, blonde and beautiful. When she laughed, she sounded as if someone were tickling her, and her laughter always sent a little thrill rippling through me. I loved the way she greeted me with 'Hallo Pussycat!' and I adored her Evening in Paris perfume, and wished I could have its little blue bottle. Aunt Mitzi and Mummy were totally different, my mother small, dark-haired, cautious and timid (except with Daddy) Aunt Mitzi tall, blonde, beautiful and who loved clothes, fashion and Raphael.

But Mummy did have one passion. When we visited Booba, Mummy played Rachmaninov and Schubert on Booba's piano. At home, she played opera on our gramophone. 'I'd run away with Gigli any time,' she used to say as he sang in his soft voice, and I'd imagine them hand-in-hand running away down a grassy slope. When Mummy sang opera with the BBC, her eyes grew huge and darkened from green-gold to black, and mouth wide open, her tongue trembled like the yellow petal on an iris; her true heart and soul gushed out of her body and I couldn't tell the difference between the BBC singer's powerful voice and hers.

But Mummy also had, like her mother, Booba, a sharp, sarcastic sense of humour, and like her mother, she saved every penny, even pennies that her friends and family secretly *shtipped* me, saying, 'Don't tell Mummy. Spend it on something you like.' But the one time I had spent a sixpence, Mummy spanked me. Every penny given me had to go into my post office bank account.

Mummy had told me she hadn't wanted to marry Daddy and hadn't wanted a child, so at home I tried to be invisible. At school I was a chatterbox, walked on my hands, turned cartwheels in the playground and was the best skipper, could jump a hundred bumps, I was a fast runner like Daddy, and always top of the class. Mr Kent talked to me, and I talked to him as if I were a grown-up. I loved school and Mr Kent: a grown-up man I could talk to every school day.

As the fire crackled Mummy sighed. 'I even won a scholarship to high school. My teacher *begged* Booba to let me go. 'No, you have to work,' Booba said. So at 14, I went to work with Zada, your grandfather, in a stinking fur factory. My dear blonde *sister, M*itzi, who doesn't have half my brains, *her*, they sent to secretarial school. Then Booba made me marry your father so Mitzi could marry Raphael, and Mitzi is *still* not married. I should have waited.'

For whom? I wondered. Did she mean for Dr Baumgarten?

She bit off the wool and stabbed the pincushion with her needle. I imagined my aunt as the beautiful princess and Raphael the handsome prince, (though he was short, dark and Jewish, and all my fairy story books showed princes to be tall, blond *goyim*). I imagined Raphael's Wicked Mother as the Queen, who forbade him to marry my princess aunt under pain of cutting him out of his rightful kingdom. Or perhaps she might turn Raphael into a useless frog, or my aunt into Sleeping Beauty. Or perhaps my stern Booba was a wicked witch who forced Mummy to marry Daddy whom she didn't love so that Aunt Mitzi, the younger sister, could marry her true love, then didn't. But as usual I said nothing and hoarded every word.

'I bet I need more make-up,' Mummy said, sprang up and ran out of our living room down the corridor to the bedroom, high heels clacking. Sometimes I dreamed that the Michael's headless dummy that I had to pass on the second floor landing, with a horrid knob for a head, knobs for arms, and three little wooden legs, clacked upstairs on its three tiny legs to our third floor flat, clack, clack, and in nightmares, the little legs of the headless dummy clacked up the stairs to eat me. Its headless body reminded me of the Dreadful Mikado who might lurk below.

Mummy, as she washed dishes in the cold-water sink often sang from *The Mikado*:

Gay little Japanese
Gay little girls from Japan
We know how to dance and sing
We know how to flutter our fans
Let everyone dance and sing
Let everyone flutter our fans
We're gay little girls from – I missed the end because of the hoot of the foghorn from the docks.
Gay little girls from Japan.

Then came the part that terrified me even though Mummy smiled happily as she sang it. Perhaps it frightened me *because* she smiled as she sang it more softly, in her low voice:

Our king is the dreadful Mikado
When we're naughty he chops off our heads
So we always try to do as he tells us
For we don't want to be dead.

Since the headless dummy on the second floor landing must once have been a naughty girl whose head the dreadful Mikado had chopped off, I was very good at home. I didn't like the idea of going to school with a chopped-off head.

Now Mummy sat at her art deco dressing table and peered into its three mirrors. 'Oh God, I look like the sinking Wreck of the Hesperus,' she groaned. 'And look at my shiny nose.'

Mummy peered in the mirror. 'Mirror, mirror on the wall, who's the fairest of them all?'

I whispered in Mumfie's elephant ear. What if the mirror spoke, and said that Mummy's sister, Aunt Mitzi was fairer? Mummy said I looked like my aunt. Suppose the mirror said I was fairer? The mirror had told the Queen that Snow White was fairest and the Queen had sent Snow White far into the woods with a woodsman who was to bring back her heart. Mummy squinted at herself through gold Tartar eyes, upturned like Booba's and mine and pursed her small, full mouth. Daddy had cut her reddish-hennaed hair into a fashionable shingle, then she'd set it with little shark-toothed clips into corrugated waves, all the rage in the '30s. Cultured pearls in her ears, pierced when she was eight days old, she told me, gleamed softly in the gas light. Mummy powdered her little pug nose and painted her small, full mouth vivid red, then rubbed her lips together. Passing a comb through her hair, she reminded me of Binkie, licking herself after sparks had ruffled her fur. Mummy looked into the mirror and chanted:

Little dabs of powder
Little dabs of paint
Make a lady beautiful
When she really ain't.

I smiled, but she didn't notice me.

'I don't know why I'm putting on powder and lipstick,' she said. 'No one's coming. Still, you never know who might pop in.'

No sooner had Mummy spoken, than three sharp bangs sounded from our downstairs' lion-head iron doorknocker. No one in the East End had a telephone nor locked the front door, so people knocked and then dropped in to visit day and night.

'It's a woman,' Mummy said, listening to the sound of high heels sharply tapping wooden stairs growing louder as our visitor neared our third floor flat.

'Cooee, it's me,' Aunty Mitzi's voice sang out silvery, as her steps grew louder.

I ran to the banister, and stuck my face between its bars, excited to see her sleek, blonde head rising closer as she passed the headless dummy on the second floor.

The dummy would let *her* by.

'Speak of the devil,' Mummy muttered.

'Hallo, Minnie, hallo, Gilda,' Aunt Mitzi said, arriving on our third-floor landing.

I smiled when she called me by my name.

'Hallo, how are you? Cup of tea?' Mummy said, coolly, as soon as Aunt Mitzi appeared. Aunt Mitzi pecked Mummy's cheek. Mummy turned away and poured more water from the sink into the fat black kettle and turned up the gas. Everyone in the East End of London kept a kettle on all day and evening for possible visitors. Blue flames shot up high.

'Hello pussycat,' Aunt Mitzi said, and bent in half to hug and kiss me; I breathed in her Evening in Paris perfume and some deeper, exciting smell rushing under it. My Aunt wore her blonde hair in soft, marcel waves like Mrs Simpson. Glossy fur pompons on her coat tickled my nose and I sneezed. '*A gesint off dir yo*,' a blessing on you, Aunt Mitzi said. Zada, my furrier-grandfather had added the fur pom-poms to her sleek, black coat, which she threw onto the kitchen chair. Underneath, a violet, long-sleeved wool dress hugged her long, slender body. Breasts small and high like Mummy's, her legs were as long as those of Betty Grable whose photograph hung on a calendar in the men's section of our hairdressing shop. Betty Grable's picture gazed at us also outside the Roxy Cinema. Deaf Daddy, head deep in, eyes glued to his adventure book in the bedroom, had heard nothing.

Mummy poured some hot water into the teapot, swished the water round to warm the pot, emptied the water and spooned in one teaspoon of tea leaves for each person and one for the pot. Then she poured hot water over black leaves and covered the teapot with a tea cozy. The cozy's 'handle' was a china doll French lady wearing a high wig, cheeks rouged and the doll's huge skirt, kept the tea pot warm. Mummy laid biscuits on a plate, and put everything on a tray.

Aunt Mitzi sat on a kitchen chair and crossed long, silky legs, but kept on her leather gloves. I supposed she was still cold. Mummy carried the tray into our warm living room, where the fire still crackled. Aunt Mitzi rose, and I, carrying Mumfie, followed.

Now seated in the living room, Aunt Mitzi opened a shopping bag and handed me a book.

'Here, pussycat, I've brought you a new book of fairy tales,' Aunt Mitzi said, picking me up as if I were Binkie, sitting me on her lap and hugging me. Mummy had hugged me once. While scrubbing the hallway floor, she sat back on her heels for a moment and had said to me, 'She's so clebber,' which I supposed was how I said 'clever' when I was little, perhaps three. And then she'd hugged me. But I was not used to her hugging me and felt stiff in her arms.

'You'll be six in January,' Aunt Mitzi said. 'This is your birthday present. It's a bit early, but since I was coming round, I thought I'd give it to you. During the week I work all day, and at night, you're usually asleep. I got off early, for a Guy Fawkes party. You like the book?'

'It's beautiful,' I whispered, stroking it and smelling its real leather cover. I'd never before seen lilac leather. Tracing the gold lettering on the cover, *Hans Anderson's Fairy Tales*, I ran my finger over the gold-edged pages. 'Thank you, aunty,' and I nestled against my aunt.

'Come, sit on a chair,' Mummy told me.

We all sat on chairs in front of our fire. Unlike Booba, we had no rosewood dining room table in our living room, so shiny that the crystal vase of flowers reflected in the table.

Mummy and Aunty Mitzi held their cups and saucers in their right hands, napkins on their laps and ankles crossed, the way ladies in Mummy's Ladies' Magazine sat, and they balanced their plates with biscuits on a napkin over the left knee.

'What brings you out on such a cold night?' Mummy asked my aunt.

Aunt Mitzi pulled off a leather glove.

'This!' she said.

A diamond ring like a star on a frosty night sparkled on Aunt Mitzi's left, third finger.

'Oh,' Mummy breathed. I gasped, too.

'A real diamond! Mazltov! Congratulations. Raphael?' Mummy asked.

Tears came to Mummy's eyes, whether from happiness or jealousy I couldn't tell. She'd never had an engagement ring, only a plain gold wedding band.

'No, not Raphael. Adrian,' my aunt said quietly. 'It's no use me waiting for Raphael. His family won't let him marry anyone unless the girl has a huge dowry. I just have to accept Adrian. He knows I don't love him the way he loves me, but he wants me without love or money. He has a good government job as a chemist, so I'd better settle down. I told him I don't want to marry for two years, and he's willing to wait. And unlike Raphael's,' her face twisted in a wry smile, '*his* family is happy to have me'.

'Mummy must be overjoyed,' Mummy said, also with a trace of bitterness.

Why hadn't Booba told us, I thought. Perhaps aunty had insisted on telling us herself.

'For years, she's been nagging me to marry,' Aunt Mitzi said. 'She'd have been happier if I'd married a rich man like Raphael, but she's satisfied with Adrian.'

'All cats are grey in the dark,' Mummy murmured. 'Or so I heard,' she added.

The sisters talked a little while longer, sipping tea. Then Aunt Mitzi rose, stretched her long body, and said, 'I'd better go, or Mama will be worried. I have to be up early for work.'

'You'll still work at the lace business with Raphael, even though you're engaged to Adrian?' Mummy asked, arching her fine plucked eyebrows.

'Of course. Jobs are hard to get. I need to save for a trousseau, for furniture, bedding and china, like all brides. Besides, I want to see Raphael suffer the way I have, waiting and waiting for him. But as much as I love him, I wouldn't marry him if he were poor. If he married me, his family would cut him off, and in these times, he might not have a job. I don't want to struggle in poverty for years, as our parents did,' Aunt Mitzi said, 'so I'll marry Adrian. And you, pussycat,' she said, touching my cheek, and now smiling, 'you will be my bridesmaid.'

'A bridesmaid?' I murmured, feeling my eyes grow big with a delight I tried to hide.

The sisters, one tall, stately and blonde, the other, Mummy, small and dark, kissed each other coolly on the cheek.

While Mummy put the cups and saucers in the kitchen sink, my aunt slipped sixpence in my hand, kissed me and like all my relatives whispered in my ear, 'Don't tell Mummy'.

Everyone knew that Mummy saved every penny, every eight-sided threepenny bit and every silver sixpence given me by her friends and relatives. I'd never forget the spent sixpence on a celluloid dolly when she had put me over her knee, pulled down my knickers and smacked my bare bottom. I hated being spanked like a stupid, naughty infant. I'd shut myself in the outside toilet for hours until she came for me and tried to hug me. I wouldn't speak to her.

But I was so overjoyed at being Aunt Mitzi's bridesmaid, another secret hugged to my skinny chest in case it annoyed Mummy, that as soon as Aunt Mitzi left, I gave Mummy the sixpence to bank.

As the sound of Aunt Mitzi's high heels tapping the stairs faded, I breathed in the warm trail of her scent that still hung in the air.

'Well,' Mummy said, back in the living room, sinking down onto the blue carpet. 'What a surprise. She finally gave up on that *mamzer*, that bastard, Raphael. I have to tell your father.'

Daddy, still reading *King Solomon's Mines* that was propped on the bedroom mantelpiece didn't hear her come in.

Mummy shouted, 'Alf, you'll never believe what happened.'

Daddy tore himself away from his book and listened to Mummy's shouted news of his sister-in-law's engagement. He raised dark eyebrows and said, 'What do I care? Your family, all except for your father, a real gent, looks down on me. They can all go to hell.'

Mummy went back to the living room. I followed, hugging Mumfie. Mummy wound up the gramophone and set the needle onto the black shiny edge of the record, playing her favourite aria, 'Knowest thou, that Dear Land,' which she'd told me came from an opera called *Mignon*.

'Well, we might as well eat these,' she said, sitting down again on the carpet in front of the fire. I curled up beside her.

I thought about her saying that Daddy looked after her and she'd never have another child, and that if she had to have only one child, I should have been a boy. I couldn't help being a girl. I didn't know how to be a boy. I didn't even know how boys were different from girls except their hair was shorter. But I tried not to be in their way.

Summers and during the Christmas Rush when everyone wanted their hair done, I stayed all day with the Lyons family and their seven daughters. They all lived in the attic over our barber shop on Vallance Road across the street from the Michaels. If Mrs Lyons had a new baby, Mummy sent me to one of my 'aunts', women I'd never met, who lived in the country. 'For your health,' she said which puzzled me, because I was never ill. She'd put me on a bus and wave me goodbye with her white lace-edge hanky. I'd arrive alone in some strange place and sit on my little suitcase in the street until some strange woman came for me. The stranger said nothing; I just followed the strange woman to her strange house.

Soon it would be Christmas. I hoped I'd be able to stay with Mrs Lyons during the coming Christmas Rush. I loved snuggling between her seven breathing girls, across their brass bed instead of lying alone in my cot while my parents worked in the shop opposite the Michaels'.

'You can stay up a little longer and help me eat these,' Mummy said, biting into a chocolate, eating half and putting the other half back in its little ruffled cup of brown paper. Her small teeth marks showed lines in each chocolate where she had bitten into it. I ate the other halves: a sweet sticky cherry filling, half of a crunchy nut chocolate, a half nougat-filled chocolate. My mouth was chocolate-warm and sticky; a luxury, Mummy said, in a Depression. We were nearing the chocolate marzipan when Mummy picked the arm off the gramophone.

'Bed time,' she said.

I hoped she wouldn't eat the chocolate marzipan while I was asleep, especially since there was only one marzipan and she didn't even like chocolates.

Springing to her feet, she scattered chocolates and their tiny brown cups over the carpet.

'Oh, look what I've done, I'm so clumsy.'

I remembered Booba, my grandmother saying in her hard voice to Mummy once, '*man kakt an falt ahrein*', and Mummy blushing hotly and crying out, 'Mama, is that a nice thing to say to your eldest daughter?' Tears had filled Mummy's eyes.

On the way home from Booba's that day, I had broken my usual silence, consumed with curiosity, 'Why did Booba say '*man kakt an falt ahrein*', Mummy? What did she mean?'

'She meant that I can do no right and Mitzi can do no wrong. I get all the blame, and Mitzi gets all the praise. Well, at least, she finally got some sense into that peroxide blonde head of hers. I just hope Adrian, her new fiancé, doesn't let her down.'

As if anyone would let Aunt Mitzi down, I thought.

Mummy led me to the bedroom, pushed me onto the empty chamber pot, and after I'd pished she shoved the *tepl* under the bed with her shoe toe. No East End house had an inside lavatory, but there were plenty of public lavatories. On the rare times we all went out together, Mummy grumbled, 'Every corner your father, the *pisher*, has to stop and 'spend a penny.' I liked to drop a penny into a slot and hear the door click unlocked.

Daddy, elbows on the mantelpiece, reading, heard nothing of our conversation.

Our bedroom, on the corner of Cheshire Street and Vallance Road had a huge oak bed with inlaid red cherries on the headboard. On Mummy's and Daddy's bed lay a fat, white down comforter; an *iberbat* and two fat feather cushions for each parent lay puffed up high. Daddy slept under the window overlooking tiny, cobblestone Cheshire Street, Mummy next to me. My white crib with white bars made an L-shape next to their bed. The front window looked over Vallance Road. Opposite, I could see our barber shop's overhead barber pole, its red, white and blue stripes, turning, turning without ever stopping. Mummy tucked me in and said the *Shema* with me. 'Hear Oh Israel, the Lord our God, the Lord is One,' we recited in Hebrew. 'Daddy will stay with you until you go to sleep,' she said, leaving. She knew I was terrified of the dark, but she didn't know why. I never told her I was afraid that the Mikado lurked nearby and that the headless dummy from the second floor might clop up the stairs and eat me. She would have laughed. But I smiled to myself over Aunt Mitzi's visit, the lavender leather-covered book, the golden-edged pages, the silver sixpence, Aunty showing us her diamond ring, and telling me I would be her bridesmaid. I couldn't fall asleep. The clock ticked in the silence.

I liked watching Daddy's short, skinny, wiry body, the same as mine. I too, like Daddy, liked running fast. He must be a good dancer. He'd told me that he met Mummy at a Jewish club dance. She'd told me that he married her on the rebound. Whatever that was.

I fell asleep and dreamed that the headless dummy clacked up the stairs on its three little legs, sounding like Mummy's clacking high heels. The dummy pushed open the bedroom door, jumped into my crib and dug its three tiny feet into my stomach. Waking with a cry of terror, I leaped into my parents' bed where, drowning in the heat of Mummy's body and the *iberbat* I fell into a deep, dreamless sleep.

CHAPTER 2

HOUNDSDITCH, PUBLIC BATHS AND GREEN HAIR *

'Eat everything. Don't stand with one leg on the chair while eating. You'll swallow a thimble, and the doctor will have to pull it out of your throat with long scissors,' Mummy said.

At breakfast, there was always a thimble on the table left from her darning. It was Wednesday.

Wednesdays – half-day closing – Daddy had hoisted our red shutters over the shop windows and locked the shop door. We were going to Levy's, the Houndsditch hairdresser wholesaler to buy shaving cream, cigarettes, after-shave lotion, Brylcream, a new shaving brush, a bone-handled open razor, condoms, flapjacks to hold women's powder, and perhaps, costume jewellery.

Mummy had gone to Wickhams, our only East End department shop. I'd been with her once when she'd gazed longingly at a sea of boring dining room tables that to me all looked the same. Daddy had waited for me to come home from school, and we left. I skipped beside him on this rare chance to be with him. Only when we were alone away from the flat did he speak to me.

'Houndsditch is where they used to throw dead dogs in the Middle Ages,' Daddy said. 'That's what Houndsditch means. A ditch for hounds.'

Children must not shout, so I looked up into his eyes and nodded, so he'd know I'd heard.

I imagined a big ditch with a hundred dead dogs, brown, white, spotted, all shapes and sizes, lying with four stiff legs in the air. Immediately, in the street, we saw two live dogs – one mounted on the other's back looked like eight feet. The top dog struggled to free himself, and looked around, bewildered. Why was he stuck and why did he look so puzzled? A crowd of women in aprons and some workmen had gathered, pointing and laughing at the dogs. Just when I had decided it was impolite to stare in case we embarrassed the dogs ('children must not stare or point'), a grinning woman came out of her house, and threw a pail of water over both animals. The dogs broke free, and each ran off in a different direction. Everyone laughed but Daddy. At the Museum of Natural History, he'd tell me all about the family life of owls and wolves we saw staring wide-eyed at us from behind glass cases.

Down three steps we went into Levy's Hairdressing Wholesalers. Inside, the windowless basement was dark and warm, its raftered ceiling loomed so low that even Daddy's head almost touched it. Cocky Levy's son stood behind a counter, the counter as wide as the warehouse.

The Levy boy, about 14 to my five, grinned at me with his crooked smile, dark eyes dancing with deviltry in a pointed, foxy and pockmarked face. Mummy told me that when I'd had chicken pox, they'd tied my hands to the crib so that I wouldn't scratch my face. I imagined itching and straining at the strings that tied my hands to the crib. But my skin, unlike Daniel's was fair and clear. However, I loved Daniel Levy's pockmarked face. The boy was slender and spry like Daddy, and even though his eyes mocked me until I felt myself blush, I liked his grin. In ten minutes, Daniel Levy took my father's order, deftly string-tied together cartons of Players Please and Craven-A cigarettes, and packed flapjacks, jewellery and condoms into Daddy's bags.

Once home, it was my job to tuck the Red Letter envelopes around our glittering mirrors for men to buy Friday and Saturday evenings. I saw a rubber fish like the condom I'd once curiously taken out of its envelope, swimming in the yellow pish of our chamber pot every morning. I never thought to ask what it was for. Children must not ask questions.

11

Daddy strode home from Levy's like Beauty's father, like a rich merchant from the East, laden down with exotic gifts: a hundred Players' cigarettes in white cartons, each with a picture on the package of a jolly sailor in a navy cap smoking a Players Please. These cardboard boxes were lighter than the Craven-A cigarettes in delightful red tin boxes with hinged lids that opened and shut. When the box was new, it was filled inside with 20 fat white cigarettes with gold tips lying neatly in a double row, 10 on top of another 10 below.

When emptied of cigarettes and men threw the boxes into the street, I picked up one. This strong, tin box was perfect for keeping my tiny doll, (the one Mummy had smacked me for buying), my gold bracelet from Aunt Mitzi and a spare humbug. The box's red lid was prettily edged with a gold and black band, and on top of the lid sat a cheeky black cat with white eyes, nose and black whiskers that grinned at me. 'Made in London, England', in gold and black, glowed below the saucy cat. Each time I opened the emptied box I read inside the lid:

'Made specially to prevent sore throats 'Craven 'A' Cork-tipped Virginia Cigarettes Are made from the finest imported matured Virginia Tobacco guaranteed pure and absolutely free from adulteration of any kind. Made in London's Wonder Factory by Carreras Limited (est. 1788) Arcadia Works, London.'

Once home, Daddy spread his treasures out on the kitchen table. Besides cigarettes and condoms he had bought creamy fake pearl necklaces and earrings, glittering marquisette brooches, flapjacks for powder, each flapjack top differently gilded, painted or embroidered and inside on the flapjack's bottom sat a fat powder puff over loose powder.

'Ladies may not powder their noses in public,' Mummy had told me. 'Ladies must put on make-up in private or in the Ladies Room. If a lady needs the lavatory she says, 'Excuse me, I need to powder my nose.'

Mummy came home, high heels clacking up the stairs and saw what Daddy had bought from Levy's in Houndsditch. She screamed, 'Alf, look at all this junk you've bought. We'll never sell it. We have to sell the old stock before we buy new.'

'If customers see new stuff in the window, they'll be more tempted to come in,' Dad said.

I looked at the two giants in my life: Daddy, who gambled, spent money, scribbled doggerel, drew pictures, went to museums and loved beauty and Mummy who dressed plainly, never took chances, saved, but loved opera. Strange, I thought, that one who so loved music had married a deaf man. But I couldn't help siding with Daddy. I also loved beauty and adventure. That was why I loved to be with Daddy and Aunt Mitzi, and why I loved fairy tales, and the new book Aunt Mitzi had given me.

Mummy was shouting at Daddy again. 'You're just like my sister Mitzi: you both spend like idiots, both like beautiful things. My mother loves beautiful things, and Mitzi is beautiful, so Mitzi is the favourite.'

'But usually boys and youngest boys are the favourite. Your brother Max was the youngest boy,' Daddy said.

'Just the same, Mitzi gets everything and I get nothing I want,' Mummy pouted and stared down at me. I looked at the floor shamefaced, guilty, because I looked like, and adored my aunt.

They had the usual Wednesday afternoon fight about spending and saving. Mummy threw a big cloud of 10 shilling notes in the air to show Daddy how he wasted money. I loved watching the green notes all flutter down. So did Daddy. His eyes twinkled with amusement.

On Thursday after school, Mummy said, 'Come on. It's time for the bathhouse, and tomorrow, Friday, you must take flowers to Booba.'

I then had no idea why we bathed on Thursday and why I carried flowers to my grandmother on Friday. I later learned that my grandparents, as did all Jews in the Jewish East End closed the shop Friday evening and Saturday because they celebrated the Sabbath: a day of rest and prayer. I didn't know the word 'Sabbath'. Mummy lit candles every Friday evening, covering her face with her hands while she murmured something in Hebrew, but never told me why. After this she put me to bed, put on the long white coat and buttoned it all the way down. I never wore any garment that buttoned all the way down (it meant goodbye) and she went to work in the shop across the street. Nor did I know that the baths on Thursday and flowers on Friday were because my grandparents honoured the Sabbath. I knew that Gentiles closed their shops on Sunday and that all the church bells pealed, but I didn't know why. Children must not ask questions.

As Mummy and I left home for the Baths that Thursday, Mummy shouted at Daddy, 'Stay in the shop, Alf. You won't hear the shop bell from the kitchen. You can book me for tomorrow. I only have one set, so far. Don't book anyone for today. We'll get back too late.'

Someone always had to stay in the shop: their real baby.

'Awight,' Daddy said, like a cockney. He'd been born in Wilkes Street, a section of the East poorer than ours he'd told me. He'd gone to work when he was 12 to support his parents.

Mummy and I left the shop's mixed sharp-sweet smell of ammonia for perms, and shaving lotion for men's aftershave. Outside, fog floated through East London, and fog-horns from the nearby docks cried hoarsely, but I loved both fog and crooning fog-horns.

We passed the Salvation Army Christian, and the Jewish Board of Guardians' soup kitchens. Long lines of men stood slouched over in both lines, caps pulled over their faces, like shamefaced little boys, hands stuffed into their pockets. What had they done wrong? I wondered why women never stood in the soup lines. Weren't they hungry, too? How often Mummy had said, 'We're lucky we have food on the table in this Depression.'

On the way to the Baths we passed barefoot children playing in the streets and Itchykoo, our young, local tramp. He never begged, but always wore the same floor-length khaki Great War overcoat flapping open, no buttons, and a back belt. He knelt at the horse trough among towering Clydesdales, their great pink tongues lapped in and out. Itchykoo knelt and lapped water with them. The name of the man who had donated the red granite troughs was chiseled in their sides, but too small to read. I had a 'lazy' right eye. Mummy said Dr Baumgarten had told her she should cover the left to make the right one work, but she never did.

Finally, we came to Bethnal Green Bathhouse. Their two marble doorways soared into the sky looking like entrances to kings' palaces in my fairy tale books. Chiseled over the towering front of one bathhouse was 'Men' and over another, 'Women,' little chiseled curls flirted around the words. Up two marble steps into the bathhouse, I felt like a small princess, especially since the women inside waited on us like obedient, if not willing servants. The ticket woman in her white overalls sat behind a strange half-door, the bottom closed, the top open, only her face, shoulders, arms and breasts showing. She reminded me of a Dutch painting Daddy had shown me one Sunday at the Art Museum.

'Two please,' Mummy said, giving the woman a few pennies. The woman took the money, face grim, perhaps because we were Jewish, and handed us two bits of paper like cinema tickets, numbers on them. She gave us each two hot, white bath towels, two face cloths and a piece of soap. Mummy had brought our own Yardley's Lavender soap.

We sat in the empty waiting room on round-backed cane chairs, the same kind as those in Dr Baumgarten's surgery, his waiting room where anyone could drop in during 'surgery hours'. On Thursdays, the Public Bath waiting room was always empty. Perhaps gentiles came, if at all, on Friday evening or Saturday. Mummy worked on those days. Perhaps gentiles were working, couldn't afford a bath, or didn't care. There was no one Jewish there either, no one at all but Mummy and me.

Soon, a plump woman in a white coat came down the marble corridor that was lined on both sides with bath rooms and said, 'Next!' the way Daddy said to customers waiting their turn in his barber shop: 'Next!' Since the place was empty, we were next, so we rose.

This woman, also unsmiling, took our tickets. She led us down the marble corridor that shimmered with modern electric lights. Following her, we passed about six marbled bathrooms lining each side of the hallway; their marble walls seemed to be six feet high. The walls didn't touch the ceiling, as they did at home and in the shop.

'Take number five,' the attendant said: I was five and a half. On entering number five, Mummy slid the brass lock across the door. Bathroom ceilings blazed with electric lights so bright they dazzled my eyes. Even the single chrome tap over a huge white bath and marble floors shimmered with light, as if sun shone everywhere. The bathhouse was sparkling clean and, though I saw no fire, cozy warm. I felt like Beauty in the Beast's luxurious palace, especially since as if by magic, water suddenly gushed out of the single inside tap, the way food appeared magically in Beauty and the Beast's palace. But I knew that the lady outside had turned a key attached to the wall outside our bathroom. First cold, then hot water gushed into our bath. Mummy sprinkled Evening in Paris bath salts into the water, and then she swished water round with her hand to mix together cold and hot water.

'Enough hot in number five, thank you,' she called out over the wall. Now I understood that the walls didn't go up to the ceiling so that the bath lady could hear Mummy over the top.

The woman outside turned off the water spigot with her key. I heard her footsteps fade. We both quickly undressed. I saw Mummy's breasts every morning when she stripped to the waist and washed under our kitchen cold-water sink. Daddy's eyes always peeked at her over his morning newspaper. Like the rest of her, her breasts were small and firm. East Londoners walked everywhere within two miles, so few were fat. Every evening, Mummy lay on the floor on her back, elbows and hands holding up her hips, and cycled her legs in mid-air as if riding a bicycle upside-down. Her stomach was flat; she had a more boyish figure than Auntie Mitzi's.

The bath water came up to Mummy's waist and up to my shoulders. A little tuft of hair grew between her legs, but none under her armpits. Even after they'd quarrelled, Mummy let Daddy shave the hair under her armpits with his glittering razor. I always bit my nails then.

As we stood in the bath, Mummy washed me down with Yardley's Lavender soap, and then soaped herself all over. And then we both lay down in the bath. Our water was warm and steamy, but as it cooled, Mummy pushed a bell over the bath.

'Yes?' came a voice from outside.

'More hot in number five, please,' she called out.

Hot water gushed in.

'Thank you,' Mummy called out, and after the water stopped, there was total silence.

A smooth, narrow wooden plank, pale brown, straddled the bath.

'You sit on the plank, while I lie down by myself,' Mummy said, draping a large warm towel around me. I sat on the plank wrapped like a present. Mummy lay full length in the bath, smiling. Was she thinking of her 'David,' the man she'd said she had wanted to marry? Was it Dr Baumgarten? Aunt Mitzi hadn't really wanted to marry Adrian, she wanted to marry Raphael, but couldn't. Mummy hadn't wanted to marry Daddy, but Booba insisted that older sisters must marry before the younger. It seemed hard to marry the man you wanted to marry.

Finally Mummy rose out of the water, white skin glistening and dripping like the picture nailed over the basin in the women's section of our hairdressing shop. The picture was called *Venus from a Shell*. Mummy rubbed us both dry and then sprinkled us both with scented talcum powder. The powder pouring down like white snow, smelled like lavender, and I felt like a crisp, clean sheet. 'Dry yourself carefully,' she always said, before showering me with talcum powder. 'Uncle Sam sat in a wet bathing suit, and now he has terrible arthritis. Lots of children die of pneumonia.'

I sneezed. 'A *gesint off dere yoh,*' she said in Yiddish. 'A blessing on you.' One sneeze and she thought: 'Pneumonia'. I hoped Mummy wouldn't cover my chest and back with that itchy, smelly pink cotton wool. But it did keep my chest warm and dry.

'Goodbye. Thank you,' Mummy said to the half-woman behind the half-door as we left. The woman looked at us unsmiling and nodded. Most East Enders were friendly and called you 'luv' except for the Fascists. Why didn't the women in the bathhouse smile, especially when they worked in such a fine marble palace? They could have a hot bath with hot, clean towels whenever they wanted.

When we arrived back at the shop, there were no men customers, but a strange woman with emerald green hair stood screaming at Daddy, 'You fucking idiot.'

I'd never seen green hair. It looked like one of the trolls Daddy sometimes drew.

Daddy leaned against his barber chair, his face serious, his dark eyes laughing like those of the Levy imp behind the counter in Houndsditch. The woman screamed at Mummy, 'I told him to dye my hair blonde and look what the bloody sod's done to me. What the fuck am I going to do with green 'air? I'll be the laughing-stock of the pub. 'ow can I go to our pub like this? You got to do somefink,' she shrieked, louder than Mummy talked to Daddy.

'*Schlemiel* idiot, look what you've done,' Mummy screamed at Daddy. 'Who told you to try and dye women's hair? That's my job. Stick to your men, you're a barber.'

Daddy said nothing but his dark eyes twinkled.

'I'm terribly sorry, Madam,' Mummy said, her own face red with shame. 'It's a dreadful mistake. We'll do all we can to help you.'

'Blimey you better 'ad. What's the idea of leaving this sodding idiot in 'ere? "Oh I can take care of you," 'e says, "you don't need to wait for me wife". You need to tie this bloke up before you go out,' she raged at Mummy. 'It ain't safe to leave 'im alone.'

'Don't I know it,' Mummy said, half to herself.

Perhaps that was why she almost never left Daddy alone in the shop. And when he came back from Houndsditch on Wednesday afternoons there was always The Big Wednesday Fight over his buying new pretty things before selling the old stuff.

The woman was still screaming at Daddy. 'If you don't get rid of this green 'air I'm going to get my big bruvver wot's a docker. 'e'll come rahnd and smash yor face in.'

'Don't worry, we'll have it all washed out soon,' Mummy soothed the woman, but though she washed the hair it stayed green. The woman screamed until blue veins stuck out of her neck.

'Please let me tie this pretty scarf on you,' Mummy said, and draped one of her own scarves over the woman's green hair. 'I'm terribly sorry, madam, the green will soon grow out. I'll return your money and some extra for your trouble.'

I saw her eyes fill with tears, while Daddy's eyes glowed with merriment. I wished that like him, I could not care if I'd made a mistake. I was very careful not to make mistakes at home or at school. But I couldn't help looking like Aunt Mitzi and being a girl instead of a boy.

Later, I heard Mummy shouting at Daddy. 'Green can't be washed out; it has to grow out. We've had to give her back her money and more to shut her up. We could lose our license if she reports us.'

Although I felt sorry for the woman, I couldn't help admiring Daddy for his adventurous spirit. He was like Jack climbing the beanstalk into the unknown. He had no idea how to dye hair but thought he'd try anything once. 'Left to you,' Mummy screamed, 'we'd starve'.

Whenever we went to the baths after that, Mummy shook her forefinger at him and said, 'Don't dye anyone's hair green while we're at the baths. You're a barber. Stick to barbering.'

He smiled his cat-like smile. He never became angry. Perhaps he just didn't care.

That night I dreamed that a doctor put scissors down my throat and pulled out a thimble.

CHAPTER 3
THE FRIDAY VISIT

Friday after I'd skipped home from school, Mummy thrust a huge bunch of long, salmon gladioli into my arms, the stiff flowers softened by a froth of yellow mimosa pompoms. The straight gladioli reminded me of my stern Booba, whom Daddy called a *vilde chaya*, a wild beast. He said she had told Mummy when to marry and had then stolen their £400 in wedding gifts. I couldn't *then* believe that this was the same stiff and stern Booba I knew, so correct and well-dressed, so careful a house and shopkeeper. But I always took flowers to her on Friday. Why, I did not know. 'Children must not ask questions,' Mummy said.

'Take these flowers to Booba, and say, "How are you, Booba?" Kiss her cheek and then give her the flowers,' Mummy instructed me, as usual.

Booba liked tall gladioli. Mummy's favourite flower was the dew-drenched violet, a fragile bunch of tiny flowers tied together, but too beautiful to live long, they soon drooped and died. My favourite flower was the tall, purple iris with a sometimes yellow petal inside the iris' mouth that reminded me of Mummy's tongue that quivered when she passionately sang with BBC singers, *They call me Mimi*.

Wearing my red dress, I walked along Vallance Road to Bethnal Green Road, passing spidery black swastikas and 'JP', daubed on filthy, damp, brick walls. What did JP mean? I shivered, knowing that Fascists hated and beat Jews and smashed our shop windows, but I didn't understand why. 'Bloody Fascists,' my parents said after a smashed window.

From Vallance Road, I turned right on to Bethnal Green Road and entered the Bethnal Green Street Open Market. Here floated the *goyishe*, gentile smells of white bread, and passing the fish and chip shop, peeping in, I heard hot oil sizzling, and smelled fresh fried fish and chips acrid with splashed-on salt and vinegar that made my cheeks suck inward. Behind Bill, vats bubbled and spat hot oil while a fresh batch of fish in one and chips in the other vat crackled as they fried.

Later, came sharp sea smells of shrimp, meaty smells of dripping, the fat from meat or from salty fried bacon I'd never tasted, smeared on a thick slab of bread, which gentiles called 'a doorstep'. Lunchtime, during the summer, mothers yelling 'Ernie!!' or 'Johnny', voices ending on a high, operatic note, flung a doorstep from the window to their barefoot children playing in the street. The boys would look up at mothers hanging out of the window and catch the falling doorstep as it dropped through air. Summers, some boys wore only an undershirt; their privates showed a teeny point of flesh sticking out under a sleeveless vest that for some, was their only garment.

As I passed the Pig and Whistle, a man pushed the latrine door outward and while still buttoning his fly, let loose into the street the pub's stink of warm piss and beer. All these *goyishe* Bethnal Green Road smells meant *home*, one part of my East London: smells of dripping, shrimp, bacon, fish and chips, piss and beer, in the gentile section where we lived among cheery dockers and cockneys. These men and women came especially on Friday nights and Saturdays – big pub nights – to 'Alf's Ladies and Gents Hairdressers' for shaves, 'aircuts and condoms.

Besides the smells, the cacophony of gentile Bethnal Green market pounding in my ears, the clop of Clydesdales' hooves as they drew giant flat carts of beer barrels, the carts rumbling over cobbled streets, the Pearly drivers' pearly buttons sewn over their entire suits, men and women sitting high over their slow horses, sang:

'Any old iron? Any old iron?
Any, any, any old iron?
You look neat. Talk about a treat!
You look so dapper from your napper to your feet.
Dressed in style, brand-new tile,
And your father's old green tie on.
But I wouldn't give you tuppence for your old watch and chain,
Old Iron, Old Iron.

Only one or two cars passed, drowning for a moment the din of cockney chatter, crying babies in prams, and barrow boys' shouting, ''ere y'ar, luvley cat meat, all fresh,' all music to my East London girl's ears.

I paused at the eel lady's stall to watch when a man stopped, and the woman dipped her hand into a wooden barrel on the pavement, wrenched out a squirming black eel, smacked it on her barrow board and with a small axe chopped it into pieces. My eyes widened as the eel's black chopped parts leaped across the board as if still alive. How was that possible? She scooped the wriggling pieces of eel into a round cardboard box that she shoved at the customer, who threw back his head, dropped the eel parts into his mouth and gulped the lot down in one swallow. How could he taste anything? Did the eel parts still jump inside him?

'Ta,' the woman said, as he handed her brown pennies and walked off.

At the next stall, the cat-food woman sliced a penny's worth of horse-meat from a chunk of meat and wrapped its slices in newspaper, the way they wrapped fish and chips, handed it to a customer, who dropped pennies on her counter.

'Ta,' said the cat-meat lady from behind her stall.

But the woman only wrapped the horse-meat in newspaper, whereas Bill, sweat pouring off him in the fish and chip shop where my friend Joycey and I went for chips, twisted yesterday's newspaper into an artistic cone into which he dropped steaming chips.

The Great War veteran, medals gleaming on his thin chest, empty leg flap pinned to his side, leaned on his crutch against the bakery brick wall and held out his one pencil, silent hope in his blue eyes. I never saw anyone stop and buy a pencil or give him money. It never occurred to me to give him a penny even if I had one. Mummy banked every penny against the Depression.

Women crowded into the bakery behind him that was owned by parents of twins in my class. The twins told me, to my astonishment, 'Our parents bring us tea in bed every morning.' Like many British husbands, Daddy brought Mummy tea in bed, but I knew of no parent who brought children tea in bed. How spoiled they were! Princes!

Passing the *trefe* butcher shop, I stared at a pig's snout and hooves, sausages, and upside-down gutted rabbits, all hanging from iron hooks like the Polish woman hanging behind a black curtain at Madame Tussaud's. Children were not supposed to peek behind that curtain, but of course, I did, and was forever sorry. Mummy and her divorced friend Gertie Franks had taken me there. The Polish wax woman hung backward, swinging slightly, an iron hook through her stomach. 'Why are you shivering?' Gertie had asked me, but as usual with adults, my eyes watched everything, my mouth said nothing. I collected sounds so I should not, when I became eight, turn deaf like Daddy.

On stalls on the curbs opposite shops, barrow boys shouted 'ere y'ar luv, lovely tomahtoes', and another called out, 'ere yar, 'ere yar, darlin' 10 a penny, 10 a penny, bootiful needles to darn yor 'usband's socks wiv.'

I loved the din and the crowds of East London's outdoor markets, the pushing and pulsating crowds, so different from our silent flat except when Mummy shouted, or played Gigli on the gramophone. But I stopped to read a big white poster showing Sir Oswald Mosley's white face, black eyes blazing with hatred, a skinny black moustache over thin lips. His furious eyes bored into mine. I read the black print under his white face that read, 'Hear Sir Oswald Mosley, Great Leader of the Union of British Fascists, Saturday 2 p.m. Outside the Salmon and Ball. Plan our march through the East End.' Without knowing why, a shiver ran through my body.

'Salmon and Ball is the bloody Fascist pub meeting place,' 16-year-old Uncle Max had said last Friday when I visited Booba. Just let them try to march through the East End, smashing Jewish shops and beating us. We'll fight the sods.' I went on along Bethnal Green Road.

Bethnal Green Road seethed with Friday afternoon shoppers, and being small, I wormed my way through spaces between bodies to get to Booba's house. Spooky eyes, reminding me of the wolf's in Little Red Riding Hood seemed to follow my red dress. I turned round quickly, looking for the wolf, and then I saw him.

Tommie Higgins, a local boy from my school, Wood Close, with shaggy black hair, black eyes, pointy ears, big yellow teeth, already smoking, a rough green wool jersey up to his chin, and torn short trousers baring dirty knees, and stinking of fart, loomed over me. 'Where you goin' Jew-girl?'

'To my grandmother's,' I said, taught to answer, not ask.

'Gimme them flahs,' and ripping the gladioli from my hands, he then gleefully pulled off the flower heads, threw them on the ground and stamped on them, picked up a plank of wood lying in the road and bounced it on my head. The flowers lay ripped in dirt. 'See 'ow yer grama likes this, Jew-girl,' he smirked.

I had no idea what to do. Jewish girls were taught to be quiet, not to answer back, and to be clever but not show-offs. Deaf daddy chased ruffian kids who shoved open the shop door making the bell jangle so loudly that even he heard them yell, 'Dirty Jew,' but he was a grown man and an amateur boxer, whereas Tommie Higgins was twice my size and looked as hairy and ferocious as the wolf who would happily gobble up Red Riding Hood as well as Red Riding Hood's grandmother. Some East End Jewish boys like my father, his brother, Izzy, and Mummy's brother, Uncle Max – who all took boxing lessons at the Jewish Boys' Club – hit back when Fascists attacked them. Still, on my visit last Friday, I'd heard Uncle Max say to Uncle Sam, 'Those bloody Fascists sods blinded a Jewish man who protested at an anti-Semitic speech last week.'

I picked up the broken blossoms and tried to put them back onto the stems, but they wouldn't stick, so from an old paper I found on the street, I made a paper cone like the fish-and-chip-man, put the broken flowers in it and plodded on toward my grandparents' house. 'Har har,' Tommie guffawed, his voice following me.

Nearing Jewish East End, Whitechapel, I breathed a sigh of relief. Walls here were free of swastikas and houses' outside brick walls didn't drip scummy water. The smells here changed from salty shrimp and bacon to Jewish smells of chicken soup, roasting chicken, salt beef, mouth-puckering pickles and pickled herring, then to salty scotch salmon, and fresh-baked crisp crusted Russian black bread with seeds, and white challah. I knew that Booba cooked on Friday afternoon, but didn't know why.

As I neared Cambridge Heath Road, a group of men, all short with shaggy eyebrows and frowns, like Edward G. Robinson whom I'd once seen at the pictures, stood in small clusters arguing loudly. A tape measure hanging around each man's neck, they were out-of-work Jewish tailors waiting for a guvnor to hire them. They talked in a mix of Anglo-Yiddish and English.

'So nu, is there going to be war?' I heard one ask another.

'Might get us out of this Depression.'

'But that *mamser* Hitler, in Germany, and here, bloody Mosley…' I heard, and then I'd passed them. I knew that *mamser* meant bastard, but what was a bastard?

Taking a short cut through a narrow, cobbled alley with iron blocks at the end, stopping traffic, I came out onto Cambridge Heath Road, and opposite was number 122: Booba's grocery shop. I crossed Cambridge Heath Road.

Walking into her shop felt like walking from dark night into a brilliantly lit palace. Or perhaps it seemed so bright in comparison to dank gentile East London and our gas-lit flat. Bright modern electric lights glittered from Booba's grocery ceiling. Marble counters with shiny cans gleamed, shining as if polished: very likely Booba *had* polished each can. Here, all the Jewish smells came together in one place: knobbly sour green pickles floated like crocodiles in a barrel of brine, and bobbing black olives winked at me from a bowl. Booba had piled on top of her gleaming glass cases, her famous black Russian pumpernickel crusted with seeds, shiny egg-brushed fresh bagels, white cream cheese, sharp, tangy chopped herring, gefilte fish, chopped liver, liverwurst, and hanging high, swung solid, red salamis, most of which Booba made fresh herself from five in the morning. West End Jews on Sundays flocked to the East End for these delicacies only available in the East End where some snobs had been born. Recently arrived refugees from Europe who lived in our poor East End also came Fridays and Sunday mornings. I didn't exactly know what was a refugee, though Booba's cousin, Zalman, had just arrived in England from Poland, crying, 'The Poles killed my wife and child.'

I loved both the *goyish* and the Jewish East End. I loved the gentiles for their 'sarky' (tart) rough humour, their fish and chips and cheery, tipsy Saturday night songs floating out of the pubs, and I felt warm and safe in the Jewish East End because my grandparents, aunt and uncles lived there, each with a sharp tongue – except for Zada and Aunt Mitzi – and for feeling protected there from the Fascist ruffians.

In Booba's shop, the smells were so delicious, and especially after my long walk, and after nasty Tommy Higgins, I desperately wanted a drink and a bagel with scotch herring, but children must not ask for food, and Booba never offered. Except with her favourite daughter, my Aunt Mitzi, everyone knew Booba to be a penny-pincher.

'Hallo, Booba, how are you?' I asked politely, as trained.

She leaned over her marble counter, her fortress, and offered me her cool cheek to kiss. '*Nu, machst a leben?*' 'Well, are you making a living?' she demanded, unsmiling. I'd never seen her smile.

I was five, didn't know how to answer. I looked at the floor, shuffled my shoes.

On either side of Booba, behind the marble counter my two young uncles Max and Sam, also in white grocer coats stood, straight as soldiers.

'What happened to the flowers?' Booba said.

'A *yok* stopped me on the way, hit me on the head and ripped the heads off. I'm sorry.'

Uncle Sam, 17, short with a little hump like lots of East Enders, but handsome, and Uncle Max, 16 and tall and handsome, a dimple in his chin like Cary Grant's, both grinned at me.

'Didn't you give him a *putsch*?' Uncle Sam asked scornfully. 'I bet you kicked that little *yok* in the bum, right? Such a brave girl!'

That was a *goyishe* thing. Gentile girls sometimes had fights. Jewish girls, never.

I hung my head.

Uncle Max, dark-eyed, laughed, his dimples appearing. 'So when are you going to bring us some flowers with heads on, poopsie? This year, next year, sometime, never?'

I blushed, but was saved from further teasing by a plump woman who rushed in holding a paper shopping bag. '*Ne Mrs* Markowitz, *vus machst du?*' Booba said. 'So, Mrs Markowitz, how are you? What can I do for you today? When's your daughter's wedding? How's that *glomp* your neighbour?' A *glomp* was British Yiddish for a *nebbish* or a useless man.

Mrs Moskowitz frowned. 'She should have a *mesa meshing*' (a strange and unusual death). '*Oy givalt*, such a *grochky*, a commotion. I explained that if I invited *her* little girl I had to invite *everybody's* little girl. Now she's so *broigus* she won't talk to me. You shouldn't know what *tsuris*, what aggravation I got,' she lamented. 'Cut me a nice quarter pound of Scotch salmon, please, Mrs Goldzummer,' said the lady and then read to Uncle Sam from a grubby shopping list. He ran back and forth behind the counter reaching up to the shelves there to fill her order.

Booba, the matriarch, she who decided her family's fate and future, presided haughtily in her grocer's white coat, her serrated knife poised over the slab of Scotch salmon. The salmon looked like a sacrifice I'd seen on a Saturday morning children's film show, and Booba looked like the High Priestess. This priestess in the film had raised her sword high in the air over a young girl lying on a slab. All the children in the cinema had jumped up on the seats and yelled, 'Kill 'er.' Then a boy stuck hot ice on my leg, and a big blister rose on it. I never went to Saturday morning pictures again. I did miss watching the man playing on the flashing rainbow coloured organ that rose from underneath the stage to the stage before the film began. Booba looked like the film's Priestess, her face severe, intense, the long knife in her hand, about to sacrifice her daughter. Silly, I said to myself. She's only cutting salmon.

With her sharp knife, she bowed her head and slantingly sliced the salmon as if it were precious, placing almost transparent slivers on white wax paper. She silently lifted the sacrificed salmon onto one curvy pan, putting little clinking metal weights in the other curvy pan, frowning like a judge as the scale's black needle teetered frantically back and forth until it came to rest on the salmon's exact weight. The salmon weighed, she looked down at my nose near the edge of her marble counter where I was sniffing the delicious salty salmon.

'Take the flowers into the dining room,' she said.

A frosted glass on top, wood at the bottom wall separated the shop from the dining room. The top glass part of the wall was etched with pretty flowers along it. In the middle of this glass-on-wood wall stood a glass and wooden door. I went through the door like Alice in Wonderland, entering a different world. Booba's dining room, unlike the 'dining room' in our flat that we called our living room, gleamed spotlessly clean and tidy. Booba's rosewood dining room table shone so brightly that the crystal vase and long-stemmed salmon-coloured gladioli and green stalks shone mirrored on the table's surface. Why did Mummy send fresh flowers, when Booba's flowers were still fresh? Perhaps Mummy, who rarely visited Booba, didn't know.

A fire in a clean grate burned summer and winter. Two great-headed tomcats, one grey, one black, slept curled on the red Persian carpet in front of it. These cats were not pets, like my kitten, Binkie, but Business Cats, with a Job, paid in mice. Every night, Zada, my grandfather, took them across the yard behind the living room and kitchen to Booba's granary. I bet Booba didn't feed the cats either, so that at night they would eat mice in the granary. The huge cats slept without stirring, but for their even breathing; they'd had a hard night chasing mice and would have another hard night, tonight.

The only unpleasant part of this silent room was the mantelpiece clock relentlessly ticking on the fireplace mantelpiece. Ticking clocks reminded me of my nightmare when the Mikado's headless dummy from the second floor clacked up the stairs sounding like Mummy's clacking high heels, jumped into my bed and dug its little wood feet into my stomach.

I glanced at the other door in Booba's dining room. This door led upstairs to her three-story house over the shop. I put the broken flowers on Booba's spotless kitchen counter and peered out of the kitchen window at her granary across the courtyard. Zada would be in there, weighing pound-size bags of *babylach*, little white beans, like the king in his counting house counting out his money. I was about to run to my Zada when Uncle Max and six of his young friends trooped into the dining room. The fire warmed the room so well that the boys took off their white shirts and dressed only in undershirts and long trousers now that they were 16, threw themselves onto the sofa and stretched their long legs. Although they'd left school, they all still studied in Yeshiva, whatever that was, after school or work. Sprawled out on the sofa and chairs, their white *tsitsit*, with twisted knots ending in fringes, hung down their chests, backs and trousers. I didn't know then that the *tsitsit* fringes and knots added up to 613 and symbolized the 613 Jewish laws for which a boy was responsible after his *bar mitzvah* at the age of 13 and he became a man. No one had invited Mummy or me to celebrate this event.

Uncle Max and his cronies, legs spread apart, smoked coffin nails, Players Please, the grinning sailor on the front of the pack. I picked out Schubert's Serenade on Booba's piano.

'Come, sit on my lap, and I'll show you smoke coming out of my ears,' Uncle Max called out, smiling. Unlike many Brits' yellow, crooked teeth, his were white and even.

His friends all stopped talking and looked at me. It was nice they were so friendly, I thought. I didn't know any big boys besides Tommie Higgins. Boys at school never spoke to girls or drank our free milk. That was 'sissy'. Some, like Tommy Higgins jumped on you when they could. But Uncle Max, only 16, was Mummy's youngest brother. So I trusted him.

'Come, sit on my lap,' he said again.

I climbed onto Uncle Max's lap, facing him, my legs bare but for short white socks hanging down one on each side of his rough trousers.

'Now watch my ears,' he said, taking a long drag on his cigarette, its end turning bright red. I stared hard at his face looking for smoke to come out of his ears.

'Oh, oh,' I screamed, as suddenly I felt a burning pain on my hand.

All his friends laughed as I glared at the angry red mark on my left hand and scrambled off his lap.

'Come on, let's all go to the Corner House Tea Dance, we'll meet girls, get cakes and whiskey,' Uncle Max said to his cronies. They put on their shirts, and as they left, I heard him say, 'We're all going to fight Mosley's Blackshirt March, right?'

'Of course. We'll stop those bloody Fascists,' said Yankel, a tall, skinny boy.

Their voices trailed off as they left the dining room, going through the shop to Cambridge Heath Road. I imagined them leaping on the deck of a red double-decker number six bus and running up the curved bus stairs without holding on to the rail to sit high up on the top deck, the way Daddy and I did when we went to the Museum. I wished I were grown up and could go with them to the fancy West End. But who'd want a girl? Zada would!

Hand smarting, I raced through the red velvet curtain separating the dining room from the kitchen, tore out of the kitchen door and across an open cobbled courtyard to Booba's granary. Lifting a heavy iron latch, I searched through motes floating through the dim granary for Zada.

Zada stood at his scale in the smoky light, sucking his lemon drops, scooping *babylach*, little white beans from a huge sack and clattering them onto the metal scale, weighing them then dropping each pound into little brown paper bags. He folded down every one-pound bag's top and placed it in a pile to give to Booba for the shop. Then he saw me framed in the door.

'*Bubbele, fleigele, zeisele*,' he exclaimed, 'little doll, little wing, little sweetness,' and sweeping me up into his muscled arms rubbed his stubble across my cheek, and gently pinched my skinny tush. I nestled against his broad chest. Always well dressed, a brown smock coat covered his beautiful grey suit.

'You sit up there,' he said, and easily lifted me, and sat me on top of a huge sack of barley, a sack so high that my head almost touched the slatted wooden ceiling. Two more great tomcats slept curled up on higher sacks, ready for their nightly mouse hunt.

Zada then continued his task for his wife. I listened to the rhythmic *swish* of Zada's little shovel as it dug into a huge sack of *babylach*, *clicks* as he dropped beans onto the metal pan of the scale, and the *swish* again as he emptied his shovel of beans into a brown bag, the *crackle* as he folded down each bag's top neatly and the *rattle* as he plonked the new bag on top of other bags for Booba. Zada was an out-of-work furrier.

Mummy once told me, 'When they first came to England, my mother, your Booba, made fur collars at home. Booba scrimped and saved until she could rent the grocery shop. As a furrier, Zada worked mainly in the winter. In Kosovo, Poland, he was in the Czar's Cavalry, but they let him out to support his widowed mother. Then he sold oil. I don't know what kind of oil.'

Zada stopped filling bags, looked at me mischievously, blue eyes sparkling, then blew into a brown paper bag until full of his air like a balloon; he gathered and closed the top of his bag of breath and smashed it with his fist, 'POP,' and we both cackled with laughter. Work done, he carried me close, his arms under my behind, mine round his sturdy neck across the courtyard back through the kitchen into Booba's dining room. Leaning against his great chest, his moustache tickling my cheek, I felt his strong heart beating. Only Zada in the whole family ever held me close to him, and he was the only person whose love I truly trusted. I could even love and admire him openly, not secretly, the way I admired Daddy and glamorous Aunt Mitzi, because Mummy never said a bad word about her father. Even Daddy had said to Mummy, 'Your father is a real gent. The others are a bunch of robbers.'

Mummy, for once, had not argued.

Carrying me into the dining room, Zada set me down. Uncle Sam came in from the shop.

He'd taken off his white coat, and his little hump rose behind his satin-backed waistcoat. He had his suits made from that East End tailor whose swinging sign said: 'Misfits a Specialty'.

'Want to play Chopsticks?' Uncle Sam asked. I didn't think this was another trick so we sat at the carved rosewood piano and played together, da da *da* tum tum, da da *da* tum tum... Then each of us took turns playing with two fingers and sang together:

Oh will you wash my father's shirt

Oh will you wash it clean?

Oh will you wash my father's shirt

And show it to the Queen?

Booba came in. '*Ne?*' 'Well?' she said. Others said, '*Nu?*' She said she came from Galicia, wherever that was, and that Galicianas said '*Ne?*' Litvaks said *Nu*; both meant 'Well?' or, 'So?' Zada cracked a raw egg on the edge of a glass, broke the egg into it, and muttered. '*Boorich*,' a strange way of saying '*Baruch*' the first word of a blessing I'd learned in Hebrew school to which Mummy took me a few times. Then he tipped his head back and I saw the raw yellow yolk disappear from the glass as it slid down his throat.

'I finished the bags,' he said to Booba, looking as satisfied and well-fed as their tomcats.

'Good,' Booba said, and looked at him, the only person she looked at with soft eyes. Everyone else (except for Aunt Mitzi) and including me, she greeted with her fierce, steely gaze. If she laughed, it was in mockery. But I could see she loved Zada as much as I did. Her own mother had died when she was two. Daddy said Booba was a witch and Zada a saint. The witch and the saint, I thought. Like a fairy story. Only men saints never appeared in Grimm's or Anderson's stories. Only witches, evil stepmothers, ogres, wizards and sometimes, fairies and fairy godmothers.

Zada sat down comfortably at the dining room table, put on his wire-rimmed spectacles, snapped open the Yiddish *Forward*, and like my father, forgot everyone else. The *Forward's* Yiddish Hebrew letters and pictures in bold sepia stood up shiny brown against shining white paper.

I imagined Zada in the Czar's Cavalry, a strong horseman on a black horse who rode up to Booba and without stopping swept her up into the saddle. Later, when Uncle Max heard me say proudly that Zada was in the cavalry, he laughed and said, sarcastic as Booba, 'You know what they did with Jews in the Czar's cavalry? The Jews used to muck out the stables.'

I felt sure that my Zada rode a strong, black stallion for the Czar. Not that this Czar was that great, but, I heard grown-ups say that he was not as cruel as other Czars. He didn't make Zada serve in the Cavalry for 25 years like other Czars so they should forget their family and their Jewish religion. He actually released Zada from the cavalry when his father died, so as to support his mother. Who supported her after Booba married Zada and ran away with him to England?

A customer came into the shop, and Booba went to serve her. Following her into the shop, I stood sniffing and looking up longingly at crusted black Russian bread, bagels, and creamy soft cheese. I knew the Scotch salmon was, of course, only for customers, and Booba would never give me a taste of that, but my mouth moistened when I thought of a thick slice of Russian black bread and butter, with a cup of tea. The customer left. The shop became empty and quiet.

Suddenly Booba pulled out from under the counter a photograph of a woman of about 40, a scarf covering all her hair. Booba leaned over the marble counter where I stood on the other side, nose to the marble counter. She held the photo for a second only.

'This is a picture of my mother. She died when I was two,' she said, and a tear ran down her face and plopped at my feet. I was so astonished at seeing my tough grandmother's tear fall and splash onto the floor that I stared at the tear and barely looked at the woman in the photograph. Quickly, Booba returned the picture under the counter. I'd hardly seen it.

'That was your great-grandmother, Golda. When you were born your Mummy was too ill to choose a name. You were supposed to be called Golda after my mother. At the last minute, Aunt Mitzi chose Gilda instead of Golda,' Booba said.

It seemed natural that aunt Mitzi 'who got everything she wanted' had even chosen my name. But I was glad. There were lots of Goldas, but I knew no one called Gilda, like me. 'Your name means 'golden' or 'God's gift,' she said. I was amazed. I never felt that I was a golden girl or a gift to anyone.

'Come into the dining room with me. Sam, mind the shop,' Booba said, and pushing his arms into his white coat he went back behind the marble counter.

In the dining room Booba said, 'See that picture on the piano?' she said. 'That's my wedding picture.'

The picture showed a handsome young woman in a black satin dress with full breasts and a tiny waist, a gold watch on a chain hanging from her breast, and heavy black hair so perfect it looked like a wig. Her dark eyes seemed to say, 'Just don't try anything with me!' Her hands held a stiff piece of paper as if saying, 'Look at my wedding certificate! He's mine!' Zada, much younger and thinner, stood beside her. An older woman, her hair covered by a scarf, sat beside Booba. So this couldn't be her own mother who had died when she was two, but must have been Zada's Mummy.

'We were cousins,' Booba said. 'It was the custom to marry '*fininsera*' one of our own family. Zada's dead father was called Shmuel, Hebrew for Samuel. So you were named after my mother and Uncle Sam. Shmuel, after Zada's father.' Booba took a roll of paper from her handbag. 'This is a copy of my *ketuba*, my marriage certificate, the one you see in my wedding photograph. It's written in Yiddish.'

Though I thought she couldn't read in any language, Booba chanted by heart, 'The bride-to-be, Chana Hochberg, – that's me, – daughter of Yehuda Hochberg, a widower, this marriage took place in 1904 in the Kosow region, near Minsk. The bride's father – my father – promised to pay for the wedding.'

Booba said, 'It says here that I promised to give my *choson*, a watch and a *tallis* – a prayer shawl – according to custom, and that the bride's father would also give the bridegroom 190 dinars. Zada's mother had several children; all except Zada died. A shame my mother didn't live to see me married.' Her eyes misted again.

His mother must have loved Zada, her only child very much, I thought. But I, too, was an only child. Not all only children were loved.

'Now I have to speak to my tenant, the refugee widow Silver,' Booba said briskly, and left the room by the other dining room door that led into the house over the shop. I peeped out of that door at her straight back as she mounted the stone stairs and heard her say, '*vus machst de?*' 'How are you?' severely, to the young widow from Poland. She was one of the first people they called 'refugees' to come to England because of someone called Hitler. The woman was cooking at a stove on the landing. Booba tried to interest our newest Polish refugee cousin, Zalman, in the widow, but he'd wept as he told us, 'Not yet; dirty Pollaks just killed my wife and child.' I was there when he said that, but was so fascinated with his leather ankle-high shoes with a zipper in the side that I hardly listened to him even though I'd never heard a man weep, and also, it was the only time that I'd ever seen Booba give anyone tea and strudel.

I was surprised at Booba suddenly talking to me and at her tears. Who had looked after her after her mother died? Her older brothers and sisters? I'd never seen her cry.

I was supposed to stay at Booba's for two hours on Fridays, but today Zada read *The Forward* and Booba had gone upstairs. I went back to Uncle Sam in the shop.

'I'm bored,' I said. 'I have nothing to do.'

'See that sack?' Uncle Sam said, pointing to a burlap sack in the corner, the sack as high as my waist. 'Count the rice.'

From the open mouth of the sack, I dutifully began counting grains of rice with my right hand, dropping them into my left, burned hand. When I reached a hundred, the rice grains barely filled the palm of my hand. There must be millions of grains of rice in that sack. It would take a year to count that much rice. I looked up reproachfully to find Uncle Sam laughing at me. Another trick. Young Uncles!!

Back in the dining room, Zada sat reading his *Forward* and sucking a lemon drop to keep his throat moist for when he sang as cantor in a place they called a synagogue. I'd never been to this kind of place. Why didn't Zada take me there? As I curled up in his lap and leaned against his strong, warm body, he stroked my hair murmuring Yiddish endearments. I loved Zada even more than Mumfie.

I was just wishing Aunty Mitzi would come before I went home, when I heard her voice in the shop. She rushed through the half-glass door into the dining room, breathless, her blonde hair, blue eyes and her sparkling smile made her look like the picture of a good fairy in one of my books.

'How's my little niece, how's my pussycat?' she exclaimed, quickly hugging me to her and kissing my cheek. The fur pompoms on my auntie's coat tickled my nose. Today, she smelled of fresh lily-of-the-valley, and her crimson lipstick must have come off on my cheek. I wondered what her new fiancé Adrian looked like. Then I saw him. Adrian stood tall behind my aunt, gazing down at her adoringly. With his dark, wavy Brylcreemed hair, thin moustache and mischievous smile, he looked as dashing as a film star, like a taller Laurence Olivier.

'Adrian picked me up from work, and we're going to see *Carmen*. I just came home to change. Adrian,' she said, turning to the stranger behind her, 'this is my little niece, Gilda.'

'How do you do,' he said, bending down and shaking my hand gently.

I immediately liked him because he was kind, and did not tease me like my real uncles.

Uncle Sam rushed in and shook Adrian's hand. 'Good to see you,' he said. 'Mazltov on your engagement to my sister. I hear you're a chemist.'

'Correct,' Adrian said crisply.

'I once thought of becoming a chemist. What are you working on?' Uncle Sam asked, for once respectful, not sarcastic.

'I'm sorry, my work is secret. The government doesn't allow me to discuss it.'

'Is it this new thing I heard about, radar?' Uncle Sam insisted.

Aunt Mitzi said, 'Sam, mind your own business.' Then she whispered in my ear, 'Look what I have for you, a new shiny sixpence, only don't tell Mummy. Spend it on something you'll enjoy. Enjoy life, pussycat. That's what it's for.'

Just before I went into the Michaels' house and up to our flat, I rubbed my face hard with my hanky. Sure enough, bright red lipstick came off on it. I threw the hanky in the street. Mummy would scold me for losing it, but it was better than if she saw Aunt Mitzi's lipstick on it. Her eyes would fill with jealousy and fury all mixed up. I ran up the stone stairs fast, shutting my eyes and feeling the walls like a blind girl when I had to pass the headless dummy on the second floor. It wasn't going to spoil my joy.

Mummy lit two candles, as she did every Friday evening, though I didn't know why. She fed me, sat me on the kitchen table, poured hot water into a *schissel* and washed me down from face to feet. She then tucked me in my white cot, leaving the gaslight on. After she left, I climbed over the rails of my cot and watched her cross Vallance Road to our hairdressing shop. She'd gone to join Daddy for the Friday evening pub customers. In bed again, alone, I listened to trains hooting on the nearby rail tracks, and the hoarse cry of the dock's foghorns.

I thought about Booba's strange tears, her coldness to Mummy, her coolness to me, her only grandchild; Zada so sweet, Uncle Max burning my hand, he and his young friends drinking at Lyons' Corner House, making plans to fight Mosley when the Fascists would gather to march through the Jewish East End. My young uncle might be careless toward me, but to fight Fascists, he also had to be brave.

I dreamed that someone left a child on our doorstep. I picked her up to take care of her, and found to my surprise that considering she was just a baby, she felt as heavy as a sack of coal. But I held her close.

Why did everyone seem so surprised that I would take care of her?

CHAPTER 4

THE OTHER GRANDPARENTS

Armistice Day, 11 November 1934 at 11am. Shoreditch Church and all other East End church bells, St Clemens, St Martin's, Old Bailey, Shoreditch and St Mary's had tolled their different rhythms 11 times. I was a cockney because I was born within the sound of Bow Bells.

Mummy threw up the bedroom window, and cold air – like bird wings – flapped our faces.

'The whole of England will be silent for two minutes. We're going to pray for the Great War dead soldiers,' Mummy whispered.

She knelt behind me, warmth from her body cupping mine, flowing into me as I stood in front of her. A rare touch. We both stared into our emptied, dead street. Nothing moved. No sound passed throughout the entire country, as if the vengeful witch from Sleeping Beauty had cursed the whole of England with a 100-year sleep.

All sounds had stopped. There was no sound of rumbling trains, no cheerful train hoot from nearby tracks, no soft fog horn from the docks, no rattle of cars and lorries joggling over old Roman cobblestone roads, no clopping Clydesdales nor high heels tapping on pavements, no wireless music, no tinkling shop door bell, no window slamming shut, no organ grinder playing, no jumping, squeaking monkey, no running water splashing, no bubbling hot kettle in the kitchen, no voices chatting, no baby wails, no mother throwing open the window calling, 'Charlie! 'ere's yer doorstep, catch!' no Pearlies sitting high on rumbling carts, singing, 'Any ol' rags, any ol' iron, any, any any ol'iron?' Silence.

This must be how Daddy listened to silence all the time. It was peaceful, but would I like it my whole life? No. I hoarded each sound, remembering every one in case like Daddy I became deaf.

Finally the two minutes passed. Mummy jumped to her feet and banged the window shut. All sounds pounded back: rumbling, hooting, bumping, clopping, neighing, tapping, music, tinkling, slamming, squeaking, splashing, bubbling, organ grinding, chatting, and wailing!

Thank God I could hear!

Mummy began making the bed and dusting the furniture, saying, 'These two minutes of silence always remind me of the The Great War. In school we had to get under our desks because the Germans dropped bombs on us.' She sighed. 'After the war I married your father. You were born almost exactly one year later, in 1929. Your birthday will be in two months, on January 9th.' She recited in a sing-song voice, 'I married your father, Abraham Moscovitch, age 25, Hairdresser's Assistant living at 91 Wilkes Street, Spitalfields, East 1, London, son of Hyman or Chaim Moscovitch, Boot Dealer. I, Minnie Goldzuman sometimes called Esther Minnie Goldzumer, aged 22, spinster, a Fur Machinist living at 50 Heneage Street, Spitalfields, daughter of Benjamin or Benzion Golzuman or Goldzumer, Furrier, I married Abraham Moscovitch.

'I came from a good family and my mother made me marry your father, a working class uneducated deaf man, so Mitzi could marry. Well, now she's going to marry a chemist, a professional man, not an uneducated deaf man, like me.'

Over the bedroom fireplace hung a huge painting of my solemn Mummy and Daddy. Daddy wore a smart, double-breasted suit, with two rows of shiny buttons, a silk top hat, and white spats probably all rented from Moss Bros. Mummy's creamy lace bridal dress with a scalloped hem fell just below her knees. Her veil, a cream lace Mantilla with scalloped edges, hung over her face like a fringe down to her eyebrows and behind her cascaded to the floor ending in a train.

Mummy sighed. 'Dad thinks my family is all middle class snobs and thieves, but his family is low class, uneducated and poor. His Mother's nice, his father's a villain.'

Each of my parents hated one of the other's parents. Why couldn't they be friends?

'Can we visit Daddy's parents?' I asked, breaking my usual silence at home. 'I've never seen Daddy's parents.'

For a whole minute, it seemed, she said nothing. Then, 'Dad can take you next Sunday'.

The following Sunday, walking through the poorest East End on our way to Wilkes Street, Daddy said, 'My grandfather, your great grandfather's Hebrew name was Eliezer Chaim or Hyman, his English name was Lewis. He was a sweet man and left me a wonderful stamp collection. My stupid father threw it into the dustbin. I was furious, but as soon as I could, I began my own stamp collection.'

Last night I'd watched Daddy's thick barber fingers grasp little bright coloured pictures with tweezers, and move them from cellophane packets each into its own tiny pocket in a big stamp book that held a different page for the stamps of each country.

'Look at this one,' he'd said, showing me a wildly coloured stamp from Italy.

Who made these pretty stamps with their beautiful colours and pictures? How did Daddy have the patience to put them in order by country as he had last night?

'I had an uncle, my father's brother, who lived in South America,' Daddy said, as we passed barefoot, grimy children playing in the streets. 'A man came into his shop and shot him. My father was born in Odessa, went to America and herded cattle like a cowboy. That's where he met my mother, an American Jewish girl; her name was then Sarah Newman. She told me he chased her until she agreed to marry him and come to England. He married when he was 25, same as me. In Russia, my father was a gunsmith, but the English Gunsmith's Union won't let Jews in, so he became a boot finisher, and now he's a grocer. His first love is guns and horses.'

So that was where Daddy got his adventurous spirit. I couldn't wait to see his father's grocery shop. Was it like Booba's? It seemed strange to be meeting this Moscovitch grandfather for the first time. Surely I'd been there when I was a baby and had forgotten. Or perhaps Daddy didn't visit his parents. Mummy rarely visited hers. She sent me instead.

'My father's three sisters, my aunts, all called Moscovitch, went to America and married there. One went to New Orleans. I don't know where the other two are.'

Since the ragged children in this neighbourhood playing in the streets shouted to each other, they wouldn't notice me shouting, so I shouted, 'Do you have brothers and sisters?'

'Me? I'm the oldest of four children; I was born September 28, 1902. I 'ave two brothers, Barney and Alec and a sister, Fanny. Until I married I lived with my parents on Wilkes Street. From age 12 I schlepped 'eavy garments for sixpence a week over my shoulder, summer and winter, not even an 'at in winter. My father took all but a penny. What could I do with a penny? We 'ad almost no food. Lucky my grandmother sent us money. She was a mystery; I don't know where she got it.

'When I was 14, I caught my father 'itting my Mum again,' Daddy said. 'I told 'im, 'If you ever 'it 'er again I'm going to wallop you.' My Mum was lying on the floor. Could you believe she screamed, 'Don't raise your 'and against your father, it's forbidden in the Bible!'

'My father is as 'andsome as a film star, but 'e runs around with other women. 'e used to take me with 'im, but I told 'im 'I don't want to go to your floosies. Stay 'ome with my mother.'

I liked my father speaking to me as if I were an adult when we went out together. I loved going out with him. It was the only time he really spoke to me and always about interesting things like Houndsditch, museums, stamps, and now about his family.

Would I like this grandfather the way I loved Zada? Daddy's father sounded wild, but I felt curious rather than afraid to meet him.

Finally, we came to a tiny corner grocery shop on Wilkes Street. Its outside walls were black with soot and oozed dripping water.

Pushing me into a dark door, Dad said, 'I'll be back in 'alf hour,' and disappeared, I guessed, to a bookie.

I stepped small through the door, and gasped. Booba's grocery shone with lights and delicacies. This grocery shop was tiny, dark and gloomy. The only light came from the open shop door. I supposed they didn't have a shilling for the gas meter, and couldn't afford electric lights. The only food on all the shelves was two tins, one drunkenly tipped against the other.

A man dressed in black trousers, a satiny black waistcoat and furious black eyes lay full-length on his counter leaning on one elbow, his hand propping up his head. He looked like Daddy only handsomer. Like Daddy, he was short and slim, but with a heavy mantle of shiny black hair. Angry, beautiful black eyes glittered at me as he lay sleek and still on the counter, reminding me of the black panther in my 'Just So' stories, or of photographs of Rudolph Valentino pasted outside the Roxy. After Daddy telling me about this gunsmith and cowboy father, my grandfather's furious eyes and silence did not upset me; I felt simply curious about this strange, silky beast. Used to being silent and watchful at home, I stood calmly under his angry stare and stared back at him. His eyes were those of a black panther.

Far from sitting in the dining room smoking Turkish cigarettes and reading *The Forward*, like Zada, Daddy's father lay sullenly on the wooden counter staring out of his open door into grimy Wilkes Street like a caged animal.

Did he know I was his granddaughter? If he did, he didn't care. Neither did he care about his grocery shop. Far from being large, light and clean like Booba's shop, stacked to the ceiling with fresh and shining tins of food, these shabby shelves were bare except for the two drunken cans. Neither were there any marble counters or glass cases overflowing with fresh breads, cheeses, chopped herring, smoked salmon, nor on the floor, barrels of pickled cucumbers, olives, nor sacks of grain in the corner. No tempting smells made my nose twitch or my mouth water. The two grandparents' shops were like Pharaoh's dreams about thin cows eating fat cows, and thin ears of corn eating up fat ears of corn that my Hebrew teacher had told us in the three or so times Mummy took me to Hebrew school. Mummy's parents had the fat cows and father's parents the thin cows; Mummy's parents had the fat ears of corn, and Daddy's the thin. I supposed grandfather Hyman or Chaim couldn't even afford to buy food for his family, let alone goods to sell. It was amazing anyone came into that shop at all. He probably thought I was a customer when my shadow darkened the door, and hated me for being only a strange little girl.

How tame life must be for him, after his exciting life as a gunsmith and a cowboy. How bored he must be, stuck in this poor slum. Was that why his eyes glittered like a beast's? As we stared at each other for a full minute, his furious black eyes reminded me of the prince trapped inside an animal in Beauty and the Beast. I knew his anger had nothing to do with me, so I felt no fear.

I imagined him in Russia, black eyes squinting down the barrel of one of those shiny pistols I'd seen on a Saturday morning American cowboy film with John Wayne, The Lucky Texan. Bang, bang, John Wayne shot dead the villain who killed his uncle and then he furiously rode his horse shouting 'Yahoo!' Once, this grandfather's life had been exciting; here in East London, nothing moved. He lay still and silent. Nor did I try to speak to him. Where was Daddy's mother? What was she like?

A door behind my grandfather's counter opened. Light from some window behind someone flooded the dark shop and blinded me, so I saw framed in the door only the dark silhouette of a large woman dressed in a floaty flowered dress. But I saw her finger beckon me. She must be Daddy's Mummy, my other grandmother. I ducked under the counter on which my grandfather lay, and padded, looking right and left into the dining room like a cat entering a new house, searching for this other Booba's shiny dining room table, the crystal vase, flowers, a sofa and piano and big tomcats asleep before a cheerful coal fire, listening for the mantle clock ticking loudly. My mouth fell open, astonished.

A vast, totally empty linoleum floor with not one stick of furniture in it stretched out ahead like an ocean. No table, not one chair, no sofa as in Booba's house, no clock. Certainly no piano. Where did they sit, where did they eat, where did they sleep?

I was so fascinated with the emptiness and silence of the room and how different it was from Booba's that I barely looked at Daddy's mother, my grandmother, Sarah. When she drew me against her warm body that cupped mine, a fleeting glance upward told me she was a tall lady with a big cushiony bosom, a ruddy face, and sandy, frizzy hair. Since she loomed so tall, and I was so small, she seemed like a giantess, her head in the sky.

She bent over me, and tenderly wrapped her large skirt around me, like a big Mummy bird nestling her baby inside its wings. Although I could not see her face behind me, I felt her large, soft body pressed warm against mine. She said nothing, but as she leaned her soft body against my skinny shoulders, she gently pressed into my hand a tiny blue glass with a tiny handle, the glass the size of a large thimble. She said nothing, but tenderly bent my forefinger around the glass handle. A dark red liquid glowed inside the glass. This grandmother's large comfortable body curved around mine as she guided my hand holding the glass to my mouth, and she tipped a drop of the liquid down my throat. The wine was so warm and sweet I immediately became dizzy, and melted into my grandmother's warm body.

Although I could see how poor she was, this grandmother, in five minutes had given me more love than Booba had ever given me. Maybe this grandmother had a loving mother who showed her how to be kind, whereas Booba's mother had died when she was two. Perhaps no one had loved Booba when she was a child, and she loved no one except Zada and Aunt Mitzi.

I looked around again at the bare living room and at the little glass of wine this grandmother Sarah had given me. I saw that Daddy was kind like his mother; Mummy, tough and bitter, like hers. People learned to be kind or hard from their mothers or fathers.

Although I met Grandmother Sarah only once, her kindness in the face of her poverty and her hard life remained forever in my memory. Grandmother Sarah had nothing and gave me everything: affection, tenderness, and drink. Booba seemed to have everything, but although her wonderful grocery shop was crammed with food, she never gave me a crumb, a drink, a kiss or a hug. I saw Booba every Friday and respected her fierce determination. But I never loved her.

I met Grandmother Sarah once, and loved her forever.

CHAPTER 5

FRIDAY NIGHT IN ALF'S BARBER SHOP

During the week, the red, white and blue striped barber pole hanging over our barber shop door on Vallance Road twirled dizzyingly night and day, day and night. But in spite of our bright pole, weekdays, only one or two customers might dribble by during the entire day. Daddy stood outside the shop on its doorstep head down, muttering out loud to the shop step, 'Fuck you, fuck you, fuck you,' for hours and hours until and if a customer came.

But Friday and Saturday evenings pub nights, even in the '30s the shop came alive.

This morning, before I left for Wood Close School, Mummy said, 'When you come home, I'll be shopping. Don't go to the flat, go straight to the shop and stay with Dad until I come for you. Mind the road. Betty Schneider crossed the rail lines without looking and the train cut off both her legs.' So I always looked both ways on the way to school.

I loved my school, Wood Close, even though from outside it looked like the prisons I'd seen on the Saturday morning children's films, with dark red brick walls and an outside stone staircase enclosed by black iron bars – I supposed so that we didn't fall sideways off the stairs onto our concrete playground. But inside, big windows let in bright light, and Mr Kent always smiled his welcome.

'Write the date, and don't forget the year, 1934,' he said, after we settled. 'Arithmetic,' he called out, and we all chanted multiplication tables from one two is two to 12 12s are 144. Then he gave us sums. I had entered his class when I was five, youngest in the class.

'Go to the front of the line,' Mr Kent always said to me after tests. I stood proudly at the head of the line, first in line every time, fingering the gold bracelet with its gold heart dangling from it that Aunt Mitzi had given me. I grinned because my aunt loved me, and I could tell that Mr Kent truly liked me.

After school I ran to our shop to stay with Daddy. There he stood on the step, hands thrust into his white barber's coat pockets all day no customers, head down and chanting to his shop step as if it were to blame, 'Fuck you, fuck you, fuck you, fuck you.' He didn't stop even when I squeezed past him. Although I was forbidden to say that word, and few Jews used it, two paint-spattered workmen passed by, one saying to the other, 'So I sez to 'er "where the fucking 'ell is the fuckin' beer I fuckin' sent you to fuckin' get?"' To me, this was normal East London cockney, but never used at home and only in the shop when there were no customers. I left him on the step and squeezed in.

Inside our barber shop, sinks and mirrors gleaming, the chrome, hot-towel urn hissed softly while six stout barber chairs sat empty, I went to my little stool in the corner of the ladies' section and opened Aunt Mitzi's book of fairy tales that she'd given me for my birthday.

Finally, a man came to the door, not at all put out at Dad's cursing, and said loudly, 'Wotcha, Alf!'

Daddy cheered up immediately, his dark eyes gleaming like burning coals and greeted Bill with, 'Wotcha,' and as he cut Bill's hair his sharp scissors 'snip, snip, snipped,' and the man's hair floated to the floor like black feathers.

Since it was Friday, and business usually picked up on Friday evening, Wally, Dad's apprentice, a young, blond, Jewish bloke, pushed open the shop door, setting the door bell tinkling. Wally came on Friday evenings, Saturdays and during Easter and Christmas rush to help Daddy. I liked Wally, because he spoke to me gently like Zada and my new Uncle Adrian and didn't tease me like my young uncles.

'Take over while I 'ave dinner,' Daddy told Wally. 'I'll be back soon.'

Daddy and I hurried across Vallance Road to our flat for Friday dinner. As darkness fell early in winter, lamplighters appeared. Grey coats floor-length, a half-belt at the back, battered trilbies covered grey old heads, and shuffling along, lamplighters carried long lit tapers from one street lamp to the next. Soon, all of Vallance Road bloomed with yellow gas-lights. Daddy and I ran across Vallance Road and up our three flights of stairs to our flat.

This Friday evening as usual, Mummy lit two candles, covered her face with her hands, murmuring something in Hebrew then sighed. Unlike Mummy and Daddy, Booba and Zada closed their shop on Saturday, but never told me why nor invited me to eat with them. Years later I learned that Jewish grandparents often invited their grandchildren to eat with them on Shabbat or holydays, especially an only grandchild. I didn't even know that the delicious dinner we ate Friday nights was a special Shabbos dinner. I thought that Mummy putting me to bed after Friday dinner, both parents leaving me alone, going to work in the shop across the street was normal.

Now in silence, all of us reading since Daddy was deaf, we ate our usual Friday evening dinner. Mummy had made chicken soup with lokshen (homemade noodles), roast chicken, roast potatoes and stuffed chicken neck. I'd watched Mummy stuff the floppy skin of the chicken neck and then thread a darning needle and with black thread sew closed the stuffed skin that now looked like a big yellow sausage. When cooked, she'd slice the stuffed neck. Chicken claws went into making our soup. Mummy loved sucking chicken legs and claws and as she read *True Confessions*, they looked as if they grew from inside her, stuck out of her mouth.

Once finished, she and Daddy put on their white, hairdressing coats and began buttoning those white coats from top to bottom. I knew they planned to leave me alone in my cot, as usual, three flights above the Michaels' grocery, the headless dummy one floor below.

The buttons all the way down their coats winked at me. When I grew up, I'd never wear any dress buttoned all the way down. Buttons down the front meant, 'Goodbye, good riddance to bad rubbish,' words with which some children taunted an unlucky child they wanted to hurt.

But tonight to my joy, Mummy said, 'If you stay quietly on your stool in the corner of the shop and read your book, you can come to the shop with us. Wally will put you to bed later.'

I now sat quietly on a little three-legged stool in the women's section at the back of the shop, Aunt Mitzi's fairy-tale book in my lap. The curtain between the women's and the men's, though drawn together in the middle, never quite closed, so I could see, smell and hear all those hairy, alien creatures: men. When they walked in, the shop door bell jangling, some had hair growing all over their faces and smelled sweaty, but they left, faces pink clean and smelling of tangy shaving lotion.

I loved the shop's mixed smells. The women's section smelled of ammonia from the perms, men's, sweet, from after-shave lotions Daddy slapped on their faces; the shop breathed out a mixed acrid-sweet smell, like Daddy and Mummy's bedroom in the morning when the yellow fish floated in the chamber pot. The two smells made me think of my grandparents, Booba, acid, Zada sweet; acid when Mummy sent me to some strange 'aunt' in some boring country place where I always felt lost, sweet when home and content in East London. Now, I felt happy sitting in my corner like Little Miss Muffet who sat on a tuffet but no spider sat beside me.

Peeping through the curtain opening on the women's side, I saw four brawny dockers sitting on our hard horsehair sofa, waiting their turn. The shop lights, doubled by the shining mirrors in front of the six barbershop chairs, set the whole shop shimmering and glittering. A gas urn for heating towels hung on the wall behind Daddy. On top of the urn sat a pile of snow white, hot towels that rippled from steam shooting up beneath them. Flickering fiercely, jet gas flames burned blue and yellow, seen through three round holes at the bottom of the urn, and steam shot hissing upward to a scalding heat to warm the snowy white towels lying on top.

Awaiting their turn, men flicked through newspapers and magazines on the sofa. If they flicked fast, it showed they looked only at the pictures because they couldn't read. The eyes of the few who could read moved slowly from left to right, sometimes mouths moving, fingers also moving along the print like children. Most had left school by age 12, like Daddy, and still could not read, though he read well. Smoke rose to the ceiling from the dockers' coffin nails. Mumfie, my velvet stuffed elephant doll, sat soft in my lap.

Jock, a regular, smoked, rolling his round blue eyes at Betty Grable on the wall calendar. Wearing a tight sweater and little white shorts, she leaned back on a high bar stool, long, bare white legs crossed at the ankle, bare feet in high-heeled shoes. Mummy said that her legs had been insured for a million dollars. I only knew pounds, half-crowns, a sovereign, shillings, sixpences, thrupenny bits, pennies and farthings, that friends and relatives tipped me with, 'Don't tell Mummy'. But a million dollars sounded like a huge treasure, especially just for two legs.

In the women's section where I sat, Mummy cut, shampooed, peroxided, dyed, set and permed their hair. Sometimes she gave them manicures, soaking jam-factory-worn fingers in soapy water, cutting their cuticles, filing their nails, dipping a wooden stick, its tip covered with twisted cotton wool into peroxide to whiten dirty nail edges, and then she'd sweep nail-polish on each nail. Few cockney women could afford a manicure. Still, Mummy complained about her 'dirty work'. She had so much wanted that high school education and clean work.

Daddy didn't seem to mind dirty men. I never heard him complain.

In the men's section, Tommie plopped down in Dad's chair. His friend Jock, waiting his turn, hurtled fat smoke rings through the shop, the rings hitting the ceiling and flattening out. How did Jock make smoke rings?

The bell over the door jangled as Bert, a stocky redheaded docker, bounced in. His arm and chest muscles stretched his blue-striped shirt thin, but his black and white check trousers held up by red suspenders perfectly fitted his narrow waist and hard belly. Jock saluted Bert.

'Wotcha cock?' Jock said to Bert, tearing his eyes away from Betty Grable's legs.

'Wotcha cock,' Bert said to Jock. 'Goin' to the Blue Whale ternight?'

'Yerss. Me and the missis. See yer there, Bert.'

Dad cut and shaved hair, the only time he moved fast besides when he chased Fascist children who shoved open the shop and yelled, 'Dirty Jew!'

Tommie Bradford sprang out of Dad's chair, shaven clean as a peeled orange.

'Gimme a Red Letter, Alf.'

Daddy pulled out one of the little inch-square red envelopes with the rubber fish inside that I stuck round the men's mirrors every Wednesday and that swam in our chamber pot every morning and that men bought Friday or Saturday evenings.

Tommy paid and tipped Daddy; most customers didn't tip a shop owner, only assistants.

'Ta,' Dad said--- he rarely spoke, but for once looked into the man's eyes, and then dropped the money into a drawer next to the mirror.

Daddy swiftly brushed down Tommie Bradford. 'Next!' he shouted not knowing, I supposed, that he was shouting.

As Jock jumped up and snuggled deep down into Dad's chair, Daddy slowly took a sip of tea Mummy had made him in the tiny scullery behind our shop, and he gazed into the distance. I wondered what he was thinking, always thinking. Customers waited patiently until he was ready, because once he started, Mummy said, he was the fastest and best barber. But she screamed at him daily, 'If you didn't charge tuppence more than everyone else we'd have more business. Why do you charge more?'

'Because I'm worth it,' he'd said quietly.

'Shave, 'aircut, singe an' 'ot towel, Alf,' Jock shouted.

'Awight,' Dad said.

Bert, on the sofa waiting his turn, struck a match, cupped a hand round the flame like a sailor in a wind and lit his Player's.

Wally whipped the white cloth off his customer, brushed the bloke down; his customer paid and tipped Wally.

'Ta. Next, please,' Wally said, dropping money into Daddy's drawer, pocketing the tip.

At Easter, and during the Christmas rush, Mummy's younger brothers, Uncle Max or Uncle Sam, whom Daddy trained, helped in our shop. Soon the Christmas rush would be on. Mummy would send me to Mrs Lyons and her seven girls while she and Daddy worked in the shop sometimes 12 hours a day. In exchange for Mummy setting her hair, Mrs Lyons scrubbed our shop floor. Bessie Lyons had thick blonde hair, beautiful violet eyes; a handsome carpenter husband, usually out of work, and seven daughters. She sat in the women's section, and was growing a fat tummy again.

'Her eighth? Silly cow,' Mummy had said. 'At least your father takes care of me.'

Of course he did. Whenever there were customers he worked hard.

Bert plopped into Wally's chair, stretched his legs and said, 'Shave an' 'aircut, Wally.'

The wireless hanging on the wall played Gracie Fields singing in her hard, pure voice, 'Wish me Luck as you Wave me Goodbye.' I hated goodbyes.

Dad threw a white cloth over Jock, snipped at the man's hair, lit a foot-long, skinny taper and singed Jock's back hairs, slathered on Brylcreem and combed the hair back until it gleamed like Cary Grant's. Daddy dipped the wooden chair all the way back until Jock lay almost flat, Adam's Apple like a white ball sticking up toward the ceiling. If only I could speak to Daddy and ask him why was that lump in a man's throat called an Adam's Apple. He read so much; he could tell me. But I'd have to shout and must not.

Daddy began 'stropping' his open razor with its yellow bone handle on a leather band attached to his chair. His razor's edge flashed under our brilliant shop lights and again, in the mirrors. He dipped the fat, badger-hair shaving brush into his shaving mug from the front of which gazed King George V with his pointy beard and Queen Mary, with her five-row pearl choker, King and Queen of our great British Empire. Daddy sloshed shaving cream in circles over Jock's face as if painting the face. Daddy lightly pinched the man's nose with thumb and middle finger, raised it and lathered Jock's stubbly upper lip. Men, like monkeys, had hair sprouting out all over them, from over their lips, chins, ears, heads, chests, under their arms and now I saw, even from their noses. My father clipped Jock's nose hair, cocked his glinting blade into a letter 'L' and elbow in the air, as if playing a violin, swiftly, with a scraping noise, swept the razor across Jock's cheek, swiftly wiping the razor's stubble and dirt on paper lying on Jock's sheeted chest. The razor moved to Jock's throat.

Jock lay back trustingly, throat stretched, Daddy's glinting razor dancing around Jock's Adam's Apple. I waited for the razor to slit the man's throat and for red blood to spout out, but Daddy deftly swept his blade along the skin without even nicking Jock, and then wiped soap and dirty stubble from his razor onto tissue paper on Jock's chest. Behind Daddy, hanging on the wall, our glittering silver hot towel urn hissed and snorted like a dragon as its leaping blue-red gas flames gushed steam up to blindingly white towels lying flat atop the urn.

Dad reached to the top of the urn, deftly whipped off a scalding towel by one corner, and with thumb and a finger tossed it from hand to hand until it cooled just enough so he could stand to hold it, then dropped it swiftly so it fell like magic into folds around Jock's face. Only the tip of Jock's pink nostrils peeked out at the ceiling. Jock lay under the hot towel, steam pouring off it up to, and hitting the ceiling and then fanning out. Jock lay as still as a dead cat I'd once seen at the pound. While Jock lay steaming, Daddy strolled over to a side table, took a leisurely sip of tea, munched on a Peak Frean chocolate biscuit; his dark eyes stared into space, thinking, always thinking. What did he think about so much? While he ate and stared, Jock, face wrapped in white looked like the Egyptian mummy Daddy and I saw one Sunday in the museum. Like the Mummy, Jock didn't move a muscle. I watched, biting my thumbnail. Could he breathe? Daddy finished his tea, walked slowly back toward the still man, and just when I thought for sure Jock had died, my father flipped off the cooled towel. Jock's face glowed pink as a pig's, his eyes popped open, and even his eyeballs looked shiny and clean.

'Cor blimey, that was a bit of all right, Alf,' Jock muttered, grinning.

'Which after-shave?' Dad asked, not hearing Jock and pointing to the dazzling red, green and blue lotions in square glass each topped with a fat, glinting square glass stopper.

'Fink I'll 'ave the red, Alf,' Jock said loudly, then lay his head down again, content.

Dad slapped the red after-shave lotion onto Jock's face, whipped off the cloth covering Jock's clothes and shook it out, scattering hair over the floor for Wally to sweep up. Jock sprang up, handsome, straight and clean, like the Beast turned into a Prince, though goodness knows when Jock took a bath. Mummy said that some people were dirty from the neck down. With a thick brush, Dad brushed down Jock's clothes.

'Ta, Alf. Tara,' Jock said, the way cockneys said thanks, and goodbye, as he paid.

'Tara,' Jock said to his other mates, 'see yer at the Blue Whale.'

The wireless on the popular channel played *Red Sails in the Sunset*. After work, Mummy turned it to the other, the BBC channel for classical music and opera.

Daddy shouted, 'Next!!'

Mummy, in the women's section, made finger waves then clamped silvery metal clips looking like sharks' teeth into Mrs Crown's hair to make corrugated waves. On the wireless a man now sang:

You Ma-a-ade me Love You. I Didn't Want to Do it, an' all the time you knew it
You made me love you, you did, yes you did, oh you did you know you did ah ha ha
Give me, give me, what I sigh for, you know you got the kind of kisses that I die for
You know you made me love you, you know you did it. You know you made me love yew.

Mummy wound the hair at the bottom of Mrs Crown's head into little snails, and poked two crossed curby grips, hairpins, into each pin curl. Next to Mrs Crown, Mrs Lyons sat under our permanent wave machine. Mrs Lyons should have had a prince, I thought. Like Beauty, she was beautiful and kind. When I stayed with her girls on Saturday, while Mummy worked or during the Christmas rush or in summer school holidays, Mrs Lyons served her seven little daughters salty meat I found out was rabbit, too stringy for me, but she bent over her girls kindly as she served them, calling each, 'lovey' and 'dear'. They were very poor, but I envied them.

Mummy chattered to Mrs Crown about the new Marlene Dietrich picture in which she had fallen in love with a monk, Charles Boyer, and the weather, a favourite British topic. But Mummy had told me, 'Never let a woman tell you any of her secrets. She'll get embarrassed, and you'll lose a friend or a customer.' But Mrs Crown, like a train, rattled on, 'So I says to 'er, I says, 'Oi, Florry, do you know that Dicky Smif's a married man? Watcha want to go out wiv 'im for?'' Mrs Crown said 'Smif,' the way cockneys spoke, not Smith.

'He's not only married his wife's got a bun in the oven; due any day,' Mummy couldn't help saying.

'That Florry don't care nuffink about Dicky's wife. Florry's a right cow, she is. 'Ere, d'you know wot she done last week?'

'No what?' Mummy said, pulled into gossip in spite of herself. I leaned forward.

'She went round to 'is wife, Mrs Smif, banged on 'er doorknocker an' said, 'In case you wants to know, me and your 'usband Dickie is 'aving it off and you can kiss 'im good-bye 'e's comin' to live wiv me.' And there's the poor wife with six kids and anover on the way.'

'It doesn't say much for Mr Smith,' Mummy murmured.

'Well, what d'you expect of a man? 'e likes to have 'is crumpet and then some on the side. Boys will be boys,' Mrs Crown laughed like a Clydesdale neighing.

A big fat black louse ran from the top of Mrs Crown's dyed brown hair down her back and without missing a beat, Mummy said, 'You're right!' and smartly snipped the louse in two with her sharp, pointed hairdresser's scissors. The two halves of black louse dropped to the floor.

How fast that louse had streaked! Like a race horse I'd seen on the children's Saturday flicks. They should have lice races, I thought.

'Florry usually comes in here Fridays for a shampoo and set, but I haven't seen her this week,' Mummy said.

'You ain't goin' to tell 'er wot I said, are yer?' Mrs Crown said, scowling.

'Cross my heart and hope to die. Now I'm going to put you under the dryer and make you a nice cup of tea,' Mummy said, hoping to shut Mrs Crown up.

Mummy covered Mrs Crown's hair, with a long, thick net, tying it at the woman's fat nape, tucked cotton wool inside the net over the customer's ears so the dryer's heat didn't burn them, and then popped Mrs Crown under the metal machine. When switched to 'hot,' the dryer roared so loudly that Mrs Crown would be as deaf as Daddy.

'My goodness, you wouldn't believe the things I hear,' Mummy said as she went behind the shop to a tiny scullery to make tea. I followed to help.

In our scullery that contained only a small gas-stove, a cold-water sink, and one shelf, Mummy kept a kettle of hot water ever ready on a low flame for the endless cups of tea we British drank. Milk cooled on the windowsill facing the yard; she poured milk into a cracked cup.

'So many customers have T.B., we don't want them using our cups,' she said, setting a tea strainer filled with tea leaves over the cup and pouring hot water over it. In the saucer, she placed two cubes of sugar, a spoon and two broken biscuits. 'Cracked biscuits are cheaper than whole. Take this to Mrs Crown.'

I carried the teacup, careful not to spill any onto the saucer.

'Ta, luv,' Mrs Crown said gratefully.

I left quickly because I didn't want lice. Mummy and Daddy tooth-combed each other's hair every evening, like monkeys at the zoo grooming each other; but I was always afraid the school might find nits on me. I dreaded becoming one of those slinking, bald children with purple spots painted on their skulls.

Mrs Lyons under the perm machine looked like the picture of Medusa Daddy had once shown me, a kind of witch with long, black snakes writhing on her head. Mummy had wound

Mrs Lyons' natural blonde hair around each thin metal curler, then wrapped a white cotton pad soaked in a strong ammonia-smelling mix over each curler, and then clipped a metal cover over each curl. Long black wires from each curler snaked almost to the ceiling, and fitted into a round metal plate. Mummy plugged the giant perm machine into an electric outlet and looked at her watch to time exactly how long Mrs Lyons should stay under it. One minute too long and smoke would pour out of the curler and shoot to the ceiling; a piece of burnt curl inside its metal holder would clank to the floor, leaving a bald spot and a screaming customer. Shivering, I watched Mummy while she poured another cup of tea in a good cup with a whole biscuit for Mrs Lyons. Mrs Lyons though poor, was clean and healthy.

The curlers and wires were so heavy that when I came with her tea, Mrs Lyons couldn't turn her head. Her arm waved out to take the cup like the antenna of those great green pretty insects that Daddy said ate their husbands.

'Oh, ta, dearie, just what I need,' she said. She stirred her tea with the spoon, but since she couldn't look down, she raised the teacup to her face. Luckily, like Mummy, I had naturally curly hair and would never need a perm.

With Mrs Crown quieted under the dryer sipping her cup of tea, Mummy checked Mrs Lyons's perm. The men murmured quietly to each other as they smoked, while the wireless played, 'T' was on the Isle of Capri that I Found Her'. The dryer hummed.

Suddenly the door burst open jangling the doorbell and in stalked Florry Dawson; the very woman Mrs Crown had been gossiping about. Under the noise of the dryer, her nose buried in her teacup, Mrs Crown didn't hear nor see Florry, but Mummy's face flushed bright red.

'Oi, Minny!' Florry called out to Mummy, and flouncing through the men's section, waggling her hips, she flung open the women's curtain. All the men's heads swiveled to stare at her big, heaving bosom, hands on her tiny waist, her big behind rocking as she stood legs astride in three-inch red heels. Long legs like Betty Grable's, but silk-stockinged, showed out of the shortest skirt in East End London. Now I understood why some men called women 'a skirt'.

'Min, I know I dint make no appointment, but can you do me, nah? I got a special date tonight, and I want ter look really smashin'.'

Florry tossed her long mane of dyed curly blonde hair over her shoulders and batted black, mascara'd lashes over emerald eyes.

Mummy shot a nervous look at Mrs Crown. 'Could you possibly come back in an hour?' Mummy quavered, no doubt hoping she could finish Mrs Crown before Mrs Crown saw Florry.

'I need it nah,' Florry Dawson insisted. 'You could do me while them uvers is under the dryer and perm machine. You ain't got no one in the basin. You could wash me 'air, set me quick and pop me under the dryer, cooncher?'

While Mummy was thinking what to say, in rushed a woman with a fat tummy.

'Oh no, not Mrs Smith,' Mummy moaned.

Mrs Smith hurled herself at Florry, grabbed a handful of Florry's hair and pulled it hard, screaming 'You cow, tryn' to take me 'usband away I'm goin' to pull all yor fucking 'air out 'till you're fucking bald.'

She tore out a handful of Florry Dawson's blonde hair, black at the roots. Peroxided hair, I knew from Mummy, broke easily.

'Sodding cow,' screamed Florry Dawson, punching Mrs Smith's stomach, 'Fuck off and leave us alone. 'e wants me, 'e don't want you.'

'Don't want me? Don't want me?' Mrs Smith screamed, 'What the bloody 'ell do you think this big belly is from if 'e doesn't want me?'

'I'll kill the bastard in your belly, bleeding bitch,' screamed Florry Dawson.

Mrs Smith grabbed out another chunk of Florry Dawson's hair.

'I'll murder your brat,' Florry Dawson screamed, kicking Mrs Smith's belly again.

Mrs Smith bent double, clutched her stomach and moaned, 'My baby!'

Florry stepped on my foot with her spike heels; I yelped and dropped my book.

Mummy shouted, 'Mind the child!'

'Bugger the child,' Florry screamed. 'Bugger all of you.'

Some of the men, even Daddy, holding his open razor, ran in from the men's side to see what the commotion was about. Suddenly, in rushed Mr Smith, a huge brute of a docker, six foot tall and five foot wide, and he shouted, ''ere, wot's goin' on?'

He grabbed his wife and Florry Dawson each by an ear, and one on either side of him, dragged them both screaming and kicking out into the street.

'Sodding bitches both of yer,' he yelled. 'Fuck off.'

Through the open shop door I saw to my horror, Mr Smith shove both his pregnant wife and Florry into the wet gutter, and then crossed the street, he headed for the Blue Whale. Daddy calmly finished shaving his customer, but Mummy stood white and rooted to the spot.

Mrs Crown had caught sight of the Smiths and Florry in the mirror and exclaimed, 'Well, blow me dahn. Did you ever 'ear such carryings on? You could knock me over wiv a fevver seein' them three in 'ere togever, fightin'.' .

'I'm burning,' screamed Mrs Lyons, smoke pouring out of the perm machine. Three curlers clanked to the floor. Smoking blackened blonde curls fell out of them.

'Oh Lord, I'm so sorry,' Mummy cried out and leapt to switch off the perm machine electricity. Two more of Mrs Lyons's metal curlers with burned blonde hair clanged to the floor.

'Don't worry, love,' Mrs Lyons said to Mummy, 'it weren't your fault. It's them new people moving into the neighbourhood. Ain't like the old days when people was respecable.'

'Thank you so much, Bessie, you're so kind,' Mummy said, her face white.

The men all went back to their side of the curtain, laughing and joking about 'females'. Dad went back to his customer, razor cocked.

Breathing hard, I picked up my book, open at *Beauty and the Beast*. If anyone tonight was Beauty, it was Mrs Lyons, and if anyone was a beast, it was Mr Smith, but there was no prince inside him.

Sometimes, a prince lay under a beast, and sometimes, a beast lay under a prince.

Mummy took off Mrs Crown's metal wave-clips and pulled the pins out of her curls, combed her hair into waves and curls then rubbed Vaseline between her hands and smoothed it over Mrs Crown's hair to make it shiny.

'Bootiful,' Mrs Crown crowed, as she primped in the mirror. She paid Mummy and left, her three chins high.

Mummy turned to Mrs Lyons and removed the cooling permanent wave curlers. Five curls had fallen off. Mrs Lyons had such thick hair that the missing curls hardly showed.

'My Gawd, I 'ope that Mrs Smith's baby isn't hurt, that rotten Florry kicking her in the stomach,' Mrs Lyons said. Mrs Lyons was such a kind lady! Mrs Lyons looked tubby in front, too. If she had another girl that would make eight girls I could sleep with when Mummy sent me to her overnight. How lovely. But if she was having another baby, would she be able to take care of me during the coming Christmas rush? If not, where would Mummy send me away to this time? I hoped it wouldn't be to One-Tit Mrs Major.

'Wally, take the child home,' Mummy said. 'Here's a shilling for the gas meter.'

Daddy said I was a silly goose to be afraid of the dark. Mummy, smiling, told me that once when the gas went out in the bedroom, I screamed so loudly that they could hear me in the shop across the street and everyone laughed.

Wally carried me home, lit the gaslight again, rocked me in his arms, dried my tears, put on my nightie and tucked me into my cot. I wished I had a big, kind brother like Wally. Wally was the only man except for Zada and my new Uncle Adrian who didn't laugh at, or tease me. But even Wally didn't know I was afraid of the headless dummy. They'd already laughed at me for being afraid of the dark, so I'd never say it again.

I lay sleepily in my cot listening to the dockers' voices coming from The Blue Whale opposite, singing, 'Daisy, Daisy, give me your answer, do,' and a beery 'Sweetest Little Fellow, Everybody Knows'. I knew all the popular songs from listening to the pub singing, and I knew from their slurry voices that the men were getting drunker by the minute.

It must be very nice, I thought, to meet your friends every Friday and Saturday night and drink and sing together and then go home and sleep together like the Lyons' girls, seven across the bed, packed warm, tight and close as kittens, their soft bodies, the sound of them all breathing quietly next to me making me feel so safe. They might be poor, but they were never lonely at night.

The ticking clock said that the time was 10pm. My parents had come home and were already asleep in their big double bed. I could not sleep.

The men and women in the pub sang one song after another, while the piano man kept banging out popular tunes on the tinny piano until the clock handles neared 11pm.

'Time Gentlemen, please,' I heard Harry McGregor shout at 11pm and, climbing over the rails of my cot and looking through the window, I saw him clicking the pub lights on and off. People began staggering out of The Blue Whale into the empty lit street, arms round each other's shoulders, kicking up their legs five and six abreast at the same time bawling:

'Oy, knees up Mother Brown,
Yer drawers is falling down.
Under the table you must go
Ei- yi ei-y ei- yi yo,
If I catch you napping
I'll tear yer drawers right orf
Oi, knees up, knees up
Don't get the breeze up
Knees up Mummy Bro-o-w-n.'

They sang and danced to *Knees up Mother Brown* 10, 12 times without stopping, without getting tired, dancing toward their homes. I sang with them under my breath while my parents slept. As their voices grew fainter I climbed back into my cot. Once more all was quiet.

What was it like to be a gentile I wondered, to speak like a cockney, go to church, not to have children call you Jew-girl, not to fear black swastikas and DP, Death to Jews painted in black on the walls, to eat eels, rabbit, pork, bacon and shrimp and spend every Friday and Saturday night in the pub, get tipsy and dance in the street, curse, and when you were a child, play barefoot in the street, eat a doorstep spread with bacon dripping for lunch, sleep snug with seven sisters across a bed.

But then I wouldn't be able to enjoy our barbershop or my grandparents' grocery sounds and smells, nor have my own Mummy and Daddy, beautiful Aunt Mitzi, my young, teasing uncles, sarcastic Booba or tender Zada as grandparents. I wouldn't have the other kind Grandmother Sarah and my panther-like father's father, the gunsmith from Russia. Without Daddy, I might never again go to a museum or to a zoo. Would I like this? Drowsy, I listened to nearby trains rumbling gently along, hooting softly, and to the soft moan of foghorns.

Daddy said that one Sunday we would visit his sister, Fannie, and his brother-in-law who was a bookie and a lightweight boxer. I looked forward to meeting this new, bookie-boxer uncle.

I dreamed that I ate squirmy eels, pink shrimps, danced in the street and said 'fuck'.

CHAPTER 6

BOOKMAKERS, BOXERS AND CROCODILE KEEPERS

It was summer, there was no school. We were having breakfast and reading. I'd just been to the library again. I was reading *Sleeping Beauty* from my book of fairy tales. Mine was propped up against the jam jar. Daddy propped his newspaper against the milk bottle, Mummy, her *True Confessions*, against the teapot. Tomorrow, I would finish reading *The Secret Garden*.

'Now run over to Mrs Lyons. I'll be working late,' Mummy said. 'Stay there all day and sleep with her girls tonight.'

Hidden in the back of our shop was a tiny winding staircase that led to the attic where the whole Lyons family lived. I once tumbled down its stairs and Mummy had stood me on the men customer's sofa, undressed except for my undershirt, even taking off my knickers in front of all the men. Horrors! She'd felt me all over and made me drink a bitter powder mixed in water.

Looking both ways before crossing, I ran across the street to our shop and now carefully up the narrow, winding staircase. All nine of the Lyons family (Mr and Mrs Lyons and their seven daughters) lived in that one, windowless room in which one huge brass bed for seven girls filled the entire room. There must have been a bed for the parents, but, so absorbed with the prospect of sleeping with the girls tonight I didn't notice one. There was no other furniture. The girls spent most days in school or outside. After school and weekends we played in the street, or in Shoreditch Churchyard: hopscotch, gobs, Oranges and Lemons, Statues, Catch, Blind Man's Buff, skipping and leapfrog. The Lyon's girls ate in the small fenced yard outside the back of our shop no matter the weather. Their 'table' consisted of crates for legs, a door standing on the crates, and she'd made seats on both sides of the table from two planks stacked across other crates. I felt quite comfortable. Chattering like birds, we girls happily sat four of us on each side of the table.

'Lunch,' Mrs Lyons called, carrying a big pot.

Mrs Lyons went round the table, pot in hand, ''ere yar, luv,' she said to her oldest, Bessie, leaning over the child, and 'Eat up, darlin'.' How I envied Bessie being called 'darlin'. Although she ate nothing herself, Mrs Lyon's tummy, like Mrs Smith's, kept growing bigger. If she were going to have another baby, would she be able, as usual, to look after me during Mummy's Christmas Rush in our shop? Last time she had a baby, I went to horrid Mrs Major.

The meat felt stringy, like pieces of rope, and tasted salty, different from the soft, sweet chicken Mummy served.

'What is this?' I asked Bessie.

'Rabbit,' she said.

I remembered the poor gutted rabbits hanging upside down in gentile butcher shops.

'Here, you have it.'

'Ta,' she said, forking it from my plate.

After lunch that Saturday, Mrs Lyons filled a large tin laundry bath with hot water, from kettles of boiled water and set the 'bath' on the 'table' in the back yard. We girls got into a line, ripped off our clothes and in turn, like a relay race, ran and jumped into the tin bath. Mrs Lyons quickly lathered each of us all over, rinsed, and then we each jumped out into a big towel she held ready. This was my second bath this week. I supposed they couldn't afford the Public Baths because Mummy said Mr Lyons, a carpenter, was always out of work. I'd once seen Mr Lyons, as handsome as Errol Flynn, but carrying his carpenter's box, his face looked sad and worried. But If I had seven big sisters to protect me like Bessie, and if I slept with them, all cozy as we'd once done, eight of us snuggled together like kittens cross-wise on the bed, not head to toe, I'd never be afraid of passing the headless dummy on the second floor landing.

We played outside on the pavement all afternoon, skipping, hopscotch, bouncing balls where the wall met the pavement, and kept score who had the highest number of hits, and drew water from a tap sticking out behind the shop's wall into the backyard, like the tap outside the bath in the public baths. There was the usual outside loo, with newspaper for wiping tushes and a chain to pull when finished.

At night, we came inside, ran in through the shop door past the Friday evening smoky shop full of men and women waiting for shaves, hot towels, haircuts, sets and perms before their big Friday night at their pub. We swarmed up the tiny staircase so fast that Dad and Mummy, working with customers, didn't even notice us. I was fast but careful on that narrow staircase.

The Lyons girls jumped into bed and we all lay across its width – eight skinny girls in a row. Bessie smuggled me in the middle of the girls where I fell asleep easily cradled by the warmth of their bodies, after hearing their soft breathing. It was such a treat instead of sleeping at home alone nightly in my cot, Mummy and Daddy working across the street in the shop, the Michaels family three flights down, and the headless dummy one flight below on the second landing. When sleeping at home, all was silent but for the mournful soft cry of the fog horns from the docks and the trains hooting as they passed on the nearby tracks, until at 11pm yoks tumbled drunk and cheerful out of the pub, singing and dancing in the street 'Knees up Mother Brown, Yer drawers is fallin' down'. How good the Lyons' girls' warm, breathing bodies felt next to mine. I wished I could go to bed with them every night.

On Sunday morning, the shops in the gentile East End closed and all the church bells clanged. Each church had its own tune, each clashing with the other. Even Daddy could hear them and called them, 'a cacophony of bells'.

Daddy was to take me to the Museum today. First, he went to the bakery across the street, to buy a newspaper, and our daily fresh rolls that we ate buttered with milk in strong hot tea. Daddy being deaf, as usual, we all read through meals. In all the books I read and films I saw, people talked while eating.

After breakfast, Mummy dressed me in my red coat and hat, Daddy put on his overcoat, stuck his brown trilby on his head. We walked down Vallance Road past Joycey's house and turned right onto Bethnal Green Road. Here, we'd catch the number six bus to the West End. I looked at Daddy's hand, hoping he'd hold it out to me, but he didn't. I didn't dare put my hand into his. All the East End church bells pealed, St Clemons, St Martins, the Old Bailey, and closest to us, the Bells of Shoreditch, where we children played on the flat graves of dead children. Each parish chimed its own tunes. Someone long ago had put chimes together for our game, 'Oranges and Lemons.' Each line of our song sounded like one of the East End church bells; the words were:

Oranges and lemons said the bells of St Clemens
I owe you five farthings said the bells of St Martin's
When will you pay me said the bells of Old Bailey
When I grow rich, said the Bells of Shoreditch

The words and beat of the song changed to a menacing sound:

Here comes the lighter to light you to bed
Here comes the chopper to chop off your head
Chip chop, chip chop, the last man's OUT.

Since I'd been born in the Stepney Green Hospital within the sound of Bow Bells, I was officially a cockney. But no one in the family except Daddy spoke with a cockney accent, I don't know why. And even he only dropped his 'h's he didn't say 'bruver' instead of 'brother'. He didn't say 'ain't got none', and he didn't say 'nuffink' instead of 'nothing'. He said 'fuck' only outside the shop and when there were no customers.

Bethnal Green Road that crowded weekdays and Saturdays with noisy stalls, open shops and shoppers was now on Sunday, silent and empty. Tossed newspapers gusted in the wind, and papers wrapped themselves round our legs while waiting for a red double-decker Number Six,

Although the gentile East End was silent on Sunday, in my head, I heard the din of the Jewish section, where Booba and Zada lived in Whitechapel. The Jewish section closed on Saturday but roared with business on Sunday. Today, Brick Lane and Petticoat Lane would be so tightly packed with people that you could hardly move. Barrow boys shouted, 'eeyar guv, missus, ten a penny, take the lot', and people's bodies warm and soft pressed deliciously against mine. I didn't like Brick Lane, though. There, Mummy sometimes bought a kosher chicken, and a woman sitting with a dead chicken in her lap plucked each feather off it until it was stripped naked. Horrible shame for the chicken flooded through me, especially when the woman plunged her hand inside its body, ripped out its steaming innards and sold the chicken with its hard, inside yolks for Mummy to feed me with. Who cared if the full yolk from inside the chicken, boiled, was a delicacy that Mummy made me eat? That chicken, once squawking and lively looked so naked. I wanted to put its feathers back on, push its insides back in and see it strut around once more, crowing proudly, king of the walk. But except for the chicken woman, I loved the rest of the lively open market. There was even a real cow and a real stable underground where a man would squirt milk fresh from the cow and sell it to Mummy warm for a penny or two. I think it was in Black Lion Yard, long gone.

However, though the gentile East End today was quiet, its busy day, Saturday, I was happy. Daddy was taking me to the museum, then to my aunt. We waited silently for the bus.

Finally in the distance loomed a tall, red double-decker Number 6 that slid into the curb, the driver a mere shadow in the small, dark driver's cabin. The bus conductor stood on the open platform next to the steel pole that ran from the bus's platform floor to its ceiling. Daddy and I jumped onto the platform, seized the steel pole, and raced up twisting stairs without even holding on to its curved rail while we reached the top deck. There we strode to the front seat of the double-decker, where we had a wonderful view of London and of people below in the street. The conductor punched the bell twice, the driver started up again, the conductor ran upstairs.

'All fares, please,' he announced, looming in the aisle over us.

'One an' 'alf to the Museum, please,' Daddy said.

The conductor took Dad's eight-sided brass three-penny bit and a penny, punched two tickets from a ticket box strapped round his neck and dropped our money into his box.

'Ta, guv,' the conductor said and ran down the steps. The bus stopped for new passengers, then he must have punched the bell, it rang twice, the signal to move on.

Sitting high up on top of the bus in the front row, like kings and queens, we were at eye level with first storey buildings along Fleet Street. I could have reached out of the window and touched white stone-carved faces of furious Greek men, stone mouths wide open roaring at us through the wide-open holes of their white stone mouths; I could have touched their angry flared nostrils, their stuck-out tongues and every beautiful curl on their white stone beards.

As we passed a bobby standing on a corner, Daddy said, 'That's a City of London bobby. The real city of London is only four square miles, and 'as its very own police force, separate from the other London Bobbies. See, 'is 'at's different from other bobbies' 'ats.'

I nodded since I surely couldn't shout on a bus.

Riding high through Cheapside passing all the big banks, now blank windowed and silent on Sunday, I stole a look at Daddy's face. His great dark eyes were brooding, his thick, black hair under his trilby, hung as glossy as his great, black moustache. What was he thinking? I wished I knew. He knew so much, but I still had dozens of unasked questions. And I so much wanted to talk to him.

The huge dome of St Paul's Cathedral loomed ahead. As its bells clanged, ca-lung, ca-lung, Christians walked up its high stone steps. I wondered what was it like inside a church? Did Jews pray? I didn't know. Mummy took me to Hebrew school a few times when I was about four years old just long enough for me to learn the Hebrew alphabet and to sing in Hebrew, *achad*, *shtayim*, *lemalah al yadayim*, 'one, two hands in the air,' as we raised our tiny, white hands. Zada said Hebrew words before he ate or drank, but instead of Boruch, as we said in school, he said, Boorich. He'd never taken me to a synagogue: then, I'd never heard the word 'synagogue'.

As we rode toward the West End, Daddy pointed out streets on the way to Tyburn. 'Men or women used to be hung at Tyburn just for stealing a loaf of bread because they were so hungry. Might as well be hung for a sheep as a lamb,' they used to say.

I nodded and stared into his soft, dark eyes, to let him know I was listening hard.

As we passed each street, he read them out loud, 'Fetter Lane, probably where they tied prisoners up, Court Street, where I guessed they had the trial. Judge Mews, I suppose where judges had their offices and Sentence Street where they probably condemned the poor sod. They all lead closer to Gallows' Square where they hung him in front of everyone. See? We passed it.'

I imagined I was that man tied up in a rattling cart pulled by horses, coming closer to death, eyes big with fright with each street passed. Daddy said, 'Before they 'ung a man they lit a candle, and that was why your game, Oranges and Lemons has a line in it, ''ere comes a candle to light you to bed.' When you sing, 'Chip chop, chip chop, the last man's OUT,' and catch a player in your arms, it means that's when they 'ung a man or chopped off 'is 'ead.'

I never enjoyed the game as much after he explained it.

Inside the stuffy museum, men, women, and children crowded together in front of glass cases behind which stood families of wolves, and owls, which animals stared at us as if we were the ones on view.

Daddy bent down and whispered, 'Do you want to urinate?' I stifled a giggle at his using such a grown up word for 'pish,' but as he couldn't hear, I shook my head and stared at my feet.

As Daddy and I walked round he told me how owls, otters, foxes and wolves took care of their children and what they ate. 'I read a lot because I can't hear. When I was eight, my ears hurt so badly I cried, but my parents wouldn't take me to a doctor.'

I remembered his parents' bare room and shelves. Either they were cruel, or had no money for a doctor.

'Then I became deaf. The teachers said I wasn't listening and 'it me over the 'ead. But because I couldn't hear, I read everything I could find. When I was 12 my parents made me leave school and go to work. I got paid sixpence a week. My father took fivepence. What could I do with a penny? I schlepped 'eavy coats summer and winter, no 'at. That's 'ow my ears went bad. I went to the library every day after work and read almost the whole library,' he said.

We stopped to look at the Egyptian Mummy all bound up with bandages, lying in a glass case. I wondered why the figure was wrapped in bandages, but Daddy looked at his watch.

'It's four o'clock. My sister, Fanny just had a baby boy. She's invited us for tea.'

Perhaps I'd met her when I was young, if so, I didn't remember her. As an only child, a baby meant nothing to me. I only knew somehow that when women had fat tummies that Mummy called, 'a bun in the oven', they were going to have a baby.

'You'd think being so poor, Mr Lyons would be more careful,' she'd sniffed.

Outside the museum, we took another bus which stopped near a quiet street with grand houses like the dolls' houses at the East End Children's Museum. My gentile friend Joycey Kennel and I used to go on Saturdays and play hide-and-seek around the glassed-in boar.

A woman whom I guessed was Aunt Fanny stood outside a big house on a marble staircase and leaned on a marble balustrade. She wore a coat with such a high fur collar and a deep cloche hat which fell so low over her forehead that all I could see were her great dark eyes. Daddy and his sister both had the dark eyes of their Russian-born Jewish father. This was family. I supposed the bundle in her arms was a chicken or vegetables from the market.

'This is your new cousin, Geoffrey,' she said.

I had no interest in horrid pink, toothless babies that looked like little pigs and that at any moment might say, 'Oink oink'. Grown ups were much more interesting to listen to.

Inside Aunt Fanny's dark dining room my fingers traced the heavy twisted wooden sides of her high backed chairs. 'They're Jacobean,' she said proudly. Why was she so proud of them?

A long, narrow table had the same curly wood on it, so I guessed the table must also be Jacobean. On the long, narrow table stood a silver tea pot and pretty china.

I was so interested in the tall, curly chair sides that I hardly ate the salmon croquettes, a favourite Sunday tea-time food served by well-to-do Jewish families. Aunt Fanny's maids, dressed in crisp white caps and aprons brought the croquettes then the cakes and tea to the table.

Fanny's husband, Izzy, my uncle, bounced into the room like a rubber ball on short, bandy legs that supported a small potbelly. Like Daddy's, suspenders held up his trousers.

'Hallo, hallo, hallo,' he called out cheerfully, so different from Mummy's family. Mummy's family, except for her and Uncle Sam with the little hump, was mostly tall, handsome, dignified, and sarcastic. Only Zada and Aunt Mitzi were kind to me.

Uncle Izzy reminded me of the nursery rhyme:

Old King Cole was a Jolly Old Soul

And a Jolly old soul was he.

He called for his pipe and he called for his wife

And he called for his fiddlers three.

I wondered whether Aunt Fanny, my father's sister, looked like her Mummy, my Grandmother, Sarah. I had hardly seen my grandmother Sarah's face swimming high above and behind me as she handed me the little wine glass, the one time I visited her in her empty shop and house. I was so busy looking at Aunt Fanny's curly Jacobean chairs that I hardly noticed Aunt Fanny.

Throughout tea, Aunt Fanny, like her own mother, Grandmother Sarah, stayed quiet. She just held her new piggy little baby and peeked every few minutes into its sleeping piggy face. Why did people make such a fuss over babies?

After tea, Aunt Fanny and Daddy left the room together with my new baby cousin, Geoffrey. 'Stay with Uncle Izzy,' Daddy said.

'Come with me,' Uncle Izzy whispered, beckoning me with a crooked finger. 'I'm going to show you my secret room.'

Full of curiosity, I ran to keep up with his short, bow-legs as he bounded up a great carpeted staircase and we came to a bright, narrow corridor. A long, skinny red rug, roses woven into it lay along the hall floor and beautiful paintings of Uncle Izzy's family hung on the walls. Taking a large, iron key from his pocket, he unlocked an oak door and flung it open.

'Look,' he exclaimed proudly.

I gasped. We stood at the entrance of a room so dazzlingly light with hundreds of electric lights, that I squinted. After the dark dining room, the room's brightness hurt my eyes.

Hundreds of tanks full of sparkling water lined the walls, three shelves of tanks one on top of the other on all four walls. In each tank, fish dressed in dazzling coloured coats, orange, purple, yellow, red, cobalt, green, inky black, striped and spotted and all in the most amazing coloured dots, dashes and zigzags darted or swam lazily like rich princes in sparkling clear water. These princes were nothing like the plain grey fish Mummy bought at Billingsgate Fish Market.

And these all had heads. Uncle Izzy laughed gleefully at my round eyes.

'Aren't they wonderful?'

'Wonderful,' I murmured. This was better than a museum. Here, every creature alive, darted back and forth, zipping in circles, diving from top to bottom flashing gorgeous colours or like the tiny frogs in some tanks they leapt from the bottom to the top, while some great, flat fish lay still playing dead on the bottom. All had different faces, fins and tails, some even had whiskers. A miracle!

Tiptoeing to the corner of the room I saw a kind of closet with a glass door through which I saw with horror and fascination, baby crocodiles crawling, smiling, yawning, jaws baring enormous teeth. I stared up at Uncle Izzy. Why did he keep such creatures? Again, I felt like *Alice in Wonderland*, that Daddy had read me, fallen into a strange new world.

'Besides being a bookie, I breed and sell exotic fish,' Uncle Izzy said, puffing a fat smoke ring from his cigar. 'Your father and I are also boxers. He's light-weight, I'm a flyweight champion.'

Daddy had never mentioned he was a boxer, though every morning he pulled out round metal springs nailed to the bedroom wall until they were almost straight, and then let them thud back flat to the wall. Although small, Daddy could lift enormous weights, worked in the shop on his feet for twelve hours at a stretch, and ran like a greyhound.

I had never even seen one fish tank, let alone hundreds, like this. I slid round the polished floor of the room, wide-eyed, peering in every tank wishing one fish would stop still long enough for me to see its beautiful colours, spots, stripes, strange fins and whiskers and eyes. They were so strange, I wanted to stay for hours. But Uncle Izzy pushed me out of the room, locked the door and said,' Have to lock the door. Can't have your cousin Pauline getting in here. Now we'll go to the nursery and see her.'

I didn't know I had a cousin Pauline. I didn't know what a cousin was.

On short, bandy legs Uncle Izzy trotted along the carpeted corridor so fast I ran to keep up with him until he threw open another oak door. In the middle of the room, a small girl of about two, dressed in a frilly frock, sat alone on a bare linoleum floor. A little wooden pole stood on a round bottom on the floor, as she tried to drop small different coloured and sized wooden rings onto the pole. I could see she needed to put the largest ring on the bottom first, then each gradually smaller one on top of it. She looked up at us with sad, lonely eyes. Why was she sad? She was lucky to have such fancy toys. My only toy was Mumfie, and I was satisfied.

'This is your cousin, Pauline. You two play together. I'll be downstairs with your father,' Uncle Izzy said, and left.

I didn't play with boring little girls even if they were cousins, and so I left Pauline and ran downstairs to the dining room to listen to the grown ups. Daddy and my uncle were talking about boxing, betting and racing, far more interesting than playing with a sad little girl. Now I understood where Daddy got his interest in dog racing and betting – from his bookie brother-in-law and Daddy's wild father.

'How's your other brother, Alec?' Uncle Izzy asked.

'Hardly see him: a balletomaniac. Meshuga about ballet, Daddy said. Aunt Fanny sat quietly holding her new baby. It was getting dark. I became sleepy.

The next thing I knew, I was trundling up narrow stairs behind the three maids. These stairs were not the same wide steps up which Uncle Izzy and I had walked to reach the fish room. This was an entirely different set of stairs, more like the narrow, bare wood and winding stairs above the shop leading to the attic. I'd never been in a house with two sets of stairs. The three maids and I all crowded into a small, brightly lit room under the roof. A great, fat, cozy bed piled high with pillows and blankets stood in the middle of the room.

'I'm Elsie, she's Flossie and that's Daisy. You're going to sleep with us tonight. Hop in,' Elsie said. The three maids giggled, put on their nightgowns, undressed me, draping over me one huge nightgown, and squashing me in between Elsie and Flossie, we all slept snug as bears.

As an only child, hugged only once a week by my grandfather, sometimes kissed by Aunt Mitzi, I loved sleeping close between the Lyons girls, and now, between the maids, their soft, warm bodies pressed close to mine on both sides, feeling like a kitten cuddled by big Mummy cats. Tucked in between the three plump housemaids, I slept as sweetly as my kitten, Binkie. At the age of five, I was so content with East End London life, with my deaf father who talked to me on the way to Houndsditch, museums, happy with my grandparents, aunt Mitzi and my new Uncle Adrian, my teasing Uncles Sam and Max and bookmaker Uncle Izzy, school, friends and teachers, the local library and Shoreditch Churchyard, the ride on the Number Six, and the vibrant markets that made me as happy as a princess. Surely I'd never lose all this?

But I dreamed that I found Mummy, so tiny that she fitted into the palm of my hand, in our sideboard drawer. She was wrapped in bandages like the Egyptian Mummy that Daddy showed me at the museum, but unlike the museum Mummy, blood seeped through my Mummy's bandages.

CHAPTER 7

ORPHANAGE *

One Friday evening, after Daddy and Wally had worked all day, shaving, cutting hair, giving hot towels, and Mummy doing perms and sets - all the locals were getting toffed up for some goyishe gentile party they called 'Christmas' - we closed our East London hairdressing shop and walked a mile or so through dark, foggy streets to Bishopsgate. Here, we often took a train from Liverpool Street Station to visit Mummy's friends, Millie Lightman and family. I used to watch, fascinated, when Milly's face twitched, how her skin became like crumpled paper and then returned to its normal shape: Mummy said that Milly had something called St Vitus' Dance. I also liked listening to Millie's husband, Lou, stammer. Why did some people stammer? Mummy called Millie's unmarried sister, Ethel, who lived with Millie and Lou, a 'Pocket Venus' because she was a tiny woman less than five feet tall and flaunted a flawless figure. She was about 20 years old.

'But with that enormous nose she'll never find a husband,' Mummy had said.

Since we often travelled by train from Liverpool Street Station to visit the Lightmans I assumed that that was where we were going. I looked forward to seeing Millie's twitch, to hearing Lou's stutter and to seeing Ethel, The Pocket Venus. Everyone in London accepted these everyday problems: such as hump backs, pigeon chests, bandy legs, necks swollen with goiters besides pock-marked faces and the limping or armless wounded of the Great World War. Aside from these, East Enders seemed strong, worked hard if employed, walked everywhere, had a wonderful tart sense of humour, drank and had babies.

Walking along Bishopsgate's festive lights and gay chatter – everyone in a good mood for this holiday they called Christmas – I skipped alongside Mummy. Shop lights blazed into the darkness, music from pubs and restaurants streamed out onto Bishopsgate as we walked the great road toward Liverpool Street Station. Everyone called each other 'luv,' and seemed excited and happy. I didn't know why. All I knew about Christmas was my parents' talk about the 'Christmas Rush' when people came to our shop to doll up for some kind of party. During the 'Christmas Rush' Mummy and Daddy worked on their feet often for 12 hours a day. They didn't eat or even go to the lavatory all day. Mummy was always constipated and put senna pods in her tea. After a long day, Daddy would rub Mummy's swollen feet and ankles while she moaned in pain. Tonight, she groaned, but said nothing. I knew her feet hurt. There was a bus to Liverpool Street Station, but no East Ender rode for a two-mile walk.

Unless she'd just had another baby, Mrs Lyons looked after me during the 'Christmas Rush', but if she had 'a bun in the oven' Mummy put me on a bus to some strange 'aunt', like horrid Mrs One-Tit, Mrs Major a widow 'come down in life' Mummy had said. Her officer husband had died in the Great War, so Mrs Major ran a school during the year, and took in children during holidays when her school closed. She'd walk from bathroom to bedroom, towel wrapped round her fat belly, one long tit hanging over the towel. Where was the other tit? She would smirk at Brian's and my confusion. Brian was the other unfortunate resident besides me.

But everyone we passed in Bishopsgate smiled and laughed, happy about this celebration.

Some were not so happy this Christmas in 1934. A huge, long poster hung from a wall along Bishopsgate. Thin, sad, white-faced children, dressed in grey, heads bunched tightly together, stared down at us. Underneath, in large words was written, 'Help Dr Barnado's Orphans for Christmas'.

Newsmen outside the station, wearing newsboy caps shouted 'Mosley's Fascists meet in the Salmon and Ball to plan march through the East End, Nazis rally in Germany, support British Fascists getcha paper, ta guv,' as people slapped down pennies and snatched up a newspaper.

Lamplighters, greatcoats sweeping the ground, swathed in wool scarves, shuffled from one gas lamp to another. Soft yellow light flared, ghostly fog floated across the lights. Just as a flash of lightning and a clap of thunder ripped through the night, Mummy and I passed under the soaring stone arch over Liverpool Street Station and ran clacking down stone steps into the Station's giant cave. Safe inside the smoky cavern, I craned my head back to look at its glass roof crisscrossed by iron bars a mile above. Here, cheeky sparrows perched warm and chirruping, inside the station, they reminded me of our cockneys gossiping on their doorsteps.

'Hurry up,' Mummy said, pushing her forefinger in my back as we scrambled onto a train. The stationmaster's whistle pierced the foggy night, as he solemnly waved his red flag up and down signaling 'Leave!' As the train lumbered, chuffing out of the station, torrential rain slapped the carriage windows, and the wind moaned like a grieving woman. The train slowly puffed off, and then as it picked up speed, rattled, 'Leaving London, leaving home, leaving London, leaving home'. Buildings outside grew smaller as we left East London for suburbs.

In our dim carriage, lit by one yellow light, sat the only other traveller, a slender woman, who wore a beige, belted Macintosh and shiny black galoshes. Her tan leather gloves lay beside her on their backs, fingers curled up like claws. The woman rested one white hand on her umbrella the handle of which glinted: a glass sapphire circle. The blue glass circle, like a wizard's eye, winked at me as her hand on it swayed to the rhythm of the rattling train. Suddenly, I feared that the sapphire glass handle would shatter into tiny blue shards that would fly into Mummy's heart. I remembered last night's bad dream. Why had I had a nightmare when I was so happy?

The train rattled over a bridge. Small for five, I shrank into the dark corner of my brown velvet seat. My little face, yellowed under the carriage light looked back at me from the window; Tartar eyes, hair parted in the middle, rain pouring down the window looked like tears flowing down my face. I clutched Mumfie, who sat in my lap.

'Did you hear about that train crash?' the woman said to Mummy.

'Yes, wasn't it awful? So many dead and injured. They found some heads and legs, but not all the bodies,' Mummy answered.

'Would your little girl like a piece of chocolate?' the woman said, leaning toward me. She tore back the Blue Cadbury chocolate's cover, and then silver foil, showing brown chocolate with a white nut that stuck out like a bone. Her thin, pale lips parted showing cold, white teeth.

'No thank you,' I said, though I loved chocolate, shrinking back into my far corner.

The women chatted about the accident during the entire journey. I sat silent, listening.

'Let's exchange addresses,' Mummy said to the woman, before the train stopped. Although no one in the East End owned a telephone, there were two postal deliveries a day.

After a time the train drew into a dark station called 'Chingford,' and we rose to leave.

'Bye, bye, drop in soon,' Mummy said, waving from the platform. The woman waved back, thin lips smiling.

The station was deserted; I had no idea where we were. Chingford could be Africa for all I knew. It was not Milly Lightman's stop, but children must not ask questions.

Large, fat snowflakes now began to fall against black tree trunks, snow clung to trees' gnarled, witch-like branches, and inside trees' elbow nooks. Snowflakes stuck to my eyelashes. Peering through sheets of snow I saw a road sign, 'Oak Hill'. We turned there.

All was silent. Not as in East London where there were always noisy shops or stalls, street chatter, cafés or pubs from which came cheery voices or people Friday and Saturday nights singing lustily to the tinny piano man's latest tunes, just silent, empty and desolate streets, bare black trees and large, faceless houses, curtains drawn. A dozen silent questions raced through my mind. Where were we? Were we lost? Why were we here?

Mummy stopped, stared up at a huge house and said, 'Aha! Forest Hall!'

Mounting stone steps, I followed her, my snowy footprint tiny in hers. She pulled a bell.

I wanted to ask whom we were visiting, but as in the Beast's magic castle, the door flew open. A thin young woman dressed in a black and white maid's uniform said smartly, 'Mrs Moss. This way. Warden is expecting you.'

We followed her to another oak door; she knocked, and pressed her ear to it.

'Come!' said a man's deep voice.

Mummy pushed me with a sharp-manicured fingernail into a large, red-oriental-carpeted room. A man in a brown tweed suit with a waistcoat, very pink skin and sandy hair, leaned back comfortably in an armchair; before him, a large, empty desk. Behind him roared a red coal fire.

'This is my child,' Mummy said. She took off my sopping wet coat, then my white angora beret. I stared around. Where were we?

'Ah, Mrs Moss, I believe. Short good-byes are best,' the pink man said.

Mummy kissed my cheek, I smelled her violet-scented breath, and she smiled her happy goodbye smile. At stations, she always waved her white, lacy handkerchief at me.

'Be a good girl,' she said, and left.

I ran after her but she'd gone and I burst into tears. A big fat nurse in a white, rustling uniform appeared and blocked my way out

'I'm Nurse Harris. Come along, then,' she said, pulling me by the hand. 'How old are you, five? Don't cry. You're not a baby any more.'

Red-faced and panting, she ran with me through a swinging baize-covered door, a diamond-shaped glass in it, then down three stone stairs. I knew from Uncle Izzy's house that this swinging, wool-covered door with a glass in it showed where the master's part of a house ended and servants' quarters, 'below stairs' began. Once down the steps, she dragged me running and sobbing along a bare stone-flagged corridor. We passed a stone-flagged kitchen on the left, and tumbled out into a round, open courtyard. As we ran across the empty cobbled courtyard, fat lumps of snow smacked our faces, then, out of the night, but lit by a pale moon and white snow, loomed an enormous long wooden shed, its roof snow-covered. Deep fairy-tale forests surrounded the long shed, branches bent under snow that relentlessly fell, now silently, like my tears.

Fat nurse Harris, breathing hoarsely, climbed three wooden steps into the shed.

Inside, through gloom lit only by flickering candles, stood a long trestle table at which sat silent, sad white-faced children, the room so long that its end disappeared into shadows. At the huge trestle table sat some forty older children aged from about six to thirteen. These stared at me silently, reminding me of Dr Barnado's Orphan children on the poster at Liverpool Street Station. Were we still in London? I didn't know. I hugged Mumfie harder.

Nurse Harris pushed me into a little seat at a small, separate table where, as my eyes became used to the dark, I saw infants, two or three, younger than me sitting dumbly wide-eyed. Cheap, sticky squares of red and green gobs of sweets sat in front of each child. I usually ate fat, gold-striped, chocolaty humbugs, with delicious toffee inside, not ugly, cheap, lumps of sugar.

I could not understand how a tall tree all the way up to the ceiling could grow in the middle of the floor. How could a tree grow inside a room? No trees grew in East London, except those green willows that leaned their breasts over me in the summer when I read my book on Shoreditch churchyards' stone benches, or played with friends on children's graves in Shoreditch Churchyard. Why did the tree in this shed have torn silver paper wound round it, little candles burning all over it and a celluloid dolly with wings on her shoulders at its very top? Perhaps this tree which grew inside the shed was a magic tree. If I touched it, I might turn into a frog.

Sleepy and now spent, my head drooped onto the table. Nurse Harris pulled me up by my arm, hurried me with all the smaller children to a room with black iron beds in it, gave me a nighty and told me to get into a bed. I hated being put to bed with three and four-year-old infants. I was five. But Mummy would come back for me after the Christmas and New Year Rush.

Next day in the nursery, I found a toy stove that really lit when I put a match to it. I was so enthralled with this new toy that I almost forgot I was lost, far from home in this strange place. But when I looked out of the nursery window, I saw only bleak, white sky, bare black trees and branches sheathed in white snow, nothing moving except for snow falling on leafless, now all white trees. Not even a sparrow flitting across the sky broke the silent sheets of falling snow. When I heard silence, I always thought of Daddy, living in his silent, deaf world.

Did he know I had gone? Did he miss me?

Nurse Harris's fat body filled the door. She shouted, 'Everyone dress and march to the common room.'

I followed the other children. It seemed that the common room was the same as the dining room: the long shed. In the common room, where we'd sat last night, a different tall, skinny nurse now rushed in, her starched apron crackling, and on her head she wore a stiff nurse's hat hanging down her back in a triangle. She carried a white enamel bowl like the *schissel* in which Mummy poured hot water and nightly washed me from head to toe before bed.

'Be quiet everyone, I have a terrible headache,' this new nurse shouted.

If she wouldn't shout, her headache might go away.

All of us sat at the long table on backless benches. We each brought her our metal bowl into which she ladled white, slimy stuff I'd never before seen. None of the children spoke to one another. Were we allowed to speak? I didn't know. Finally, I had to speak to someone.

'What's this?' I whispered to a thin girl next to me.

'Porridge,' she whispered. 'Ain't you never seen porridge before?'

'No.' At home we ate fresh rolls, butter and drank hot tea for breakfast.

I tried my porridge. It was cold, lumpy and tasted like sand that had once got into my mouth at Brighton.

'We don't get no milk nor sugar,' she whispered.

I was so hungry I ate, except for the nauseating lumps, which I pushed to one side. As we ate, the skinny nurse walked along the table hitting our backs with a stick shouting, 'Sit straight!'

'Who's that?' I asked the girl.

'Sister. Don't cross 'er.'

Sister rushed round the table, her thin face cold, hair covered with a white nurse's sheet that hung down her back over the apron straps crossing her back that joined her crackling starched white apron at the waist.

I sat straight.

Through windows all along the common room, thick snow still fell over the forest. I imagined Hansel and Gretel lost in it, and then finding the witch's sugared house.

'You there, go into the kitchen,' Nurse Harris said to me. 'You,' she pointed to the blonde girl next to me, 'show her where it is.'

'Cum on, foller me.'

'What's your name?' I asked.

'Violet,' she said, running on bowlegs in front of me.

Violet was a head taller than me, her hair blonde; her face, pale and thin. Large but tragic eyes gleamed like jewels in her white face. We ran out of the dining room, into the snowy courtyard, and through the stone corridor through which Nurse Harris had dragged me last night. This time, the kitchen was on the right. I wished that I could run past it to the end of the corridor, leap up the steps, swing through the baize door with the glass diamond in it, jump into the main house and magically find on the other side of the servants' door, my grandfather, Zada, in his warm granary. There, he would smother me with warm kisses, his stubbled face grazing my skin and I could hear him murmuring '*Bubbele, zeesele, fliegele,* little doll, little sweet, little wing.' I wished I were nestling into his strong arms instead of going to this strange, stone kitchen. Far, far in the distance, I could see steps leading up to the baize door with the diamond-shaped glass in it that I'd come through yesterday. Beyond the baize door was the warden and then the front door and home, right outside it. If only I could get to that front door, I would run. But then what? Like Gretel lost in the forest, I had no idea where I was, or how to find my home. And I knew now, that like Snow White's stepmother, my mother didn't want me. Also, Warden, like the Wizard of Oz, or skinny Witch Sister, would surely block my escape, point their fingers and shout, 'Go back!'

Did Daddy notice I'd gone? Did Booba and Zada, Aunt Mitzi know where I was?

Mummy said so often, 'You're so pale, you need country air.' She'd probably told them that too, and they thought I'd gone to the country for my health. But I was strong and healthy.

'This way,' Violet said, grabbing my hand. It was the first time anyone here, but for fat Nurse Harris, had touched me. Violet's bony hand in mine, I clutched Mumfie with the other.

'Other side of that baize door is Warden, where you must of cum in,' Violet said. 'You won't see 'im again unless you done somefink wrong or if you ever leaves.'

I looked at Violet sharply. 'How long have you been here?'

'Since I wos four, when me muvver died.'

'How old are you now?'

'Eight.'

'When's your father coming for you?'

'Don't 'ave no farver. 'e's dead too.'

I began trembling. Violet had no mother or father. Violet must be an orphan. Every child's face looked pasty-white like those on Dr Barnado's poster. This must be an orphanage. I had a Mummy and a father, four grandparents, six uncles, two aunts. I am not an orphan, I wanted to scream. What am I doing in an orphanage? Did Daddy know I had gone? Hansel and Gretel's father had given in to whatever their stepmother wanted. But this was my own mother, not a stepmother. Only in fairy tales did stepmothers send children away. Surely Mummy wouldn't leave me here until I was eight? For three more years? No. She'd be back after the 'Christmas Rush' after all the gentiles visited her for sets or perms for Christmas and New Year, then the shop would be 'dead,' and I'd soon be back in my little cot next to Mummy and Daddy's great soft bed. I squeezed Mumfie hard. A few grains of his sawdust fell out onto the floor. If all his sawdust fell out he'd be empty. Then I'd be truly alone.

Violet pulled me into a huge stone-flagged kitchen, as spotlessly clean and tidy as Booba's, my grandmother's, but Booba's kitchen was warm and shiny. Here, a long, bare, pine table stood in the middle of a stone floor, a plain white china bowl stood on the plain table, and arms folded over chests, sullen sister and a plump, friendlier looking woman both of them in white aprons stood behind the table. The woman with a large bosom must be Cook. Sister stared at us with cold, blue eyes.

'Come. Drop a sixpence in the Christmas pudding, and stir it,' Sister said.

Sister held out a shiny sixpence and a wooden spoon.

'Drop sixpence into the pudding?' I asked, though one must not ask questions.

Neither did she answer, but shrugged impatiently.

I'd never heard of pudding, let alone dropping money into food.

'Look at your food while eating, or you'll pick up a thimble and swallow it, then the doctor will have to pull it out with a long pliers,' Mummy said, when I couldn't take my eyes off my book while eating. And what was this thing called pudding? At home we ate fresh white rolls or black bread and butter, homemade gefilte fish, or Mummy's fried fish bought at Billingsgate open fish market, ('look under the gills, if they're red it's fresh') peeled and cut potatoes to fry chips, made chicken soup, cooked delicious roast chicken and roast potatoes, and stuffed and sewed closed the skin of a chicken neck. We never ate 'pudding'. Whatever was it?

'Hurry up,' Sister snapped. 'We haven't got all day.'

My chin barely up to the table, I stood on a stepstool, and peered at a dark, round ball in the bottom of the bowl. I dropped the shiny sixpence into it then tried to stir but the ball didn't move. Mysteriously, my sixpence disappeared. Violet in turn dropped her sixpence into the pudding and stirred the hard ball.

'Go back to the common room,' Sister said.

In the common room Nurse Harris shouted, 'You two, into the kitchen,' for two other children to stir the hard ball. I had lost even my name. We were all 'you'.

We 'you's' were eating plum pudding. I feared swallowing the sixpence, and a doctor would have to pull it out with long pliers, but finally, my tongue found, and pushed a metal coin out of my mouth and into my hand. I licked off the brown pudding.

'Cor blimey, sixpence,' Violet said, with shining eyes. She still didn't smile. I'd never seen her, nor anyone in the orphanage, smile. To Violet, sixpence seemed to be a lot of money. I was used to my grandparents, uncles, aunts and Mummy's friends all *shtipping* me eight-sided brass threepences that stood up on one side by themselves, silver sixpences, shillings and even half crowns on birthdays and Chanukah. I gave all to Mummy as she'd ordered me to, to bank. If I didn't she might spank me again.

Next morning, Sister, starched skirts crackling like cold fire, came into the dining room, carrying lumpy porridge. 'Quiet, you children, I have a splitting headache.'

When I grew up I would never eat porridge or eat and drink from enamel plates or mugs. I longed for fresh rolls, butter, for china cups and saucers, lump sugar, sugar tongs, for sooty London and home. If only I could speak to my father or grandfather, even see and hear the men's voices in our barber shop instead of this all-women-and-children place.

Sister passed behind us, whacking backs with her stick. 'Sit straight.'

Fat Nurse Harris shouted, 'Put on your coats and hats and line up in a crocodile.'

'Where's a crocodile? I don't see one,' I hissed to Violet.

'It's two by twos, stupid,' Violet whispered.

We went to the hallway outside the kitchen where forlorn coats and lonely galoshes hung. Each child silently put on a coat, hat and boots. Violet shoved her hand into mine. Looking behind, I saw a long, winding double line of children. It was true: we did look like the crocodile's tail that Daddy had shown me in a picture in Kipling's *Just So* stories about crocodile tears. As Nurse Harris marched ahead, swinging her arms like a soldier, her big bum joggled up and down, and her flat shoes looked like paddles. I thought of Mummy's tiny size five high-heeled shoes with little bows on the front. What was Mummy doing now? Did she remember where she'd left me? I felt like lost Binkie when we'd found her mewling in the street. Did Daddy notice I'd gone?

We walked silently along snowy pavements. I hated marching in-step, in twos and in formation, we were like prisoners I'd seen on the Saturday morning films. I hadn't realized that before the orphanage I was free to walk where and how I wanted, run, jump, leap, and turn a cartwheel, somersault, whirl, race, move slower or faster than all other children and even grown-ups. Here, an invisible drum beat out our pace, to which we had to keep time. I hated marching to everyone else's beat. I wanted to run out of the line. Where were we going? A thin winter sun glimmered white through gnarled, black and bare branches. I hated that white sun like the eye of God. Why had he left me here?

Great white flakes began falling again, winds driving wet snow into our faces.

I wanted to be home in London in front of our roaring coal fire, toasting a great slab of white bread on a long toasting fork, slathering on it thick butter and jam, the bread deliciously hot. I could taste the toast, butter and strawberry jam melting on my tongue. Binkie would be curled up in a black ball in front of the fire, Daddy reading *The Daily Mail*, Mummy reading *True Confessions*, crunching on her pink sugared almonds. From outside, we'd hear the rumble of carts, clops of Clydesdales' hooves, the hoot of trains and the low moan of dock fog horns.

Here, there were no shops, no cars, no rumbling lorries, horses and carts, no comforting train hoots, no beautiful mournful cry of ship's foghorns at London's docks. I felt deaf, like Daddy. Except for Violet, these streets and people were all strange. We saw no grown-ups except Sister, Nurse Harris and cook, no father, no men, only little boys with runny noses. No grown-up had spoken to me except to order me what to do. All faces at the table looked alike, pale, with no expression, like ghost children.

'Stop,' Sister now shouted, outside a huge red door. Everyone stopped on command.

'Go inside,' Nurse Harris ordered.

We marched through a red door into an enormous room, as high as Liverpool Street Station. At least it was warm. I craned my neck to look at its ceiling. On one side of the great room I saw with amazement a gigantic red truck. First a tree, and then a truck inside a room. How did the tree and the truck get inside? Had I fallen into some magic country where trees and trucks grew inside houses?

'Hallo, Children, Merry Christmas,' shouted a huge, fat man dressed in red and white. 'Ho, ho, ho,' the fat man in red shouted. This must be an evil wizard from a fairy tale come to eat us up, like the giant in *Jack and the Beanstalk*. But no, he laughed happily. Several men dressed in smart black uniforms with rows of shiny brass buttons helped us take off our coats and led us to a long trestle table like that in the orphanage, but white tablecloths covered these, and tables here were piled with plates of chocolate cakes, green biscuits, and red jellies. From the ceilings hung blue, green, and yellow paper chains. Next to each plate lay strange fat red or green rolls of paper tied near each end with coloured string.

That tree again; growing in the middle of the room. How did it get inside? In East London, trees only grew outside, and then, mainly in Shoreditch Churchyard or Barmy Park where once, Joycee said, crazy people used to live, and that's why they called it Barmy Park.

'Sit down, children. There's jelly, blancmange, cakes, biscuits and lemonade. Eat as much as you want. And pull your crackers, too,' the man in red shouted.

'Pull it wiv me,' Violet said, holding out her red roll of paper in bony hands.

'Pull it where?' I said. 'What is it?'

"ere, take 'old of the other end and pull,' Violet said. 'You don't know nuffink.'

As we both pulled, the roll of paper broke in two, I heard a loud 'crack,' a spark flashed, and I fell backward off the bench. For the first time, Violet laughed a cackling laugh like a chicken before the chicken man cut its throat in Brick Lane Market. With great dignity I climbed back on the bench. A red folded paper and a cheap green ring fell out of the paper cracker onto the floor.

'Mine,' Violet said, diving for them. She unfolded a red paper hat, stuck it proudly on her head, and then slid the green ring on her finger. 'Look, I'm married,' Violet said, turning her skinny finger this way and that. The cheap green stone looked nothing like Mummy's thin, gold wedding band.

'Let's pull your un, now,' Violet said. My cracker was green with a gold tassel on it, quite pretty for paper. Violet and I pulled it. I hated the 'crack' and feared that the little spark that flew out like the sparks from our fire at home would burn me as it had Binkie. Out popped a folded piece of greasy blue paper, which I now knew was a folded paper hat, and a tiny folded paper umbrella with coloured roses all over it. The umbrella, at least, was pretty.

"Ere's your 'at, it's a pointy one,' Violet said. She unfolded and stuck it on my head. I snatched it off, but cradled the tiny umbrella in my palm. I'd seen such umbrellas in pictures of Japanese ladies.

'Let's eat,' Violet said, and shoved red jelly into her mouth. Other orphanage children also gobbled food, eyes darting, searching for the next tasty morsel.

'Don't stuff your cheeks, you little pigs,' Sister said.

Sister and Nurse Harris began talking to a group of men who stood near the trucks and whom I now realized must be firemen. I'd never before seen nurse or sister laugh, nor even seen their teeth, sister's large and horsy, Nurse's little front teeth split by a gap. Nurse's small eyes glistened with merriment, and her brown, frizzy hair stood on end like a golliwog's as she chatted happily with a skinny fireman. Mummy, a hairdresser, should set her hair.

Finally, the firemen sat down, drank foaming beer with Sister and Nurse Harris, leaving all of them with a frothy moustache, and the children finished their food. I would not eat. If I ate with them, I would be like the orphans. When Mummy came to take me home they'd see I had a real mother.

On our way back, heads down against driving snow, we saw laughing children sledding down hills, mothers and fathers cheering them on. Why should they be with their parents and me, left in an orphanage? I thought angrily. When would Mummy take me from this prison? If only Mummy were here to give me a cozy hot water bottle and to tuck me into bed, saying the *Shema* prayer with me. Daddy might even read me a story. Being deaf, had he even heard us leave? Did he miss me? Did Zada notice I had gone, or did Booba miss me bringing her flowers on Friday? No. Mummy told everyone I needed country air.

'Everybody up, it's Christmas,' Nurse Harris said, coming into the infants' nursery.

Instead of the usual lumpy, dry porridge, a single fat, pink sausage sat across each white enamel plate. For the first time, an enormous silver knife and fork instead of the porridge spoon sat on either side of the tin plate. All this cutlery for one sausage, I thought. So much washing up. I'd seen pink sausages like these hanging in Christian butcher shops, but I'd never eaten one.

Other children quickly cut their sausages into pieces and greedily ate them. I cut mine slowly and tasted it. Although cold, it was delicious. Perhaps it was pork. I didn't know. Although not religious, we ate only kosher food. Booba told Mummy to buy meat from her kosher butcher. Mummy always obeyed her mother, the way I always obeyed mine, but for once by spending sixpence.

After Christmas breakfast, Sister pushed us into the hateful crocodile. 'March!'

We marched like soldiers, not knowing where. 'Stop,' cried Sister. 'Church.'

This soaring building she called 'Church' was almost as high as Liverpool Street Station. Inside, towering pointed pipes looked like sharks' snouts. Each snout had sharp little holes in it that looked like a mouth that would eat me. Thunderous sounds crashed out of the mouths, the noise rolling over our heads without stopping for a breath. Low notes sounded like an anguished giant; high notes squealed like Binkie if we accidentally stepped on her tail.

Scanning the walls, my eyes opened horrified, riveted on a life-size statue of a man hung high, naked, except for some *schmatte*, a rag, covering his hips, his arms stretched out sideways. Some wicked, horrible Ogre had hammered his poor hands to the wood with horrible black nails; his feet crossed each other and some ogre had hammered thick, black nails through both his feet. Who could have done such a terrible, disgusting cruel thing to him? His head hung down as if he were ashamed or dying. It was a terrible, frightening statue, worse than Madame Tussaud's Wax Museum, where I'd peeked behind a curtain that children were not supposed to look through and had seen a wax figure of a Polish woman hung upside down, an iron hook stuck through her belly. Who were the terrible people who had nailed this man to two pieces of wood? I couldn't bear to look at him so tortured, but since being at the orphanage I could no longer cry.

Nurse Harris opened her big mouth and sang in a man's voice, her face red, giant bosoms straining against her apron. Sister sang in a high voice. Violet kicked me.

'Ouch,' I whispered. 'Why did you do that?'

'Why doncha sing like all of us?'

'Don't know the tune or words.'

'Ainchoo Christian?'

'No. I'm Jewish.'

'Oh. A Jew girl. Well, I'll teach you the words.'

She showed me the place in a book called: Hymnbook. They were singing to God or to the British Empire. I didn't know the difference.

'Land of hope and glory

Mother of the free,'

A lot more words followed then they ended in a tremendous chorus,

'God who made us mighty,

Make us mightier, yet.'

I supposed we were asking God to give us a bigger Empire. I would rather hear Mummy sing 'Knowest thou that dear land?' from *Mignon*.

Back in the orphanage, Sister gave me paper and a pencil.

'Before lunch, write a letter home. Don't forget to date your letter December 26th 1934.'

No other children wrote letters or mentioned parents. For that matter, I'd never spoken of mine. I was ashamed that mine, like Gretel's had dropped me here, like a package Mummy dropped at the post office Wednesday afternoon's half-day closing. I hugged Mumfie, but another tiny trickle of sawdust slid from his leg, so I stopped hugging him or he'd lose all his insides. If I could only find a needle and cotton, I'd sew him up. We'd learned to sew and knit in school.

'I'll write our address the first time,' Sister said.

She wrote swiftly:

Forrest Hall
Oak Drive
Chingford
Essex

I wrote: December 26, 1934

Dear Mummy and Daddy,

How long will I be here? Violet says there are ghosts here. Today we had a sausage for breakfast and went to church. Please send me some humbugs.

'There are no ghosts here,' Sister said, tearing up my letter. 'Write a new letter.'

'There are ghosts. I seen them,' Violet said.

'Be quiet you children, I have a splitting headache,' Sister said. I wondered why she didn't take aspirin like Mummy.

I missed the Public Baths with Mummy, my silent father, our lively hairdressing shop Friday nights and its mixed sharp and sweet smells of ammonia for the perms, shaving lotion for the men. I missed our kindly giant, Medusa-like black permanent-wave machines, Wednesday afternoon shopping with Mummy in Billingsgate's fish market or with Daddy in Houndsditch, Brick Lane, and I yearned for Petticoat Lane and Brick Lane open-air markets. I missed my kitten Binkie, chicken soup and fried fish and chips, the fish and chip shops, my best friend Joycey Kennel, my gentle Zada, glamorous Aunty Mitzi; I even missed my flinty Booba and my two, teasing uncles, Max and Sam. There were no grown-up men here to talk to, to listen to or even to tease me, no men customers smelling wonderfully of tobacco and beer, no pubs' familiar stink of beer and piss, only small, scared, gentile boys. Shut up in the orphanage, I missed the freedom to wander East End Roman roads with Joycey, peering into shops, meeting Jews and Gentiles, hearing my grandparents speak Yiddish even if I didn't understand it all. Here at the orphanage, nights were silent as if everyone were dead. Except for Violet, no child spoke to me, nor did they speak to each other. Each child was an island. Each child played alone. I knew no one's name but Violet's. Until bedtime, we saw no adult except Sister who brought food or hit our backs straight. Nurse Harris took care of nursery.

One day in the nursery, Nurse Harris called me over to my bed. Bending down so her breasts almost touched me, shoving her red face and gat-teeth into my face, she chanted, 'Now we are six, we make our own bed. This is how you make a hospital corner.'

That was how I knew that it was my birthday, 9 January, and that I was six, and that the New Year, 1935, must have begun. And though the Christmas and New Year rush had come and gone, Mummy had not come for me. When would she come?

Now that I was six, I slept in a big dormitory with other big children in a high, black iron bed. Upstairs, past the curved wood balcony beside the warden's office on the first floor, twenty of us girls and boys slept on each side of the dormitory. None of them spoke to me nor did any of them speak to each other. Violet must have slept somewhere else.

'Everyone go to the cloakroom for hats and coats,' Sister said, as we finished our porridge. 'Form a crocodile! March!'

We passed mothers walking with their children to school. I wanted to shout, 'I'm not an orphan. I have a real Mummy and Daddy.' Only I couldn't show them my Mummy and Daddy.

My new school, a large, light-coloured one-story building, looked completely different from my old, dark red brick Wood Close School in London. Instead of the London cement playground, this school was surrounded by grass, most of it covered with snow. A few tender white and purple crocuses with tiny yellow tongues pushed out of white winter snow and peeped at me, cheering me a little.

In London, in school, I'd always been a chatterbox, friends with the teachers and top of the class. Here, in this country Christian world and school, no warm Mr Kent talked to me. I'd never again be top of the class. As the only Jewish schoolchild, I was silent. I had no friends except Violet and she was not in my class. My mind stopped working or thinking.

We all stood in a large room for morning prayers.

'Would you sing us one of your Jewish songs?' Miss Lawson, the teacher asked. How did she know I was Jewish? I couldn't see any difference in the way I looked from the other children. Well, perhaps my Tartar eyes like Mummy's and Booba's slanted up a little, but not much. Nurse Harris, who daily walked us to school, must have told the teacher. I wished she hadn't. I didn't want to be different. Also, there might be Fascist children here as in East London who would hit me and say, 'Take that, Jew girl'.

'Stand in front of the class,' the teacher said. 'Sing a Jewish song.'

Gentile children all sat cross-legged so low on the polished boards of the floor, that standing, made me feel tall and lonely. Like Mummy, I had a strong, deep voice.

I sang a haunting song in Hebrew, learned from Mummy: '*Shuvi nafshi.*'

Be at rest, Oh my soul, for the Lord has dealt kindly

with you. You delivered my soul from death,

my eyes from tears and my feet from stumbling.

I shall walk before the Lord in the world of life.

I trust even when I cry out: 'I am greatly afflicted.'

Even when I say, 'all men are deceitful,' I have faith.

But at that time, I didn't know the meaning of the Hebrew words. Had I known, I might have burst into tears or laughter.

Children sitting perfectly still on the hard boards of the wooden floor, listened. I knew the song sounded as sad as I felt. After I finished: dead silence. No one clapped. When grown, I thought of Jewish and African slaves whose captors ironically always expected them to sing.

Without yet knowing my people's history, I felt sadder having to sing when sorrowful and to strangers who did not know me or my people, but saw me as a curiosity, an amusement.

'Thank you,' said Miss Lawson politely. 'Sit down.'

About a week later our class again stood in the large, dark hall, clumped together.

'I'm going to pick children to act in our school play,' Miss Lawson said.

My cheeks grew warm, I jiggled with excitement. I loved acting. At home in London, I had often acted in school plays. I'd played a Queen in the last play, when that scamp Joseph Singer had pulled my throne out as I was about to sit down, and I'd tumbled to the floor. Even he hadn't spoiled my acting. Perhaps Miss Lawson would pick me to be in the play. They'd see how well I could act. They'd notice me.

'Now I don't want anyone to put up a hand and ask to go to the bathroom,' Miss Lawson said.

To my horror, a puddle immediately appeared on the floor directly under my feet. I'd never ever wet my knickers. The only Jew in the class, and I'd wet my knickers.

'Hurry up, I never did, a big girl of six wetting her bloomers, you're a disgrace,' Nurse Harris scolded, rushing me from school. I hung my head, ashamed. How had it happened, and in front of everyone? And after I'd just sung them a Hebrew song and everyone knew I was Jewish. Now they'd never know I was a good actor or ask me to be in a play. They'd think I'd pish on the stage in the middle of the play.

Fat Nurse Harris, puffing and panting, dragged me, a humiliated child, by my hand back to the orphanage. I staggered along, legs apart like a Saturday night drunk, the long, wet, orphanage bloomers rubbing my soft inside thighs, making them sore.

'Hurry up,' Nurse Harris shouted.

As we came to a main road, I saw a crowd of men and women standing in a circle staring at something on the ground. Through a parting in the circle a brown horse stood in front of a wooden cart. The horse's head hung down like mine, as if he felt as ashamed as I did. A woman lay on the stone road beside the cart on her back, her arms outstretched almost like the statue in the church but flat, not hanging like the man nailed to wood. Suddenly the pale skin on the woman's face, neck, arms and legs parted and red blood seeped out from hundreds of her seams.

I slowed, dragging my feet to look back over my shoulder. I felt as if I too had been run over by a huge cart and horse, my seams opened, my life-blood seeping out like the woman's, like the sawdust seeping out of Mumfie's seams.

Nurse Harris jerked my arm. 'Come on,' she said. 'Don't dawdle.'

CHAPTER 8

THE ATTIC *

Two days later, when Nurse Harris had sent most children to bed, only Mary, Violet and I stood, bored, in the now vast and empty shed that was our dining and common room. Mary was the only other girl besides Violet that I knew in the orphanage and I knew her not because she was friendly, but because she was unfriendly. Mary, at thirteen, the oldest and biggest girl in the orphanage was as fat as she was tall; her few claims to beauty were her long, thick, hair and her mole.

Thin and small at the age of six, my sole enjoyment in the orphanage was to stand directly in front of fat Mary, look up and see beneath her chin the brown mole as big as a sixpence and as brown as a halfpenny. No one but me, not even fat Mary knew it was there.

Mary, like many cowards, liked taunting small Violet.

'Who said you could stay up so late?' Mary demanded of Violet. 'You're only eight, you should be in bed.'

'Nurse Harris hasn't called me yet,' Violet stammered like Lou Lightman.

'I'm telling you to go to bed,' Mary said, moving closer to and towering over Violet.

'I don't fink I'm supposed to go up until I'm called,' Violet quavered.

Mary pushed Violet hard so that she fell, legs sprawled, the long, red orphanage bloomers I hated and wetted, blooming in sight.

Someone slapped fat Mary's face.

I felt no impact. I'd never in my life slapped anyone. Mary was twice my size and could easily have hit me hard or just sat on me. I wondered why she didn't. Cowards were not used to anyone fighting back. As usual, there was no adult in the room.

'I'm telling,' Mary screamed, rushing out.

Nurse Harris's huge bulk, panting, her red face filled the doorway.

'You certainly like to cause trouble, don't you?' she hissed through the gap between her front two teeth. 'First you wet the school floor and make me come for you and now you've smacked Mary. You'll be bathed with the nursery children, and go straight to bed.'

Nurse Harris shoved me into a bathroom I'd never before seen. Two baths stood side-by-side, four claw legs on the bottom of each bath, a narrow aisle between them. Nurse Harris barely fit in, but she squeezed in between the two baths to tend to each infant. A tiny little nursery girl aged about two sat in each bath.

Nurse Harris lifted a scrawny child out of one bath with one fat arm. The wet, slippery child clung terrified to Nurse's wet arm like a baby monkey to its mother in the pictures Daddy had shown me, and with her free hand, Nurse Harris rubbed the baby down hard with the towel. Although rough, I could see that Nurse Harris worked hard; her face bloomed redder than ever.

'Get in the bath,' she panted. Grimly, I edged into the same water that the nursery child had bathed in. Mummy, at the public baths, would never have let me bathe in someone else's dirty bath water. I felt humiliated being bathed with babies, especially since I'd turned six in January, and now slept in the big boys' and girls' dormitory.

Nurse Harris threw me a bar of stinking, red carbolic soap that only poorest East End gentiles used. I longed for our fragrant Yardley's Lavender soap and Mummy's closeness when we bathed together at the all-marble Bethnal Green Public Baths. I wished our bath-lady were here to pour fresh water into the bath, and that afterwards, Mummy would shower me with her scented talcum powder that came down like snow. I did, however, love these baths' fat claw feet. It had been worth smacking Mary's face (though my hand did it on its own) just to see these beautiful claw feet on the two baths. They also reminded me of home, where we'd now acquired a dining room table with claw and ball legs. I'd loved lying under that jungle lion-legged table.

Another nursery child sat in the other bath playing with the stinking carbolic soap. Its bitter smell made me feel lonely for our London shop with its familiar sharp and sweet scents of ammonia Mummy used for perms mixed with the sweet smells of Daddy's after-shave lotions. I missed the comforting sounds of my grandparents' Yiddish. If only I could sit in my Zada's lap and he could cuddle me and murmur sweet nothings in my ear. He didn't know where I was imprisoned. I bet Snow White's mother also told everyone that Snow White's disappearance was due to her being 'frail' and needing country air. Fairy tales did not say how stepmothers explained their daughters' sudden disappearances. I had been turned into an orphan.

Nurse Harris bent low over me, roughly scrubbing my back, face, neck and body with the washcloth, her hot breath on my face. Although I didn't like her, I saw as she leaned down with her face so red, panting, that she seemed so tired, she seemed to be ill.

The next day Sister came crackling in her starched apron and cap into the dining room carrying the usual white, enamel bowl of porridge and as usual she cried out, 'Be quiet, you children, I have a splitting headache. Today, it's worse. Some children and Nurse Harris have come down with scarlet fever. I have to do all the work myself!'

No wonder Nurse Harris seemed so tired last night. She really was ill.

The following morning I had a high temperature and ached all over. A red rash covered my body. 'Sister,' I cried weakly, the first time I'd ever spoken to her.

Nurse Harris had caught scarlet fever from the small child she'd bathed, and I had caught it from her. If only I hadn't slapped Big Mary; but she'd knocked down my only friend, Violet.

I awoke in a strange bed in a strange dormitory with many other children. Plump and pretty young nurses rustled in starched aprons up and down the long room, carrying thermometers, food and chamber pots. I guessed this was a hospital. I waited for Mummy to come, but none of my family came. I don't know how long I was there, but soon, they sent me back to the orphanage.

Weakly, I followed Sister's rustling, starched apron and white 'V' headdress hanging down behind her back and her white, crossed-over apron straps as she clacked upstairs. But she didn't stop at the first floor where all we 'big children' slept in the long dormitory. We came to another, smaller, winding staircase. There had been two staircases in rich Aunt Fanny's house. This narrower staircase, I now knew, led to what used to be a maids' attic, a nursery or both. I'd seen this house plan at the Children's Museum showing a model doll's house of a rich lady.

I climbed the stairs slowly, weak from scarlet fever and time spent in bed, and following her blue skirt and white apron, panting up the narrow stairs behind Sister. She never looked back, spoke to me or turned to help me. I thought of running downstairs in the opposite direction and out the front door. But I didn't know where I was, in which direction to walk, nor how to get home to Liverpool Street Station. I'd know my way home from there. But how could I find Liverpool Street Station from Chingford? We'd only left the orphanage to go to church, to the firehouse and to school. Where was the train station? I'd need money to get on the train. Where was my sixpence from the Christmas pudding? I didn't know, and in any case, I felt so weak.

At the top of the small staircase, we came to a plain wooden door. From under the long, blue dress beneath her starched apron, Sister pulled out an iron key, rattled the key in the lock and threw open the door. She pushed me into a room in the orphanage I'd never before seen.

The small but warm room's walls, ceiling and floor were all made entirely of plain blond unfinished wood. The ceiling sloped inward to meet low, bare walls. The room was strangely warm, and full of light coming from two windows set into walls at right angles. One window looked out onto what seemed to be the back of the house, where a long, narrow fenced path like the one I'd seen at Aunt Fanny's house stretched below. At Aunt Fanny's house, this long fenced path had an arch on which a sign said 'Tradesmen's Entrance'.

There was no furniture in the room save the usual black iron bed with white sheets tucked in tightly with hospital corners and one white pillow. In the centre of the room stood a bare wooden table and a wooden chair, and on one side stood a small table holding a white china wash bowl and a plain white jug full of water for washing myself. A chamber pot squatted under the bed. The bare room held no books, toys, not even my doll, Mumfie. Before it became an orphanage, this plain room must once have been the maids' room, or a nursery in a mansion. The doll's house in the Children's Museum had shown nurses, babies and maid dolls in these attics. But Aunt Fanny's attic, when I had visited had been cheerful, with bright curtains and a huge soft bed where I'd slept snug between kind, chattering maids. This attic was bare, silent and lonely.

Alone in this third story empty attic, I looked out onto the back of the orphanage seeing only crisp, white snow etched on the pointed tops of the high fence enclosing the Tradesman's path below. Nothing moved. There were no footprints on the Tradesman's path. No birds flew or sang: total silence like 11 November Armistice Day, but not for two minutes thinking of the World War dead. This was to be a long terrible silence, like being deaf.

'Get into bed,' Sister pointed to the bed. 'You'll be quarantined here for six weeks.'

I heard the rasping key turn in the lock, and the clacking of her shoes fading away as she ran down the stairs.

Darkness fell, shadows lengthened, silence stretched forever. I fell asleep on the iron bed.

In the morning, weak, I crawled out of bed, limped barefoot in my white flannel nightie to the window and looked down again at the long, snow-topped fence bordering each side of the glistening white path. This path had remained untouched by man or beast. There were no footmarks, not even a cat's footprint or the lines of a bird's claw on the tradesmen's path. Nothing. I was totally alone, locked in the room at the top of a house. I couldn't see or hear anyone and no one could see or hear me. There were no books to read, no one to talk to, no sound to listen to. Suppose they altogether forgot I was here? Mummy, if she ever came, would never know where I was unless Sister told her where to find me. I pressed my nose to the window and waited for hours to see Mummy, Daddy, anyone, come up that empty iced and desolate path. I yearned for a bird to alight on the fence, for a footprint, any sign to let me know I was not totally alone. I watched that path all day as the white winter sun rose above the roofs, and then sank down, and the moon peeped out; I watched, hoping to see a butcher, baker, grocery man, Mummy, even Daddy, but no one came down that fenced path. Nothing moved, nor made a mark in the snow. It lay, untouched on the ground. Even the trees were too bare and icy for the birds to sit on. I murmured to myself:

The north winds will blow, and we shall have snow
And what will poor robin do then, poor thing?
He'll sit in the barn, and keep himself warm
And tuck his head under his wing, poor thing.

Only Maisie, the scullery maid, three times a day, rattled the door as she unlocked it, pushed a tray of food inside on the floor, and scuttled away.

'Stay, stay with me, don't go away,' I wanted to cry out, but I said nothing. My tongue stuck to the roof of my mouth from not talking for long days and nights.

The days and nights passed in total silence and isolation, agonizingly tedious. Locked in, a prisoner, I lost count of time. I pressed my face to the cold window where my breath made a little steam circle. I wrote my name in the steam to see if I were alive. I was deserted, forgotten. I had no way of knowing how long I'd been there nor how much time had passed. More white snow fell, blanketing the house and path, deepening the silence. Was this how my deaf Daddy felt? Did he know where I was, and did he, my grandparents, aunts, uncles and friends miss me?

Why hadn't anyone come to see me? I walked around the room, licked my finger, etching my name on the frosty window, along the bare wall and chanted:

Nobody loves me

Nobody wants me

I'm going to the garden to eat worms.

Big fat slimy worms

Long thin skinny worms

I'm going to make a samwich out of worms.

Weeks later, it seemed, Maisie threw on the table two *Rupert the Bear* books, blank paper, a pencil, scissors and some leaves, and then ran out. I fell on the gifts joyously, immediately traced the brown leaves on paper and cut out their shapes. Grateful to see *Rupert the Bear's* joyous brilliant red, blue and yellow colours, Rupert, as sweet and adventurous as my Mumfie in his elephant books, I read both *Rupert* books in 10 minutes. I liked the pictures of the golliwog, a black cloth doll, wild hair sticking out all over her head like Topsy and big, round, saucer eyes. After the monotone brown of the attic and the endless white snow outside, the white sheets and white water jug in the attic, my eyes hungrily devoured Rupert's brilliant reds, blues, yellows and greens as if I were licking ice-cream. Sitting alone at the bare table with the vividly coloured books to read, and scissors to cut out leaves, I actually felt happy.

The sun peeped out of the white sky for a moment, and then disappeared. The next day the white sun stayed longer. Snow on the tall fence along the tradesmen's entrance slowly began to melt. I'd been in the orphanage about four months, I guessed, since about 24 December, but it felt like a year. It must be February or March of 1935.

I could understand the Beast waiting so long for Beauty to come back, finally lying down alone to die of loneliness. Had I been punished by a witch and shut up in a castle turret? Did anyone say what this prince had done? Perhaps a prince would ride by and rescue me. No prince came. No one but Maisie came with food and then ran away. No one explained to me why Mummy didn't come or write, that I might be contagious. But why didn't she write? I felt deserted, totally abandoned.

The sun shone a little more yellow, more snow melted. The sun shone warmly through the window. I grew a little stronger, but felt achingly lonely. I'd been in the attic for six weeks.

Suddenly one day with no warning, Mummy and Aunt Mitzi both appeared framed in the attic door. I was so astonished I didn't know what to do or say. I'd waited so long for Mummy to come, I'd given up hope. Now she'd not only come, she'd come with glamorous Aunt Mitzi. I remembered that just before Mummy dropped me in the orphanage my aunt had visited and told Mummy that she'd become engaged to Adrian, hugged me, and said '*You*, pussycat, will be my bridesmaid.'

Now, like magic, Mummy stood in the doorway of my attic prison, petite, dark haired and dark-eyed, her sister, Aunt Mitzi tall and slender, blue-eyed and blonde. I'd rarely ever seen them together. Total opposites: Mummy, cautious and plain, my Aunt Mitzi, bold and beautiful. I didn't even wonder or care why they had come together when Mummy so envied her sister. Speechless, I flung myself into Mummy's arms and buried my face in the two little mink furs at her neck; their beady little glass eyes stared at me. Silently I begged her to take me home.

But Mummy sat casually chatting to Aunt Mitzi as she had done with the strange woman on the train to this Chingford orphanage.

'Not such a bad trip, here, was it?' Mummy said to Aunt Mitzi.

'If I'd known it was such a short journey I wouldn't have bothered bringing a book to read,' my aunt said. She nodded to her book on the table that had on its cover a picture of King George V and Queen Mary.

So I wasn't so far from home as I'd thought. And I could see they planned to have a nice chat between themselves and leave me in this hateful place.

If I didn't get out now, I never would.

My heart suddenly lost all feeling, as if it had been left in the freezing path outside and had turned to an ice snowball. Suddenly, I felt only a cold determination to escape this deathly lonely room. My mind long dead came alive as I plotted how I could get out. Even the aunt whom I'd adored was ready to leave me in the orphanage. The only weapon I knew might move my mother and aunt's cold hearts was a tear. I didn't feel like crying; I hadn't cried since the night Mummy dropped me at the Chingford orphanage. Now, I squeezed my face up, whimpered, pretended to wipe tears away, and by thinking hard about crying finally squeezed out two tears.

'I want to go home,' I sniffled. 'Please! Won't you please take me home?'

I wasn't miserable, I was furious, but I hid it. Who wanted an angry child? I had to make them pity me. Between fingers over my eyes, I watched their faces.

The two sisters, the dark and the blonde, looked at each other over my small head. Mummy sat completely still, only her green eyes moved, watching her sister's blue eyes. After a long, long moment Aunt Mitzi gave Mummy a tiny nod. The fact that Aunty and not Mummy decided to take me home infuriated me even more. But I hid it.

'I have to get Mumfie,' I said.

It was a terrible risk. They might leave without me. But I couldn't leave without Mumfie, nor without showing the other children that I had a real Mummy and a beautiful blonde aunty. And they had *both* come for me. At least, they had come to see me. The children would not know these two planned to leave me. I was not an orphan like them. I had a *real* family. I could shed my shame the way Daddy told me a snake shed its skin.

I burst out of my hateful attic prison, ran wildly free, now full of strength, clattering down the narrow stairs out of the house, I ran across the courtyard and into the common room.

The children sat silently at the table eating from their white enamel plates, backs upright, Sister with her stick stood like a witch behind them. 'Sit straight,' she said, hitting Violet.

I ran past all their straight backs, and ignoring even Violet, sped past an astonished Sister to the end of the room where on the stage, Mumfie lay in a cubbyhole. All the children's heads turned silently, curiously, to watch me. Seeing them eating from the hateful white enamel plates and mugs, I swore that I would never, ever in my life again eat or drink from an enamel tin plate or mug. I flashed Fat Mary, I was sure, a look of sheer joy and triumph. Someone had come for me. I wasn't an orphan like her, with her brown mole under her chin. I belonged, I had a family.

The two sisters, one dark and small, the other, blonde and tall, stood framed like a photograph in the dining room doorway, waiting for me.

'See, they have even come for me, two of them,' I wanted to shout to all the orphans.

I ran to Mumfie, snatched him up, and hugging him to me, ran out again, past the silent children all staring wide-eyed at me. Mary's face held her usual sneer, this time mixed with tears. Brimming with joy to know that I had not one, but two relatives who had come to take me home and that all the children could see I had a Mummy and an aunt waiting for me, I sped back through the common room to my mother and aunt at the shed door. I enjoyed having them wait for me, the way I'd waited for them. Running down the room toward freedom, I stopped only to kiss Violet's cheek. She burst into tears. 'Don't leave me!'

But I felt so giddy with joy and power, even Violet could not stop my mad rush to freedom and home. I ran and threw myself into the arms of my waiting Mummy and aunt, into their warm bodies, into their Evening in Paris scent and fox furs. Looking back at the children, I saw faces twisted with longing, wistfulness, jealousy and pain. Violet wept, face resting on her skinny arm on the table. I felt sorry for my friend, but my heart was bursting with joy at having a family, showing the orphans that I was not an orphan, and at finally leaving the orphanage.

Sister, for once, said nothing. She had never dealt with a family.

I was away and free, riding the train toward home in mute ecstasy, while Mummy and Aunty Mitzi chatted and ate, between them, an entire box of Black Magic chocolates, never offering me one. I didn't care. I stared out of the window at my furious reflection, afraid to let them see the terrible, silent victory on my face. This time, unlike the train ride to the orphanage, which had been in the middle of a raging storm, the sun shone onto my attic-white face that was reflected in the train window. Only I could see the terrible rage on my face. I closed my eyes and raised my face to the sun, which warmed my cold eyes but not my cold heart.

The journey home was short. I realised Chingford was only a half-hour from home. It had just seemed endlessly far away when we left in the dark storm last year, when I was young.

That night, tucked up in my little white crib next to Mummy and Daddy, I slept peacefully with Mumfie under my cheek. I'd had my way. Justice had been done. I was home.

For how long, I didn't know. But being home now was all that mattered.

I dreamed that there were twin sisters, exactly alike, like golliwogs, only with white instead of black faces. Both had enormous round black eyes glittering like the tinsel around the orphanage Christmas tree. Although much taller than me, and with children's faces, their doll's eyes stared straight ahead. They were blind, but laughing and chattering to each other. They didn't seem to care that they were blind. They spoke to each other over my head without seeing me. They were so big and I, so small between them, they didn't even know I was there.

CHAPTER 9

SHORT TRIUMPH *

Joycey, myself, and our schoolmates played almost daily in Shoreditch Church's graveyard. Once more I became leader in our games and in class, once more I enjoyed visiting the library, Petticoat Lane, my grandparents, my aunts and teasing uncles and happily called for my friend Joycee Kennel across the street on Vallance Road.

'Joycey!' I'd call up the stairs, and she'd stick her blonde, Shirley Temple curls over the banister and shout in her lovely cockney, 'Cum up.'

Upstairs, her four brothers still slumped round a card table, eyes miserable, playing cards.

'They're unemployed,' Joycey said as always, humbly, as if it were her fault.

Across the stairs, I heard a noise like a running tap and saw her mother pishing in a pail.

'Hallo,' she called out cheerfully, and still pishing in the bucket, 'How are you?'

Joycey and I went on long rambles through East London and to the Children's Museum, once more played hide-and-seek around the glassed-in boar and stopped to peer into the four-storey doll's house behind glass. Tiny doll grown-ups, children, maids and even toy dogs filled each room. So that was how rich people lived. The museum's doll house had a basement with a big kitchen, the next story held a huge dining room, a plush sitting room and a library; the next storey, bedrooms, and the top floor held a nursery, the nanny's and the maids' rooms. But I knew that house with the two sets of stairs and an attic. I'd now been in it first, in Aunt Fanny's house, the second time, in the Chingford orphanage that at one time must have been this man's mansion.

In May 1935, a beautiful summer's day, Joycey Kennel and I went to see King George V and Queen Mary ride through the decorated East End, thick crowds cheering for their Silver Jubilee. I climbed up a lamppost to see over the heads of grown-ups and Joycey tunnelled between grown-ups' legs to the front of flag-waving mobs. I saw the king and queen in their open carriage riding through and waving their hands to us East Enders, our walls hung with Union Jacks, our streets full of tables covered with white cloths and heavy with cakes and drinks.

As before being left at the orphanage, some Sundays Daddy took me to museums. Once more I was delighted with life. I was now six, and very grown up. I didn't think about the future.

Sometime in the summer, Mummy dropped me back at the orphanage. It seemed hopeless to protest. Like the worm, I didn't stand a chance. She had first dropped me at the orphanage last December 1934 during heavy snow and darkness. The half a year I'd been there felt like years. Now, aged six, it was late summer of 1935. To my surprise, on entering, I found the great shed, our formerly dark common room and dining room, flooded with light. All six large windows had been taken out of their frames. Outside loomed a ragged garden full of Jack-in-the-Beanstalk green trees I'd never seen during the winter. They'd been bare and covered with snow. This garden had been there almost like *The Secret Garden,* that I'd just read, but instead of hidden behind a secret gate and shrubbery it had been hidden by huge piles of snow.

Children now played on a rough wooden seesaw among great, ancient trees.

Violet had disappeared. A child sidled up. 'Your friend died.' I felt sadder.

Big Mary, fatter and taller than ever, wearing a cheap, ugly green dress, sat crouched on an empty window frame. She looked like a huge frog. Her bum hung outside over the garden, her fat legs dangled inside the room. I had not grown much and could still look up and see that great, beautiful brown mole under her chin. I detested Mary, but loved her mole.

As soon as I opened the door, a great smirk split her face. Her brown eyes lit up with such joyous triumph, I thought she would burst, and green bits of her would fly all over the shed.

'Thought you were going home for good, but they tricked you, just took you back to shut you up 'til they could get rid of you again. They don't want you.' she crowed.

The other kids grinned.

I rushed at her, seized her by the ankles and pushing her feet up with all my strength, shoved her backward out of the window. Shoes appearing upended in the empty window, I heard her thump as she landed in the stinging nettles.

'Stinging nettles! I'm telling!' Mary screamed, from the ground under the window. She climbed back and panting, red faced, heaved her froggy bulk over the windowsill. 'You little kike, I'm going to get you for this.'

I was astonished that considering she was twice my age and size she hadn't hit me. I was still only six and she was 13, perhaps 14 by now. But I was so angry with Mummy and Daddy for dropping me like a package back in the hateful orphanage, that fat Mary crowing over me was the straw that broke the camel's back.

I'd just arrived, and I was already in trouble. What to do? There was no escape.

For some reason, no one punished me. After exciting London, I would die of boredom and loneliness here. No wireless, no news, no music, no pictures, no museums, no parks, no pleasant Mr Kent, no library, no Booba and Zada, my grandparents, no barber or grocery shop with people coming and going, no pubs, no king and queenly glitter driving in a fairy tale carriage through the East End: only silence and boredom. Children didn't speak to each other and adults called us all 'you'. Also, there was not one Jewish person in the entire area.

There were many Jewish orphanages; why didn't Mummy send me to one of those? Crafty now, I guessed that if I were in a Jewish orphanage, some visitor might recognize me, and Mummy would have to explain not only why I was hidden in an orphanage, but in a Christian orphanage. Perhaps a Jewish orphanage wouldn't take a child with a full family? And how often she had said to me in front of others, 'You're so pale and skinny, you need country air,' as if she were doing me a favour and was the kindest mother in the world. But though pale like Daddy and his father, I was the best skipper and student in the class. And even Violet had gone.

Violet had sobbed, 'Don't leave.' Like Beauty leaving the Beast, I had left, but I hadn't come back in time and she had died of loneliness. I knew loneliness. If I could have cried for Violet, I would have. But I could no longer cry. No one would ever make me cry again. Fear as well as joy had almost disappeared. Back in the orphanage I again lost all feeling.

One day Sister shouted, 'Everyone put on a nightgown.'

We followed her to a large room, another I'd never before seen at the orphanage. This house was always a surprise, with new rooms always popping up. Perhaps this enormous room had once been the grand living room or ballroom Joycey and I had seen in the museum's doll's house. We stood barefoot, single file on a cold, shiny black floor. I stood last in line. Peeking around our line I saw a long narrow table on wheels, the table covered in a white sheet. Sister, a doctor (I supposed from his white coat) and nurses in white, stood all round the table.

'You. Come here,' Sister said to the first in line, a boy. 'Lie down on the table.'

The adults all leaned over him, so we children in the line couldn't see anything of the boy. What were they doing to him? Since he didn't scream, they couldn't be hurting him. In a few minutes the boy disappeared behind a black curtain at the end of the table.

'You, next,' Sister called the girl next in line. There was silence for a few minutes, and then this girl disappeared, too, like magic. Where did she go? Six, five, four, three, two, then it was my turn. I climbed onto the table and lay down. Now I would find out the mystery. Sister pressed a black, rubber thing over my nose and mouth. 'Breathe!' she commanded.

I awoke in bed in a long, hospital ward. All around me stretched white beds, in each of which lay a pajama-striped child, my age, six or seven. While young, pretty nurses bustled back and forth, children chatted with each other, exchanged comic books or just stared into space. A nurse brought me some red jelly, then ice cream, both special treats, given to children only on Christmas or after their tonsils were pulled out. My throat hurt a little. Now the mystery was solved. We'd all had our tonsils out. I didn't recognise any of the other children from the orphanage. But then, we never played together, my only friend, Violet, had died. Mary was not here, I didn't know the other orphans, and anyway, the orphanage faces had all looked the same.

Licking my spoon, I suddenly noticed all the other children's hair was even shorter than my shingle. Then I noticed that though I wore a white nightie, they all wore striped pajamas. To my horror, I realised that I was the only girl in an all-boys' ward. The boys giggled to each other and pointed at me. If only I could disappear. Worse was to come.

'Nurse,' I hissed, to a passing young woman, 'I need a chamber pot!'

She trotted back and placed a pot on the floor for all the boys to see and left. Those horrid boys nearly fell out of bed straining to watch a girl lift her nightie and show her behind. There was no way to relieve the ever straining urge without getting out of bed, onto the floor and lifting my nightie. Slithering out of the bed, pulling the flannel nightgown down over my behind, I tried to push the pot and myself under the bed, but the bed was so low that even the pot wouldn't go under. The boys leaned out of their beds, staring at my tush the way a cat looks at a mouse, waiting for me to lift my nightie. I clutched my stomach that began to cramp from holding everything in. Frantically, I tried to keep my behind covered while forced to lift the nightie so as to press down urgently which I did, to great relief, now racking my brains how to wipe my behind, pull down my nightie and get back into bed without the accursed boys seeing my tush.

The nurse hadn't given me any toilet paper, and in any case, I was not going to wipe my sticky behind in front of all those giggling hooligans. I wrenched my nightgown down, leaped into bed, where to my dismay, a brown streak immediately spread across the bottom white sheet.

'Tut, tut,' the young nurse said, but mercifully didn't say out loud that I'd stained the bed. But I had to stand barefoot on the cold floor while she changed it. Didn't she understand my acute shame at being in a ward of all boys in the first place and worse, having to use the chamber pot in front of them? Adults were there to torment, not to help children!

I threw myself into the bed, pulled the blanket over my head, refused supper and wished I were dead.

Not Mummy, Daddy nor anyone in the family visited me in the hospital.

Soon, I was back at the orphanage.

On my return, I saw that about six new, big, tall boys, aged 12 to 14 had arrived. Their faces lean, thin mouths in bitter, straight lines, they paced restlessly on muscled legs round the common room, hands thrust deep in trouser pockets like gangsters in films.

One day in the common-room, Ernie, one of these big boys, dragged Peter, aged seven, to the wall. He shoved Peter against the wall, raised Peter's arms, laced his long, bony fingers into Peter's, and then bent Peter's fingers all the way back. I heard a crack, a scream from Peter, and then I saw blood spurt between Peter's joints under his skin. I didn't know you could bleed inside. I shrieked, sped outside to the kitchen, the nearest place where there might be an adult. Ernie pounded after me shouting, 'If you tell, I'll break your fingers too.'

Ernie chased me, but I was faster.

Rushing into the kitchen, I cried to Cook, 'I think Ernie broke Peter's fingers.'

Cook large and strong, collided with Ernie, took hold of him by one ear, and dragged him screaming and kicking to the warden's room. The warden, his pink face black with fury, dragged Ernie into the common room and threw him on the floor. Warden carried a big stick with a rusty pointed nail sticking out of it.

'Face the wall, hands on the wall above your head.'

Ernie rose from the floor smirking, sauntered over to the wall and leisurely raised his hands to the wall. The warden slammed the stick, nail first, onto Ernie's skinny rump. Thwack!

'Here's one for each finger you broke,' the Warden shouted. Each time he struck, Ernie howled like a wolf. On the tenth, Ernie ran out of the room screaming.

I never found out what happened to Peter.

In the next couple of days, a few children disappeared until I was the only one left. Mummy came, and silently, we walked to the train. On the train ride she ignored me. I didn't care. I was going home. I felt justice and triumph. She couldn't get rid of me. This had been the longest year of my life. I believed I would never again feel fear or love. I left all feelings at the orphanage. I would never again trust grown-ups, especially the ones I loved. They were the least trustworthy. Grown-ups hurt you the most. None of them save Mummy, who sent me away in the first place, had ever written to me or visited me while I was in the orphanage or in hospital. But of course, everyone believed I was in some wonderful country place. Mummy had probably even convinced Daddy of this 'fact' though he might not have cared.

Mummy must have told everyone that she sent me to fresh country air for my health. Perhaps she even believed it herself. But I couldn't stop wanting Mummy to love me: I was six.

CHAPTER 10

THE CABLE STREET BATTLE *

Sunday I walked the mile through the sooty slums of London's 1936 Jewish East End to pay homage to the matriarch, my grandmother, Booba. Mummy had dressed me in my autumn red hat and coat. In spite of that, a little shiver ran through my body. Suppose the Wolf was hiding behind the forest of old East End buildings. Suppose the Fascist boy jumped out, banged me hard over the head with a plank again, giving me a headache and shouted, 'Jewgirl!' Then there were my two young uncles, who worked in Booba's grocery shop. What new mischief had they prepared for me? They'd never dare laugh at their sister, Aunt Mitzi. Finally, I had to face my grandmother, Booba, she whose acid tongue could melt wallpaper, and who studied me from head to foot to see everything on me was perfect. After this inspection, she always bent down over the marble grocery shop counter, and offered me her cool cheek to kiss. For kindness, I would need to find my grandfather, Zada, who would sweep me into his strong arms – he'd been in the Czar's Cavalry – and whisper '*Bubbele, zeesele, fliegele,* little doll, little sweet one, little wing,' hugging and kissing me, his stubble scratching my cheek.

A girl of seven, small, but wiry, like my deaf Daddy, I walked the mile safely this time. 'You only weighed five pounds when you were born,' Mummy told me. 'I never wanted to marry, Booba insisted, oldest had to marry first, so my younger sister, Mitzi, could marry. She always gets what she wants. I never wanted to have a child, especially in the Depression. Daddy wanted a boy.'

My fault I was born, I thought. My fault I was not a boy.

As I entered Booba's spotless grocery shop, glittering under new electric lights, Booba stood in her white coat at the counter, a long serrated knife in her hand, staring at the white scale with two pans hanging on either side: Queen of Judgment over the half-side Scotch Salmon glistening coral on her white and green marble counter.

'*So nu? Machst a leben?*' she said in Yiddish. 'Are you earning a living?' Always tongue-tied with Booba, I smiled, shyly and looked at my Shirley Temple shoes.

Daddy told me Booba had stolen her sister Frieda's fiancé, their cousin, Benzion, planning to run away with him. ''You can't go away with him without being married,' Great Aunt Frieda told me she'd said, years later. '*You* want me to be married, *you* make the wedding,'' great aunt Frieda told me my grandmother had said, 'and I baked all day and made her a wedding. And you think she ever thanked me?' Frieda had said highly indignant. I didn't blame her. Could this be the same stern grandmother who often told me severely, 'Only dogs eat in the street'? Once, when I was older, she laughed sarcastically to me, 'Mrs Greenberg next door complains her husband never makes love.' I understood that the opposite was true for Booba.

My two young uncles in their white, grocers' coats stood on either side of this ferocious grandmother. If she had met the wolf of Red Riding Hood, she would have eaten the wolf; no wolf would have eaten my grandmother.

Booba commanded my uncles, 'I'm going inside. Watch the shop.'

As soon as she left through the frosted glass door connecting the shop to the dining room, disappearing into another world like the Queen of Alice in Wonderland, Uncle Max began striding up and down behind the marble counter, waving his hands at Uncle Sam.

'I can't stand here doing nothing. I've got to go. Didn't you see on the newsreel last night,

Hitler's thugs in Berlin cutting off Jews' beards, making them lick the ground, beating them and laughing? Mosley, Hitler's arse licker, is trying to do the same, here. You heard on the wireless, the government gave the bloody Fascist Blackshirts permission to march through the East End of London today. You can bet these hooligans will smash our shops and beat Jews, like the Nazis. My pals decided it's our duty to stop them. We're all going. I'm leaving now. *You* look after the shop.'

'Mama won't like you going,' Uncle Sam whispered, glancing fearfully through the open door at Booba in the dining room, knowing Booba's sharp tongue.

Booba stood in the dining room behind the shop, arranging her favourite gladioli, which, like her, stood imperious and cold. The crystal vase's reflection shimmered in the polished dining room table.

'What shall I tell Mama?' Uncle Sam asked.

'Say I took Gilda for a walk,' Uncle Max hissed, tearing off his white grocer's coat, snatching my hand, and hurrying me out of the shop.

'Wait,' Uncle Sam called out, running after us, but Uncle Max and I were already on Cambridge Heath Road, walking fast, where to, I had no idea. I was thrilled that Uncle Max was taking me out. Usually he teased me unmercifully. He'd never before taken me for a walk.

So I didn't ask where we were going. I had to run fast to keep up with his long legs. I was small for seven, but sturdy, and the best skipper in my class. I felt very daring to be doing something Booba would have surely forbidden. As I caught sight of my reflection in a shop window, I was glad I was wearing my red hat and coat because the October day was chilly, and Mummy had told me that Jewish people wore red for protection against evil. My face in the windows appeared as usual, pale, my dark hair short and shingled, and I had the same green, gold and Tartar shaped eyes as Booba, Mummy and Aunt Mitzi except hers were blue. I didn't care that some children in school trailed me in single file chanting, 'Chinky Chinky China'. I liked having different eyes.

Uncle Max hurried along holding my hand. Suddenly, dozens of other young men tumbled out of four slum side streets where old houses stood, damp glistening on the soot-blackened bricks. They came rushing out, their feet hitting East End cobblestones left by the ancient Romans, Daddy said, and all of them merged into one mass going in the same direction.

'Where's everyone going?' I asked.

'Cable Street,' Uncle Max said between clenched teeth, for once not teasing me.

A shout rose from all the men's mouths, getting louder as they joined another crowd, chanting, 'They shall not pass, they shall not pass.'

'Who shall not pass?' I asked Uncle Max.

'The bloody Mosley Fascists,' said Uncle Max, sometimes stopping with other young men to rip white posters showing Mosley's sneering, upper class, moustached, white face above spidery swastikas, off walls and lamp-posts. I was used to seeing swastikas with JP; Jews should Perish smeared in black on the school brick walls opposite our house. But what did 'perish' mean? The posters said something about a Fascist march on October 4, 1936. Oh, was that today?

Cars, rarely seen in the East End, drove slowly down the street, loudspeakers on top blaring, 'Keep out Fascist Mosley. Keep out the Blackshirts'.

Other men in groups poured out of all the grubby little side streets carrying signs on sticks and banners saying, 'ILF, International Labour Party,' and 'Young Socialists'. I was surprised that they dressed as well as Daddy. Some wore suits or hand-knitted pullovers under their jackets against the crisp October day; others wore white shirts and ties; many sported bowlers, trilbies or caps. I'd never seen so many men in one place, all carrying banners saying; Union, Labour, Communist, Socialist. The unionists were brawny union dockers, but the others were ordinary men from the Labour Party, communists, socialists, skinny sweatshop Jews, some bearded with yarmulkes or hats, some clean-shaven with or without hats or caps. All surged forward like one giant man.

'So many men coming from every street,' I said. 'Is the king coming again?'

'I told you. We're going to stop the Fascist march,' said Uncle Max, his lips still pressed together, his dimpled chin sticking out. It was hard to keep up with these Daddy-Long-Legs so I held tightly on to his big sixteen-year-old hand.

Other young men who went to tea dances at Lyon's Corner House with Uncle Max, running the same way, said, 'Wotcha Max,' their faces grim. He just nodded grimly to them.

As we ran I saw the words, 'They Shall not Pass,' whitewashed large, on the walls, lampposts and pavements. Black words painted on white sheets hung out of windows, just the way they had when King George V passed through the East End in his gold coach for the Jubilee, only the signs then read, 'God Save the King.' Now the sheets all said, 'THEY SHALL NOT PASS'.

'Look, a trolley's stuck at Gardner's Corner,' I said, pointing (forbidden, but I was so excited) to a bright red double-decker Number 65 tram for Blackwall Tunnel. People inside the trolley stood packed together downstairs, all up the winding stairs leading to the upper deck where I loved to ride, and on the upper deck, so many people were jammed together they couldn't budge. White faces and noses from inside pressed against the tram glass. Limp hands hung out of the windows like monkeys' from a cage, except these hands were white and not hairy. Men's bodies outside the red double-decker pressed against it on all sides so that no one inside could get out. A low rumble became louder and louder as we ran. Then the noise grew into a roar, and when we finally turned the corner into Cable Street, my mouth dropped open in astonishment. Hundreds, perhaps thousands, of young men pressed so tightly together they could hardly move.

On one end of Cable Street stood shoulder to shoulder fierce, booted Blackshirts, and at the other, the Jewish East End facing the Fascists, banners flying, stood unionists, communists, socialists, Jews all united, roaring, 'They shall not pass, they shall not pass'. I was trembling with excitement and the fear that I would lose Uncle Max. Then what would I do? I couldn't see any women or children. I was the only child in the crowd. A huge man in front of me crushed my foot with his.

'Oh, my foot!' I cried, hopping in pain.

'Up you go,' said Uncle Max, hoisting me onto his shoulders. I had a wonderful view of everything from up there. I felt as tall as a clown on stilts.

A cordon held back the 'They Shall not Pass' men: our side. I bent down and caught a glimpse of Uncle Max's mouth wide open shouting, 'They Shall not Pass'. We were still behind the cordon, and in front of it, a long line of blue uniformed police sat straight and grim-faced on prancing horses. All the white horses looked as if they, too, wore a uniform. The police pulled on their horses' reins while trying to keep our surging crowds at their backs, behind them. The animals' heads jerked, perhaps from the bit; their eyes rolled wildly showing the whites. I felt sorry for the horses. At the other end of Cable Street, the Blackshirts waited for their leader, Sir Oswald Mosley, to begin their march, faces sour and angry. Where was he? I wanted to see this ogre, but was afraid to see the hatred, which in Daddy's morning newspaper burned so fiercely in Mosley's black eyes.

'He's late,' muttered Uncle Max, pushing against the cordon, touching a horse.

'Get back,' the police shouted. Uncle Max pulled on me, looking around for his friends.

'Why are the police keeping us back?' I asked.

'They want a clear space for the damned Blackshirts to march. The Fascists are waiting for Mosley to come and lead them. He's probably chatting with his Nazi friends Goebbels and Hitler and his Nazi girl friend. They're all visiting. He doesn't care about his wife.'

I had heard Mummy's customers in our hairdressing shop gossiping about married men like Mr Smith who ran around with other women like Florrie, so I wasn't that surprised.

My uncle and his friends' crowd growing bigger every minute, booed the Blackshirts, who stuck their white, black-sleeved hands, pale white fingers pointed in the air and shouted hoarsely, 'Heil Hitler,' then sang a rowdy song and stamped their heavy leather boots. I couldn't understand the words. 'What are they singing?' I shouted.

'That's the Horst Wessel song,' Uncle Max shouted over the noise, 'one of the 'Master Race's' disgusting songs about the joy of seeing Jewish blood spurting from the knife.'

I didn't know who Hitler was or what a 'master race' was, but the words, 'Jewish blood spurting' frightened me, and reminded me of the time I cut myself and red blood poured out and wouldn't stop and I imagined I'd be empty. The noise of the chanting 'They Shall Not Pass' began to drown out the Blackshirts' singing. I wanted to put my hands over my ears but couldn't because I was holding on to Uncle Max's head, and would fall into the angry crowd.

The police from their high seats on their horses suddenly began swinging truncheons and hitting men on our side, over the head. These men howled; every now and then a man fell down, bleeding, but the crowd picked him up chanting, 'They shall not pass, they shall not pass'.

'We have to break the police line,' Uncle Max shouted to his friends around him.

Hundreds, perhaps thousands of young men shoved and pushed against the police cordon and the prancing horses.

'The police are bloody Fascists, too,' I remembered Mummy saying. 'No use calling them when the Blackshirts smash our shop windows.'

I'd always thought the blond Bobbies on the corner of each street were kind. They helped children and old ladies cross the street, but these Bobbies stared at us behind the line with hatred.

What had we done wrong?

I wrapped both arms tighter around Uncle Max's head.

'You're covering my eyes, I can't see,' he said sharply.

Suddenly I heard the crash and tinkle of breaking glass, the way I heard it when the Fascists just last week threw a brick through our shop window, yelling 'Dirty Jews!'

Three men ran out of a building carrying a young woman screaming, 'Oh my Gawd! Oh my Gawd!' blood pouring down her face and legs, sharp pieces of glinting glass sticking out of her bloody back.

Horrified, I burst into tears.

Uncle Max lifted me off of his shoulders and held me gently against his chest, like Zada. I curled my arms around his neck and buried my face in it.

'I want to go home,' I sobbed.

'Sha, sha, it's all right,' he said. 'That's where I should have left you. I'm an idiot. I didn't know there would be such a mob. Look, there's Toby Frost's flat. It's lucky she lives on Cable Street. I'm going to take you up to her flat and you stay there until I come back for you, all right?'

He hoisted me back onto his shoulders and because he was so tall and strong, shoved his way through the chanting, jostling crowds until we came to Toby's downstairs door. The Frost family lived over Gronofsky's tailor shop on the second floor. The sign over Gronofsky's hanging by a chain swinging in the wind read:

S. Gronofsky & M. Lightning
Suits made to Measure
Misfits a Specialty

We had lots of misfits in the East End with bandy legs, pigeon breasts and goiters. Toby Frost's brother, Harry, had a huge hump.

The Frost's downstairs front door was, as always, open. Uncle Max put me down, and we rushed, two at a time up the old, shaky wooden stairs to the Frost's flat. He burst through Mrs Frost's glass-paned kitchen door.

'Look who's here…' Mrs Frost began. 'What a noise down there?' Then seeing me, small and shivering behind him she said, 'Are you *meshuggah*? You're crazy to bring the child!'

'Here, look after her, I'll be back,' Uncle Max said, and clattered down the narrow winding stairs back to the crowds. I stood at the top of the stairs watching his back disappear. Mrs Frost flung up the window from the bottom. The crowds roaring below sounded like, I imagined, a terrible sea storm. I put my hands over my ears.

'A *meshuganne*, a madman, bringing a child into this!' Mrs Frost called out to his back, but he wouldn't hear because of the shouting. She closed the window; the sound became fainter, came back to me and stroked my hair. 'There, there, *kinderle*. Don't cry, child.'

Mrs Frost's daughter, Toby, with the wart on her nose was Mummy's friend. Toby told us her mother had married an older man who had died, and left her mother a poor widow. Toby worked as a seamstress in a sweatshop and supported her mother and her brother, Harry. I liked Mrs Frost's soft, brown eyes and long, dark hair, which, gathered in a soft knot at the nape of her neck, looked like a hank of silk.

She dried my eyes with a white handkerchief. 'He's only a child himself, 16, but he ought to know better. Come, *kinderle*,' she said to me, 'sit, and I'll make you a nice cup of tea.'

Harry came into the kitchen. 'Mum, turn on the wireless. I want to hear the news.' Harry's humpback was the largest I had ever seen. He never went out because the children tormented him so, but all day he sat at his bedroom window, watched the street or read the newspaper and books, or went into the kitchen and listened to the wireless. The BBC announcer was saying, '…three thousand of Sir Oswald Mosley's Fascist followers have gathered, here in Royal Mint Street in their uniform black shirts and boots, just like Hitler's followers, to march through the East End of London. They have been impatiently awaiting the arrival of their leader. Sir Oswald was supposed to have arrived at 1:30 p.m. but he is two hours late. Fights have broken out between the BUF, The British Union of Fascists, and anti-Fascists here in Royal Mint Street with both sides throwing bricks, bottles and stones. All available police in the London metropolis are on active duty. Police reporters, an autogyro and aeroplane surveillance say that over 100,000 people and 7,000 police have gathered in Cable Street through which the BUF obtained police permission to march today.'

'Marvellous,' Harry said. 'This will make history! I'm going back to my bedroom to watch out the window what happens. I hope we kill that *mamzer*, Mosley.'

I knew that *mamzer* was Yiddish for a bastard, but I wasn't sure what a bastard was. Someone really bad?

Mrs Frost sat me at the kitchen table. A black kettle always purred over a blue and orange flame on the gas stove in the East End, for visitors. Mrs Frost boiled milk on the gas stove, picked the skin off the top, poured hot milk into the white cup, and then boiling water through a tea strainer. She dropped in two lumps of sugar and stirred it for me, the spoon clinking against the inside of the cup. I shivered from excitement and fright. All those thousands of men, looking so angry; the police whom I thought were my friends, hitting Jewish and union men on the head, the enormous white horses with their long, beautiful swishing tails. It was exciting and confusing. However, after a sip of strong, sweet tea, I felt better, and then dashed over to the kitchen windows to look for Uncle Max. Would the police hit him on the head? Would he fall? How would I get home?

The crowds below were, in places, so thick no one could move except to sway back and forth. Looking out the kitchen window, I could see Harry's head hanging out of his bedroom window. His hump almost higher than his head towered over his poor twisted body. For sure, Gronovsky made his suits. Mummy said that Harry had a hump because when Mrs Frost was pregnant she fell down the stairs. I ran to Harry though I was a little afraid of him. He looked the way I imagined the Beast, in *Beauty and the Beast* looked. But when I dared look into his brown eyes, they seemed, like the Beast's, intelligent and kindly.

'Can you see my uncle? What's happening, Harry?' I asked.

'A wonderful thing is happening,' he said, his brown eyes shining. 'Mosley's Blackshirts are trying to march through the East End to beat Jews and smash our shops and thousands of our boys are fighting to stop him. If only I could fight myself.'

'Aren't the police going to stop Mosley?'

'Stop them?' Harry laughed, 'Come here. Look out of my window. Do you see our British police stopping them? They're *helping* them, trying to clear a way for them. In Leeds the Fascists called a rally, the Jews came out in protest. The Blackshirts hit a Jewish bloke so hard they blinded him. Guess who they arrested? Jews. The British police and most of the *goyim* sympathize with the Fascists. Don't you see the signs on all the walls on your way to school, 'JP'. It means 'Jews should Perish'.

I did see the signs and the swastikas, but I didn't know what perish meant and didn't like to ask. What does a swastika mean? I knew it was something bad against Jews, and the black, spidery swastika made my heart miss a beat, but I didn't know exactly why.

Searching the crowds from the Frost's second story window, I couldn't see Uncle Max anywhere. I would never find him in the thousands of men below who, jammed together were still chanting, 'They shall not pass'.

I heard a crack as a stick hit a man's head. He fell, but his mates picked him up and surged forward angrily against the police, pushing against their horses. The horses pranced, their sharp hooves clicking on the road as the police tried to hold our side behind the cordon. Dozens of other police on foot stood further back behind the anti-Fascists in case, I supposed, my uncle and his friends broke out from the back of the crowd. There seemed to be almost as many police as Fascists and anti-Fascists, except the police wore blue shirts, and the Fascists, black.

'Look at that. Everyone came out together. Mosley's against unions, so all the union dockers came out. He's Fascist, so the socialists and communists came. He's anti-Semitic, so the Jews came. For once they're all united instead of fighting each other. Look. Look over there,' Harry shouted. He leaned out the window. A roar went up from the crowd below, and all the men below turned to look where Harry's long finger pointed.

'Look! Our boys have broken through the police cordon. They're trying to turn over a lorry on Cable Street to make a barricade so the Blackshirts can't march through our Jewish section!' Harry shouted, pointing to a crowd of men pushing the side of an enormous lorry. Strong Irish dockers, labourers, muscles bulging, Jews in beards, men in derbies shoulder to shoulder all pushing together, strained to overturn the huge lorry. It rocked back and forth, back and forth, until finally the men all put their shoulders to one side of it and one shouted, 'One, two three, *heave*,' and the lorry crashed over on its side with a thud, wood splinters flying, glass windows shattering, and a great cloud of dust went up all round it and the men who pushed it over jumped back so as not to be hit by the flying glass and splinters. Everyone on our side roared with delight.

Then our men behind the overturned lorry lying on its side like an elephant, threw piles of corrugated iron, chunks of old beer barrels left by coopersmiths, planks of wood and glass bottles over the hulk. The dockers, using their giant hooks ripped up pavements, smashed them into pieces and threw a hail of broken stones over the barricade at the mounted police. The police horses reared up, neighing.

'Why are they throwing stones?' I asked Harry.

'I told you already. To keep Fascists and the police from getting through Cable Street to the Jewish East End,' he shouted, eyes blinking fast. Did I imagine it or did his hump quiver?

I suddenly saw Uncle Max behind the barricade on our side throwing a hail of shiny little black balls over it.

'Ball bearings,' Harry muttered with satisfaction.

The police charged up to the overturned truck and the men in front of it, but just before the horses reached them, their hooves slid on the metal ball bearings and they fell squirming, neighing, screaming, upside-down, black hooves waving in the air. Policemen went flying in all directions. One policeman fell, his horse on top of him. His bobby's hat fell off as he lay there, blond, his tall helmet on the ground. Clutching his stomach, he moaned, 'Oooh, oooh.'

I felt sorry for the horse; I wasn't sure about the policeman. Was he a friend or not?

'Ha, ha,' laughed the men on our side of the barricade. 'Bloody Fascist bobby.'

After six or seven tries to ride their horses forward toward the lorry, the police finally turned back, scowling. The crowds cheered. They began again roaring, chanting, 'They Shall Not Pass,' over and over and over again.

'They had police permission to march but we're going to stop them.' Harry crowed joyously. 'Oh, I wouldn't have missed this for anything.'

The roaring from the street was so deafening even my deaf Daddy would have heard it. I wondered what Mummy would have said. She thought I was with Booba all this time so she wouldn't be worried. She'd never dream I was with the Frosts on Cable Street in the middle of a big fight. I was so excited I bit my nails down to the cuticle. Mummy would be cross with me.

'Come away from the window and finish your tea,' Mrs Frost said to Harry and me. 'I'm worried about Toby; I hope she isn't caught in this crowd. It's no place for a woman.'

'Don't worry Mum, she said she was going to see her friend Sadie in Epping. That's miles away,' Harry said.

'*Gotze Dunk*,' thank God, said Mrs Frost, wiping her hands on the white apron she always wore, as she finally came to the window with us, to look. She was just in time to see a burly policeman smartly smack a young Jewish man with his stick. The man fell down, covering his face so the policeman couldn't hit his eyes. Blood spurted from his head.

'*Oy a broch!*' a curse on them, Mrs Frost cried, and running for empty milk bottles, came back, threw up the window and rained six milk bottles down on the policeman's head, hitting him with each one. The policeman looked up and shook his stick at her. She stuck a long, pink tongue out at him, and her bun came undone, her silky hair tumbled below her waist. She looked like a girl. Who would believe that the quiet Mrs Frost would be so cheeky? A real cockney, full of spunk.

Noticing movement in other houses on our floor level, I saw more women in white pinafores framed in their open windows throwing bricks, bottles, and water on the tall hats of the policemen and screaming at them words which only women coming out of the pub used. Instead of being quiet Jewish women as usual, they were being bold and brave fighters. The police, Jewish women, everyone and everything had changed. I was in a different country, and totally confused. I just knew that together with his friends, Uncle Max and all our side had stopped Mosley marching through the Jewish East End. I felt so proud of him, and all those brave men below. I was not used to feeling proud.

A loud buzzing overhead made us look up at the sky. Some strange things, not blimps, were flying overhead, besides a small aeroplane.

'Autogyros,' Harry said, 'counting the people, probably. Ha ha,' he crowed, 'with that lorry blocking their route the lousy Blackshirts will never be able to get to us. Turn up the wireless again, Mother,' he said again, 'let's hear what they have to say.'

'The crowd is…wait, a bulletin has just come in from the Metropolitan Commissioner of Police, Sir Phillip Game. Sir Phillip says that owing to the violence already evident between the BUF and their opponents, the Commissioner has decided that this march would be impossible without serious riots and bloodshed. It cannot, therefore, take place. The Commissioner has sent a police escort to lead the British Union of Fascists, the BUF procession in the opposite direction, along the Embankment, to Temple Underground Station. However, outbreaks of violence between Fascists and the Young Communist League are reported in Trafalgar Square. The Young Communist League had its own meeting there today protesting the rule of Generalissimo Franco and in support of the Spanish Republic.'

'Christ, the whole world is turning Fascist.' Harry said. 'But thank God we stopped this march.'

Somehow the news had reached the 100,000 protesters gathered below and a great roar went up as they cheered their victory and threw their hats and caps into the air. Harry caught a bowler as it sailed past our window and stuck it on his big head. With the hat and his hump, he looked stranger than ever. The men below started dancing arm in arm in the streets, singing *Knees up Mother Brown*, the pub song gentiles sang and danced to in the streets when the pubs closed on Saturday nights. Harry turned up the sound on the wireless.

'So far, there have been 84 arrests and 80 people, including 15 police, have been injured in the crowds.'

'You can guess who they're arresting,' Harry said. 'Jews first, then Communists, then dockers. Those bloody Fascists can forget about getting drunk tonight at the Salmon and Ball.'

'Is that a pub?'

'Yes. It's their favourite meeting place near Trafalgar Square where the Fascists rally and jump each other up,' Harry said. 'They'll be crying in their beer tonight.'

Uncle Max, a red cut on his left cheek, finally came leaping up the stairs. We walked home along with thousands of men, some bloody, but victorious against Mosley's Fascists. Women poured out of houses to greet their heroes. Men and women danced in the street. This time, as they laughed together, I skipped in front of Uncle Max and his friends on the way back to Booba's house.

Mummy had become worried when I didn't return on time, and had walked to Booba's to find out what happened to me. As Uncle Max and I walked in, Booba ranted and raged at him for going, and Mummy shouted at him for taking me, but both were too relieved we were safe and about the outcome of the battle to be seriously angry. After all, except for that cut on Uncle Max's cheek, neither of us had been hurt. Still, it had been exciting to share the Cable Street adventure with my young Uncle Max.

The next day, on the wireless at breakfast, the Fascists claimed it was all outside Communists who came and fought them, but Mummy said hotly, 'Bloody liars.'

'Still,' Mummy said, 'Hitler has many supporters in England and Germany and in Italy, under Mussolini. Even the Mufti Arabs support Hitler. We're in for trouble.'

My cousin Zalman, a Polish Jewish refugee from Hitler, had already arrived in England. 'The Pollaks killed my wife and child.' I'd never seen a man cry. For the first time, I saw Booba give someone tea, strudel, and some gentle words.

The next day, Uncle Max came to our house. He sometimes helped Daddy in our barbershop. After closing shop, we sat in the kitchen, drinking tea before a roaring fire.

'The BUF is forbidden to march in their black shirts and leather boots now, and Mosley might be imprisoned in the Tower of London,' Uncle Max shouted, so deaf Daddy heard.

'That evening after we beat the Fascists, we all danced in the streets and shouted, 'Down with Mosley, down with the BUF,' Uncle Max crowed. 'After the Fascists' humiliation at Cable Street, we Jews who rarely go into pubs, joined the gentile dockers, unionists, socialists and communists with a beer in celebrating the victory for democracy.'

I wondered what that was.

'Too bad everyone doesn't come out against the Nazis in Germany as we did here with the Fascists,' Daddy said.

'The Nazis would have shot every anti-Fascist,' Mummy said. 'It's bad enough our police side with the Fascists. If they carried guns, like the Nazis, they would have shot us all.'

'Well it's not the end of the Fascists nor of the Nazis,' Uncle Max said. 'The Fascists and Nazis are getting stronger all over Europe. It's not the end, it's just the beginning.'

My uncle's face had changed from a laughing, teasing boy's face to that of a serious man.

His was now the stern face of a soldier.

CHAPTER 11

AUNT MITZI'S WEDDING *

'Alf are you ready?' she shouted at Daddy.

Daddy now wore 'tails' and striped trousers, spats and a silk top hat all rented from Moss Brothers. Smart and severe; he looked just like his own enormous wedding picture that hung over their bedroom fireplace.

'When we get to the shul someone will give you flowers to hold,' Mummy said.

I didn't know what a shul was, but said nothing. I would find out.

We always walked, rode the bus or trains, but for the first time in my life we went in a taxi. I sat luxuriously on the soft seat, between Mummy and Daddy.

'The Great Synagogue,' Mummy said, grandly. 'The Spanish and Portuguese.'

'Wot, the one on Duke Street?' the taxi driver said.

'Yes please,' Mummy said.

'Cor,' said the taxi driver. 'Ain't that the place where the geezers wear silk top 'ats?'

'The synagogue officials always wear silk top hats and many other men also, on a Sabbath or a Jewish festival,' Mummy answered. 'It's the main synagogue for Jewish royalty,' she said proudly. What was it like in a synagogue? Surely, she herself hadn't been married there. Daddy said that Booba had given Mummy an inexpensive wedding in the Great Spitalfields Synagogue next to the wholesale fruit and vegetable market. Then, according to Daddy, Booba, after stealing her sister's fiancé, had also stolen his £400 in wedding gifts. But if Booba was so naughty, why was she was always telling me what to, or what not to do?

'Only dogs eat in the street,' Booba always told me. Even if she were not with me, the rest of my life if I put anything in my mouth in the street, I always heard her voice in my head, 'Only dogs eat in the street,' and I stopped. Her words were branded like fire in my head.

The taxi stopped outside a tall building as high and wide as Liverpool Street Station, but inside, light flowed in from three-story stained glass windows and carved poles soared from floor to ceiling, the pillars passing balconies on each side of the enormous room. Great chandeliers hung low from the high ceiling. Gazing up, my head rested on my back. (Photo-Ausubel. p.435). It was certainly a more cheerful and beautiful place than the Chingford church.

'Look at those 'uge Sephardic columns,' Daddy exclaimed. 'What a great synagogue!'

It was the first time I had been in a synagogue. It was far grander than Chingford's church and bright, filled with light and colour and no sad man hung nailed to two pieces of wood.

'Look at the balconies, up there. That's where the women pray on shabbos Saturdays. The men sit downstairs on these polished benches. But since this is a wedding, not a service, men and women can sit together. How bright it is,' Daddy said.

Mummy said, looking at the heavy chandeliers. 'I heard that when this synagogue used to be lit by candles it took four hours to light them all. This shul is 300 years old.'

Men in elegant, shiny silk top hats walked like princes down the two aisles toward a raised platform like the one in the orphanage. But instead of being at the end of the room like the stage in the orphanage, this one was in the middle of the huge room. Instead of being made of rough wood with large gaps between the planks (down which I'd lost Aunt Mitzi's gold bracelet, never retrieved) like the orphanage stage, carpeting covered this little platform but for a rim of polished wood round its edges. A waist-high banister stood all around the platform, I supposed, so no one fell off of it. A tall desk covered with satin stood in the centre of this stage.

'What's that for?' I whispered to Mummy.

'That's where the cantor sings the prayers or someone reads from the Torah,' Mummy said. 'It's called the '*bima*' a stand, or a platform.'

'And what's that arch at the back with a light burning over it and the velvet curtains with marks embroidered on it in front?' I whispered.

'That's where they keep the scrolls of the Torah. Every word on the Torah is handwritten by a *sofer*, a scribe; he's a special writer of Hebrew words. The light over the Torah is called the *Ner Tamid*, The Eternal Light. Like the Torah, it's never allowed to go out. The Hebrew words under the Eternal Light are the first word of each of the Ten Commandments.

I didn't know what the Ten Commandments were either. I knew Booba had given all her children a good Hebrew education, but I didn't know Mummy knew so much. Booba and Zada seemed to be religious, and all Jewish parents in the East End, as far as I knew, sent their children to cheder. Mummy had taken me to cheder a few times, and I now recognised the Hebrew letters on the velvet scroll covers. Daddy seemed to know nothing about religion so I supposed except for lighting the Friday evening candles and eating kosher food, Mummy had stopped being religious too. I knew we were Jewish. If we forgot, the Fascists reminded us.

On the little platform, four poles held up a satin cloth.

'What's that little tent on the platform for?' I whispered, too excited to keep silent.

'That 'tent' is called the '*chuppa*'. It's like a little house that the bride and groom will soon live in together. Remember, when you grow up and go out with boys, you're never really married until you're under the *chuppa*.'

'What do you mean?'

'Don't take fancy words and promises from men and give them everything they want. They're only serious when they agree to go under the *chuppa*. Save yourself for this man.'

Daddy had told me about a girl he knew who had given a big engagement party.

'Her fiancé didn't even show up. Everyone went to look for him, and found him in the arms of a prostitute. His fiancée committed suicide,' Daddy had told me. I supposed that was what Mummy meant when she said you weren't really married until you were under the *chuppa*.

By now, people arriving had filled the synagogue; all my relatives on Mummy's side came, but none of Daddy's relatives. Either they hadn't been invited or they had nothing to wear for a posh wedding. Every guest wore a black silk top hat, tail coats, waistcoats with white bands around their waists, white ties, a white carnation in their buttonhole and a gold pocket watch on a gold chain across their waistcoats and striped trousers. Women wore long dresses. In spite of the summer warmth, some women wore fur capes.

'Show offs,' Mummy muttered, 'but good for Zada. Furriers have no work in summer.'

From somewhere hidden, music played and a choir sang in Hebrew. A man mounted the steps of the *chuppa*. He wore a tall hat and a long black robe, over which he had draped a fringed shawl ending with black stripes, reminding me of a zebra. He stood on the *chuppa* and began chanting with a rich voice sounding like one of Mummy's opera singers, but in Hebrew.

Mummy led me to the back of the synagogue and opened a door. Behind the door stood Uncle Adrian, his older brother, Sidney, best man (who was the worst man?) and his other brother, Wally. Also standing there were Uncle Adrian's two sisters and his mother and father. Mummy handed me a bunch of white carnations.

'Now walk down the aisle slowly with these flowers in your hand. Go up the steps onto the *bima*. Aunt Mitzi and Uncle Adrian will come up the aisle to the *bima*, and the rabbi will marry them. When he's finished, I'll beckon you with my finger like this,' and she wagged her finger back and forth. 'Come down quickly and sit with me.'

I walked down the aisle all alone, feeling very small, my bare shoulders cool, proud of my silver topped dress, the white tulle skirt poofing out as I walked, shoulders straight, carrying the bouquet of white flowers. Guests watching me were murmuring, 'Ooh, how sweet, how pretty!' My pale cheeks, I was sure, flushed with happiness. I didn't need country air to put colour in my cheeks. I just needed someone to say I was pretty. I smiled like the Cheshire cat.

Since I'd come home from the orphanage, happy to be in London and with my old friends and my relatives, I'd almost lost my shyness. But as I walked up the steps to the *bima* I feared tripping over my long dress and spoiling everything. The other bridesmaids, Uncle Adrian's sisters, followed me up to the *bima*. I was amazed to see that although they were old, at least 18 or 19, they both wore the same dress as mine. They had breasts, so they didn't need shoulder straps to hold up their dresses.

Uncle Adrian's brothers, his sisters, my Uncles Sam and Max joined us under the *chuppa*. It was getting crowded but I liked being close to people. Why didn't Mummy come up?

Uncle Adrian walked tall and proud down the aisle, his short mother and father supporting him on each side because Mummy said he and Aunt Mitzi had fasted before the wedding. As he mounted the *chuppa* steps, his face looked like Binkie's after she licked the cream that came at the top of every bottle of milk.

Aunty Mitzi now stood framed in the door at the back of the synagogue, Booba and Zada on each side of her. There was a loud, 'Oooh,' as everyone admired Aunty Mitzi's long, shimmering column of white satin. It was so simple, heavy beading glittering only at the boat neckline and around slashes baring each shoulder. The starkly simple dress showed off her tall, slender figure. As she walked, a long, long train swept behind her; her face, not laughing as usual, was serious. Perhaps she was thinking if she'd been richer and had more *nadn* instead of just being the daughter of Polish immigrants, she would now be under the *chuppa* with Raphael, her boss's son, the man she really loved and who loved her. She stood still beside Adrian.

Suddenly, there was silence. The rabbi began reading from a scroll he held in his hand, I heard him say the date of the marriage, the location, London, Aunt Mitzi's name then Uncle Adrian's, then I heard Uncle Adrian repeat Hebrew words after the rabbi saying, I supposed, that he was taking Aunty Mitzi as his wife. He placed a wedding ring on her forefinger, a funny place for a ring, but that was where Booba wore her ring in her wedding photograph. Booba lifted the veil over her younger daughter's face and put a silver cup of wine to her lips. Aunt Mitzi drank, then Uncle Adrian stamped on the glass at his feet, and everyone shouted, 'Mazltov!!' 'Congratulations!'

Mummy beckoned to me, so I ran off the *bima* only just in time before guests stampeded up to the little platform, hugging and kissing Aunt Mitzi and Uncle Adrian, laughing crazily and shouting 'Mazltov', and wishing Booba and Zada and Adrian's parents Mazltov and *nachas*: congratulations and you should have much happiness. To Aunty Mitzi and Uncle Adrian's unmarried sisters and brothers everyone was saying, '*Mirtza shem badir*' that I'd heard meant God willing you should soon get married, too. And they were all saying, '*Off simchas*,' 'we should meet only on joyous occasions.' Some were crying and laughing at the same time.

Only Mummy didn't go to the bride and groom.

She sat in her seat, tears falling, whether from joy or grief I didn't know. Her dark gold eyes opened wide and tragic as if she remembered that Booba had made her marry my father eight years ago because Aunt Mitzi had wanted to marry Raphael. Perhaps she remembered that Aunt

Mitzi gave up waiting for Raphael and had only just married Adrian. Mummy said that she had married Daddy for nothing. On Mummy's face I saw sadness as if she were thinking that had she waited, this David might have asked her to marry him. Neither sister had married her true love. Mummy's face twisted with what I thought was envy. Even if Aunt Mitzi hadn't married her true love, Uncle Adrian was taller, handsomer, and far more educated than Daddy. And no one had to shout at Uncle Adrian for him to hear. I looked at Mummy and Daddy sitting together, both looking serious and sad. But I couldn't help feeling happy.

I saw a flash of Uncle Adrian's tail coat and of Aunty Mitzi's white satin gown before they disappeared into what Mummy told me was the 'Yichud' the 'alone room' for the bride and groom to break their fast. But Booba told Mummy, Daddy and the rest of the guests to hop into cars outside to go to the wedding lunch. Later, there would be a wedding tea before the evening dinner and dance.

Booba said to Mummy, 'You and Alf go to the lunch hall. We'll meet you there.' To me she said, 'Gilda, you come with me and the family. We're going with the bride and groom to Boris to take photographs.'

Wasn't Mummy and Daddy family? Why weren't they invited to come with us to be photographed? But children must not ask questions.

My grandparents, uncles Sam and Max and I climbed into a great car, which said on the bonnet, 'Daimler', the car in which the King and Queen drove in. I felt very posh being in a King's car. I felt like a princess in a fairy tale.

'Where are we going?' I asked Booba. I sat on Zada's lap. Since the time Uncle Max had told me to watch his ears then burnt my hand with his cigarette, I had been careful not to sit on Uncle Max's lap. But Zada held me close and gently against his solid chest. Leaning against him, I felt beautiful, loved and secure. I had never felt so happy.

'I told you. We're all going to take photographs, and then we're going to La Boheme Ballroom for lunch, and dinner,' Booba said. So Mummy and Daddy were not coming with us. I couldn't believe Booba had sent them straight to the lunch hall. Perhaps there was some truth in Daddy calling Booba a *vilde chaya*, a wild animal. I felt sad for Mummy, Daddy wouldn't care, but I couldn't help feeling proud that I was going to be in the wedding photographs.

Boris, the famous photographer, posed Aunt Mitzi tall and straight as a queen, Uncle Adrian even taller, like a prince, behind her, Adrian's left hand in his tuxedo pocket. The hand in the pocket surprised me, as adults always told boys to keep their hands out of their pockets when speaking to their elders. Of course, Uncle Adrian was neither a boy, nor speaking to his elders. Still. Boris stood me in front of my aunt and uncle, my head came up to my tall aunt's waist. Uncles Max and Sam, and Uncle Adrian's brothers and sisters who'd suddenly appeared stood on either side of bride and groom. I felt that Booba had hurt Mummy's feelings, but what could I do? Booba was matriarch, a word I'd only recently learned in a book I'd read.

Boris took only a little while to pose us and take our photographs. We left the photographer's studio and scrambled back into the waiting Daimler. When the car dropped us off, we entered an enormous room with hundreds of white-covered tables, each with a huge basket of fruit or a vase of flowers in the centre. There was one big, long table with an arch of flowers over it.

'Where will we all sit?' I asked Mummy.

'The bride and groom and parents sit at the long table. We'll be sitting close by.'

Mummy turned to Daddy and said loudly above the babble of hundreds of people talking in Yiddish, English, Polish or Russian, 'Alf, go and look at the cards on that table, and see which number table we're sitting at.'

Chattering wedding guests crowded through doorways into a huge room. Waiters in white coats and black bow ties stood near each table. I looked for Cousin Alex, our cheerful refugee cousin waiter with the gold tooth, but he wasn't there. Then I caught sight of him, only he wasn't a waiter, he was now a guest, wearing tails like other men guests, smiling and cheerful, his gold teeth flashing, talking fast in Yiddish and waving his hands like European refugees. We English were taught to keep our hands still. Zalman was not there, I remembered, Mummy had said that if the Nazis had just killed his wife and child, he couldn't go to a wedding for a year.

Aunty Mitzi and Uncle Adrian arrived for the lunch, breathless. Adrian, grinning, held Aunty Mitzi's hand as if she were a prize. Aunty Mitzi smiled, though not with her usual smile that looked like bubbles springing to the top of the seltzer bottle with a handle that a man delivered to us every week. We all sat. Aunt Mitzi, Uncle Adrian and all the relatives, except Mummy, Daddy and I, sat at the head table. My family sat at a separate small table. The rabbi made what sounded like a blessing over wine and bread, and the waiters began serving. At each place lay a little booklet, a gold tassel through its centre.

'Look at this menu,' Mummy said, opening it. 'It's marvellous.'

'Cover Page,' Mummy read out loud.

'It says, This Dinner given on the occasion of the marriage of:

Miss Mitzi Goldzummer

To

Mr Adrian Hart.
Sunday, June 3rd, 1937
at
La Boheme

I traced the first initials of my aunt and uncle, 'M' and 'A' intertwined at the top of the page and enclosed in a circle.

'MENU'

Mummy read:

'Cocktails
Cantalope Melon
Hors d'Oeuvres Varies
Fillet of Soles, Lemon Sauce, Sweet Cucumber
Vermicelli Soup and Rosies
Tomato Soup and Meat Patties
Schnitzel, Mushroom Sauce, French Beans
Tongue with Blintzes

Tangerine Ice
Roast Chicken, French Sticks, Mixed Vegetables
Macedoine Apple Sauce
Asparagus with Sauce
Ice Pudding, Preserved Fruits
Black Coffee

Catered by Madame A. Blumstein
1 Devonshire Rd, Mare Street, E.9 Phone Amherst 4353.

'Wine List' She read:

'Love and health to all – Macbeth'
Whiskeys: White Horse, Johnny Walker, Black and White, John Haig
Brandies: Three Star Martels, Hennessy Liqueurs:
Cherry Brandy, Kummel, Benedictine, Green Chartreuse,
Yellow chartreuse, Advocaat, Crème de Menthe
Wines: Fine Old Muscat, Superior Sauterne, Old Port
Wines and Spirits supplied by the Host.

'Your mother probably used our four hundred pounds she took from our wedding gifts,' Daddy grumbled. Mummy turned the page of the little cream book and continued reading:

'Music During Dinner
by
Musicant's Band
Toastmaster Wally Hart

'Wally is Adrian's older brother,' Mummy said to me.

The other husbands and wives were chatting and laughing together with guests at their table. I thought Mummy was reading the menu out loud to look as if she were talking to Daddy. Mummy cast the head table a burning look. Her face turned red.

She turned back to the menu. Turning the third page she said loudly to Daddy,

'Toasts
The King
The Bride and Bridegroom
The Parents
The Guests.'

The last page was empty but said at the top, 'AUTOGRAPHS'. Why, I wondered.

Mummy closed the little booklet; I touched the silky tassels that hung in the back of the booklet. I wished I could have it, like the marzipan, but Mummy tucked it in her satin bag.

We began eating but I was so tired that somewhere, sometime, I fell asleep just as someone was saying, 'they're going to hold the Olympic Games at Berlin in July, no Jews allowed to compete, bloody Nazis,' and I awoke only to feel Mummy pulling off my bridesmaid's dress and tucking me into my cot.

As I fell asleep, I thought I was having a wonderful time in London, at home. I had my best friend Joycey Kennel with whom I roamed East London on Saturdays, played with friends after school on the steps of Shoreditch church, I went to the library every day, enjoyed reading at home during meals, Mummy had once taken me to an acrobat and tap dancing class, I'd seen King George V and Queen Mary in the Jubilee Festival, and today, I'd enjoyed Aunt Mitzi's wedding. London was the most exciting place in the world. I loved every minute of it. Nothing could make me unhappy, though I'd heard rumbles of war with Germany.

But surely, strong Britain with our great Empire would beat anyone, even the Nazis.

CHAPTER 12

THE LAST SUMMER OF PEACE *

As she washed a fuzzy peach, Mummy sang one of the latest 1930s songs.

The way you smile and hold my hand
To let me know you understand,
The wind and rain upon your face
The blessed thrill of your embrace
Remembering all those little things
All of a sudden, my heart sings.

Mummy's rich voice, throbbing with passion and longing, poured through our tiny East London kitchen. I wondered if she were still thinking of David, whoever he was, because I'd never seen Daddy hold her hand except while he danced with her at Aunt Mitzi's wedding. That was not the same as holding hands. I wondered if her 'David' was Dr David Baumgarten, who, towering over Mummy when he came to see Daddy had held Mummy's small, white hands in his great paws, looking down into her green-gold, upturned eyes. But David was a common name.

As Mummy cut the peach in half, a brown worm slithered out and fell into the sink. She turned the tap water on harder and faster; the worm swirled round, struggling against the circling downpour, but finally, caught helplessly in a swirling torrent, the water sucked the worm down the drain. Poor worm, I thought. It had fought hard, but didn't stand a chance.

When she offered me half of the peach I couldn't eat it, mourning for the worm that had fought so hard and lost.

'Your teacher just spoke to me,' Mummy said, turning to me. 'Although you're only seven, your marks were so good that you're going to miss a class and pass up next autumn to the class above. You're so clebber,' she said, imitating the way I supposed I had pronounced 'clever' when I was young. She knelt, so that our faces were the same height, took me in her arms and gave me a rare hug. Her warm body pressed against mine, I felt my face flush with joy.

'That's good, some colour in your cheeks,' she said as she stood up. 'You ought to get away from this dusty London summer and get some country air. I'll write to Aunty Ellen.'

I didn't have any Aunty Ellen; she must be one of the many friends Mummy sometimes sent me to 'for my health', though I was never ill except for the time I'd caught scarlet fever from Nurse Harris in the orphanage. I didn't want to go away again. I wished I hadn't blushed.

My pleasure at the hug and my blush faded. I'd have far rather stayed in sooty exciting East London than go to a lonely country place where nothing ever happened, where I knew no one, and where the 'aunt' might be a giantess like Mrs Major who walked from bathroom to bedroom, a towel round her waist, only one tit hanging over her waist, jeering at my confusion. Mummy stripped to the waist and washed herself every morning. I knew women had two breasts.

Who cared about sooty air? London was my air. It didn't matter to me that Mummy had told me she didn't want a child, especially in the Depression, and that if I had to be born, I should have been a boy. I had London, school, Joycey, a library, friends, grandparents, aunts, uncles and Daddy. That was enough for me. Daddy, though deaf, talked to me always, when we went out together, and some Sundays we visited museums or his brother, Uncle Izzy. My friends at school, teachers and Zada, my grandfather, loved me. However, I knew that like the worm that had swirled desperately against the relentless water, there was no hope. If Mummy wanted to send me away again, I would be swept down a gurgling drain like that worm.

'You'll love it there,' Mummy said, 'Aunt Ellen lives at the seaside.'

I'd been to Brighton, once, when I was young: two or three. I remembered dirty sand, an oily sea and slimy, cold, green seaweed clinging round my legs.

If Mummy wrote today, her letter would reach this stranger, 'Aunt' Ellen in the morning. We'd have an answer within two days.

Sure enough, the next Sunday, closing day, Mummy led me by the hand to a one-level green, country bus and not to my favourite red, double-decker London bus to the West End.

'Put her off at Hythe, please,' she told the driver, handing him a small suitcase.

'Up you go, young lady,' he said, swinging me up the three bus steps.

As usual, she said goodbye with her violet-perfumed kiss. She only kissed me when she said 'Goodbye' sending me from home. I stared out the window at my white-faced reflection in which her waving white hanky flashed as the bus pulled away from London. I watched her goodbye handkerchief waving until the bus turned the corner and she disappeared. But it was really me who disappeared, vanishing, becoming as usual, like the worm, invisible.

'Good riddance to bad rubbish,' I imagined her saying happily, the way urchins chanted at other children whom, for no particular reason, they forced to leave their group. She took good care of me while I was at home, but I thought she couldn't stand having me at home for long.

After riding, it seemed, for hours, the driver said, 'This is where you get off, miss.'

He carried me and my tiny suitcase down the bus steps, and left me on a hot, deserted, utterly flat sand, not one street, not one building and not one person in sight.

This was gentile, desolate, country even if it was near a beach. Country streets were always empty and silent, not filled with shops, carts, barrow boys who shouted their wares; where people, horses, dogs and cats barked or meowed as in London. The silence was as heavy as the hot, silent sun that burned my head. I sat on my suitcase and put my head in my arms on my knees. Where was I? As usual, I had no idea where I was. It was Hythe, but where was Hythe? How far from home was I this time? Who and where was 'Aunt' Ellen? What did she look like? Had this new 'aunt' forgotten me? What to do if she didn't come? I was in Nowhere, haunted with Nowhere. I had been to Nowhere so many times.

The sun and the dead silence that I so hated, the flat, dull sand, burning sun and empty view exhausted me. I hunched small on my suitcase. Were Hansel and Gretel or Snow White ever left on sand near a beach? No, they were left in forests with tall, shady trees, not in a desert.

I sat alone in the hot sun for about an hour. Only twittering birds looking for nesting places broke the silence. I had hated silence since being shut up alone in the orphanage attic during my six-week quarantine.

The red ball of sun began sinking. Soon, it would be dark. Even the birds had stopped singing. I longed for a cool drink and a thick slice of white bread and butter. Tea time had gone.

Finally, loping along the flat sand, a tall, lean woman, I thought, in her early 40s and dressed in a blue flowered cotton frock, broke the empty horizon. Without pausing in her step, she said briskly, 'Come along,' and strode off. I followed her long strides, mine, two to her one, lugging my suitcase. We walked without a word for about a mile until we came to a row of stone yards. Each house and yard, only separated by a wire fence between them, looked exactly the same. Entering a stone yard through a gate, we passed a shed like the one at the orphanage, only smaller. I looked over my shoulder at the low shed. Was this to be another orphanage?

Left to right: Paternal great grandmother, bride Chana Hochberg (maternal grandmother) and groom Ben-Zion Goldzummer.

Esther (Minnie) née Goldzummer and groom, Abraham/Alfred Moskovitch (later Moss), wedding 20 March 1928.

Gilda in frilly sleeveless white dress aged about five with mother.

Gilda's mother, Esther, with her mother, Chana (seated) c.1928.

Gilda aged three and a half, last left on bicycle.

Shoreditch Church where we used to play after school. Extant.

Brick Lane Market on a Sunday c.1935.

Billingsgate open fish market, see fish weather vane top left of building c.1935.

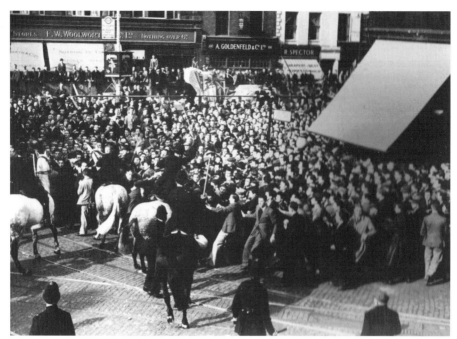

The Cable Street Battle, fascist–anti-fascist fight, 1936.

The Cable Street Battle showing double-decker No.65 bus unable to move.

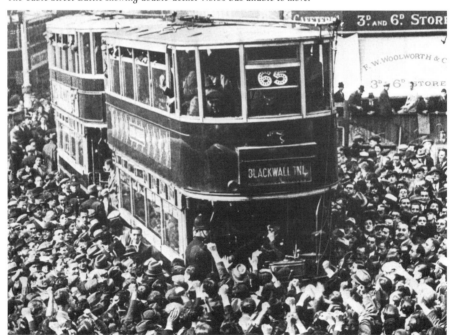

Cable Street Battle scene showing overturned lorry blocking Fascist march through Jewish East London: Gronofsky Tailor sign: 'Misfits a Specialty'.

Aunt Mitzi's wedding, Gilda as a bridesmaid, 1937.

Aunt Mitzi and Uncle Adrian's wedding picture at Boris' Studio.

Last summer of peace. Aunt Ellen and Gilda at Hythe, Folkestone, 1939.

Last summer of peace, Gilda with Aunt Ellen's daughter and husband, Hythe, Folkstone, summer 1939.

War: Uncle Max, front-centre, seated on camels in Egypt fighting Rommel and Mufti Axis.

Uncle Max on leave from Egypt for wedding to Sylvia Delin.

War: Uncle Max, a British soldier in Egypt fighting Rommel and the Mufti.

THANKFUL . . . a group of Jewish 'Kindertransport' children at Ely Jewish Boys' Home in 1943.

13a

Remembering Ely's role caring for Jewish boys

BY John Morgan

Email: editorial@elyweeklynews.co.uk

Jewish Boys' Free School evacuated to Ely c.1941.

Ely Cathedral 1941.

Great Chesterford train station.

The White House Refugee Hostel, Great Chesterford, 1943–45.

Great Chesterford Refugee Hostel – Mrs Shapiro holding child, Gilda back row fourth from right, 1943–45.

Bishop's Stortford train station: Hertfordshire and Essex High School 1943-45.

White House Hostel Back of White House Study, Bay Windows. 1945 - Children, numbered from left to right: Second Row from back: 4 - Rosel Koehler, 5 - Helga Beer, 6 - Norma Huberman, 7 - Nurse Rita, 8 - Mrs. Koehler, 9 - Marta Jellinek, 10 - Ruth Koehler, 11 - Eva Groner. Front Row: 3 - Selma, 5 - Cookie, 7 - Gilda in white blouse.

White House Hostel - Children, numbered from left to right: Back Row: 1 - Cookie, 2 - Marta Jellinek, 4 - Helga, 5 - Gilda in white blouse, 6 - Selma, 8 - Mrs. Koehler, 9 - Eva Groner. Front Row: 2 - Rosel (Lilly) Koehler, 4 - Norma Huberman, 5 - nurse with two children, 7 - Ina Falk.

New Wardens Koehlers, left to right, Ruth Koehler, Lilly, seated, Mrs Koehler, with dog Schatzi, Bernard, standing, Eric seated with hat and brother Alex at far right.

The White House, Great Chesterford, Garden, Ponds, Orchard – 1943 – Gilda seated on bench.

Nurse Rita's wedding with bridesmaids Norma and Helga.

The Boys – Eric, Alex, Joey and Herman arm in a sling from fall.

The White House front 2007.

Author addressing school in Stanford 2007.

Hopewells and Campbells, White House residents, Great Chesterford hosts 2007.

Gilda in doorway about to address the Great Chesterford community 2007.

Gilda with Coco Chanel c.2010.

Maybe this 'aunt' was a widow like Mrs Major, or poor, like Mrs Lyons with seven girls. Mummy probably paid them. Why else would grouchy Mrs Major take in strange little girls and boys she hated? I hoped this Aunt Ellen had both tits or if not, she didn't, like Mrs Major, purposely show me her one tit then laugh at my shock.

After passing the shed, we came to a back door. The same green and white awning hung over every back door along the row of small houses. Aunt Ellen opened the back door and we came directly into a small, bright kitchen. Left of the kitchen ran a hallway with only one door off it. As soon as we entered the kitchen, that one door flew open, and a young man of about 20 popped out. He quickly closed the door behind him. But before he closed the door, I glimpsed like a photograph, an unmade bed piled high with plump, white pillows, white sheets and a rumpled white bedspread. The young man was a very handsome goy, a gentile, with golden skin, and blonde curly hair falling into his sky-blue eyes. He smiled at Aunt Ellen with the whitest teeth in his bronzed face. But although handsome, his right arm and hand hung in a white sling with layers and layers of white bandages wrapped around the hand and over his shoulder. Where his fingers should have been, the bandages lay flat against his knuckles. I could see that on his right hand he had only a thumb and no fingers. The white bandages over this man's missing fingers were unraveling and trailing behind him like a bride's veil, but his face glowing into Aunt Ellen's eyes, he seemed not to notice. He must be her son.

He smiled a warm, loving, but guilty smile at Aunt Ellen. Why did he feel guilty?

'Hello, Tom,' Aunt Ellen said to him, gently. 'Come and have your tea, then.'

He sat at the small kitchen table, opposite me, but had eyes only for his mother. She had to be his mother, he'd come out of the only other room I could see. Aunt Ellen boiled water on the gas stove and made tea, poured some hot water in the teapot, swished it round then emptied the hot water. She spooned four teaspoons of black tea into the pot, one spoon for each of us, one for the pot, and poured boiling water over the tea, then popped a blue tea cozy on the teapot. While the tea steeped, she poured milk from a little jug, the jug covered by a little net I supposed, against flies. Round the edges of the net she had sewn pretty little beads to weight the net down. She had set out three cups and a bowl of sugar cubes. From a large loaf, she sliced thick slabs of white bread, quickly buttered them, and then spread the slices with thick strawberry jam. Since there was no label on the jam jar, she must, like many countrywomen I'd read about, have made the jam herself. I bet she stored her jam in that shed outside. I saw no other children, so the shed was not for orphans like me.

Bending her tall frame over the kitchen table, Aunt Ellen cut Tom's bread into squares, as if he were a child. I saw that he couldn't cut with his left hand. He looked lovingly at his mother.

Tom and I both gobbled thick, fresh bread, butter and jam, and took huge gulps of tea with milk and sugar, but though I looked at Tom he never once looked at me, only at his mother.

Tea finished, Aunt Ellen took me out of the house to the shed in the back yard. I thought she was going to show me her jars of jam. It was now dusk, and the moon smiled faintly as it drifted through silvery clouds. A breeze lifted my skirt and a whiff of salt sea air filled my nostrils. We must be near a beach. Aunt Ellen opened the shed's creaking wooden door.

'You'll be sleeping here,' she said.

'Here?'

It had been a surprise to eat in a shed when at the orphanage, now I was to sleep in one?

I peeped inside. In the middle of the shed stood a high bed with white sheets and a plump pillow; a funny place for a bed, but it looked snug and comfortable. I worried about being alone outside the house when darkness fell, though the fat, white moon would shine in the window.

However, I felt so sleepy that my eyelids drooped over my eyes. Aunt Ellen put on my nighty, cozily tucked me in, and then left, closing the shed door, quietly. Suddenly, I noticed a spider web and a small, black spider over the shed's little window. Yet for the first time in my life, I didn't feel afraid, neither of the spider nor of the dark. Nor was there any headless dummy here. Though she spoke little, and he, not at all, Aunt Ellen and her son Tom seemed so kind and happy together, that I fell into a deep, dreamless sleep.

The next day Aunt Ellen's daughter, Gladys, a grown woman, came over with her new husband, Ken, and their dog, Flossie. Gladys was plump and jolly, with large breasts and a deep cleavage, as Mummy called it, and giggled at everything Ken said. As plump as she was, Ken was thin. I chanted under my breath:

Jack Spratt could eat no fat

His wife could eat no lean.

And so between the two of them

They licked the platter clean.

Flossie, a brown, bony, mongrel with a deep cleft between her eyes ran busily to each member of the family, greeted each one with a lick and ran to the next, as if she thought she was a human.

'There's a real beach at Folkstone,' Gladys said, 'we're going there today,' and she handed me a black wool bathing suit and a white rubber cap.

We all, except Tom, travelled together on a bus to Folkestone. It felt strange, but nice to be out with a whole family and a dog. The beach was nothing like slimy Brighton I'd faintly remembered. Here, clean, fresh sea lapped clean sand, the sky, as blue as Tom's eyes, the air smelling fresh and salty sent shivers of pleasure through my body. I quickly changed in the bathing booths into my heavy wool bathing costume, which hung on my skinny frame. Gladys pulled the rubber swimming cap over my bobbed hair and a squeaky white rubber tube over my shoulders. I thought I looked as plain as Flossie, but I didn't care, because everyone was so kind to me, I felt joy creeping from my heart to my face until I felt myself foolishly blush. This time, Mummy couldn't send me away for blushing, because I was already away.

Ken, skinny in swimming trunks, put his hands in the water under my tummy and holding me up, joked to Gladys, 'She can swim, but not on top of the water.'

I laughed.

Then he sang:

'Oh, Jemima look at your Uncle Jim

He's in the bathtub learning how to swim

First he tries the breast stroke then he tries the side

Now he's under the water, swimming against the tide.'

When I later sang the silly song to Mummy she said, 'That's the Smith's Chorus tune from *Aida*.' Gladys tucked her frock up into the elastic legs of her long bloomers and waded into the water up to her plump knees. Gladys and I giggled as we splashed about, Ken still holding me up under my tummy. Aunt Ellen sat quietly nearby on the beach, curved into a stripy rented deck chair, her lean face shaded by an enormous straw hat. Ken and Gladys standing in the water clasped their four hands together, and made a chair for me to sit on. I put my arms around their necks and sat on the 'chair' just as if they were my parents or my big brother and sister, if I'd had any, and I kept laughing out of pure, silly joy. I couldn't remember when I'd laughed so much and for no reason. Wasn't I silly? Aunt Ellen stood up and with her box camera snapped me sitting on Ken and Gladys's hands, and snapped me sitting with bony Flossie. In a way, Flossie reminded me of Aunt Ellen, not pretty, but quiet and very kind.

'Come out now, the water's getting cold,' Aunt Ellen called. She towelled me down, wrapped me in a warm, dry towel, and then we all sat on a blanket in the sand. Aunt Ellen opened a straw basket and brought out fat roast beef sandwiches with piccalilli and sand. She took more pictures of Gladys kneeling on the blanket, head thrown far back, tipping a dark bottle of brown Guinness into her mouth.

I could hear Booba, my grandmother saying scornfully, 'Only dogs eat in the street.'

Was eating at the beach as bad as eating in the street? I didn't know.

And kneeling in the sand and drinking beer straight from the bottle?!!

'How prost!' 'How vulgar!!' I could hear Booba saying.

'Here, have a swig,' Gladys said, offering me the bottle of Guinness.

I wasn't keen; it reminded me of East Enders singing drunkenly and dancing in the streets five abreast, kicking up their heels to *Knees up Mother Brown* on Friday and Saturday nights. It was all right for them. Jewish people didn't go to pubs, or sing and dance drunkenly home through the streets. But Gladys was so nice, I didn't know how to politely say no. I took a small swig. It was so bitter I pulled a face, 'Ugh.' Gladys and Ken rolled around in the sand laughing at me. Aunt Ellen, sitting in her striped deck chair, watched, smiling. Like my deaf Daddy, she didn't speak much, but unlike him, she listened; she heard everything.

Aunt Ellen also tucked her skirts into her bloomer leg elastic, and like a crane, on her long, long legs, waded into the water, where I stood. Standing tall behind me, she leaned down and wrapped her arms across my tummy, reminding me of Daddy's mother. Gladys took a snapshot of us like that.

Somewhere, they found a donkey, and lifted me screeching with excitement and fright onto his prickly, hairy back. Aunt Ellen snapped a photo of that skinny, delighted little girl, too.

Then I thought of Tom. My usual silence at home had totally gone.

'What happened to Tom's hand?' I asked Aunt Ellen.

'He was holding a metal stake in the ground while someone swung a pickaxe to drive it in. They missed. He lost four fingers,' Aunt Ellen said, matter-of-factly.

I shuddered. How often I had watched a kneeling man holding a metal rod in the ground, while another man swung a heavy pickaxe, and how many times I'd thought: suppose he misses? How it must have hurt poor Tom. That was probably why Aunt Ellen was so tender to her son.

'Why didn't Tom come with us today?' I asked.

It was something new for me to ask questions. I barely spoke at all at home.

'Tom can't go into the sea until his hand heals,' Aunt Ellen said. 'It could get infected.'

'Pity your brother couldn't come,' I said to Gladys.

Gladys threw her head back and roared with laughter. 'He's not my brother!'

Aunt Ellen lowered her eyes and blushed. Who was he, then, since he always came out of her bedroom? I supposed they had only one bedroom and shared it, the way I slept in my parent's bedroom.

When we came home, sandy, gritty and sunburned, Tom came out of Aunt Ellen's bedroom. He must be her son. He gave Aunt Ellen his great, radiant smile, his teeth so white in his bronzed skin, his blue eyes shining, but as usual, he said nothing. Daddy couldn't hear. Could Tom speak? I never once heard his voice. How did his voice sound?

A few days later, Aunt Ellen and I, just the two of us, rode on a bus to Portsmouth. The sun shone, a gentle breeze riffled our hair.

'Portsmouth is the biggest port in southern England,' Aunt Ellen said as we walked on the boardwalk. 'See the barbed wire? That's to keep the Germans from invading us.'

I didn't exactly know what 'invade' meant, and in any case, an enormous, dark grey ship, with grey guns sticking out all over it like a huge hedgehog, loomed over us. It was as tall as the orphanage church organ had been, no, taller, and so high, I almost fell backward craning my neck to look up at it. Where the church organ had little mouths in the middle, the ship's guns had little open mouths at the end.

'That's a battleship,' Aunt Ellen said.

Suppose this enormous ship with all its guns fell down on us? But around us, hundreds of sailors, their square, white-ribboned navy collars rippling in the sea breeze, strode along the boardwalk, each with a girl wearing a sleeveless cotton frock, her arms bronzed and glowed, short white skirts whipped about golden legs. The girls and sailors passed us chattering and laughing and didn't even see Aunt Ellen and me, nor looked at the gigantic battleship.

Somewhere nearby a tinny gramophone was playing a song I knew and a voice sang:

All the nice girls love a sailor,

All the nice girls love a tar

For there's something about a sailor,

'Cos you know what sailors are,

Strong and breezy, free and easy

He's the ladies' pride and joy.

Falls in love with Kate and Jane,

Then he's off to sea again-

Ship Ahoy! Sailor Boy!

Aunt Ellen bought me a stick of pink rock about a foot long, wrapped in wax paper so my hands never became sticky. I just peeled the wax paper down as far as I bit. The outside of the rock seemed painted bright pink, the inside, white, but at the top and no matter how much of the rock I bit off, I still read 'Portsmouth' in clear, pink letters. I couldn't understand how they got the word 'Portsmouth' to go all the way through the whole rock.

'We brought you some rock, Tom,' Aunt Ellen called out as we came home through the back door into the kitchen.

Tom came out of Aunt Ellen's bedroom and smiled at her with his wonderful shy smile. She, as usual, ducked her head, lowered her eyes and smiled as if she had a secret. I thought it was sweet how mother and son loved each other. Gladys had said he wasn't her brother, but he had to be. Why else would he be coming out of Aunt Ellen's bedroom every morning? Weren't there any other bedrooms? I never saw any room but the kitchen and the shed, and I never saw past that door in the hallway, so I didn't know if there were any other bedrooms. There might be only one. Was that why Tom had to sleep with his mother and I slept in the shed?

The next day I dressed, ready to go on my usual morning ramble with Flossie. Gladys had left Flossie to 'visit' with us. Aunt Ellen was still in her bedroom. As I helped myself to corn flakes and milk, Tom came out with his usual beautiful smile on his face. For once he had come out of the room when I knew Aunt Ellen was in there. They must have only one bedroom; that was why they shared. Though the white sling still held his fingerless hand, the bandages floating apart again, his sky blue eyes shone as if there were a light behind them. For someone who had four fingers cut off his right hand, he seemed terribly happy.

90

I called out, 'Flossie, come on, girl,' and she ran up to me, licked my hand and followed. It was wonderful to have a dog that followed me wherever I went and did whatever I wanted and that I was never alone. Flossie and I walked to the blackberry bushes Aunt Ellen had told me about. I would pick some for her to make a pie for tea. I would fill the straw basket I'd brought.

Busily, I began picking fat, juicy blackberries that grew in thick clusters on low green bushes. Suddenly, the bushes stopped, and Flossie and I came to a large, empty stone circle. The place was dead silent.

I couldn't see anyone, but an invisible man's voice shouted as through a bullhorn, 'Get off the target area!'

What target area? Were they shooting arrows? I wanted to ask, but could see no person and no bull's eye. I felt strangely frightened. Was someone shooting? At what? I imagined myself shot, falling down, down, and dead or wounded so I ran, calling, 'Flossie, home.'

At home, Aunt Ellen said calmly, 'They're having target practice. You'd better not wander over there again, you could get shot.'

I liked her for being so calm and kind. Mummy and her family were always so excited, so clever and sarcastic. Aunt Ellen dealt with each situation in her quiet, efficient way. She was a million miles better than one-tit Mrs Major.

But I still loved London, soot and all. I had to admit I liked the sea here, providing Aunt Ellen and Flossie were nearby, and if we stayed only a few hours. After that I longed for East End buildings, cheerful cockneys, the clop of Clydesdales, the rumble of lorries, cars on cobblestone, the train's hooting song and at night, in bed, the haunting mournful sound of the fog horn from the nearby misty docks.

It was time to go back to school for the autumn, to my new class and new teacher. I was sorry to leave the sea and Aunt Ellen, but looked forward to being in London. I wanted to see my Zada, Aunty Mitzi, my two, no, my three uncles, and my best friend, Joycey Kennel.

Saying goodbye, I gave Aunt Ellen a hug.

'Go on with you,' she said, patting my shoulder awkwardly. 'Come for Christmas.'

But soon after I returned to London, that September of 1939, England declared war on Germany. We London children were to be immediately evacuated to the countryside for six years. I never saw Aunt Ellen, Tom, Gladys, Ken or Flossie again.

Unknowingly, I'd just had my last summer of peace.

PART 2

WARTIME ENGLAND 1939–45

CHAPTER 13

WAR AND EVACUATION: NEWMARKET 1939

After I returned home, I went back to Wood Close Elementary's dark red brick school with its prison-like iron railing enclosures. Most of my classmates' parents were rough East End Irish dockworkers and labourers, often unemployed and toothless. The custom among poor gentile cockneys was, while young, to pull out all healthy teeth – no anesthetic – and to wear glittering false teeth.

A few Jewish sweat-shop workers' children attended our school. Jewish red-faced Rosie always arrived late, right cheek bulging with a humbug. Mr Kent placed her standing, facing the class, where she stood, head hanging with shame, her right cheek nevertheless bulging. She would not surrender that humbug.

'Throw the humbug away,' Mr Kent said mildly, every morning, and every morning Rosie stood, head hanging in front of the class and then threw her humbug in the waste basket. But Rosie never took her lunch into the lavatory. If she did so by mistake, she then threw it away. Her cleanliness so impressed me that I never again took food with me into the lavatory.

One or two children's parents – mine and the twins whose parents ran the bakery and, astonishingly, brought them tea in bed in the mornings – had small businesses. Such children like us were clean, fed, free of lice and carried handkerchiefs. Almost all the other Wood Close children were hungry, scrawny, scruffy, ragged, itchy, pigeon-breasted, bandy-legged, lice-ridden fighting ruffian boys and girls who constantly wiped runny noses on their sleeves.

One of these ruffians, Peggy, sat next to me in class. One day while we were taking a test, Peggy whispered, 'Copy from me or I'll bash your head in after school.'

I copied from her.

'Why did you copy from her? Her answers were wrong. You know the right answers,' Mr Kent said, puzzled.

Like Rosie, I hung my head. But it was an unspoken rule never to 'tell' on anyone.

Perhaps they thought I *had* 'told'. Outside school that afternoon, a ring of 15 children awaited me. Someone pushed me into its middle, empty but for Peggy, her fists up.

'Fight, fight, fight,' the children chanted.

It seemed unjust that Peggy had made me cheat, given me wrong answers and now wanted to fight me. What to do? I looked round for help, or for a teacher. Nothing. I had no idea how to, and no interest in fighting. A rough Irish boy, a miniature James Cagney, who always grinned at, but never spoke to me, stood outside the ring, arms folded, looking sympathetic, but made no move to help me. James Cagney would have helped a girl in distress. 'Fight, fight, fight,' the children chanted. Peggy closed in. I searched desperately for escape.

Seeing a tiny gap in the ring, I dove into it and under. Like Daddy, I was a fast runner. For some strange reason, no one followed me and the next day, everyone had forgotten.

While puzzling, this suited me. It taught me never to cheat, though I had no reason to.

I should have learned to fight, I was strong enough, but Jewish girls didn't fight.

The first child refugees from Nazi Europe began arriving at school. Silently, in the concrete playground, one small girl stood alone, staring at us British girls playing hopscotch. She had sad blue eyes and clutched a piece of her skirt to her mouth into which she stuck her thumb and sucked it. She knew no English. We knew no other language, except some Jewish children like Pearl Snopkovsky knew Yiddish. I knew almost no Yiddish. My parents, both British-born, knew it but only spoke it when they didn't want me to understand what they were saying. We didn't understand this lonely girl's sorrows and no adult introduced her to us. In 1939, adults rarely explained anything to children. If only I had gone to that poor, lonely child.

I'd loved my first Wood Close teacher, kindly, tweedy Mr Kent. After the orphanage and my return to London, I liked Mrs Thackeray, my next teacher. Often, she left the room. Me in charge. 'Stand on the chair and listen to children take turns in reading,' she said, then left the room. Once, she smacked me over the head by accident (she didn't see my face) for misspelling 'exhaution.' During silent reading, she crept up to my seat and laid a tiny Chinese umbrella on my desk. My dignity as top girl in the class was affronted. I never spoke to her again.

After Mrs Thackeray, I skipped a grade and arrived, the youngest, in Miss King's class. Miss King, with hair cropped like a man's dressed in a man's suit and tie and was totally flat-chested. She looked like Sir Oswald Mosley, the Fascist leader and sneered at cockney accents. 'Oo, wo' a lo' a little bo'uls,' she smirked, for 'Oh, what a lot of little bottles.' Although she'd copied the cockney accent correctly, and although I did not speak with a cockney accent, neither did I like an outsider sneering at our hard-working, hard drinking dockers and labourers, men and women with a wonderful tart sense of humour. They tumbled along life slaving for low wages, accepting or laughing at everything, so I didn't like Miss King's snobbish sneering.

Today, Miss King asked the class, 'What is a rectangle?' My hand shot up.

'Yes?'

I stood to answer and said, 'A figure that has four equal sides.'

As soon as I said it I knew I had made a mistake.

'Wrong,' she said triumphantly. 'Give the correct answer.'

Although I knew the correct answer, my tongue stuck to the roof of my mouth and I stood dumb. She waited, smirking. For a full, numbing silent minute, the entire class sat motionless, holding its breath.

'Come here,' she ordered.

I walked down the six rows of steps, each row on a different tier, and coming to her desk, I looked up at her questioningly. What did she want? She turned my right arm over showing its soft, white underside. All the children in the class ducked their heads but watched from under their eyebrows. The only sound was that of 10 stinging slaps on my arm.

'That's for wasting the class's time,' she said. 'Sit down.'

Although the slaps didn't hurt that much, I felt indignant, ashamed and humiliated at being slapped in front of all the other children. This new class didn't know I'd always been top of the class and had skipped a class. Teachers smacked only dummies and dunces. And I had skipped a class.

That night, hundreds of tiny red blisters sprang up on my inside arm. I hadn't told Mummy that Miss King had slapped me; I'd never told her Mrs Thackeray had hit me, even by mistake. Teachers often slapped or caned children but none had ever deliberately slapped me.

Puzzled, I showed Mummy my blisters.

For the first time, she came to school with me. 'I want to see the headmaster,' she announced. I was thrilled that Mummy had come to school for me; the first time she'd ever stuck up for me. Surprisingly, a teacher immediately led us to the headmaster's office.

I'd never seen the headmaster, didn't know who he was. Like the orphanage warden he lived in some secret realm. Two strands of hair across his bald pate, Mr Hollingshead leaned back in his armchair, face sullen, as Mummy told him 'Miss King has no right to slap my daughter.' I had never heard of a parent coming to school and challenging the headmaster. Most East End parents gave their caned child an extra slap for having been in trouble at school, so most children didn't report slaps or canings.

I felt enormously proud that Mummy had not only come, but had even stuck up for me. I wanted to laugh as Mr Hollingshead, being ticked off by Mummy, sulked like a naughty boy.

'Do you want to stay at Wood Close or transfer to Buxton Street?' she asked me, in front of Hollingshead.

'Transfer,' I said, eyes dancing at having a choice of any kind, and doing the dirty on snotty Miss King and greasy old Hollingshead.

At this new school, Buxton Street, children were clean and didn't fight. Even my teacher was a buxom, blonde, Jewish mother, not a mannish, skinny Miss King. There was no snobbery. For once I was not the only Jewish child among hostile, some openly Fascist children, and a sneering Miss King. My new headmistress was skinny, but kind Miss Crawford.

I had only been in the new school for a week, when Miss Crawford called all children into the assembly hall. Her horse-face sad, bags under her eyes and lines running from nose to mouth, she climbed onto a sturdy wooden school chair. Sorrowfully looking down at us from this great height, her eyes filled with unshed tears. What could be the matter?

'England has declared war on Germany,' she said sadly. 'You will all be evacuated immediately to country foster homes. Each school will be evacuated to a different country village. In case of invasion, we don't want the Germans to know where you are, so your destination is a secret. You will only know where you are when you get there. Go home and put one change of underwear, a nighty or pajamas and soap into a pillowcase. Take a stamped postcard to send to your parents so they know you are safe. Be back here in half-an-hour. Run.'

That was how, when war broke out, I was evacuated with Buxton Street School instead of with Wood Close Elementary School.

I raced home passing the 'JP' – Jews Should Perish signs on dank slum brick houses, crossed the railway tracks, burst into our empty barbershop and told Mummy, 'We have to pack a nighty, underwear and soap in a pillow case and be back at school in half an hour.'

Mummy showed no surprise, ran upstairs to the bedroom, packed my things which made only a little lump at the bottom of a pillowcase, and handed me the pillowcase.

'Why do I have to go away again?' I cried, one foot out of the door.

'London might be bombed at any minute. It's not just you. The government wants to send three million city children to the country. Germany is going to bomb London, especially the East End. The Germans know that many Jews live in the East End and that the docks are in the East End. They want to cut off our food supplies. The government is sending East End children first because we live near the docks and our government is afraid that poor, East End families will loot, so they're evacuating you first,' she laughed sarcastically. 'That's how much they trust us. Do you have your identity bracelet and gas mask? You'll be safe in the country,' she said gaily, as if I were going to one of my many 'aunts'.

The government had already issued children with gas masks. My new friend, Nora Eglash and I had tried on the black masks in front of my parents' bedroom full-length wardrobe mirror. Our reflection had shown goggle-eyed monsters like those in the Saturday morning films. 'Phew, they stink,' Nora's muffled voice came through her gas mask. 'I can't breathe.'

Mummy had bought me a little silver bracelet inscribed with my new identity number. She pinned a luggage tag with my name, address, and identity number to my coat, the way she labelled one of the string-tied brown-paper parcels that she took to the post office on Wednesdays, half-day closing. She was so quick and ready with my belongings. I thought she must have known from the wireless that I was coming home early only to be evacuated.

'Goodbye,' she said, as I left, not even kissing me as she did when she left me at the orphanage for two years when I was five. How long would I be away this time?

Hundreds of other children, all of us carrying our pillowcases and gas masks in a cardboard box hung over our shoulders by a string, ran through grey streets toward school, feet pounding ancient Roman cobblestones.

Strange women, black bands on their arms, suddenly sprang out of side streets. 'Run,' the women said, running beside us. 'Faster.'

As we ran through the streets, gas masks bouncing on our hips, men with big square cameras ran beside us. 'Wave goodbye,' they shouted, 'Smile! You evacuees are going to be in the newspapers!!' Who cared? No one smiled. I hadn't even said goodbye to Daddy, to my grandparents, nor to Uncle Sam, Aunty Mitzi or Uncle Adrian. I'd just been bridesmaid at Aunt Mitzi's wedding, dressed in a fancy silver lamé dress with white gloves and a silver bow in my hair, and now I was running through the streets jostled by thousands of other children, to be evacuated; sent away again from my London to live with strangers. And again, I didn't know where I was going. Always a stranger!

At school, our teachers shouted, 'Form a crocodile.'

Nora Eglash, like me, a skinny, dark haired Jewish girl, snatched my hand. Pearl Snopkovsky behind, took Sarah Lampel's hand. As we marched in twos toward Liverpool Street Station, I glanced back, and again thought that the curved line of children in twos really did look like the picture of the crocodile in Kipling's *Just So Stories* that Daddy used to read me.

My best friend, Joycey Kennel and I had often walked the mile or so to Liverpool Street Station. At least before leaving London I'd see our favourite haunt. I bet *her* mother would keep her at home, bombs or no bombs. Her three always out-of-work depressed young brothers would probably like Uncle Max, join up. Instead of being unemployed they'd become soldiers. Daddy was not drafted because he was deaf nor Uncle Sam because of his hump. Uncle Adrian was doing some essential secret chemical research and Uncle Max had already become a soldier. I had said goodbye to none of them.

Thousands of London school children streamed toward the station all carrying a pillowcase and gas mask except for one tiny girl who, clutching her mother's hand clung with the other to a pink china potty, a nursery rhyme painted on it.

'Where we goin'?' a small boy asked a bigger boy.

'I dunno, seaside, I fink. I took me bucket an' spade.'

'Nah, I 'eard someone say we wos goin' to Sweden.'

'That was Swindon, not Sweden, you idjit.'

I squeezed my eyes shut. I didn't want to leave home, my grandparents, aunts and uncles, or lose the long Saturday rambles through London's East End with Joycey Kennel or the Sunday visits with Daddy to Brick Lane, Petticoat Lane, the museum or to Uncle Izzy with his brilliantly tropical coloured fish and crocodiles. Daddy said that Uncle Izzy wouldn't be able to buy any more tropical fish; ships were now to be used only for troops.

A long line of people stood outside the vet's cuddling their dogs and cats.

'Poor Toby, with rationing we won't even have dog food. Forgive me,' a woman wept, hugging her puppy.

The dog licked Lil's face and whined, as if he knew his fate. Mummy had once given me half a crown and told me to take our cat to the vet's. After the vet took our cat, I saw six glass-topped boxes lining the walls with dead cats lying in them. Poor dog.

'There, there, Lil, war'll soon be over, we'll get another dog,' her husband said, patting her shoulder.

Along the way, posters in huge black letters read, 'The Blackout is now in force. No chink of light must be seen from any window after 7:47 p.m. Volunteer for the ARP. The Air Raid Patrol'. The ARP in their steel bucket hats nightly banged on windows. 'Seen a chink of light, missus,' they'd shout. 'Draw yer blackout curtain.'

'*Alter kakers*, old shits, too old to join the forces,' Booba sniffed when I'd paid her my last visit the Friday before. I didn't then know that I would not see her for years, and that I would return, a stranger, and edged out by Aunt Mitzi's son who became their favourite grandchild.

'They're bound to bomb London, us being the biggest city in the world,' I heard one mother saying to another. 'I 'opes we don't get it like Spain and China. 'Orrible.'

Would we have to get under our desks when bombs dropped, the way Mummy had, during the Great War? Overhead, enormous grey blimps 'Flossie' and 'Blossom' floated in the grey sky. The blimps' ropes that moored the great balloons were supposed to entangle low-flying German planes. As we ran through old East London Roman roads, boys in white open-necked shirts, short trousers, jackets, high socks and school caps, streamed alongside us. We girls, like Shirley Temple, wore white socks, strap shoes, short coats, and coloured ribbons in our hair. Some girls' dresses, like mine, hung below their coat hems. We were all growing.

Newsmen in grubby newsboy caps stood outside sooty Liverpool Street Station shouting, 'Getcha Daily News. England evacuates: thahsands of children leaving London daily.'

Six-inch tall letters scrawled on stands outside the station read: 'August 30, 1939, Children of Britain Evacuated. London Prepares for German Bombing.' Hundreds of people dropped pennies on stands and snatched a paper, before diving into the bowels of the Station.

People jammed the great stone entry arches at the station's entrance. Women with black armbands as if in mourning jabbed us children forward and we clattered down two flights of stone stairs into the cave-like station. The station echoed the noise of chuffing trains coming and going, shrill whistles as trains left, people shouting and running, greeting or waving goodbye to each other, sounds that thrilled me as always. But we were leaving all this. Through the smoke, I glimpsed as in a snapshot, grubby men in a dusty station cafe wolfing ham sandwiches, pigs in blankets and pork pies, and for the train ride, women wearing white gloves choosing magazines, newspapers and the last chocolates from Smith's Stationers before rationing began.

A mysterious sign over a sooty door said, 'Night Boat Train to Paris'. But no one came in or out of that door. When I grew older, I'd pass through that door and I'd ride that Night Boat Train to Paris, wherever it was. A sudden shove from the jostling children brought me back to the present. Long lines of children, like me, lined up on the stone platform.

Mothers, some still in aprons, and a few fathers stood behind waist-high black iron railings, waving their children a last goodbye. A woman pushed open a gate in the rail, crying, 'Maisie, Maisie,' to the little girl with the pink potty.

'No parents in children's lines,' shouted the black armband woman pushing her back.

'Mummy, Mummy. Take me home,' Maisie wept.

'Maisie,' her Mummy called to her child, but the arm-banded women shouted, 'Stay back. Parents shouldn't even be in the station.'

There was little chance that my mother or father would come to say goodbye. I hadn't said goodbye to anyone except Mummy. No one would know where I was. Stinging tears sprang to my eyes. But British girls didn't cry. And since the orphanage, I'd forgotten how to cry.

I gazed up giddily at the station's smoky-glass ceiling, as high as St Paul's Cathedral. Sparrows flew among the iron girders, chattering like cheeky East Londoners. I always thought of sparrows as cockneys, and of cockneys as cheeky sparrows. The enormous, sooty black trains, which Joycey and I loved to watch when we walked here Saturday afternoons, chugged in and out of the giant station, puffing white steam and hooting. Why was steam white, I wondered? Their shrill train sounds echoed against the glass roof and bounced back to us. If only my deaf Daddy could have heard this music.

Steam trains had music of their own, the chug and soothing rhythm of the wheels, the comforting engine hoots along with foghorns from boats at the docks that I used to hear at night when lying drowsy in bed alone on the third floor flat over Michael's grocery shop. While I was away at the orphanage, my parents had moved to a new house and shop further down Vallance Road near the railway tracks. I was rid of the headless dummy on the second floor. Tucked up sleepy and safe in bed, I still listened to the trains and foghorns every night.

Now we were leaving for another unknown place, another strange, boring country village, and another strange gentile family with strange accents, language, customs and food, all so different from my East End Jewish family, and from East London. No new stranger would be as nice as 'Aunt' Ellen in Hythe.

A long train, usually full of happy passengers visiting friends and family, now stood empty and silent, its black-framed open windows staring at us. Black, instead of tan shades now hung at every carriage window, and I expected black tears to fall out of their black window eyes. 'The trains' window shades are pulled down at dusk, because if German airplanes see any light they'll drop bombs. But trains are now so black,' Mummy had laughed, 'that at night, people can't find them.'

I imagined an invisible train standing on the tracks, people blindly feeling for it, like Blind Man's Buff, only instead of catching a person, they caught a train.

Thousands of jostling, jabbering children crowded the platforms. For most East End cockneys it was their first time away from home, a train ride a big adventure. By age five during Easter, before Christmas and New Year, and every summer, I'd travelled on trains or buses to Chingford Orphanage or to strange 'aunts'. I was an old traveller but hated leaving home again.

Nora Eglash pulled my sleeve. 'Blimey, look at all them sandbags,' she said.

'See the tape across all the windows in the roof?' Pearl Snopkovsky, said, staring upward. 'Me Mum said that's to stop glass from flying when the bombs drop.'

I shivered. Only rain or snow dropped from the sky. What did bombs look like? I imagined huge black pointy lumps like pieces of coal, falling and hitting our heads.

Mothers stood behind the rail holding children under four, too young to be evacuated. I'd heard that some mothers left for the country with their children, while the fathers joined the services. Those men too old or not fit enough to fight stayed in London to work. Dad, because he was classified 4F and not called up, would have to do 'essential work', go where the government said they needed a barber. But Uncle Max, only 19, only 10 years older than me was already a soldier. Before leaving, he'd come to see us in his rough Tommy's uniform. Did Booba or anyone see him off? No one had so far come to see me off.

Women stood on other platforms, mothers, wives, girlfriends, hugging and kissing soldiers, sailors, airmen. Women were sobbing, 'Goodbye, Darling.' Other servicemen hugged their children and wives before that last goodbye.

More children's mothers had rushed to the station without even taking off their aprons and now stood behind the black railed barriers some with tears running down their cheeks, waving goodbye to their children. One woman cried into her husband's shoulder, his arm around her waist. Some mothers, I heard, couldn't bear to come to the station to say goodbye. A mother dashed out from behind the iron railings, and snatched a little boy of about five out of the line.

'I can't let you go,' she wept, carrying the child back.

'You can't do that,' said one of the black armband women but the mother shoved her away. 'He's *my* child,' she cried, and hugging him close, ran out of the station. I looked at him enviously. *His* mother wanted him home.

Mummy suddenly appeared behind the black rail laughing and chatting with another woman, already exchanging each other's addresses on the backs of used envelopes. 'Drop in for a cup of tea, we love having visitors,' Mummy would be saying. She didn't say that Daddy was deaf and would not join them; that the woman would be added to my list of 'aunts'.

Two tagged boys aged about 14 stood sad-eyed, waiting on the platform for someone to come and get them. Jewish refugees from Europe wearing jackets with belts at the back, trousers tucked into socks, big caps on their heads, faces sad, were arriving every day.

The crowd of English evacuee children round me suddenly surged forward, as a black-banded woman pushed us forward shouting, 'Everybody on,' and hundreds of British children surged into an empty, black train. They leaned out of windows and waved goodbye to their mothers. Mummy waved me goodbye with her white, lacy goodbye handkerchief.

I was leaving home again, but for once, it was not Mummy's idea. Uncle Max once told me, 'I remember when you were three and your mother sent you away, you looked so pretty in your little angora beret.' I didn't remember being sent away at age three. But after age five and finding myself in a Christian orphanage on Christmas Eve, I remembered everything.

The stationmaster's clear, high whistle pierced the din of chattering children and shunting trains. He waved his red flag up and down. I took one last look at Liverpool Street Station. On another track, beside the khaki-dressed soldiers and sailors in navy saying goodbye, the usual last-minute businessmen passengers ran past the ticket collector, shoved their tickets into his hand, rushed up to the moving train, doors still hanging open for last minute riders, and like acrobats, leaped onto the running boards, coattails flying, slammed wooden doors shut, pulling the window's leather strap which let the window bang down, and leaned out grinning, waving goodbye to friends or family. Passengers arriving at Liverpool Street Station on other platforms spilled out of train doors like unwinding balls of wool, growing smaller and smaller as our evacuee train steamed out of London, it seemed, forever.

Strange children I didn't know sat in my carriage. Nora and Pearl had disappeared. I sat with a scruffy girl, with Maisie and her potty and a band of big, ugly boys.

'Cor, I ain't never bin on a fuckin' train, 'ave you, Nobby?' one of the big, ugly boys grunted, scratching his head.

Scrawled on his nametag in large, untidy letters, I read Titch Dawson. Titch, meaning small, was the cockney nickname for someone very big or for someone really small.

'I wos once on a train ter Brighton,' Nobby said.

'I want my Mummy,' sobbed Maisie, sucking her thumb and hiccupping.

'Oi, you, nipper. Shut up or scram. We don't want that racket in 'ere,' Nobby shouted, wiping his snotty nose on his wool sleeve, while another boy of about ten, white-faced, stared silently at his own reflection in the window. Maisie on her chamber pot still sobbed.

I sprang up, left the carriage and walked down the corridor. Where were the adults? Nowhere. This was an orphanage on wheels, with no adults to protect small children from big ruffian boys. Since Ernie, in the orphanage had broken little Peter's fingers, I feared big boys.

In the next carriage, five nine-year-old boys were fighting happily with one another while two others engaged in a distance-peeing competition, arching rainbows through the open window. Further down, a group in a carriage sang lustily, 'Ten green bottles, 'anging on the wall'. Others ate the sandwiches their mothers had packed. I didn't have a sandwich. No adult was in sight. They must still be at the station organising more evacuees.

We were leaving London because of war. What was war? To me, war was a game we played on the steps of Shoreditch Church after school. One of us ran to the top step of the church, waved and shouted, 'I'm the King of the Castle and you're the dirty rascals!' Then we'd fight with wooden swords. That was war.

I wished there was just one grown-up on the train. I feared being alone with big boys in my carriage and feared going to another carriage. I thought we were supposed to stay in the carriage the black-band women shoved us into. In any case, all the other carriages were chock full. How many children fit into this train? Perhaps a thousand. Children were small. There had been no adult in the room when Ernie broke Peter's fingers at the orphanage and there was no adult on the train. I stared at Titch. Suppose during wartime all adults disappeared and big, nasty boys ruled the world?

The train wheels clackety-clacked past the soot-blackened houses of the East End of London, sooty wash hanging across grimy back yards. After a while the grimy houses and washing changed to clean, like Mrs Awful-One-Tit Major's house. The train wheels clacked out the rhythm, 'far from home, far from London. Staying with strangers, staying with strangers, leaving London, leaving home'. The train sped on, taking us ever further from London, family and friends. 'Clackety-clack, leaving London, clackety-clack, far from home, clackety-clack, going to strangers…'

We passed clean houses, and then almost all houses disappeared. No houses, no shops stood cheerfully in these wide, open spaces, only endless, boring green fields with cows and horses lazily chewing the grass as our train chuffed by. I thought the orphanage in Chingford had been country, but now I saw it hadn't really been country at all. There had been houses next to the orphanage, we had gone to a local school and to a Christmas party for orphans at a firehouse and on Sundays, Sister had taken us to church. In Chingford, I had seen no fields, nor the roaming animals I now saw. This must be real English country, worse than Chingford.

From the train window, miles of empty green fields and leafy trees, cows, sheep, flashed by, the autumn sun glinting between leaves, and here and there a few houses stood alone in the middle of a field. Who did these people talk to? Where did they shop? I supposed these houses in the middle of nowhere were farmhouses.

'Peter helps father milk the cows. Pam helps Mother bake bread in the kitchen,' we'd read in our schoolbooks. The closest I'd come to a cow was the one in Peterson's Milk Company in an underground stable at the bottom of Black Lion Yard in East London; a London cow. Toby Frost, Mummy's friend had once taken me there. The man had pulled the cow's udders and milk spurted out right in front of us and into a pail that the man held under the cow. He'd given us each a glass of fresh milk for a penny. The milk was warm. But I hated milk. I liked tea.

'Wot's them animals?' Nobby now asked, pointing to white, woolly creatures and taller brown and white beasts wandering in fields near the train. 'Are they goin' ter eat us?'

'Them's sheep and cows.' Titch said. 'We eats *them*.'

'I ain't nivver bin on a train nor seen a field nor sheep nor cows,' Nobby said. 'Looks like they got six sides.'

'Well you seed 'em now so shut yer gob,' Titch said, scratching his head. I moved away from him. Who wanted a shaved head dabbed with purple?

The train flew clattering past stations, a white sheet thrown over their names in case of German invasion, until after about two hours, the wheels screeched as the train slowed. We all jumped up and crowded at the window. The train suddenly gave a last squeal and jerked backward. Nobby and Titch fell down.

'Get your fucking bum off my face,' Nobby growled at Titch.

'Snot nose,' Titch said, amiably.

Who would be my foster Mummy and father? I wondered. Would they be cold, like Mrs One-Tit Major or friendly, like 'Aunt' Ellen? I'd never had a foster-father. In all the places Mummy had sent me to, a woman had lived without a husband. Mrs One-Tit Major and Aunt Ellen had no husband. Would my new foster-mother have a son, who like hers, was missing four fingers, and who slept in her bedroom?

While I was thinking all this, the train squealed to a stop at a station. Once more, I was in a strange place, with no idea where I was. How far from home was I this time?

Home. Had bombs dropped? Did Daddy or my family notice I kept disappearing? Did they think I was magic, or did they just not care? But everyone must know about evacuation. For once, my family knew the reason I'd left London.

As the train drew into the unknown station, a line of tweedy women stood on the platform. Before the train even stopped, they shouted, 'We're your billeting officers. We'll take you to your new foster parents.'

The train squealed to a stop, gave a final huff, as if fed up with us evacuees and ready to disgorge us and return to London. How I wanted to go back to London, to family and friends.

'Everyone off,' shouted the tweedy women on the platform.

We all jumped down to meet our new foster parents who probably hated Londoners.

CHAPTER 14
FIRST FOSTER MOTHERS – NEWMARKET

Thousands of children's shoes clacked on stone platforms and hundreds of train doors slammed as we jumped out of the train and closed doors, as if closing the door to London.

'Line up single file,' a woman from the platform shouted. 'Show your identity number.'

The black and empty train chugged away blowing a farewell mournful hoot. The train was surely going back to London for another load of evacuees and refugees. Refugees like Anne Penner our first refugee at school, or like those boys at the station this morning who landed in London would also be evacuated from London's expected Nazi Blitz. Suppose, like these refugees, we might never see our parents again. What would it be like without Mummy and Daddy? How would I live without exciting London, my family and friends? Nothing happened in the country. Country people might hate Londoners and Jews.

Across the train tracks on a far platform, two women sat at two tables, a pile of objects on the table in front of each. These two women's mouths turned down, their heads drooped.

A black armband woman on our platform shouted, 'Go down the ladder on this side of the platform, cross the tracks, and climb up the ladder to the platform on the other side of the tracks. Run past those two women with your pillow cases held open, but don't stop. Move!'

The women pushed us quickly into single file. 'Hurry up, hurry up,' the black armband women cried out. What was the hurry, I wondered. It was like the orphanage Christmas party at the Chingford firehouse when I was five. 'Hurry up,' cried the firemen making us run round in circles for no good reason. 'Run,' the black armband women cried, tears filling their eyes.

Why were they crying? We were the ones separated from our families, sent to strangers far from home because of some adults' war. But not knowing where we were, or where we were going, as so often in the past, I felt lonely. I no longer had Mumfie to hug. I was too old for him.

I ran, once more an anonymous child, behind the other children in single file, climbed down a little wooden ladder nailed to the inside of our platform, frightened that a train might come along as I crossed and cut off my legs, the way Mummy told me a train had cut off Sheila Cohen's legs. Gingerly, I crossed the tracks looking both ways, making sure to step over the rails, climbed up the little ladder on the other side of the tracks and stepped onto the opposite platform. Here sat the two women with glum faces behind long, white covered tables. Why did the tables have white tablecloths on them? Everything seemed dreamlike. I understood nothing.

As I ran past the first woman, holding open my white pillow case, she threw in it a bar of chocolate. The second woman threw in a bar of soap – they probably thought all London kids were filthy – and Daddy had told me soap had fat in it and that fat was needed for war. 'It's guns or butter,' he said, 'soap will soon be rationed'.

The women must have practiced that throw because they never once missed our pillowcases. I hated all these women because as in the orphanage, their faces sour, none of them spoke to us, we had no names and I was again, lost.

'Come along,' said a strange woman sharply, the way Nurse Harris had said, 'You're five, you're not a baby.'

I was nine, but I felt the same as when I was five and suddenly separated from my family, friends, school and from London; again I had no idea where I was, where I was going or for how long. The only difference was that this time, I was not the only child sent to the country. This did not console me because at least, these children had always lived with their families.

A tight-lipped woman divided us into groups of twenty and turned us over to another group of women in tweed jackets, tweed skirts, tweed hats and flat shoes, so different from Mummy's smart high heels. Each of these women wore a pin with WVS' on it that I soon learned meant 'Women's Volunteer Service'.

'We are your billeting officers,' said a woman to my group. 'Follow me.'

I had no idea what a billeting officer was. My billeting officer strode along so fast our group had to run to keep up with her. Along a street on a steep hill called Bakers Row, she banged on doorknockers.

'Take a London evacuee?' she asked at each door.

One woman, a child clutching her skirt said, 'No,' and slammed the door shut.

At the next house the woman said, 'Only want a blonde little girl. No boys.'

The billeting officer pushed a weeping little blonde girl separated from her brother inside the house. We continued up the hill, pushing children into doors like our postman dropping letters into our house. It was beginning to get chilly. I was cold, tired and hungry. Soon, because of the black out, there'd be no lights. Even bicycles and cars put black paper over their lights; they could hardly see where they were going. Mummy had already been knocked down in the dark by a bicycle. Now I understood why the women with the black armbands arms kept telling us to hurry. Darkness was falling. I saw that women chose blonde and blue-eyed children.

No foster mother wanted me. My stomach ached from hunger. I shivered in the cold.

The billeting officer knocked on the door of a little house, number 15, as small as a witch's house.

A tiny old lady opened it. Was she a witch?

The billeting lady asked her 'Will you take an evacuee?'

The little old lady saw me standing alone and cold and took pity on me. 'Come along, dear,' she said in a trembly voice. 'My name is Mrs Ancliffe and this is Mr Ancliffe.' Her false teeth wobbled so much as she spoke that I feared they would fall out. A small man of about 60, older than my Zada shuffled over in slippers to join his tiny wife at the door. I didn't think witches had husbands, so I stepped inside, and the billeting officer vanished.

At home there would have been a roaring coal fire, here the grate was empty. Against the chill, the man wore a hand-knitted woolly sleeveless Faire-Isle sweater. The old man's blue eyes blinked behind large glasses.

'Come and have some tea, dear. You can sit in Tim's seat,' my new foster mother said.

I wondered who and where Tim was. Probably called up. Perhaps Tim was a cat.

The old lady drew me to a low couch and table. Darkness had almost fallen, but she didn't turn on a light. As she poured, the lid of the brown teapot in her trembling hand wobbled. Cold and hungry, I was grateful for hot tea and the two slices of bread and butter or margarine.

'You see that picture up there?'

She pointed to a sepia picture of a young, unsmiling soldier in a khaki uniform, hair stiff and short, standing at attention as stiffly as his hair.

'We had a little boy once, Timothy, but he was killed in the Great War. Now they call it the First World War. That's him. He was our only child. He died in the war to end all wars, in 1918.' The cup in her hand shook. 'Now we're at war again.'

The young man in the brown picture stared at me. I wondered if he didn't like me sitting in his seat. His parents were so old he must have died a long time ago in the war to end all wars. Mummy also thought there would never be another war. Hadn't we heard Neville Chamberlain on the wireless only the week before saying that Hitler wanted peace? Then why were bombs going to fall, and all of us children rushed out of London and evacuated to country foster homes?

I remembered in London, the Great War veteran standing daily on one leg, leaning on his crutch in Bethnal Green Road, his thin chest decorated with a dozen medals, all day holding out one pencil, never selling one. Seeing the picture of a young son who had actually died in that war, I saw war wasn't just a game we played with stick swords on the steps of Shoreditch Church after school. War was when Mummy crouched under the desk and bombs dropped and the pencil man had his leg shot off and Mr and Mrs Ancliffe's son had died and they hung him flattened on the wall and they'd cried. I imagined Timothy shot through the heart and falling down crying out, 'Mama,' and then lying still, and now he had turned into a flat brown picture staring at me as if it was my fault that he was dead and I was alive sitting in his chair.

'Time for bed, dear,' Mrs Ancliffe said, though I was still hungry.

Mrs Ancliffe took a candleholder, lit a candle, stuck it in the holder and led me to a door with an iron latch on it. When she pulled the door open I saw to my surprise, a steep, narrow staircase. No London houses had a door in front of a staircase. What was it for? As we climbed a narrow staircase in flickering light, our shadows darted along narrow walls, looking like fearsome dragons about to leap on us. We entered a small, low-ceilinged bedroom.

'This was Timothy's room,' Mrs Ancliffe said. It was another attic with slanting walls.

We fished my nighty out from the bottom of the pillowcase. I gave her the bar of soap. As I was hungry, I kept the chocolate. The wavering candlelight cast jumping shadows over all the attic walls. I undressed and put on my nightie. Mrs Ancliffe tucked me snugly into a soft bed. At least she was kind. Perhaps it wouldn't be so bad being evacuated in the home of such a nice old lady. I hoped she'd leave the candle. Mummy and Daddy knew I was afraid of the dark, and never left me alone in the dark.

'Goodnight, child,' she said, and she took the candle downstairs, leaving me in pitch-black silence in this strange house. There was no electric light. There wasn't even gaslight. I hoped Timothy didn't mind me being in his bed. I felt his ghost beside me shift. Alone and too upset to sleep, I stayed awake until dawn, and then ate the chocolate from my pillowcase: almost the last chocolate I ate for years.

The next day, after a breakfast of tea and one slice of bread and margarine, the Ancliffes switched on their ancient wireless. At 11am Prime Minister Chamberlain, who had returned triumphantly from Germany waving a paper showing Hitler's promise of peace now said that Hitler had invaded Poland and that England was at war with Germany. Mrs Ancliffe burst into tears. Mr Ancliffe stared out of his big glasses with misty eyes at the flattened sepia face of his dead son, whose ghost had lain beside me last night.

'There, there, Mother,' Mr Ancliffe said, patting Mrs Ancliffe's shoulder.

The second evening at the Ancliffes, for dinner, we again ate two slices of bread and margarine. Used to my mother's home-made fried fish and chips or on Friday evenings, roasted chicken, and with a healthy appetite, I became very hungry. But children must not ask for food.

After 'dinner', we sat on the couch.

'You see that little cupboard?' Mrs Ancliffe pointed to a low, latched door about three feet high. 'Once when our Timothy was naughty, we shut him in that cupboard. Later we saw something wet trickling out. D'you know what it was?'

'No,' I lied.

I was sure he'd wet his trousers but it wasn't polite to say so.

'That little scamp had opened the homemade wine we kept there. He rolled out dead drunk.'

The old couple laughed until tears rolled down their cheeks and then they cried.

At bedtime I was again afraid of Timothy's ghost and couldn't sleep until dawn. But the next day, exploring nearby streets, I found a tiny crooked sweet shop, and with the sixpence Mummy had given me I bought my favourite humbugs; then I began to feel more at home.

Two days after arriving at the Ancliffes, the billeting officer came.

'You're going to the Pettits,' she said. She didn't say why.

The billeting officer led me away as if I were a prisoner. Although only about 30, she wore steel rimmed glasses, a tweed suit and hat, a bun at the nape of her neck and thick, flat shoes. We came to a real town with shops and cars, but suddenly a large field appeared.

'Why is there a field in the middle of the town?' I timidly asked the woman.

'This is Newmarket Heath or The Commons,' she answered, our feet swishing through sweet-smelling green grass. A tiny man dressed in brilliant pink, green, yellow, and blue, with a coloured cap to match, raced by on a horse, so close that the animal's rough hair pricked my skin. I jumped back. 'What's the matter with you? It's only a race horse,' the woman said.

She didn't understand that we were London city children and that the only horses we knew of were the rough Pearlies' dray horses or great, gentle Clydesdales that slowly pulled beer barrels, not horses with strange little men on them, racing by as if chased by lions or tigers.

A little further on, a black Indian Chief in a beautiful long feathered headdress stood on a wooden box shouting to a crowd of men, 'I've got a horse!'

I'd never before seen a man who was black all over, nor an Indian chief, except in books. Did they have speakers here, as they did in Hyde Park in London, where anyone could stand on a soap box on a Sunday morning and say anything he liked? Men crowded round this Indian Chief, every few minutes handing him money. He'd said he had a horse, but where was it?

'Who's he?' I asked the billeting officer. 'Where's his horse?'

'That's Prince Honolulu taking bets,' she said. 'He's a famous bookie.'

Oh, I thought, Uncle Izzy is a bookie, though he doesn't dress like an Indian chief.

'The Commons we're walking on used to be the place where people in the Middle Ages grazed their sheep. Now it's more of a meeting place,' she said. At least she talked to me.

Back onto pavement, we passed more small men dressed in different bright colours and brightly coloured caps. We'd left the small town, and now passed only houses and small men.

'Who are they?' I asked. Perhaps midgets lived in this part of England.

'Those are jockeys,' said the billeting officer. 'Except for Ascot, Newmarket is the biggest horse-racing centre of England. You'll often see our horses racing across the Commons.'

I wished I could go to a horse race, the way Daddy went to dog races. He'd love horseracing. Did Daddy miss me? Did he even notice I had left? We came to 45 Lowther Street.

Mr Pettit, my new and second foster-father, was a tall, broad, slow-moving man of about 40 who hardly ever spoke. 'The strong, silent type,' Mummy would have called him. He was a labourer. When he did speak, he stopped to think first. A sepia picture of him as a soldier in World War One hung on the wall. But he was alive, with a curly round scar in the back of his neck.

When he saw me looking at the picture of him, he spoke to me for the first time.

'In the Great War I got a bullet in the neck,' he said proudly, pointing to his curly scar.

Mrs Pettit, plump and kind, had two children. 'My older son, Alec, is away in the army, and Ron, two years younger than you, is seven.'

My first night there, when I went upstairs to bed in the pitch dark, a great white ghost jumped on me shouting, 'Yaroo.'

'I'm not scared,' I exclaimed, heart beating. 'I don't believe in ghosts!'

'Ha ha, it's me,' Ron shouted, pulling off the white sheet.

Next day, he yelled, 'Come on, let's play the piano.'

Before the war, I'd had piano lessons with Mr Bannister, an unemployed pianist who used to play for silent films. Always dressed in a raincoat with a cigarette dangling from his one tooth, we'd moved from scales, to The Volga Boatmen, to Strauss waltzes. Then war broke out. That finished my musical training. I wished I could play Schubert and Rachmaninoff like Mummy. Ron had had some lessons, too, unusual for a country boy.

In the country, the 'front room' in every house, faced the street, the way our 'living room' that we never used in London faced the street. At home, we now had a piano, and so did the Pettits, but in both houses, no one used these 'front rooms' except to play the piano. Any entertaining was done in the kitchen. Ron and I could both pick out tunes and play by ear. We banged out together, singing as we played:

Roll out the barrel,

We'll have a barrel of fun,

Roll out the barrel,

We've got the Huns on the run,

Sing, boom tarraral,

We'll have a barrel of cheer,

Now's the time to roll the barrel

'Cos the gang's all, here.

And

Run Rabbit, run rabbit run, run, run,'

We'll get the Hun with our gun, gun, gun

We'll get by without our rabbit pie

So run rabbit, run rabbit, run, run, run.

Then we banged out and sang:

Bless 'em all, bless 'em all, the long and the short and the tall,

Bless all the sergeants and W.O. ones

Bless all the corporals and their blinking sons,' cause I'm saying goodbye to them all,

As back to their village they crawl,

They'll get no promotion this side of the ocean

So cheer up my lads, bless 'em all.

Although my father was 4F, the government sent him to Wales to do 'essential work' as a barber in a veteran's hospital. He wrote me only two letters during the six years of the war. The first letter read:

'There was a bunch of Fascists standing around and one said to me, 'Ha, look at the Jew boy.' All his friends were standing round him, laughing at me. One of them pushed me. I walked over to the ring-leader and clouted him one in the face so he fell down in a heap. They never bothered me again.'

I was proud of my father for standing up to bullies. I supposed that since he now lived in Wales and not with my mother, he could write to me, and I could write back, but he was there only for a month. He was a fighter, my Dad.

I wished all Jews, including me, learned to fight the Fascists back as they did at the Cable Street Battle. In my childish innocence, I thought the war would stop Fascism, but now I learned that Fascists still lived in England and Wales and were trying to hit my father.

Mummy had also been sent on essential war work. She wrote every week:

'The government made me a Lady Almoner, a kind of receptionist in a London V.D. clinic.' She didn't explain what V.D. was but I knew it was some illness. 'The soldiers have to take sulphur baths, and it makes them all yellow.'

The government sent people not in the services, wherever needed for 'essential work'. During this time, my parents had to close the business. Uncle Adrian was also sent on 'essential work' in a government chemical laboratory. His work was so secret, that only his brother Wally knew what it was, and 60 years later, Wally took this secret to his grave.

At 6 o'clock, the Pettits turned on the wireless to hear the news. 'I wonder where our Alec is,' Mrs Pettit said to Mr Pettit after the news, her face sad. 'I pray to God he's safe.'

That night, Gracie Fields sang on the wireless in her hard, high, perfect voice:

Wish me luck as you wave me goodbye,

Cheerio, here I go, on my way,

Wish me luck as you wave me goodbye,

With a cheer, not a tear, make it gay.

Give me a smile I can keep all the while

In my heart while I'm away.

'Till we meet once again, you and I,

Wish me luck as you wave me, goodbye.

I didn't then know that Gracie Fields was an ardent Fascist or I would not have enjoyed her singing. Vera Lynn, long hair over one eye and with that special break in her voice sang:

We'll meet again, don't know where, don't know when

But I know we'll meet again some sunny day.

Keep smiling through just like you always do

Till the blue skies chase the grey ones far away.

And will you…please say hello to the folks that I know

Tell them – I won't be long.

They'll be happy to know that while I'm away

I'll keep singing this song.

We'll meet again, don't know where, don't know when,

But I know we'll meet again some sunny day.

'I heard that Joannie Greenwall got her hair caught in a munitions machine. Fair scalped her,' Mrs Pettit said to Mr Pettit one evening as he scooped fresh farm peas onto his fork.

'Oh aye. They're all copying that Vera Lynn with her long hair.'

'Women working in factories all have to put their hair in turbans, now,' Mrs Pettit said.

'Oh aye,'

Suddenly, turbans became a new fashion. Everyone was wearing them.

Although the weather grew colder in October of 1939, coal and coke were rationed along with many foods and clothing. In the winter, if we left the only heated room in the house, the kitchen, with the fire in it, our white breath steamed out into the dark corridor. Why was breath white, I wondered? We wore double sweaters in the house, and took to bed with us stone hot water-bottles for our feet.

'You'll have to get used to margarine, Father, and that's getting hard to get,' Mrs Pettit said in November of 1939. 'They've rationed butter to two ounces a week.'

'You'll have to do with cheddar, Father, there's no other cheese,' Mrs Pettit said, later.

'And what's wrong with cheddar, Mother?' Mr Pettit said. He always called her Mother, so I didn't know her first name. I knew his first name because she often called him Andrew.

There'd been few cars in the streets of Newmarket when I arrived. By winter there were almost none. We went everywhere on foot or on bicycles. Mummy had sent me money for a bicycle. I found out that I was evacuated to Newmarket because each school was sent to a different country town. Buxton Street School had been assigned to Newmarket.

At first we used Newmarket church for school, then an old, empty house. Someone gave us cheap fabric, lent us sewing machines and girls learned how to use the machine. But I pricked my finger, dropped blood on my garment, had nowhere to wash it and never wore it.

Gradually, we resumed lessons held in odd buildings lent to us by the town. We held exercise classes in the local park. Once, I showed a schoolmate an acrobat I'd learned in my one acrobat class. In the park, I lay on my back, my legs bent, arms in the air, supporting Trisha. Trisha lay on my knees and arms, her arms wide out as if she were flying. I imagined we looked like a beautiful statue together, but no one passed, or saw us.

Many nights, the Pettit family played cards or cribbage together. I had never done anything with my whole family, so I enjoyed these family times. By January of 1940 when I became 10, I was a card expert and had become the Pettit family's crib score keeper. I loved moving the tiny, smooth ivory pegs, and being once again an important person. For so long I had been unimportant. The Pettit family was quiet and kind, and Ron was a lovable scamp. Mrs Pettit made even bedtime a happy family time.

'Time for bed,' Mrs Pettit said every night, and made us all hot chocolate with a thick slice of bread and marg and a chunk of sharp cheddar cheese. I felt like Flossie, a mongrel, not pretty, but frisky, lively and adopted by this quietly kind family.

Once a week Mrs Pettit heated up kettles of water in the kitchen. A great tin bath stood on boxes in front of the fire. I stayed in my room while Ron took his bath and after he went up to bed, Mrs Pettit set drying racks around the bath, hung towels on them to give me privacy, and I had my bath. There was already a shortage of soap and no aromatic perfumed soap like the Lavender or Evening in Paris soap I was used to at home. Wartime soap had no smell.

That first Christmas away from home I, like everyone else, hung a stocking on the mantelpiece under the Christmas cards. I'd never done this before. This was a far pleasanter Christmas than that at the orphanage. I had Ron for company and I was also company for him. His big brother away in the army, we became what I imagined to be like brother and sister.

A new song came out for Christmas. Ron and I picked it out on the piano and sang it:

I'm sending a letter, to Santa Claus,

A letter I hope he'll receive,

Oh I wonder if he, will please remember me,

When he comes on Christmas Eve.

I've got a lot of letters and playthings like other girls and boys

But I want my soldier Daddy, he's better than all the toys,

And so I'm sending a letter, to Santa Claus, to bring Daddy safely home, to me.

The Pettits were anxious about Alec.

I hadn't seen Mummy or Daddy since I'd been in Newmarket, for about two years. It was now 1941. Mummy wrote to me regularly.

One morning I received a letter.

'The Blitz has started in earnest. Bombs are dropping every night, many people killed. Some of my friends are dead. The Germans are aiming for the nearby docks. I refuse to go into shelters or the underground at night. If I'm going to die I want to die in my own bed.'

Sheltered from the bombing in the quiet countryside, this letter had little effect on me. But less than two hours away from Newmarket, Mummy said London was being bombed to pieces. I didn't want to even think about it. I still couldn't imagine bombs falling. What colour were they? What shape? I was busy at school, and after school, playing at home with Ron.

At Easter of 1941 Mummy sent me two new cotton dresses, a tartan and another. A new dress, with clothes rationing, was a big event. I felt strange celebrating Easter with a new dress. Even though I didn't know what Easter meant, I knew it was some Christian holiday. Slowly, I was becoming Christian. All Jewish education stopped during the war, unless some Jewish children stayed with their parents, had private tutoring, or were evacuated with a Jewish school. I had no contact with Jews except with some girls at school, and no Jewish adults played any role in my life. At what must have been Passover, a Jewish woman took some Jewish girls, including me, to a strange house where we ate matzo and a hard-boiled egg, but I for one, had no idea why. I'd never before eaten matzo.

One beautiful evening in the spring of 1941 Mrs Pettit skewered on her hat with a hatpin. She and Mr Pettit were going to the pub. I assumed they would leave Ron and me at home, but Mrs Pettit called out, 'Come on you two.'

Ron and I leapt out of the house and skipped along with the Pettits. Mrs Pettit showed us the Ladies' Section of the pub where an empty and silent room stood behind a frosted glass door. Unlike London, where women went to the pub, the country pub was a man's place, almost like a club. Mr Pettit often stopped in after work for a 'quick one' and a chat with other men.

In the Ladies' Section, Ron taught me how to play shove'appeny (shoving a halfpenny). He showed me how to place the hapenny (half a penny coin) at the bottom of a long, shiny board on a table, and to nudge the coin sharply or gently with the heel of one's hand so it shot forward. We had to land the hapenny exactly in one of the squares at the end of the board, and each square earned a different number of points. Ron, of course, kept winning. I didn't mind. He was the younger brother I'd never had.

Another day in summer, the Pettits took us to their 'Victory Allotment'. Because of great food shortages and rationing, the government leased lots to people. The Pettits had planted fruits and vegetables. Posters all over urged, 'Dig for Victory'. We often passed healthy Land Army girls in their khaki jodhpurs and sweaters, boots pressed down on pitchforks, planting vegetables or gracefully throwing hay into the air making a hay stack: their faces happy.

At the edge of Mr Pettit's allotment. I picked up a small green, hairy fruit from the ground. 'Ooh, look, what a tiny little apple,' I said to Mr Pettit.

Mr and Mrs Pettit exploded in laughter.' That's not an apple, that's a gooseberry, you gooseberry,' Mr Pettit laughed. That was the second time Mr Pettit spoke to me. We picked a basket of gooseberries and Mrs Pettit made a gooseberry pie with no sugar; sugar was rationed, I suppose because it came from abroad, and all ships were needed for war. I came to like tart gooseberry and rhubarb pies. Lack of sugar possibly saved our teeth from cavities.

One Sunday afternoon, Mrs Pettit gave Ron and me a whole iron bucket of winkles. Ron showed me how to dig them out of the shell with a long pin. Being Jewish, I'd never eaten shellfish. I didn't really like the taste, nor the gritty feel of the winkles, but I liked digging them out and Ron's special closeness, the warmth of his body next to mine. No one, except by accident, had touched me for two years.

Another day Mrs Pettit gave me a taste of her homemade elderberry wine. After two sips I became dizzy and staggered about. Homemade wine had a powerful punch, at least, for a girl. I now understood Mrs Ancliffe's tipsy Tim. The Pettits laughed at me, but in a kindly way.

In summer, if we went to bed early, Mrs Pettit allowed Ron and me to read comics in our own beds until dark. At the top of the stairs to the right were the Pettit's and my bedroom. I had to pass through the Pettit's bedroom to get to mine. Left of the staircase was Ron's bedroom which I never saw. Summer nights, Ron and I would each take a huge pile of comics upstairs. Since paper was rationed, Mummy sent me used comics all of them printed in black and white. We each went to our own bedrooms and read until it was so dark we couldn't see any more. Ron and I would call out and chat to each other across the stairs, but never saw each other's bedroom.

One comic was about a fat boy, Billy Bunter, who went to a posh private boys' school. The boys had pots of money that they spent at the Tuck Shop. Here, they bought treats for their midnight feasts. Another comic was about a rascally scamp of a boy aged 11 called William, always getting into and out of trouble. In 1940 Richmal Crompton, the author, published a war book with William in it called, *William and the Evacuees*, more about William than about us evacuees. Mummy sent comics about girls' escapades in girls' boarding schools. Boarding schools sounded wonderful – but seemed to be attended only by wealthy Christian girls.

One day Mrs Pettit cut string and unwrapped a brown paper parcel, 'Look, my sister sent me a birthday gift, Oh, pre-war soap! How lovely it smells,' she exclaimed.

The soap was oval, like a small blimp. I touched its smooth and silky ovalness. We all sniffed its wonderful rose-like scent that immediately reminded me of Mummy, Aunt Mitzi and London. My aunt had never written to me since I'd been evacuated. Nor did anyone else in the family, besides Mummy, write to me except for Daddy's letter telling me not to answer him and not to tell Mummy he'd written to me. I didn't understand why I couldn't write to my own father, but Mummy had a fiery temper, so I didn't answer, as I wanted to.

But smelling Mrs Pettit's beautiful soap reminded me of London, family and home.

'It smells wonderful,' I said, holding the smooth, scented oval to my nose, breathing in its perfume. Mrs Pettit gently took it from me and went with it upstairs. I just had to smell that wonderful soap once more. Where could she have put it?

That afternoon I crept upstairs into the Pettit's bedroom. Although I always passed through their bedroom to get to mine, I'd never before stopped in it. But now, I had to smell that soap again that reminded me of home and pre-war 'luxuries'.

A rough wooden chest of drawers stood near the Pettit's window. Might the soap be in there? Stealthily, I pulled out the creaky top drawer, and started feeling inside clothes for the hard oval-shaped soap. Suddenly the blankets on the bed reared up, and I nearly fainted with fright. I thought that finally, I was going to see a real ghost.

Mr Pettit's enormous grey head appeared over the top of the sheets. 'What are you doing in our drawers?' he thundered.

'I'm looking for silver foil for the war effort,' I lied, quavering.

'Next time ask, and keep out of our drawers,' he said and went back to sleep. I hadn't known he napped on Saturday afternoon.

That was the third and last time he ever spoke to me.

Why did I lie? What could have been more innocent in our luxury-starved, austere life, and separated from London, city life and my Jewish family than wanting to smell again, home's perfumed soap? I yearned for pre-war scents. No one could find perfume any more. I hungered for colours. All young men, now in the services, wore khaki or blue. Women dressed in blacks and browns, austerity: the fashion. Suddenly, I bitterly missed the excitement, the scents and colours of London city, my Jewish parents, relatives and friends.

Alone in my bedroom, I cried quietly, not sure why, for that which I'd loved and lost.

CHAPTER 15

WARTIME LONDON:
BLACKOUT AND BLITZ

At the age of 11 in 1940, I sat for the National British High School Entrance Examination in Cambridge. One could only enter British high schools after passing this examination. Lifelong status in England was then almost fixed by age 11. I'd pass this examination and go to high school, a scholarship permitting.

Mrs Schiff, a Jewish social worker, took me by train, about a 15 mile ride, from Newmarket to Cambridge. Cambridge bore the closest resemblance to London that I'd seen for two years. We even passed young men rowers wearing boaters, reminding me of rowers on London's Thames. Cambridge's enormous old mediaeval buildings loomed over us, and college students zipped by on bicycles, black gowns fluttering out beside them like crows' wings. I didn't notice any women students. There were piles of bicycles everywhere. Mrs Schiff said that students picked up any bicycle, rode it, and left it in another pile near their class building. Many students had been called up, volunteered or served in 'essential' secret work. 'Some even work on decoding enemy messages,' she whispered.

Mrs Schiff took me to a restaurant where we ate tinned tomato soup. Going to a restaurant was a big luxury after two years of home meals in Newmarket. We then went to a large hall where hundreds of students my age sat for the exam.

I easily passed the exam, and was admitted to Spitalfields Girls' High School, the high school nearest my East London home. Some Spitalfield girls or their parents chose not to be evacuated, and attended the original London school, in spite of nightly bombing. However, much of the school was evacuated to Ely during the war. I would be going to high school in Ely.

Since I had done well, and my parents' income was low, I won a government scholarship that covered school supplies, the school uniform, plus a living stipend. When war ended, I would go to Spitalfields Girls High School in London where it stood next to the ancient, medieval wholesale Fruit and Vegetable Market. I loved this market, where before the war I'd watched its men workers gracefully walking with six or more round baskets of brilliantly coloured fruits and vegetables on their heads. They'd cheerily call out 'Good morning' to me. I wished I could go to the London Spitalfields. I didn't care about bombing, but Mummy wanted me evacuated, so I would have to attend the evacuated branch of Spitalfields.

'Spitalfields High School, sometimes called Central Foundation Girls' School is evacuated to Ely,' Mrs Schiff told me. 'You'll be leaving your Newmarket foster parents and going to new foster parents in Ely. Before being admitted to Spitalfields, you must go to London to buy your high school uniform.'

I was excited about going to high school, about going to London, seeing my parents and relatives and buying my new school uniform. In the 1940s, only upper class girls wore a high school uniform. However, since mediaeval times, the guilds and London County Council had provided full scholarships with living expenses for excellent students from low-income families like mine. 'We could not have afforded the tuition and the uniform otherwise,' Mummy wrote.

Miss Crawford, Buxton Street Headmistress, sent for me on Thursday. Since war and evacuation, she'd grown thinner; new lines ran between her nose and mouth.

'Congratulations on winning high school entrance, and a scholarship,' she said. 'As you know, only troops may travel by train. I have obtained special permission for you to go to London tomorrow to buy your uniform. On Sunday, take the early train to Ely. The billeting officer will meet you and take you to your new foster-parents.'

It was thrilling to be in London again, in spite of the still smoking ruins left by heavy German bombing. But everyone in London went about business as if bombed out buildings and smoking ruins were normal. British spirit high, no one complained.

'We're used to it,' Mummy said. 'Happens every night. We just do what we have to do.'

Since I'd never experienced bombing, I supposed it couldn't be all that bad.

I visited Booba and Zada, my aunt and Uncle Sam, although Uncle Max was in Egypt fighting Rommel at Tobruk, Daddy and Uncle Sam were 4F, unfit for duty. Aunt Mitzi's new husband, Uncle Adrian was not drafted because he was doing essential secret chemical work. Aunt Mitzi still worked for Raphael. Even though Aunt Mitzi had married, Raphael had not. The government had changed his imported lace business into a uniform factory. All was austerity now. No lace, perfume, colours, no silk stocking; silk was used for parachutes.

Due to nightly bombings, whole streets of shops and houses lay in rubble and since there was a serious shortage of housing, Aunty Mitzi and Uncle Adrian lived at the top of Booba's large house. Booba told Mummy who told me in her weekly letter to me that the newlyweds argued a lot, especially over the bedspread. Modern Aunt Mitzi wanted blankets; Uncle Adrian wanted the old-fashioned *iberbat*, the large, feather-stuffed, toasty cover I loved: what a silly argument! I wondered if Aunt Mitzi still loved Raphael, and gave poor Adrian short shrift.

I had not seen Booba, Zada or Aunty Mitzi for the two years during which I'd been evacuated to Newmarket. Neither had any of them written to me. I ran to my Zada. How I'd missed my grandfather's hugs and kisses. '*Bubbele, zeesele, fliegele*,' he'd called me, little doll, little sweet, little wing. But now, I was too big to sit in his lap. He only lightly kissed me. I was a stranger. War had separated us. His coolness hurt my feelings, but I didn't know how to say so. He hadn't seen me for two years. I was now 11. I could no longer cuddle up in his lap.

As usual, my grandmother offered me her cheek but did not kiss me, nor, although we hadn't met for two years, did she offer me even a cup of tea. I remembered how my other grandmother, Daddy's mother, had wrapped me close in her skirts and given me a sip of her home-made wine, so I loved her. But I only had a weekend in London. Was she still alive?

'You've grown,' Uncle Sam said, staring at my pinprick breasts, making me blush.

It was wonderful to be in London again especially in the fancy West End. London's West End teemed with soldiers, sailors, airforce men, Polish and French Free Fighters who had escaped Europe, Australian soldiers, the Jewish Brigade, most servicemen with a girl on each arm. We passed thousands of young women in the rough khaki uniform of the WATS (Women's Armed Training Service) or the WRENS (Women's Royal Naval Service). The WRENS looked smart in their navy, brass-buttoned suits, white shirts, navy ties, and tiny white-trimmed tricorn hats. Chattering crowds, rumbling cars, honking taxis, the roar of buses, bursts of laughter from restaurants and pubs as doors opened and closed were all music to my ears famished for gay London sounds after quiet, boring, country Newmarket.

As a WREN passed, smiling up at her beau, Mummy shouted above the din, 'If the war goes on long enough you'll be able to be an officer in the WRENS. The WRENS only take high school girls. You'll look wonderful in a WREN uniform.'

I looked at her, surprised. I didn't know much about war, but I thought thousands of young men in the forces were daily being wounded and killed in battle. The Pettits had said that two hundred British, mainly Londoners were killed every night in German bombing raids. I knew vaguely, that Hitler was killing Jews. Surely we'd want the war to end soon. Why would Mummy want war to go on long enough just for me to wear a smart uniform? But excited about being in London and soon going to high school in a new town, Ely, excited about buying my new high school uniform, I forgot her strange remark.

I'd only been in the West End of London once before the war when I was about four years old. I remembered perfumed women in long, rustling evening gowns and gleaming fur coats, men in silk top hats and tails, the flash of their white-fringed silk scarves, couples sweeping into glittering cars driven by chauffeurs. 'Home James,' or 'To the Ritz, Carl,' I heard them order their drivers. I remembered dazzling lights, glittering restaurants with uniformed doormen outside and an enormous electrically red-lit silhouette of a gigantic Johnny Walker on the wall of a hotel, his outline as tall as the whole building, his long, red-lit legs ceaselessly walking while he raised his silhouetted-in-red-lights top hat. Such a luxurious life had disappeared with war, and with the blackout, so had lit-up-in-red-lights Johnny Walker. At night, now, all streets were dark, but we'd be home by dark.

In the West End as in the East End, piles of sandbags surrounded big buildings and tape, criss-crossed all shop windows in case of flying glass. Mummy had written that after a slow start, the Germans, in 1940, had nightly begun bombing London. 'The Blitz' she called it.

'Two hundred thousand incendiary bombs dropped last night,' she'd written. 'All the windows upstairs are broken. We've had to board them up until the end of the war.'

I tried to imagine fires falling out of German planes onto London, but I could not. But I could imagine the sound of glass crashing, because before the war I'd often heard glass breaking when Fascist hoodlums smashed our shop window.

'You can only go to high school because the scholarship pays all your fees, and gives you a stipend to use for your school uniform,' Mummy shouted above the wonderful din as we shouldered our way through the crowds of servicemen and their girls. Everyone seemed to be going in the opposite direction from us, kept bumping into us, grinning, and saying 'Sorry!'

'They're all desperate for a last fling before they go back to the front,' Mummy said.

I imagined the lively young airman we'd just passed, lying dead.

We passed a serviceman on crutches, reminding me of the man from the First World War with one leg who stood against a wall all day on Bethnal Green Road holding out one pencil. Would this soldier end the same way? A still acrid hot smoking building, now a pile of rubble, made my eyes water. With all this destruction happening, buying a high school uniform seemed unimportant. 'Why do we even have to wear uniforms?' I asked.

'You should be proud that everyone can see that you go to high school. Not many girls or boys pass that entrance exam. Besides, a uniform also makes girls equal. No one can tell rich from poor, because everyone wears the same clothes,' Mummy said. 'Your school has a wonderful reputation. The Spitalfields Vegetable Market guildsmen started it in about 1500 for clever children whose parents couldn't afford to pay for a high school education. Barrel makers' guilds began Coopersmith's, and the Skinner's guild began Skinners' High School. Each school has its own uniform and colours so people can recognise which school you belong to.'

I was surprised Mummy knew so much about schools, but she was passionate about opera and education. 'You're lucky to go to high school,' she reminded me again. 'I won a scholarship but even though my teacher begged my mother to let me go, Booba forced me to go to work in a stinking fur factory. How I cried,' she told me again.

Finally we entered a crowded Marshall and Snelgrove, the only West End shop that sold our school uniform. I'd never been inside such a posh shop before and I doubted Mummy had. For once, she fell silent as if we East Enders had no right to be in such a posh West End shop.

'Can I help you Modom?' a tall, well-dressed lady with an upper class accent said frostily. She looked to be in her fifties. The younger, single women were all in the services.

'We need the winter and summer uniform for Spitalfields High School,' Mummy whispered, unlike her usual loud voice.

'Yes Modom,' said the lady.

She returned with a huge pile of clothes over her arm. After her initial frostiness she became friendlier. For winter we bought two uniform beige blouses, the school green and red-striped tie and a pleated gym tunic to go over the blouse; the lady tied a braided 'girdle' ending in two tassels round my tunic's waist. We bought the school's navy blue school blazer with gold buttons and with a shield over the pocket reading, 'Spe, Labore, Fide,' 'With Hope, Work and Faith,' and a green sweater edged with red stripes at the neck and wrists for winter. I'd need it, since coal was rationed, winter was coming, schools had no heat and would be chilly. We bought the black velour with a green and red hatband, school hat, a shield at its centre. The woman brought thick, lisle stockings, a garter belt to hold them up, and solid brown brogues with a fringed tongue hanging out. Even though the uniform was hardly pretty, I was thrilled with this new booty. Few East End girls then went to high school. Everyone would see from my uniform that I had passed the entrance exam for high school and must be intelligent.

'You'll need this one-strap indoor shoe,' the woman said. What were indoor shoes?

I felt a huge change creeping over me, as if I were changing from an East London girl into a rich, Christian girl at a boarding school where the comics showed they all wore a uniform. But my dress was a disguise. Underneath, I was still a cockney.

'And now, for the summer uniform,' the woman said. What? A different uniform?

The summer uniform consisted of a pretty emerald green cotton dress with a cream collar, a cream panama hat with the green and red band round it. Instead of heavy lisle stocking and leather shoes we'd wear socks and sandals, plimsolls for gym, tennis, hockey, and netball.

We bought a tennis racquet and a hockey stick. Although athletic, I had never played team games, only skipping, leapfrog, catch, hide-and-seek, statues and gobs. The idea of playing with a partner or partners, or on a team for tennis or hockey was a foreign, Christian upper class forms of sport I'd read about in books and comics about rich girls in boarding schools.

The clothes probably cost at least a hundred, possibly two hundred pounds. We couldn't possibly have done it without the scholarship and stipend money, Mummy said again.

Back home on the number six bus, I ran across the street to my friend Joycey Kennel and showed her all my new high school clothes. But she said, 'Me and you can't be friends no more. We're going to be too different,' she said, and she walked away as if we'd never been close friends for years. I ran after her.

'Joycey,' I pleaded.

'You'll be having posh friends, and I'll be working in the jam factory. Goodbye.'

Joycey was right. I would be studying intensively for the tough Matriculation examination taken at age sixteen, and if passed, Higher School Certificate Examination at age 18, without which one could not even apply to college. But these exams were so far off, and I was so excited about my new school clothes, I hardly thought of them. I'd miss Joycey, but I was about to enter a new world. I didn't realise as Joycey did, I was about to enter the middle class.

That night in London, a deafening wail like an animal howling in pain signaled an air raid warning. I was getting into bed when I heard the siren, and then the roar of overhead airplanes.

'Are those German planes?' I asked Mummy.

'Our Spitfires give a steady hum, the Junkers and Messerschmitts go throb, throb, throb, throb, like a heart beating loudly,' she said.

That was how my heart was beating while Mummy casually darned Daddy's socks.

Suddenly I heard a deafening WHUMPF, the house shook and I jumped off the bed. 'Mummy,' I screamed, leaping into her arms.

'Downstairs into the cellar,' she said. Daddy slept, for once his deafness useful.

Mummy and I raced downstairs. Coal for our fires was piled in a space under the stairs and closed in behind a door. Once a month, our coalman, carrying a huge sack on his back, bent forward and tipped the open sack of coal right over his head and coal showered straight into the coal 'cellar'. Mummy now opened the iron latch of the door and shoved me onto a pile of coal. Following me, she closed the door. Lumps of coal jutting into my behind, Mummy crouched over me. For once I felt her warm body close to mine. The bombs kept WHUMPING down one after the other. I shivered and whimpered. Suppose the house fell in or caught fire. Suppose our house became a heap of smoking rubble like the one I had seen this morning, and worse, would we be under burning rubble, legs broken? I'd never go to high school or become a WREN.

'Can we go to the Underground?' I asked in a trembly voice as another whump shook the house. 'I hear hundreds of people sleep in the underground station every night.'

'I refuse to join that riff-raff,' Mummy said. 'They sing, cook, talk all night and pee in stinking pails in the corners. You don't know who you're sleeping next to. If I'm going to die, I'm going to die in bed.'

Did I have to die there, too?

Bombs rained down with thumps, whumps, whines, explosions, followed by crashes of glass exploding, rumblings of houses falling broken to the ground, shouts of those running outside, caught in the raid, fire and ambulances screaming by, ack ack guns clattering at Messerschmitts overhead. Our house rattled and shook, our shop windows first exploded into smithereens followed by a delicate tinkly sound as smaller pieces of glass fell. My head rattled and pounded from noise. But Mummy's warm body curved over mine. Did she really love me? Was she protecting me or was this the only way we'd both fit into our coal cellar?

Finally, throbbing Messerschmitts turned tail and with a roar flew back to Germany, Spitfires chasing them with staccato gunfire. Silence, then a mournful All Clear wail sounded. Faces black with coal dust, we peeped outside the coal cellar and then went to the front door.

The moon and stars, as always eternal, shone and glittered. God was in his heaven, together with searchlights that still criss-crossed the skies looking for enemy Jerries. In the distance toward the docks, red and orange flames licked the sky, it looked as if all of London was aflame and smoking like a giant chimney. Acrid fumes filled our lungs. On our street, firemen were already hosing small pockets of incendiary bomb fires.

'They always come on a moonlit night,' Mummy said. 'I think they got the docks. I hope my friends, the Frosts are all right. We'll go round and see them in the morning.'

After breakfast, bleary eyed, we both walked a half-mile to Chana, Gertie and Harry Frost. Where the Frost's flat had stood, we now saw only a pile of smoking debris and the jagged outline on the second floor of their narrow staircase; a toilet teetering at the edge of stairs where the wall had been shattered. I was surprised to see an indoor toilet in the East End. Shards of glass and furniture lay tossed in rubble. ARP and other rescuers were digging through the smoking debris. They pulled out a crushed bowler; I hoped it wasn't the one Harry had caught during the Cable Street Battle. Then they found a bloody, severed hand. Harry's ring was on it.

I vomited.

Mummy approached the diggers. 'Did you know the Frost family? Do you know if some of them went to the shelter last night?'

'I don't fink they went to the shelters,' the grimy cockney said. 'Ain't no chance they came froo this. This wos all on fire last night it wos. Full of fire engines and ambulances. They took away 15 dead. You relatives or somefink?' he asked.

'Just very old friends,' Mummy said, tears streaming down her face.

I began to cry, too. I remembered Harry's joy when we East Enders won the Cable Street Battle against Mosley's Fascists. We'd won that battle, but Dunkirk, and the Blitz had followed; it looked as if we were losing the war. I felt ice-cold with dread. Suppose the Nazis really invaded England? They'd already killed thousands.

How did girls who stayed in London go through this every night and still go to school at Spitalfields the next day? Londoners had become so used to war and bombing, they treated it cheerfully and as if normal. But although I loved London and hated evacuation and the country, I was not as sure that I could live through horrific nightly bombings like last night's, and also risk being killed like the Frost family.

'You still want to live in London? Be glad you're evacuated to the country where it's safe and quiet. Tomorrow, you'll be evacuated to Ely, to new foster-parents,' Mummy said.

I nodded sadly. Tomorrow, I would go to a strange town, Ely, and again be billeted with my third stranger foster-parents.

If only England would soon win the war and I could come home to my beloved London.

Neither wish seemed likely to come true. But tomorrow, I'd be off to Ely and a new life.

CHAPTER 16
ELY AND HIGH SCHOOL EVACUATION

On a dark, blustering Sunday night in September of 1941, Mummy and I arrived at Ely station. Ely in East Anglia boasted one of England's most famous historic cathedrals. I'd read that it was 537ft high. It sounded enormous, but who cared, I would not be going into it. I thought a cathedral was a big church. I had only been to one church, when I was at the orphanage. I didn't want to go again because I dreaded seeing that poor, tortured man, head hanging, hands and feet nailed to old pieces of wood. These figures moved me to tears with compassion for the man, hatred for and fear of such inventive torturers. I felt the shame of being hoisted high, for everyone to see, and terrified that someone might sometime nail me to wood and I'd die of shame before I died of nailing. Did they nail women to crosses? Also, I'd feared the thunderous groans coming out of little organ mouth looking like shark's mouths that might eat me. I was so afraid of churches that I didn't want to go to Ely with its enormous cathedral. But my London high school was evacuated to Ely, so I had no choice. I would never enter that cathedral.

Except for the Ely stationmaster, the station and surrounding flat countryside was deserted, not a soul was in sight. I groaned. I was back in the hated, boring countryside. The skinny stationmaster was just putting bicycle clips over his old trousers' cuffs at the ankles (with war, cuffs had been cut out to save fabric) before swinging a leg over his bike to go home for his tea. Dinner in London was called tea in the country. There, they had dinner at lunch time. They were all backward. The stationmaster gave us directions to Miss Winifred Fry's house. Miss Fry, the school's history teacher was to take me to my new Ely foster home.

It was lucky the stationmaster was available, because we didn't meet one person on the way to Miss Fry's. We'd have had no idea how to find her. I shivered as a chill wind whipped Mummy's and my skirts. Newspapers gusted up from the ground wrapping themselves round our legs as we passed the single town square with shops and one cinema, all closed, pitch black hulks. With the blackout, only searchlights scouring for enemy planes, and a half-moon faintly lit our way. Suddenly, Ely Cathedral, reaching the sky loomed over the whole town and seemed to follow us through every space between houses, black and as ominous as a monster.

Why did I often feel terror? being devoured by a headless dummy, church organ mouths, battleship gun snouts, and now feared that monster Ely Cathedral would fall and crush me?

We fought our way through the wind to a tall, narrow house on a street called, The Vineyards. Mummy knocked on a door flung open to a brilliantly lit, warm room. After walking through near pitch black, the lights almost blinded us, and after the cold streets, fear changed to joy as the warmth engulfed us.

'Come in, come in,' said a lady with a generous bosom, milky blue eyes set in pink skin, skin that reminded me of the old warden's at Chingford's Christian orphanage. She smiled, showing large, buck teeth. 'I am Miss Winifred Fry and this is my sister, Miss Abigail Fry.'

Abigail Fry, a younger, surlier version of Winifred Fry, wore dark brown hair braided in Victorian circles over her ears. Bent almost double, muttering to herself, she was clearing away remains of tea and cake I yearned for. Two girls dressed in my school shirt, tie and tunic, stood feet apart, backs to the fire, hands linked behind their backs like lords and stared at me coldly.

Though unfriendly, I had to admit the girls looked smart in my new school uniform. They looked almost as smart as the WRENS that yesterday, Mummy had so admired.

'Mrs Moss, come to the fire, you must be frozen. Move away, gels,' Miss Fry said.

The two girls, pouting, dragged their feet three inches from the fire. Before the fire stood a table on which rested a large Monopoly game board. 'The girls and I were just having a game of Monopoly. Have a cup of tea, and then we'll show you the way to the Lupsons, your new foster-parents. Abigail,' Miss Winfred Fry commanded her sister, who now snarled at us as she cleared plates, 'please bring Mrs Moss and her daughter a cup of tea.'

Abigail shot her older sister a murderous look, but bent over in a servile walk and mumbling, scuttled crablike to I supposed the kitchen. Returning shortly, she shoved two cups of tea with milk, no sugar, at Mummy and me.

'We're very grateful, thank you so much,' Mummy gushed. 'It's terribly cold for September, isn't it?'

Weather was a British cover for all pauses in conversation or embarrassments. I didn't care. I gulped my hot tea, feeling pleasurable warmth stealing through my frozen limbs.

'Oh, it's a little colder than usual. We're used to it. We've been here for two years, you know. Are you ready?' I gulped my tea down. 'Good, then Abigail will show you the way to the Lupsons. It's time for you to go, too, gels,' she said to the two silent, staring girls.

Abigail, muttering, put on her coat, pulled a decrepit old hat onto her head and skewered it on with a hatpin (right through her brains, I thought), and then she led us back into the dark, blustering night. I didn't blame even Abigail for not wanting to go out tonight. The half-moon, cold and forbidding – I never did like the moon much – stared pale and icy through searchlights that forever criss-crossed dark skies. I longed for cheery London, bombs and all. In the dead silence of Ely we walked for about half a mile.

'This is the Lupson's,' mumbled Abigail, stopping at a low door, and disappeared into the blackout night, all windows black draped so German bombers saw no light.

We knocked. A grim young woman with a greasy face and straggly black hair opened the door. Silently, she stood back to let us in. Behind her, smoke poured out of a frying pan where she was cremating four chips. Mummy introduced us to the Lupsons and then said, 'I have to catch my train, goodbye,' and as usual, vanished into the night. In the strangest of places, she always knew her way back to the station.

A man and a young girl of about 10 sitting at the table waiting for their dinner stared at me. I had come from nice foster parents, the Pettits in Newmarket, and assumed all foster parents would be friendly. So far, no one had said a word.

'Are you cooking chips, they're my favourite,' I said, trying to break the ice. Mrs Lupson stared at me with cold eyes.

The girl came over to me and rummaged in my hair with her hands.

'If you're looking for nits, I don't have any,' I said.

'Where's your horns? Ain't you got horns?' the girl said.

'Come and sit down, Elsie,' Mrs Lupson said.

'I thought all Jews had horns,' Elsie said, her grey eyes cold. She'd assumed all Londoners must be Jewish. Anyone Jewish must be horned. The idea came, Daddy had told me, from Christians who mistranslated the Bible. 'It said there that Moses came down the mountain with rays of light coming from his head. The Christians translated 'rays of light' into 'horns'. Some artist called Michael Angelo had painted Moses with horns coming down the mountain holding the Ten Commandments. So it was logical for all Jews to have horns like the devil right?' Daddy said, laughing. I couldn't believe Elsie really thought that Jews had horns.

Mrs Lupson put out four greasy, blackened chips for me. That was dinner. She then showed me by candlelight, just like Mrs Ancliffe, only not kind like Mrs Ancliffe, up to a tiny room. My new foster-mother and father had not spoken one word to me. I wished Elsie had not.

After Mrs Lupson left me, I saw by the light of the moon, another girl in the bed, probably, another evacuee. The sleeping girl's tousled hair and long, dark lashes lay black against her white cheeks. Thank God I wouldn't have to face the Lupsons alone tomorrow, I thought, undressing quickly in the cold room and climbing into bed with her. The girl slept on.

In the morning, I saw that though she was very serious, spoke quietly and never smiled, my bed companion had a dimple in her chin. She told me she was an Irish Jewish girl, Moira from Dublin. I'd never met an Irish Jew. I dressed for the first time in my school uniform; Moira showed me how to knot the school tie.

The Lupsons gave us cold cereal with very little milk, bread and tea for breakfast. Mrs Lupson and Elsie scowled at us. Mr Lupson seemed nice, but kept glancing from his wife to Moira and me as if he needed his wife's permission to speak to us. Why did they take evacuees if they disliked us so much? It must have been for the small allowance and extra rations the government paid them or the government told them it was their duty. Many foster-parents assumed, I learned later, that all Londoners had lice and or, were Jewish. Neither was true.

The day was cool but bright and sunny; Ely didn't seem as depressing as it had the night before. However, as soon as we left for school, Ely Cathedral loomed over every building. Wherever I went, that gigantic cathedral towered over me, there was no escape. My old terror of the organ pipes falling on me and sucking me into their little mouths, returned. But as long as I didn't have to go into the cathedral I remained calmly morose.

The Lupsons lived close to the school, Archer House that had probably once been a former private home. The school was also opposite the market square and my first day at school happened to be market day. Farm men and women came in from the surrounding countryside and set up stalls in the town square. The one Ely cinema faced the town square. Things began to look livelier. Perhaps Ely wouldn't be so dull.

Since most foods were already rationed, the stalls bore mainly locally grown, I supposed, fruit and vegetables. But this market was not like London's Brick Lane or Petticoat Lane's open markets. Now those were real outdoor markets where you could buy anything from gold watches to shrimps to knickers! Lively hawkers shouted their wares and made jokes. Here, sellers were silent. However, in Ely, a contest was in progress. Everyone was singing this song to anyone they met:

'Kkkkkatie, my beautiful Katie,
You're the only one that I shall ever adore.
I've hunted and sought you, and now I've caught you,
So I'm claiming my five-pound-bond-reward.'

Apparently if you sang this song to the right, anonymous person, you would win a five-pound-bond reward. Everyone was excitedly singing this song to total strangers. Luckily, I'd arrived on market day and during a contest. It made the dour Lupsons and looming Ely Cathedral slightly less depressing.

Moira had shown me the way to Archer House, which was only just down the street from the Lupsons. She went to a different school, one that was evacuated from Dublin to Ely, so we parted. The British, I remembered, feared that Ireland might join the Germans, but also, Dublin might be bombed.

I arrived at an ivy covered building, and followed a stream of uniformed girls inside. Not knowing anyone, I stood lost in a large hallway, afraid to move until I changed into indoor shoes.

'Where do we change shoes?' I asked a fat, pimply girl with frizzy hair.

'Follow me,' she said, taking enormous strides.

'Are we supposed to take big steps in this school?'

'I take big steps to save leather for the war effort,' she said grimly. 'I'm Rita Gillis.'

Rita, one of the few friendly girls showed me my cubbyhole, my name on it: Gilda Moss.

Copying Rita, I changed into my house shoes, put my outside shoes in my cubbyhole and hung my coat on my hook above the shoes. We had done this in the orphanage.

'Prayers,' she said, and I followed her to a large room. Hundreds of girls dressed in my school uniform sat in rows, hands folded in laps, feet crossed at the ankles, as ladies were supposed to sit. Curiously, I looked round, not finding one familiar face except Rita's. My new green and red sweater itched horribly, and I couldn't scratch so I squirmed.

Suddenly every girl stood up as a stout older woman with short, curly grey hair strode in.

'That's Headmistress. She's an Australian, Miss Menzies,' Rita whispered.

Miss Menzies' enormous breasts, unusual in schoolteachers and headmistresses, were firmly packaged in a drab dress. Once, she must have been a pretty girl, but since women high school teachers (but not men) in England were forbidden to marry, she was a spinster.

'Good morning gels,' she said, with an upper class accent.

'Good morning Miss Menzies,' everyone chanted.

'Sit down.'

We said some prayers, then stood and sang a hymn which a firmly corseted woman banged out on the piano. The girls chorused:

'What heroes thou hast bred, Oh England, my country,

Amid the gallant dead, that is thine

Each with undaunted heart, playing his gallant part

Making thee what thou art, mother of mine.'

Then we sang:

'I vow to thee my country all earthly things above

Entire and whole and perfect the service of my love.

The love that asks no questions the love that pays the price

That lays upon the altar the dearest and the best

We also sang:

God who made us mighty, make us mightier yet.

I didn't feel all that nationalistic. It was only three years since the Cable Street Battle where some Fascists that constantly smashed our shop windows, daubed swastikas and JP's all over the East End walls, had tried to march through Cable Street to smash Jewish windows. By now, Kristallnacht had taken place in Germany in 1938, two years after The Cable Street Battle. In Germany, there had been no unified opposition to the Nazis as there had been against the Fascists in London. It was ironic that the first attempt to march through the Jewish section had occurred in London, not in Germany. People seemed unaware that before and throughout the war, there were active British Fascists. My grandfather, Daddy's father, could not practice as a gunsmith in England because Jews were excluded from the gunsmith guild. I felt wary of all British gentiles. And why did we sing hymns asking God for a bigger Empire? We already had India, Israel, other countries, and the British refused Jewish refugees into Israel.

'Sit down, gels,' Miss Menzies said.

We all sat. I squirmed in the rough wool jersey, longing to scratch my back.

'Sit still,' hissed Rita Gillis.

'Something dreadful has come to my attention,' Miss Menzies said, as I thought that if I couldn't soon scratch, I'd scream. 'A foster mother has complained that one of our gels placed a sanitary towel under her bed. This is a most awful occurrence. What will our kind foster parents think of Londoners if we behave in so irresponsible a manner?' Her voice trembled with horror.

I didn't yet have my period; I wasn't sure what a period was, so I could only guess at what she meant. I knew that once a month Mummy boiled bloody rags on the gas stove in a special pot. She'd said I had torn her womb and that was why she bled so much. She'd stir the bloody rags with a wooden spoon until the water turned pink and the rags turned white, but I didn't know where the blood came from, nor what exactly was a sanitary towel, I waited for Miss Menzies to tell us, and to tell us where you did put the bloody thing so that when I began my period, I would know what to do with it, but Miss Menzies rambled on about this girl's terrible crime, and never did say where the blood came from, how to find a sanitary towel and what to do with a bloody one. I was as much in the dark as before.

To a march thumped out by Miss Senior, the music teacher, we marched out in twos. Miss Senior, stuffed into a tight satin dress, looking like a sausage, I expected that at any minute mounds of her would burst through the seams. I followed my classmates, all of us marching like soldiers to Miss Senior banging unlike my mother softly rippling the keys.

I found myself in a dreary first form room with 25 other 11-year-old girls. Mummy was right. With identical uniforms, no one could tell rich from poor girls. No one here would know I came from Bethnal Green, only a notch above the poorest parts of the East End.

Everyone had to take French, besides English classes. Choices for a second foreign language were Latin or German. I had heard Latin was hard, so I slipped into the German line even though we all hated Germans, but thought it would be easier than Latin. I was marching with the other German linguists-to-be when a firm hand took hold of the back of my collar and tugged me roughly, out of the line.

'You're in me Latin class,' said an Irish voice.

I twisted my head to see who was holding a fistful of my collar. A slender woman of about 40, her piercing blue eyes bored into mine: her prey. High cheekbones framed a Roman nose and thin nostrils, and her Irish red hair with a middle part fell into natural waves that gathered in a small bun at the nape. She wore expensive high-heel shoes, Mummy judged people by their shoes, and dragged me by my collar to her Latin line. I groaned.

Later, Mummy wrote that Daddy wanted me to be a pharmacist and had signed me up for Latin. Normally he had nothing to do with my education except for showing me encyclopedias, books, taking me to museums and when we were out, telling me about history, animals and London. Probably it was Mummy who had decided I should be a pharmacist and learn Latin. No one had consulted me, but that was normal.

Months after, we had thoroughly learned Latin grammar, and intensively studied Horace, and Tacitus' Agricola. At the age of 18, we must pass Latin with honours to even apply to college.

'Decline hic,' Miss Brady said.

'Hic, haec, hoc,' I said.

'Faster,' she rapped me sharply on the knuckles with her wooden ruler. 'Now repeat.'

'Hic, haec hoc

Hunc, hanc hoc,'

School began at 9am. There was a short break at 11. The market square right opposite school, our 'playground', had a little alley where we could buy hot cross buns.

'I bet they drop the raisins in here from the top of Ely Cathedral, there's so few of them,' Bertha Goodman laughed, licking the thin sliver of rationed confectioner's sugar atop the bun.

Today, the twice-weekly market was crammed with stalls all around the edge of the market square. Farmers came in with produce that were welcome with stringent food rationing. Our ration book allowed us two ounces of meat and two of butter a week, one egg a month, clothes, petrol, coal everything was rationed so Ely bought or grew all the vegetables it could. Women arrived early and waited in long queues to buy fish before the fishmonger ran out of his supply. Troops were fed first, civilians received what was left or grown.

'Not fish again,' we'd groan, the third time in a week. We ate a lot of bread, potatoes, fish and vegetables, a healthy, though starchy diet. I learned to eat whatever was put before me, happy to feel full, no matter how boring the food.

The market was crammed with people and noise, which, being a little more like London city life, cheered me. Today, on the other side of the market square, I spied a good looking boy of about 15, blond, dressed in the pale grey school uniform of Ely Cathedral Boys' High School. As the boy looked intently at the one stall selling marbles a passing friend of his called out, 'Hallo, Paul,' I sneaked all the way round to his side of the market, pulled his grey scarf and streaked back to my place opposite, sure he couldn't know who'd done it. But no sooner had I arrived at my opposite lair than he threw me a mischievous smile. I knew that a rich, gentile boy from Ely Cathedral Boys' High School would never speak to a Londoner or a Jewish girl, so I might as well show my true colours. Cheekily Cockney, I smiled back at Paul.

One morning as I was leaving for school in my neat uniform, gas mask in its cardboard box on a string slung across my back, Elsie Lupson, my foster-sister sat on the front porch in bare feet, lazily combing her hair and examining the comb. We both cordially hated each other.

'Looking for nits?' I yelled at her on the way out.

The next day the billeting officer came for me.

'After school, pack your things and go to this address.'

On my way to school I sang, as I had when locked up in the orphanage attic.

Nobody loves me

Nobody wants me

I'm going to the garden to eat worms

Big fat slimy worms

Long thin skinny worms

I'm going to make a samwich out of worms.

Even though I didn't like the Lupsons and hated Elsie, tears trickled down my face as I dragged my shrinking cardboard box of clothes. No one wanted me.

The billeting officer came for me five more times to move me from foster families, each cold and unfriendly. Finally, a billeting officer took me to the Barnards. By now, I was 12. The three generation of Barnards lived in the house. Mr and Mrs Barnard, the grandparents, in their late fifties, owned the house, an old, low, rambling country place with no decoration, pictures or mirrors to brighten the drab beige living room sofa. With war, no one could buy new furniture but I was sure the Barnards wouldn't, even if they could. The back yard through which we came and went was empty of flowers or trees save for one fragrant lilac tree in a back corner.

The only other item in the back door was a tall wooden barrel for catching rain water.

'In case the Germans invade and cut off our water,' Norma said.

Norma, the Barnards' widowed daughter, about 30, her husband killed in a London air raid lived with them together with Norma's eight-year-old twins, Beryl and Roger.

Mr Barnard, the grandfather, was tall and slim, with brown hair turning grey, a lock falling into his blue eyes as if in memory of a flirtatious youth. Although he spoke quietly, his eyes 'flashed' daredevil. A dandy, he always wore a shirt, tie and suit with a waistcoat, gold watch on a chain draped elegantly across his long, elegant torso.

'I fought in the Great War,' Mr Barnard told me. 'I got poison gas from the Germans; doctors took out my eyeballs, cleaned them then put them back.'

I believed everything he said.

I'd been hearing about the Great War from Mrs Ancliffe, Mr Pettit, and now, Mr Barnard all of whom had been or fought in 'the war to end all wars'. Since we were now enjoying the second, younger men called The Great War, the First World War. A sepia picture of dashing Mr Barnard in his khaki World War One uniform hung in the front room, the room which in every country house faced on the street, a gloomy aspidistra at the window.

Gracie Fields often sang in her hard, perfect voice, a song, and 'He's got' – here she always paused – 'the biggest aspidistra in the world', and everyone laughed. I didn't know why.

Mrs Barnard, tall and angular, reminded me of 'aunt' Ellen of Hythe to whom Mummy shipped me during the summer and Christmas 'rush' in the shop. But whereas Aunt Ellen's angularity was softened by her kind eyes when she looked at her son, Tom, Mrs Barnard's head was always bowed over the sink scraping carrots, her eyes always downcast, her mouth always pressed into a tightrope. She wore drab grey cotton dresses, always covered with an apron, and never spoke except to call us in a monotone, to meals. Like Mrs Lupson and other foster parents, she never spoke to me. There were no cozy playing cards, no family around the kitchen table evenings sharing bread, cheese and cocoa before bed as there had been at the kind Pettits. Foster-parents in Ely, so far, had been like its cathedral, tall, cold and unfriendly. The exception was Norma.

Norma was a jolly, bouncy merry widow, the only one in the family who spoke to me.

'Silly bugger,' she said to me, 'when our house in London got a direct hit, he didn't die from the bomb; he died of a heart attack, while I came to with a bowl stuck in my head.'

Norma, like her father, was tall, with long legs, and wore her hair in a straight bob parted in the middle, thick bangs over her forehead. A small waist emphasised her plumpness. When Bill, her Tommy boyfriend chased her round the front room sofa and tickled her, her brown eyes sparkled, she giggled like a schoolgirl.

Bill, a Tommie private, wore rough British khaki. He looked to be about 38, stocky and crude. His broad impudent and florid face, bold eyes and coarse laugh, repelled me; he ignored me, but he seemed to make Norma happy and I liked Norma. Many British men were away fighting, so perhaps Norma had little choice. I thought from my lofty 11-year old perspective, that they were silly, but Norma was the only kind person in that family and if she wanted to be silly, fine.

Every evening, Mr Barnard, swaggering slightly, left home for the pub, leaving Mrs Barnard, angular and bitter faced, crouched before dinner scraping vegetables over a sink, and after, washing dishes in the sink. No one helped her, and surprisingly, she never asked me. In any case, we high school girls had three hours of homework every night. But Norma didn't.

Just outside, left of the back door entrance stood that huge wooden barrel brimming with rainwater that was to play a significant part in my life. Clear droplets trickled over its brown sides, and dripped to the ground, past the metal bands, leaving small, shining puddles.

'It's good to have in case the Jerries cut off our water, and it's great for washing your hair.' Norma said, as she scooped out a bucketful.

I didn't then know, thank God, of the German plan to invade England in 1940 and later.

The privies, too, as in most country homes (also in East London), were outside in the stark plain yard, save for the lilac tree. I arrived at the Barnards in spring when the lilac tree was just blooming. Every day when I came home from school, I'd bury my face in its blossoms and breathe in its scent. I still missed Mummy's and Aunt Mitzi's perfume. The war had eliminated most make-up, face-creams and perfume. Lipstick was hard to find, so Norma melted the stubs of two old lipsticks and poured them back into a lipstick case. Here they hardened into one, new lipstick. She used Rennet, a blue clothes' wash whitener, for blue eyeshadow. When, like many women, she couldn't find any silk stockings with the seam up the back, she went bare-legged and drew the 'seam' and the back bottom square of the 'stocking' up her legs with a dark pencil.

The highlight of the week was Sunday High Tea. At this meal, about five in the afternoon, we enjoyed a once a week feast of potted meat, potted shrimp, fresh scallions, radishes, lettuce, tomatoes, and carrots, cheese, pickled beets, piccalilli, thick slabs of white bread and margarine, jams, jellies, slabs of ration-buttered bread and strong, hot tea. We could eat as much of anything as we wanted. The lucky child got to eat the hard stalk of raw cabbage or broccoli; delicacies to our wartime palates. We also drank the water in which vegetables had been cooked. If really hungry we ate a mashed potato sandwich. Except for the shortage of fruits and fats, we were on a healthy though fatty diet. But some people, Miss Menzies for instance, developed a vitamin deficiency that turned her nails green. Mummy sent Miss Menzies some butter to cure her deficiency. Miss Menzies would have been horrified had she known she was eating black-market butter.

The twins' and my bedroom, at one time one huge attic room, had been divided into two rooms. We shared a window. A large space between our dividing wall and the shared window allowed them to constantly stick their heads through this opening and spy on me.

By the age of 11 I was already obsessed with Joan Fontaine whom I'd seen in *Rebecca*, with Lawrence Olivier when I'd played hooky from school. I often did not come back to school from lunch and went instead to a film, the only wonderful experience in an otherwise turgid and lonely evacuee's life. I imagined myself grown up, swathed in glamorous clothes like those of Joan Fontaine or Hedy Lamar, in Laurence Olivier's arms. If only I could be as beautiful as those two exquisite women and have a romance with someone as wonderful as Lawrence Olivier. If only a handsome man loved me, I would be so happy. So every night I smoothed Pond's face cream, bought secretly in Ely's Woolworths on Fore Hill during lunch break. If any prefect saw me, she might report me.

I was small about 5ft 1in, slim for age 11, and I still had a short bobbed haircut parted in the middle, upturned eyes, a small, retroussée nose, and small breasts. But I was shy, quiet and serious; I had no friend and no adult to talk to. Moira was the closest to a friend I had, but since I'd moved from the Lupsons I no longer saw her. Nor did it ever occur to me to confide in anyone. My feelings, stifled by the orphanage, had begun to bloom when back in London and with the Pettits, but with evacuation to Ely, at my loneliest, I didn't even know I was lonely. I hid all feeling from others and from myself. My heart had once more frosted over, except that I longed to be beautiful. I thought that beauty would make me lovable. Every day I searched my face in the small mirror I'd bought in Woolworth's. Was I pretty? No. My face was more intriguing than pretty: upturned green-gold eyes, a short nose, a long upper lip I resembled Wendy Hiller.

One day Bill just disappeared. Had he left her or been shipped out? Did he have a wife and was only 'leading her up the garden path'? Norma walked around red-eyed. I didn't dare ask why, though when we passed, she looked me full in the face, as if she was bursting to talk. If only I had said, 'What happened to Bill?' she would probably have been glad to talk to me. I was afraid of seeming nosy. I think that since I was quiet and serious, she saw me as a younger sister in whom she could have confided. I never saw her speak to her parents. Mr Barnard, except for meals, was always at the pub with his friends; Mrs Barnard with a secret bitterness, only spoke to call us to meals. I wished after, I had said, 'Norma, what happened to Bill?' But I was afraid to intrude, and waited uselessly for her to confide in me.

The next day was so momentous that I forgot about my only friend. I found a clear round, red spot, vivid against my white knickers. I went to Mrs Barnard who as usual stood crouched over the kitchen sink, mouth a straight bitter line, scraping carrots that sounded as though her skin was being scoured. For the first time, I spoke to her and showed her my knickers.

'I don't know where this blood comes from, I'm not cut and nothing hurts me,' I said. For once she spoke to me. 'Put this in your knickers until the blood stops,' she mumbled in a monotone, handing me a white piece of cotton wadding.

That was my introduction to menstruation. True I had seen Mummy boiling those bloody towels, and true I heard Miss Menzies expound about the awful girl who had put a bloody napkin under the bed and giving London evacuees a bad reputation, but I didn't connect either of these with my own spot of blood. Well where did you put the bloody thing? Miss Menzies never did tell us, nor did Mrs Barnard. There was no one I dared ask. English people were trained not to talk about bodies at all unless ill. And then you only spoke to doctors or intimates. I had no intimates. It didn't occur to me to write and tell Mummy or to ask Norma about my bloody spot. I only spoke to Mrs Barnard about it because I thought I'd cut myself but couldn't see where. It was alright to talk about cuts. After the first spot of blood there was no more. It was very mysterious. I took the nearly clean napkin, wrapped it in newspaper, put it in the dustbin and washed the blood out of my knickers. I'd begun my period. I now felt grown-up.

'But where do I get sanitary napkins for the next time?' I whispered to Rita Gillis, and she pointed me to Woolworths, our Mecca. I went into Woolworths, shuffling along its bare, wooden floors, looking around furtively in case a boy or man should see, I whispered across the counter, 'sanitary towels please', paid, surreptitiously stuffed the package in my school satchel, ran out like a thief, and hid them in my drawer under my blouses. If the terrible twins found sanitary napkins they'd ask a million questions and tease me to death. Never having had sisters or brothers, growing up in institutions and foster homes, I did not take teasing in stride. I wished I could have confided in Norma, but because her eyes were red-rimmed, I didn't.

I decided she must have found out that Bill was married (I didn't know whether he was or wasn't but as he ignored me I thought the worst of him) and she'd told him to leave. That didn't mean she didn't miss him. Perhaps he'd been shipped abroad. Soldiers moved a lot. I saw few Tommies. I felt sorry for her but didn't know how to console her. No one had ever consoled me, nor had I seen consolation. How did you do it? After two weeks, her reddened eyes paled, but she lost her excited smile, her special giggle and bounce. I was sorry to see Norma, the only happy Barnard so sad. The whole family, except for rascally looking Mr Barnard was sad.

One day, Moira, the Irish Jewish girl who was still billeted at the Lupsons called for me. 'Tomorrow is Yom Kippur. We don't eat all day. If you like I can take you to shul, to a synagogue. The London Jewish Boys' Free School is evacuated to Ely on Barton Square. They have Yom Kippur services. Want to come with me?'

'Thanks,' I said. I didn't know what Yom Kippur was. Except for Aunt Mitzi's wedding I'd never been in a synagogue. And that was not for services. I knew more about churches and Christian hymns, but knew nothing about Jewish religion. Although religious, my grandparents had never offered me a bite of food let alone invited me for a meal, had never taken me to a synagogue or taught me the first thing about Judaism. My parents practiced nothing except that Mummy bought kosher food because Booba made her, lit candles on Friday evenings with no explanation, then went to work in the shop. I couldn't have cared less about religion, but welcomed anything that broke the utter tedium of Ely. Five minutes after passing the one squared High Street, the view turned into vast, flat stretches of grass, trees and the River Ouze. There was no one to talk to, nothing to see, no music or wireless, no one to touch or hug, kiss hello or goodnight or goodbye, and nothing interesting ever happened as it did in the shop at home, or with my relatives in London. Foster parents' children received all the attention while I, as an evacuee, was ignored or treated as a nuisance. I was bored to death in Ely and had a personal feud with Ely Cathedral. Miss Winifred Fry took us on gushing 'historical' tours of the cathedral, slathering over Ethelred the Unready's flat stone tomb on the cathedral's floor, on top of which lay his statue, arms piously folded over his stone cold chest, his wife likewise entombed in stone, piously praying next to him even while dead as a doorknob. I knew every tomb and stone inside Ely Cathedral and the poor man hanging nailed up to two pieces of wood. Everything in it was dead. I longed for laughter, chatter, for touch, talk and companionship.

So when Moira invited me to a Yom Kippur service, I immediately said 'Yes'.

Moira and I walked a long way to the outskirts of Ely. Nevertheless, huge Ely Cathedral loomed over us at the interstice of every building as if it were following us. Miss Fry had told us repeatedly that nothing held it together. While this might be an engineering miracle I constantly worried that the monster would fall apart on me, but there was no escape from it.

Finally, we came to a large country house called Old Hereward Hall in Barton Square. A sign outside said 'Jewish Boys' Free School'.

In front of the house sprang thick grass, poppies and tall, lush trees. A pretty girl of about 14, with long, dark wavy hair, pale skin and dark eyes, wearing a brilliantly flowered prewar dress, sat high in the fork of a tree. Below her, three boys of about 14 to 16 stood gazing up at her like bears that had found a pot of honey but didn't know how to reach it. She smiled down at them mischievously.

'If anyone wants me, come up and get me,' she said, in a clear voice, and laughed a tinkly laugh. I gasped. How daring she was! Would I ever be that sophisticated when I was 14? The boys looking foolish didn't know what to do but stare up at her. Moira, solemn, ignoring all, entered the white-painted house fronted by a bay window. I followed.

Inside, we came to a spacious front room, bright from sunlight still pouring through its enormous windows. The room was cleared of all furniture, its walls painted clean white. About 100 men and boys were, I thought, praying. Some swayed from side to side, some from front to back, some stood still, faces buried in books; some turned eyes beseechingly toward heaven. Some wore a white, black striped shawl over their shoulders. All wore a small round cap on their heads. There was a babble of manly, pleading voices. It was all arresting. I stared.

When I was five, I'd had a few sessions in Hebrew school, but when Moira gave me a prayer book, I found to my surprise that I remembered the Hebrew letters and could read, if slowly. The Hebrew was on the right, English on the left side of the book. While Moira was *davening*, reading the Hebrew prayers with heartfelt devotion, I whiled away the time reading the English next to the Hebrew and admiring the boys.

One boy stood out among the others. Taller than all the others, slender, and with large, dark eyes and dark, curly hair, he prayed passionately, with his whole body and soul. I'd never seen passion in a man before. His, entranced me.

'Who's that tall boy?' I whispered to Moira.

'Joseph Singer,' she said, 'Shush.'

Suddenly all the boys and men fell down on their knees and elbows and bowed their heads to the floor. Moira and then I, following suit, also fell to the floor.

'What are we looking for?' I whispered to Moira.

She looked at me with pity. 'We're bowing to God, only one time in the year on our hands and knees, asking forgiveness for our sins,' she hissed, our faces pressed to the floor. Through no fault of my own, I was truly ignorant about Judaism.

'What is this place?' I asked Moira during a break in the praying.

'It's a Jewish boys' refugee hostel. These boys escaped from the Nazis to London. They're alone here; their parents couldn't get out. Well, some could get out, but most countries wouldn't let them in. Most of them don't know if their parents are dead or alive.'

I looked at Joseph Singer with compassion. Alone without parents. Poor boy. If only I could comfort him. He was so handsome. Immersed in prayer, he didn't once look in our direction. How I admired him!

The next day, Moira and I stayed there fasting and praying the whole day. Well Moira prayed and I looked about me fascinated with this new world of boys, men, fasting and passionate praying. Since leaving London, there had been no passion in my life. Moira had brought me back to it. Moira had taught me to give up bacon, and now, like her, I fasted all day. Not a drop of food or water had passed my lips. This formed a bond between Moira and me. In Moira, I had finally found someone with principles. I'd never met anyone with principles; a code of ethics, devotion to a higher power. I wanted to be like Moira. And I wanted desperately to know Joseph Singer and for him to know me. Mine was a most innocent crush on a handsome and spiritual young man. I loved what he represented: devotion, commitment, passion and responsibility, all the qualities missing from my life. And he belonged somewhere, I did not.

When I returned to the Barnards that evening and had eaten, I thought long and hard about Joseph Singer. He reminded me of that little scamp in kindergarten, also called Joseph Singer, who during a school play in which I played the Queen, had pulled the chair from under me before I sat down. But it couldn't be the same boy grown up, because the earlier Joseph Singer was an East End-born English Jewish boy and this one was a refugee. I loved this refugee Joseph Singer and all he stood for, on sight.

The next night I sat on my bed in the little attic room, and by candlelight, dipped my pen in ink and wrote in my best handwriting:

'Dear Joseph:

You don't know me, but I think you are the most wonderful boy I've ever seen. I am an evacuee, and live on Chandler Street. Your admirer.

I put this missive in an envelope and licked it shut. I wrote his name on the outside. I wasn't going to post it. That would take too long. I had to tell him how I felt immediately. It was about 10 o'clock. Everyone in the house slept. I crept out, closing the unlocked door, quietly. Save for the searchlights scouring the skies for German planes the streets were dark, silent and deserted. Even the skies were deserted; no planes, neither our Spitfires nor enemy Junkers or Messerschmitts tonight flew overhead.

Swiftly, I sped like an arrow through dark, deserted streets to the refugee boys' hostel. Their door stood wide open. Everyone left their doors unlocked then, even in London. This presented a problem. How could I drop my letter through the letter box if the door was open? A mat lay on the floor just inside the open door. I was afraid to go inside in case someone caught me loitering in a boys' hostel. We evacuees were not supposed to be out at night at all. Girls were forbidden to speak to boys or men. The longer I stayed, the more danger there was that someone still awake might see me. This refugee house was silent, everyone asleep. The only sound was my heart beating as I stood indecisively on that mat, staring into the pitch black hostel, wondering what to do with my letter. Should I take it back or leave it on the mat?

I thought I heard footsteps. Taking a daring step, I dropped my letter on the doormat inside the front door and ran all the way home. I didn't see a soul en route. When I entered, the Barnards' the house was as still and quiet as I had left it. I removed my shoes and crept stealthily through Beryl and Roger's room into my own, closing the door with agonising slowness so as to make no sound, I undressed silently and slid into bed. I had a wonderful dream about Joseph Singer holding me in his arms and saying, 'I love you, you're the only girl for me'.

Two days later Miss Menzies called me into her office.

'Why did you write Joseph Singer a letter?'

It was a stupid question. Obviously, because I liked him. I stood silent and proud of my love. I was willing to suffer for it. I was the beautiful heroine in a film, being persecuted by an old spinster who had never known love.

'You will be sent to Coventry. You are not to speak to any girl nor is any girl in the school allowed to speak to you for two weeks. You are banned from assembly for two weeks. You may leave.'

I left, chin held high. They weren't going to break my spirit. Joseph Singer had probably received my letter by now and knew of my love. But it had been stupid of me to say I was an evacuee and which street I lived on. There was only one other evacuee on my street, Jocelyn Theilkuls. She was a *shiksa*, a gentile girl with a huge mop of wild, chestnut hair, totally flat-chested unlike most of us in the first form with our proud bosoms. Jocelyn wore enormous tortoiseshell goggles the lenses so thick you could hardly see her eyes and she was a swot, spending all her time studying, never wasted words, and looked at everyone as though at an insect under a microscope. There was no way the letter came from Jocelyn Theilkuls. It had to be me.

I bore my exclusion stoically. I was the beautiful heroine suffering for her love. During school breaks I wandered alone around our 'playground', the empty market square in front of Ely's one cinema, looking at pictures of Laurence Olivier and Hedy Lamar outside, trying not to look alone. But gradually, I noticed that although girls didn't speak to me as ordered, they circled me with a kind of awed respect in their eyes. I began to realise I was to them, a romantic plucky heroine. I had done something they'd dreamed of, but not dared do. They all seemed to know what I'd done; Miss Menzies must have told them a horror story as she had done about the sanitary napkin. She must have told them of my crime during morning assembly while exiled, I stood outside. I was already lonely. I couldn't get much lonelier, so being exiled hardly mattered. I wondered whether she had told the Barnards about the letter. They never mentioned it. Perhaps this event prompted Mr Barnard's behaviour toward me, later. I didn't think of telling Mummy.

Joseph Singer's Headmistress of the Jewish Free School also called me into her office. I hadn't realised he was still at school. He looked as if he were 17 or 18. Children could then leave school at 14. Some had to; their parents couldn't afford to send them to our paid high school. Some children couldn't pass the stiff high school entrance examination. Apparently, Joseph Singer had passed, and probably had a scholarship. So my hero was intelligent, too. I was surprised a boys' school had a headmistress.

We girls all knew Joseph's headmistress, a short stout Jewish lady whom we called Old Sally Wetlegs. She was known to have a habit of saying, 'I do see your point,' which we dirty-minded little girls interpreted as her saying, 'I can see your little dickey,' though I had never even seen a dickey beyond an eighth of an inch tip sticking out of an East End ragamuffin's undershirt as he played barefoot in the street during summer. We nevertheless all burst into gales of laughter when we imitated Old Sally Wetlegs' 'I do see your point'.

I stood before Joseph Singer's headmistress. Old Sally Wetlegs gave me a long harangue ending with, 'You do see my point, don't you?' It was all I could do not to burst out laughing. Altogether I thought I must have done something pretty daring, since not one, but two headmistresses had called me into their offices. I felt quite proud. I was a grown up, experienced woman who knew how to express her love, the way Joan Fontaine had expressed it in *Rebecca*. Except everyone I didn't want to speak to had spoken to me, but I had yet to speak to Joseph Singer.

The two weeks' Coventry passed easily, there was no verbal exchange but there were many satisfying and knowing eye interchanges between the girls and myself and when it was over I had, without the subject ever being mentioned, several new, admiring friends.

I never did speak to Joseph Singer.

But as my period ushered me into womanhood, Moira's and Joseph Singer's passionate prayers revived my desire to belong, and slowly, later, ushered me into Jewish life.

CHAPTER 17

GIRLISH DIVERSIONS

This quiet cathedral town, Ely, was unbearably quiet for a London girl like me. I cordially hated it. My only escape from its boredom was to quietly leave school after lunch and see a film. Attendance was called only in the morning. The cinema was directly on the market square, a hop, skip and a jump from Archer House. Here, in the dark, watching Clark Gable, Lawrence Olivier, Vivian Leigh, Hedy Lamar and Greta Garbo I could dream of love.

Soon, there was another distraction from Ely's utter boredom. When the Allies finally began beating back the Germans in the summer of 1943, and hope soared that war would soon end, Ely began holding civilian Saturday night dances. Tommies and Yanks regularly held dances in their own canteens but Spitalfields forbade us even to speak to a soldier. Besides, I was regretfully under 16, some mysterious age under which we were forbidden to have dates. If only I were 16! Tommies treated us as children, but Yanks asked me out and I had to refuse.

However, one of the few pleasures our school did give us teenage city girls was weekly ballroom dances. We danced in Ely Corn Exchange, the only Ely building with a polished floor.

I was 14, Lily Cohen was 15. Watching Lily dance with other 15-year-old girls from her own class I saw her lead so well, I knew I would easily follow her. I imagined her dancing to the Big Bands in those enormous London ballrooms where Benny Goodman played, *In the Mood, Night and Day, These Foolish Things, Praise the Lord*, and *Pass the Ammunition,* or *Mister Watchacallit whatcha Doin' Tonight* starting softly then gradually building the sound to roaring full blast, dancers clapping and screaming as jitterbugging, they flung their bodies high and low.

If only Lily Cohen would choose me for a partner. Like most girls from Spitalfields, and like me, Lily Cohen was a Jewish East End girl: unlike me, a math whiz. Tall, big boned, strong, she was a terror on the hockey field. When I saw this 15-year-old-Attila the Hun with her 15-year old *zaftig* team thundering toward us from the other end of the field, slashing hockey sticks right and left like swords, threatening the lives of our smaller 14-year-old team, I dove into the bushes until the end of the game. No one seemed to miss me.

On the other hand, Lily was a wonderful ballroom dancer. Older girls, like Lily Cohen, contemptuously ignored younger girls, so I was honoured but nervous, when on the dance floor, Lily, face grim, thyroidal eyes bulging, bore down on me, wordlessly grabbed me round the waist, schlepped me close belly-to-belly like a Basque dancer, and swung me onto the floor. Just as I imagined a man would, she pushed and pulled me firmly as I, her willing slave, thrillingly and in perfect time, followed her every step.

I especially loved dancing the tango with Lily, our solemn cheeks pressed together, heads thrown back, eyeballs staring up at the ceiling, our two joined arms stretched forward, and her right hand firm behind my back, both of us sliding and swooping to *Jealousy*. As we danced, I sang under my breath to the *Jealousy* tune:

Leprosy, I think I've got leprosy,

There goes my eyeball; it just fell in your highball

Oh throw it back please will you?

Leprosy, I caught it in Tennessee

While I was dancing, with a girl from Paree.

I wasn't sure whether I'd learned the words somewhere, or made them up.

At the end of the tango, Lily, unsmiling, held out her left arm out while I 'dipped' on it so far backward that my hair touched the floor. Although we were supposed to remove school hats inside, Lily kept hers on; it sat on the back of her head like my bookie uncle's hat even while we danced.

'Lily keeps her hat on by willpower,' Miss Nureyev, our gym teacher in silky pleated shorts, said acidly.

I didn't care, as long as Lily danced with me. She was mine. I'd have killed anyone else she danced with. As she led me in a fox trot, waltz or tango, I'd shut my eyes and imagine I was tall, blonde, Ginger Rogers in the arms of tall, skinny Fred Astaire instead of being a brown-haired, petite, 14-year-old evacuee with minimal curves in the arms of…? I'd open my eyes to see Lily's bulbous, staring brown orbs, her stolid face, and school uniform hat stuck on the back of her head. Reality returned, and I was dancing in the arms of a muscular 15-year-old math whiz in Ely's Corn Exchange. If only I were two years older, I could dance with Tommies and Yanks in British or American army canteens.

Oh, the tragedy of being 14!

'Wanna go to a movie?'

'We're under 16," headmistress Menzies told us to say when herds of lonely Yanks drifting through Ely passed us herds of London evacuees. Miss Menzies never said why we should say we were under 16. We were amused and equally ignorant as to why, after we told them our age, Yanks scurried away looking worried.

By 1943, Ely finally joined the world and held weekly dances for civilians. Lily now spoke for the first time. 'There's a dance competition in Ely tonight. Want to enter?'

'Oh yes,' I breathed.

'Call for you seven sharp. Dress up,' she snapped.

That night I wolfed our tasteless boiled fish and spud supper and told the Barnards I had to meet a school friend (true) to study for a test (sort of). Secretly, I lipsticked forbidden red onto my mouth, spit on my eyelash brush, rubbed the wet brush into an old box of black mascara cake and stroking upward, I turned my long brown eyelashes to long black. I changed into my one rationed flowered dress and black-market two inch heels that Mummy had sent me, covered my clothes with my school coat, pulled the school uniform hat low over my face and ran outside. Surely, underneath the uniform I now looked 16?

In the dark yard, lit only by searchlights a man's silhouette appeared.

'Who's there?' I whispered. Searchlights lit up a man's silhouette.

'Lily?' I gasped. 'Who cut your hair?'

'Come on,' she said roughly, pulling me by the arm. 'I'm now Lawrence.'

'Where did you get a man's suit?'

'Borrowed from my older foster brother. Have to sneak it back.'

At Ely's dance, held in a church hall, Lawrence paid half-a crown for each of us and shoved me through the blackout curtain hanging over the door. Inside, bright lights scorched my eyes and I trembled with excitement as real, grown up men, also Tommies, RAF's, Yanks, Aussies all with lady partners whizzed round the floor waltzing to a band playing Strauss' *Blue Danube*. I'd learned to play it with an unemployed silent film pianist, just before war broke out. Lawrence swirled me fast round the entire edge of the crowd, firm hand on my back as an MC tapped couples on the shoulder: 'Out!'

The music changed to a fox trot, a polka, and Lawrence and I danced every dance. The band played a jitterbug. Lily, big and strong, slung petite me over her shoulder, between her legs, showing my black-market satin knickers at which sight women jealously sighed 'Ooh!'

Only two couples now stood on the floor, when the band struck up *Jealousy*.

'A tango,' I breathed.

Lawrence's thyrodic eyes glittered briefly as he swung me into our most exotic tango steps ending in an extravagant dip, me, arched backward over his strong hockey arm, my head and throat flung all the way back like a ballerina's.

Rising when the music stopped, we found that we were last on the floor and everyone was wildly clapping, cheering and whistling.

'You've won a war bond and a box of chocolates for the lady,' announced the MC. I wasn't sure which one of us was the lady.

'Thank you,' I said, in case Lily's voice gave us away.

Lily bowed and I curtsied to the crowd. Clutching our war bond and precious chocolates, we rushed from the hall like two Cinderellas, two teenage schoolgirls forbidden by our school to be out at night. If discovered, the dance MC would have confiscated our prizes and at school: scandal, lectures, 'sent to Coventry', no girl allowed to speak to us, nor Lily and I to each other for three months; or we could be expelled.

My foster parents didn't care when I left or returned to the house or where I went.

We scampered to Lily's foster-home, sat down outside it on the stone curb in the dark and ravished the whole box of chocolates, our first for years. Lilly kept the war bond. She drew her school clothes out of the bushes, changed into our uniform and glided, swathed momentarily by searchlights, into the pitch-black house.

Lily never alluded to our escapade. However, during this long, six-year war, even if I danced only once a week in Lily's arms, her bulging eyes fixed in space, and Bookie hat on the back of her head, I felt for a brief time, that I belonged somewhere.

Sunday's tedium was also broken one day by Yvonne de Bled. Yvonne, a year my senior, was the acknowledged school princess. At 15, she was blonde, blue-eyed, with perfect white skin, round breasts, a tiny waist, and long, shapely legs. She wore the fashionable pageboy-style blonde hair turned under from ear to ear, not a hair out of place. Every girl in school admired, and tried to befriend her, but her blue eyes remained aloof. This made her mysterious. We lonely, young high school girls often developed innocent crushes on older girls like Yvonne.

Yvonne had transferred from some other school, perhaps even from Belgium, the rumour went, and though a year older than our form, she was scholastically a year behind, so Miss Menzies put her into our class. Because of the clothes' ration, transfer students didn't have to buy our school uniform. Yvonne wore her own, perfect 'civilian' clothes instead of our heavy shirts, ties, gym tunics and thick brogues that hid our beautifully developing curves. Yvonne's figure in the hand-knitted lavender cardigan and skirt, the sweater clinging to her full breasts and small waist, was the envy of all younger girls. The girls in our class so adulated her that while adoring Yvonne we didn't pay much attention in class, so even though she wasn't ready for it, Miss Menzies moved her into the class ahead. This was where she should have been in the first place.

This dream girl had never spoken to me, so I was amazed when one day she slid at my side in the street and asked, 'Would you like to go for a walk with me on Sunday?'

'Y-y-yes,' I stuttered, overwhelmed at the honour bestowed on me by the Princess.

'Call for me at four,' she said and walked off.

Though I had never been to her house, everyone knew where this exalted person lived. When the clock drew near to four on Sunday afternoon, I dashed to the door.

Almost trembling with awe I knocked on Yvonne's door precisely at four. Her foster mother's house, considering a princess lived in it, seemed as dull as mine.

'Goodbye,' Yvonne called back over her shoulder, to someone I couldn't see, probably her foster mother. As she came through the screen door, her beautiful lavender sweater clinging to her pretty bosom, I felt silly in my blouse, tie and gym tunic. I had grown out of my one pretty dress and had only the stodgy uniform to wear. As we walked, Yvonne neither looked at me nor spoke to me. I couldn't help but wonder why, among all her admirers, she had chosen me to accompany her.

I didn't know where we were going, and just blindly followed this Princess. Princess stared straight ahead. I was so basking in the honour of having this sought-after girl ask humble me to go for a walk with her that I didn't notice in which direction we were walking. Then I realised we were going to Ely Park, a big, hilly park in front of the monster Ely Cathedral.

Ely Cathedral loomed over the Park beside a lake; many green hills rose throughout the park, each dotted with brown cow dung patties left by some 20 free roaming cows. One of the few girlish pleasures we younger girls enjoyed was rolling down the park's green slopes, skillfully twisting our bodies, dodging cow patties, always landing at the bottom of the hill, triumphantly unsullied. It took special practice to arrive at the bottom of the hill clean. Yvonne, so perfect would have been disgusted had she known how we younger girls amused ourselves.

Yvonne and I entered the park. A group of tall boys aged about 16 stood at the top of the tallest hill. They were exquisitely dressed in the cashmere wool uniform of the Ely Cathedral Boys' High School. These boys, with their well cut grey flannels and blazers and their thick, blond hair looked the way I imagined upper class gentile Englishmen appeared. I had never spoken to one of them. The boys stood on top of a hill like kings and princes, chatting and languidly playing conkers in pairs. Paul, whose blazer jacket I had mischievously tugged at the market on my first day in Ely and the most handsome, lorded all, at the centre of the group.

One boy in each pair held a conker or chestnut pierced through the middle and threaded onto a tough string. A knot at the bottom of the string stopped the conker from slipping off. Paul stood still with his conker hanging down from the string in a plumb line while another boy swung his own conker against Paul's, and tried to smash it. Paul whirled his conker by the string, to strike another boy's. Paul looked up a moment to smile at Yvonne below.

'Come on, Paul, old boy, don't take all day,' his partner said.

Yvonne waved to Paul, and without breaking her stride, or speaking to me, she made a beeline up the hill to him. Paul took time to smash his opponent's conker, took possession of it, and then turned to greet Yvonne with his white, lazy smile.

So this was the goal of our 'walk'. I was simply a decoy so her foster-mother let her out.

Yvonne and Paul spent the next hour together on the grassy slope under ancient leafy oaks, heads close, frequently bursting into laughter. I sat alone and bored at the bottom of the hill as cows ambled about dropping fat, steaming cowpats.

I'd been an idiot to be taken in by Yvonne's sudden friendship. Why should a princess suddenly befriend a lowly peasant if not to use her? Her foster mother probably knew about Yvonne's popularity with boys, and had forbidden her to go out. Yvonne had used me, pretending to her foster mother that she was going for an innocent walk with a girl. I wouldn't have minded had the Princess told me, or made any attempt to speak to me, but she'd totally ignored me.

After an hour I saw her look at her watch and at Paul. No doubt her foster mother had told her to be home for sanctified British teatime at 4pm. I sauntered up the hill with a smile.

'Isn't it time to go,' I asked.

As she looked at her watch again, I slid behind her and shoved her hard down the slope.

Yvonne, unpracticed like we 14-year-olds in how to swing around cow dung patties, wailed as gathering momentum, she rolled over every possible brown cow dung patty. By the time she reached the bottom of the hill, her perfect creamy skin, blonde hair and lilac sweater and white skirt were plastered with stinking brown cow dung from head to foot.

'I'll tell your foster mother you clot,' she screamed, as Paul burst into laughter.

'Why don't you call for me sometime,' I said, and skipped home.

At least this Sunday, Ely had not been such a colossal bore.

CHAPTER 18

DEATH IN THE FAMILY *

January 1941. Snow fell relentlessly like linen sheets that covered Ely Cathedral. The River Ouze became one sheet of ice. But even ice-skaters swirling gracefully failed to cheer me. I hated being evacuated to Ely.

No one from London wrote to me except Mummy. Daddy had written only once in the two years I'd been evacuated, but had scrawled at the bottom, 'Don't answer this, and do not tell your mother I wrote to you'.

Why was a child, especially an only child forbidden to write to her own father? I didn't know, and didn't dare ask Mummy. Daddy had asked me not to tell. We had moved out of the small flat over the Michaels' shop into a shop with our own house over it. Mummy wrote:

122 Vallance Road
Bethnal Green
London, E.2.
12. 3. 1941
Dear Gilda,

It's bitterly cold, snowing almost every day. The war news is very depressing. Thousands of soldiers, sailors and airmen are daily being killed, wounded or missing in action. Every single night the Germans bomb us to smithereens. The windows and roof have fallen in but thank God no direct hit. In any case I refuse to go to a shelter. If I'm going to die, I'll die in my own bed.

If the Germans invade England, don't tell anyone you are Jewish. Go and live with gentiles.

I didn't understand why she wrote that if the Germans invaded I should say I was not Jewish. She'd been complaining that I was becoming like a *shiksa*, a Christian girl. Now she wanted me to pretend to be one if the Germans invaded. What did she want me to be? As usual, she'd enclosed a pound note. She always sent money.

A month later, out of the blue, Mummy suddenly appeared at the Barnard's front door. It was the first time she'd visited me during the two and a half years I'd been evacuated. She wore a brown wool coat, with little fox furs draped round her throat, the beady eyes of which seemed to stare at me inquisitively; their little mouths foolishly clamped onto their tails. As if a smart fox would be caught looking so silly. A brown felt slouch hat, which she nervously kept tugging down, sat low over black mascaraed lashes. Mummy blinked away tears.

My foster-parents, the Barnards, in spite of the cold and her two-hour journey from London did not invite her in. There was nowhere to go on a Sunday; even Ely's one tea shop, Lamb's, closed on Sundays. We walked alongside Ely Cathedral that loomed over the iced river, but could not even sit on the benches. The benches were so totally encased in ice that they glittered like Christmas presents lacking only a red ribbon and a sprig of holly. Had we tried to sit on them, we would have slithered off. In any case it was too cold to sit. Mummy and I faced each other, eyes tearing from cold and misery.

Nearby, blond, British boys from local elite Ely Cathedral High School in their elegant pale grey caps, blazers and trousers, red cheeked, Paul among them, hurled snowballs at each other, target hits punctuated with gleeful, boyish yells.

Mummy's breath streamed out white like the steam from Daddy's hot towel machine. Why had she come after so long? Finally, she spoke.

'I came to tell you your Uncle Adrian is dead. There was an explosion in his laboratory. He was blown up.'

Just then, Paul slammed a hard, ice-packed snowball into my bare nape, the blow jolting me forward in the snow to my knees. I burst into tears, whether from news of Uncle Adrian's death, the icy snowball, Paul's perfidy or all, I didn't know. Mummy ignored my tears. Although we had not met for two years, she'd neither hugged nor kissed me.

'He was working on a secret chemical formula. It could have been sabotage, we don't really know. Aunt Mitzi is pregnant, she's expecting Adrian's child. She wants to marry Raphael, her boss's son. You know she's been in love with him for years, even before Adrian.'

'Well, why didn't she marry him instead of Adrian?' I said, rising from my ignominious position and sniffling. Had Mummy come to Ely just to tell me about Uncle Adrian's death? I was deeply sorry he'd died, but she could just as well have written it in her last letter. I thought that after two years away, she'd come to see *me*. She hadn't kissed or touched me, even when Paul's snowball drove me to my knees and I'd wept hot tears. Shortly, she'd say, 'I have to catch my train,' run to Ely's station, return to exciting London and forget me the way she'd visited, and then tried to leave me in the orphanage when I was five. She broke into my thoughts.

'I told you. Raphael's family is wealthy; they wanted a girl with money. Your Aunt Mitzi hadn't enough *nadn* so his family forbade the marriage. However, with government compensation from Adrian's death, Mitzi will have enough *nadn*. Isn't it ironic? Only problem is she's pregnant.'

'Why is that a problem?' I asked, like the innocent I was.

'Well of course she doesn't want to go into a new marriage with another man's baby,' Mummy said scornfully, as if to an idiot. 'Aunt Mitzi asked me to help her get an abortion.'

'What's an abortion?' I asked, still feeling even more stupid.

'It gets rid of the baby so it's never born. It's not legal. Somehow Booba heard about it, came round to the house and knocked on my door. I didn't know why she came, she doesn't visit me much.' I forbore to make a comparison. 'I open the door, give her a big smile, and what do you think she does?'

'What?' I asked since it seemed I was supposed to.

'She smacks me hard across the face,' here Mummy began to sob, 'and she says to me, "how dare you try to murder my grandchild, I never want to see you again," and she storms off'. Tears dropped from Mummy's eyes turning to ice and falling to icy ground with tiny clashes.

'The abortion wasn't even my idea, it was Mitzi's. I always get the blame in my family. Mitzi can do no wrong and I can do no right.'

I felt sad. I hadn't been close to Uncle Adrian, still, I liked him. He was young, handsome, clever and happy, and he'd always spoken to me kindly, and as if I were a grown-up.

Mummy was speaking to me as if I were a grown-up. She seemed to want my sympathy, but wasn't it usually the child who came to the mother for sympathy? No one in the family had ever offered, nor had I thought to ever ask anyone for sympathy. But I saw that now my mother had no Mummy or family, and only a deaf husband who despised her family, to turn to. I was her only family. Whenever hurt, I never expected their sympathy so I didn't know how to show it. I had shown Violet sympathy when I slapped Mary, the bully, in the orphanage; but when Mummy finally came to the orphanage, making her take me home had been so important, I hadn't stopped to comfort my weeping friend, Violet.

'I have to catch the next train back,' Mummy now said, as usual.

The local boys had gone home to roaring fires, tea, toast and jam and their families. Alone, stiff with cold, I left the frozen park and canal and trudged back through Ely's deserted streets to the Barnards. Gigantic Ely Cathedral loomed like a grey cloud through every space between buildings. Mummy had stayed an hour and then left, back to the bustle, the warmth of London and the East End. I wished I could have gone with her but remembered the *whumping* sound of the bombs, the one night I'd visited. That was why I was in 'Timbuktu' (which is what we called any primitive place far from London).

As I walked back alone to the Barnards, I kicked snow, head bent low, hair falling into my eyes, I longed for someone to love, or for some creature who would love me.

Then I remembered. Jocelyn Theilkul's foster mother had kittens to give away. If only I could have a kitten like Binkie, some creature to cuddle and call my own and that would love me whether I were beautiful or not. I'd had no word from my idol, Joseph Singer. Perhaps he'd been forbidden to contact me. Perhaps he'd never read my letter. A kitten would ease my loneliness.

Arriving home, I saw Mrs Barnes bent over her sink scraping carrots. 'Jocelyn Theilkul's foster Mother's cat has had kittens. There's an adorable black one. May I have it?'

Morosely scraping carrots at the sink, to my surprise, she nodded her head once.

I immediately ran across the street and banged Jocelyn's knocker.

Jocelyn's skinny body, giant mop of curly hair and thick glasses appeared round the door opening. Even though it was Sunday she wore our hateful school uniform tunic, tie and blouse.

'What?' she said looking down her nose through her thick glasses. Jocelyn could say 'what' as if it were an insult.

'My foster mother says I can have a kitten.'

Without a word, Jocelyn turned her back on me, returned and shoved in my hand a tiny ball of black fur, one white spot between her eyes, about six weeks old. The kitten mewled.

'Oh, she's darling,' I said, and cradled her, so soft and needy, to my breast. She soon snuggled against me, purring. Jocelyn who lacked sentiment of any kind, anxious to get back to her swotting, a star student, shut the door in my face. I didn't care. I was thrilled with my sweet little kitten, a warm, breathing creature on which I could shower my love and which in turn would love me.

The snows cleared, the days were now almost spring-like. The Barnard's only beautiful possession, the lilac tree in their back yard, burst into sweet-smelling buds. I thrust my face into the buds and drank in their scent.

In the Barnard's yard, in front of the barrel of rain water – water in case the Nazis invaded – I tried to teach Binkie to jump over a stick, but she preferred racing round the yard, skidding to a stop, sticking her nose into the lilac tree's buds, tail high in the air, showing her tiny pink tongue that licked my face in the mornings and that lapped milk, in and out, in and out, in the afternoons. She was the happiest creature I'd ever seen, full of the joy of living. Just seeing her delight in life, I felt some pleasure seeping back into my old, 14-year-old dried-up veins. With spring, the sun shone and the kitchen door always stood open. Binkie now came into the house, raced over the back of the settee, pounced on invisible mice, skittered along polished floors, then lay head on paws in deep sleep. She was a darling puff of black fur that slept against my face at night, her minute body breathed warm against mine. If I put my fingers gently to it, I could feel her little heart beating. She was so tiny, so fragile. I was her protector, the first living creature that belonged just to me, that loved me and that I loved in all the nearly three long years I'd been evacuated; and she trusted me.

About two weeks later I came home from school and immediately ran into the yard to find Binkie. I didn't see her anywhere.

'Have you seen Binkie?' I asked Mrs Barnard, dour at the sink, peeling potatoes.

'Mr Barnard drowned her,' she said without looking up from her potatoes.

I went upstairs to my room. Fully dressed, I slid into my narrow bed and lay absolutely still. I thought of tall Mr Barnard sweeping my tiny Binkie up in one hand and carelessly dropping her into the full barrel of rain water that Norma said was so good to wash your hair in, and in case the Nazis invaded. I saw Binkie terrified as she splashed into the water with all four little legs outstretched, clawing desperately with tiny paws to find something, anything solid to hold on to. I heard her anguished mewling for help, saw her struggling for breath, gasping for air which only let in more water, her pink tongue hanging out, her little white teeth wide open with fear, her beautiful soft fur sopping wet and dragging her down, down into that hateful barrel of water, her lungs filling. I saw Binkie sinking to the bottom, my innocent little kitten who had so joyously loved life, still, on the bottom of that hateful barrel.

Why had he drowned her? Had she torn the settee? Drank too much of the milk ration? She could have had mine. If they hadn't wanted her any more why hadn't they at least let me try to find another home for her? They'd given me a taste of joy, some solace during this horrible war, then as abruptly snatched it away. Mrs Barnard had told me so casually, so brutally, of the kitten's drowning. She knew how I loved Binkie. The kitten was so full of love and life, dour Mrs Barnard couldn't stand watching her happiness. I couldn't cry; my heart lay like stone under my ribs.

I heard the click of the iron latch on my bedroom door, but didn't look to see who had come in. I didn't care. A tall figure loomed over me, darkening the room.

'I expect you're upset about your kitten,' Mr Barnard said pleasantly, as if he were saying, 'It's tea time.' He'd never before entered my bedroom.

I lay dumb, still as a corpse, but then looked up at him towering six foot four over me like monster Ely Cathedral. I stared him full in the eye. I didn't cry. I hadn't cried since I was five except at Cable Street and when Mummy told me of my uncle's death and the icy ball felled me.

As I lay under my blanket Mr Barnard looked slowly over the length of my body. He wore his neat grey suit with the waistcoat and the gold watch and chain, looking so respectable. What did he want? Was he going to apologise for killing my kitten? It wouldn't help. She was dead. My kind uncle Adrian and sweet kitten Binkie had both been killed, both lives snuffed out.

'Stand up,' Mr Barnard said, very softly.

Children were taught complete obedience to adults. I stood.

He was six foot four and I was five foot one. Even sitting he stared down at me and his body began trembling all over. Whatever was wrong with him? Did he have a cold or a temperature? Seated, legs apart, standing me between his knees, he pulled me closer. Why? Was he going to hug me and try to make me feel better because he'd drowned Binkie? He put a shaking hand up my skirt and stroked the inside of my bare thighs. His hand wandered higher than my thigh and clutched me. He was shaking and panting, fingers trembling.

I was strong, and furious that he'd drowned Binkie. With all my strength I shoved him back, wrenched myself away from his hateful hand and flew down the stairs, out of the house and into the yard. The twins were playing hopscotch there, jumping in and out of chalk squares as I dashed between them nearly knocking them over. My face must have been crimson.

'What's wrong?' Beryl asked curiously.

'Your grandfather put his hand up my skirt,' I blurted, running into the street.

Next day, the billeting officer came and took me away from the Barnards. No one ever discussed the incident with me. It never occurred to me to tell Mummy or some adult. The Barnards probably told the billeting officer I'd caused too much trouble with the kitten and had to go. In fact, my next foster-mother, Mrs Gotobed, my sixth or seventh, a widow who believed her dead husband visited her every night, accused me of 'having caused trouble' at the Barnards. 'You'd better behave here. I won't stand for any nonsense,' she said by way of greeting.

Although I didn't like the Barnards except for Norma, who had disappeared, being moved from the Lupsons, four or five other foster-parents and then from the Barnards made me feel even more unwanted than I felt before evacuation. Mummy had continually sent me away before the war, and now, during war, every foster parent but for the Pettits had sent me away.

I felt so alone. I must be totally unlovable. But who needed love?

I didn't need anyone. Neither would they get me down. But although I didn't like the Barnards, except for Flo, being moved through no fault of my own made me feel as though the injustices of wartime were some sort of skin affliction. Scabies itched, you scratched and they bled then they turned you out for bleeding, the way Mrs Gotobed did when I caught scabies.

No one wanted me. I had a mother and father, four grandparents, five uncles, no, now four uncles, two aunts, but no family; I'd suffered two deaths in one week, and I'd survived. I was strong. But my spirit, like Binkie's, was sinking into the deep water. A spark of resistance reminded me I was a tough, British, East End cockney. Churchill had said, 'We shall *never* surrender'.

Now, in 1943, we Allies were winning the war. An evacuee, I would fight on, winning my own war against adults. I would survive not because of, but in spite of adults. Come spring, like the lilac tree in the Barnards' dirt yard, I would bloom again.

CHAPTER 19

WHITE HOUSE REFUGEE HOSTEL

For a while, the Germans stopped bombing London. Many London parents thinking the war was ending brought their children home. We did not then know that the lull was because the Nazis were preparing to invade England while killing millions of Jews in concentration camps.

So many Spitalfields High School girls left Ely and returned to London that the evacuated Ely branch of the school closed. I joyously returned home. I was now 14, blossoming into a young woman. Of course, I was also delighted in thinking that war was ending, and that my strongest wish, to return to London and my family had come true. Since I had begun high school while it was evacuated to Ely, I'd never entered my real, London, Spitalfields High School building, though I had often, before the war, adored nearby Spitalfields market.

The open market without walls or doors, just poles on which rested a tarpaulin cover, allowed us to see inside, green apples, oranges, purple grapes, red tomatoes, green beans and peas, white onions, all fresh and glowing as if painted on a canvas. What a sight to see men walking gracefully like ballet dancers, balancing five or more round straw baskets of vegetables on their heads, not even using hands to keep baskets in place! The market opened about 5am, selling wholesale fruits and vegetables (though still rationed) to restaurants and hospitals, so that by school time at 9am its men were beginning to pack up. Now, the old and poor arrived to pick wilted and discarded vegetables off the stone floor or to buy damaged or surplus fruit and vegetables cheaply. Sometimes a compassionate wholesaler gave away free produce. Fruit from abroad was still rare as ships still served mainly war needs.

Although I was delighted to be home, Mummy grumbled, 'Your former bed in the upstairs dining room can't be used. Bombs smashed the windows, and the roof. The upstairs is full of debris. There's nowhere for you to sleep.' I didn't question Mummy's word about my bedroom's destruction nor how they passed through mine without falling over the debris, so I never even looked upstairs. But she had rented the downstair's spare room to two Polish Free Fighters, Polish airmen who had escaped Poland and formed their own army in England. I never found out what they did, because they stayed in their room all day. But they frightened me.

'Mees Moss, I not know you hev such big, pretty girl,' one said, looking at my breasts making me blush hot anger. They'd come again to our kitchen and knocked, 'to borrow sugar'.

Russians and Poles were the reason Booba and Zada had left Poland. They were known for killing Jewish men and raping women. So why did Mummy rent a room to Polish soldiers? It never occurred to me either, to ask Mummy to give me that room, nor to ask why she rented it at all. During wartime, hairdressing businesses boomed. Almost everything, food, clothing, silk stockings, coal, fuel was rationed except for hair care. The shop was busier than it had been before the war. So surely Mummy didn't need the money.

But I sensed that a girl of 14 with my now shapely figure was an embarrassment to her social life. Mummy, though cold to me, was witty and sociable and held nightly court in our kitchen crammed with friends. They drank tea, crunched biscuits, laughed amid the few bombs.

'You'll have to sleep on the kitchen couch,' Mummy said.

Mummy's friends had no compunction about sitting on top of me as I tried to sleep, chattering until one in the morning. At school, red-eyed, I was too tired to concentrate. However, I loved London, even its ruins, and looked forward to passing those cheerful Spitalfield men gracefully balancing baskets on their heads. Even their hand-woven baskets were a beautiful rich brown, a feast to eyes hungry for the brilliant red, green, yellow and gold colours of fresh fruit and vegetables amid khaki and blitzed buildings. Mornings en route to school, the men also greeted each other with, 'Wotcha cock!' and us girls with, 'Mornin' Miss'.

Booba had forbidden the whole family to speak to Mummy and me. To her, Mummy was a murderer. Aunt Mitzi must have told Booba that the proposed abortion of Adrian's child was Mummy's idea. The only family member who talked to us was Uncle Max. Much later he told me that he knew Mummy was the family scapegoat and Aunt Mitzi the favoured child, even though he was youngest and a boy. But Uncle Max in 1942 was far away, a soldier in Egypt, fighting Rommel, and when war ended, he stayed behind in charge of demobilisation of soldiers.

At night there were still a few bombing raids. First we'd hear the buzz, buzz, buzz, of the Messerschmitts, so unlike the steady, soothing roar of our Hurricanes and Spitfires. I'd only been through one night of bombing three years ago, so it came as a shock when one evening I went alone to see a film. Suddenly, the siren wailed, then bombs whumping, buildings crashing, and glass splintering with an almost pleasant tinkling sound. The screen turned pale grey as if the film stars had died and disappeared; and then it silently crumbled down to the stage. The screen crumbling and the terrible silence felt more ominous to me than a bomb. For a minute no one moved. But we walked silently to the nearest exit. During mass panic rushes to Underground shelter, if anyone fell, hundreds of others trampled the fallen to death. So we all walked slowly, single file out of the still cinema, even our footsteps muffled by the carpeting. Outside, I ran home, bombs falling, houses exploding. terrified of being blown to pieces or wounded for life.

Mummy rushed me into the coal cellar under the stairs. There we crouched, her body covering mine. I hated the new whistling bombs. They screamed as if tortured while coming toward London then there was a minute's dead silence when their engines cut off and then the bomb fell, exploding like thunder and lightning, killing 200 Londoners a night and finally, 60,000 Londoners, the majority Jewish. Then came another breathless, heart-beating silence until a doodlebug fell with a thunderous crash of buildings falling and people screaming. Our house shuddered. Finally, the all clear sounded. We crawled out of the coal cellar covered in coal dust.

Mummy now suddenly became concerned about my religion. 'You're getting too *goyish*,' she'd said, 'you're swinging your hips about, staying out late, wearing too much make-up, and eating all kinds of non-kosher chazer. You need a Jewish environment.'

'Isn't home a Jewish environment?' I dared ask.

'You're going to a Jewish refugee hostel.'

'I'm not a refugee, Mummy,' I protested. 'I was born in England; so were you.'

'You'll do as I say.'

Mummy had never before been concerned about my religious life. I didn't think it would have mattered to her had I become Christian. Since I was obviously blooming with vitality in spite of late nights, she could no longer claim I was pale and needed country air. I supposed I was ruining her social life. A 14-year-old girl would make her seem older. So now the stated reason for sending me away was 'because you're becoming Christian'. This was true, because I had never had a Jewish education before the war. Even before the war, Mummy had sent me away to Christian homes or orphanages. During the war, most Jewish education stopped.

Apparently, the only Jewish places in the country were Jewish Boys' Schools like the one Moira had taken me to for Yom Kippur in Ely, and where I had dropped my ill-fated letter to Joseph Singer, or Jewish refugee hostels.

One of the few and minor aids Britain provided during the Jewish mass slaughter in Europe was to accept 10,000 Jewish children refugees. Britain (and the US among many other countries) refused to take the other two million Jewish children so the Nazis killed them. Millions of Jews were denied entry to countries that could have saved them. The Nazis murdered them in cold blood. Poles, the French under Pétain, many Slavic, besides Arab countries gladly helped the Nazis. Even in Holland, a man reported Anne Frank to the Nazis who killed her. Britain occupied Israel and refused entry to desperate Jewish refugees on the very shores of Israel, heartlessly sending them back in boats to certain death. A few landed as shown in the film, *Exodus*. Roosevelt refused to bomb train tracks that carried millions of Jewish prisoners to death camps. 'This isn't a Jewish war,' Roosevelt and his anti-Semitic State Department, declared.

The relatively few children the British accepted forced European Jewish parents to make a terrible decision: to send their children away, even if the parents could not escape, knowing they might never see their children again. The *Kindertransport* was organised at short notice in 1939 shortly before war broke out to send 10,000 Jewish children under 14 out of Nazi Europe and into England. These 10,000 young children arrived in England days before Germany closed its doors and preferred to murder rather than let Jews (who could) leave the country. Why does a country that wants to be rid of any group not simply let them leave? Why do other countries not give asylum? Jewish organisations helped the few refugees and housed *Kindertransport* children in foster-homes or refugee hostels. Refugee children who had arrived in London were evacuated like British children and billeted with private gentile foster parents. Nunneries took in some, and converted many Jewish refugee children to Christianity. Some Christian institutions to their credit took in but did not destroy the children's religious identity. Child refugees of four or five were often too young to even know they'd ever been Jewish. A few found out years later.

There were about 30 Jewish refugee children's hostels all over England and Wales. Mummy chose one called The White House in a tiny village, Great Chesterford, in Essex, about 12 miles north of Cambridge and about two hours by train from London. I would be the only British Jewish child in the orphanage, once more, a stranger.

The only live human was the usual country stationmaster clipping on his bicycle clips over his trousers. As in Ely, one leg was already slung over his bicycle, to go home for his tea.

The landscape again stretched far, green and empty; nothing moved, there was that awful country stillness and silence that I so hated: no people, no houses or shops broke the endless flat, desolate land and there was no sound. I felt as deaf as my father. 'Can you tell us how to get to the White House, please?' Mummy asked the stationmaster, giving him her charming smile.

'Oh you be wanting them there refugees. There be only one road,' and he pointed it out.

We began to walk. Although it was only September, there was a cool nip in the air. England lay peaceful and green for miles around. Stretching green fields only meant to me loneliness as we crunched, me glumly, Mummy happily, along an empty stony path.

'You'd never know there was a war on, here,' Mummy said.

'Well we've had four years of rationing, blackouts, searchlights and evacuation.'

'You should be thankful you didn't have to go through the bombing,' Mummy said.

In the distance I could now see softly undulating green hills, and green farms, white farmhouses tucked away at the centre of little valleys. Slow-moving horses, sheep and cows grazed in the fields over which hung a light mist. It was picturesque, if you liked country, or if you were evacuated with your own family, or if you lived with a kind family like the Pettits.

Soon, we came to the church the stationmaster told us we'd pass. I grudgingly liked its rough, uneven stones and its blunt, square crenellations. This church would not tower over and follow me wherever I went, as had Ely Cathedral. We passed the one General Shop, closed, in which large window stood a rake, a pair of boots, a straw hat, and a burlap bag of potatoes. I imagined the pungent smell of damp sawdust on the floor and a side of salty bacon hanging inside. We passed a silent, old green-painted pub with green bottle bottoms for windows, like one out of a Dickens' story. It would never be interestingly rowdy like London cockney pubs.

Soon after the pub we came to a beautiful big white house, stone, with a contrasting dark brown, ark-shaped roof. Over the cheerful red door hung an old-fashioned pull-bell. At least, I thought, the house looked pretty. So had the witch's in *Hansel and Gretel*.

Mummy pulled the rope, and we heard the bell jangling inside. I hoped the house was as pleasant inside as it was out. I was tired of grungy foster homes, smelly kerosene heaters and cold foster parents; but I also worried about what the Warden and his wife would be like. I'd almost never lived with Jews. Would a Jewish warden and staff be as cold as Chingford orphanage's Sister and Nurse Harris or the Christian foster parents I'd lived with so far, cold, except for the Pettits? What were Jews like to live with? I didn't know any except my own family, and they were always fighting. Meanwhile, Mummy said, Mitzi had had the baby and married her true love, Raphael. Raphael had adopted the baby. I was no longer the only grandchild, or anyone's grandchild. The new baby, my aunt's, would now be the favourite.

In this hostel, I'd be the only British Jewish girl. Would these refugees accept a British-Jewish girl, or would they be unfriendly? Would I be a stranger my entire life?

The Times lay on the front step. I picked it up. 'Russians Whip Germans', said one heading. 'The Allies have Landed in Italy', said another. 'Bombing Tapers off. Evacuees Pouring Back into London by the Thousands.'

What was I doing here, then? I was being unloaded, an unwanted girl.

The door opened suddenly. A petite woman in her 30s with dimpled cheeks stood there, smiling. Her dark hair parted in the middle and fashionably rolled up all around below her ears, framed a heart-shaped face. Warm amber eyes above which soared thin, plucked, Marlene Dietrich eyebrows, smiled at us. A tiny boy of about two, with a mop of dark curly hair and huge dark eyes, peeped out from behind her skirts as he clutched her leg.

'I'm Mrs Shapiro. Do come in,' she said, smiling.

'You're so kind,' Mummy said charmingly, pushing her sharp-nailed finger in my back. Inside, we stood in a spacious, empty hallway, and opposite the front door behind us stood a fireplace in which glowed a warm, crackling fire. I'd never seen a fireplace in an entrance hall. The hall's ceiling soared above us, two stories high, its height only broken by an open-railed wood balcony running all around the entire first story. Behind the railed-in balcony, I glimpsed two open doors and some cozy beds reminding me of glimpses of Aunt Ellen's and her son's bedroom. The enormous hall, in which we stood, with its brightly burning fire, reminded me of the Beast's Palace, except that here there was no Beast. Perhaps this had been the home of a lord, or a great family. It was the third largest house I'd been in: Aunt Fanny's, the Chingford orphanage, and now this mansion. Surely, the floor had once been polished or carpeted but now it was simple, clean and bare wood.

Right of the entrance, a stately, curved staircase shone brightly, lit by two-story windows right of the staircase. I imagined the former mistress of the house sweeping gracefully down the stairs in her long, silken dress, dashing husband in evening dress behind her.

At the top of the staircase the balcony hung over the entrance hall fireplace. Older children aged 10 or 11 leaned over the balcony rail, watching Mummy and me as if they were a balcony audience watching us on a stage. I'd seen a balcony in the cinema when skipping school to watch films. The children's faces showed wide-eyed innocence and friendly curiosity. So far, this was a far warmer reception than I'd had in Chingford orphanage, or from most foster parents.

I also immediately wanted to explore this house with all its nooks and crannies. Looking up again, I saw to the right of the balcony a separate narrow winding staircase leading up to a third floor that I now knew led to an attic where the maids slept, and the nursery was kept. Although curious but wary of small flights of stairs and attics since my imprisonment in one, and fall down another, Mrs Shapiro's and the children's warm smiles promised friendliness.

However, I still had to meet the Warden. Would he be like Chingford's warden and say to Mummy, 'Quick goodbyes are best'? Mummy always left quickly anyway. And I was no longer a helpless infant, but a war-weary young woman, used to 15 or more different billets.

'Come into the study and have a cup of tea,' Mrs Shapiro said, putting her arm through mine. I was thrilled that she treated me like a grown-up and a friend rather than a nuisance.

She opened an oak door, and we entered a panelled study with a huge bay window that ran the entire width of the room. Light from an enormous garden that stretched endlessly outside flooded through this window, warming the severe oak paneling. A man wearing a grey suit, white shirt and navy tie sat in an armchair and, like my father, immersed his head in his book. He puffed contentedly on a pipe from which rose an aromatic scent. This man now stood, his thin face serious, his horn-rimmed glasses framing dark, intense eyes.

'This is my husband, Aaron Shapiro,' Mrs Shapiro said, looking at him with a melting, dimpled smile.

'How do you do; please sit down,' Mr Shapiro said to us, shaking hands with Mummy.

As he rose, I saw Mr Shapiro's deep chest and wide shoulders. His short hair fitted like a dark cap over his head on which he wore a little black velvet kipa, like those that had covered the heads of refugee boys and Joseph Singer in Ely during Yom Kippur services.

Mr Shapiro's dark eyes bored into mine as if he could see inside me. He looked a little like a Russian bear, like Dr Baumgarten, strong, courageous, and intense.

But his voice was gentle. 'How was your journey? Was the train packed with troops?'

'It was packed…' Mummy began, when someone rapped knuckles on the door. A tall lady of about 38 in a flowered dress, black hair long and loose as a Gypsy's, dark eyes pretty, but ringed with black circles, carried in a tray of tea and biscuits. I was glad adults didn't, as they had in the Chingford orphanage, wear stiff nurses' uniforms.

'This is Mrs Bramson, our cook,' Mrs Shapiro said.

Mrs Bramson smiled to Mummy, handed round tea and left, humming, 'Waltzing, waltzing, high in the clouds,' the latest Deanna Durbin song.

'Mrs Bramson's English; she was married to an American pilot shot down over Germany and killed. She's not really a cook; she's just helping us out during the war. It's hard to find help with most young women in the services, Land Army or on essential work,' Mrs Shapiro said.

I remembered Helen, an adult young woman who was billeted with me at Mrs Gotobed's foster home. Helen had been sent to Ely on some sort of secret essential work and always, after lunch, before returning to work, she went into the front room with the aspidistra and hammered out Rachmaninov's piano concerto that became Churchill's Victory signal. Ta ta ta tuuum.

'I'm so sorry to hear about Mrs Bramson's husband,' Mummy murmured, sipping tea. I drank mine gratefully, my tension ebbing away. True, this was another orphanage, but it seemed completely different from the cold Chingford orphanage. First, I was already in love with this graceful house. Second, since everyone was Jewish, I didn't have to worry about anti-Semitic children poking in my hair for horns; third, our welcome had been warm and friendly. Fourth, unlike the children at the old orphanage, the children here looked happy, friendly, well-fed, and unlike at Chingford, they chattered to each other. Mr and Mrs Shapiro seemed to love each other, and for once, I felt safe and protected. Like these refugees, I no longer had a family. Or I had one, but was exiled from it. Zada used to love me, but I hadn't seen him for years. Of course, these loved children wouldn't understand. I didn't understand it either.

Another knock on the oak door, and a young woman of about 20 bustled into the room. Seeing her nurse's uniform, I froze. But she was not tall, thin and sour-faced like Sister from the Chingford orphanage, but small and pleasingly plump. Her deep brown eyes shone brightly in creamy skin, her black, curly hair shone thick and glossy. As she smiled, showing sharp white teeth, she reminded me of a friendly, efficient beaver. Her blue uniform with its white apron didn't crackle coldly like Sister's, but sat softly on her small, plump body. Even the little white cap perched on her head seemed soft. The sun coming through the window caught the sparkle of a diamond engagement ring on her finger.

How normal everything seemed, a husband, wife, child, a widow, and a young fiancée.

'This is Nurse Rita,' Mrs Shapiro said.

'How do you do,' Nurse said with a strong foreign accent, shaking Mummy's hand with her own small one. I supposed she herself was a grown-up refugee working at the hostel.

'Now you have met our entire staff,' Mrs Shapiro said.

'How do you manage to keep the place so clean?' Mummy asked.

'The children all have *toranut* – duties,' Mr Shapiro said. 'They all make their own beds and are responsible for their own rooms. Older children take turns setting or clearing the tables, washing and drying plates and putting them away, peeling potatoes or vegetables. Each morning two older girls fetch the day's milk from the dairy. Three other big girls like you go to high school, so they are exempt from duties during the school year. But you'll have full duties during the school holidays,' he said, looking at me severely.

'Of course I want to do my share. Are there any other girls my age?' I asked.

Mrs Shapiro smiled. 'At 14, you're now the oldest. There are a few others aged 12 to 13. Three of them, Selma, Cookie and Helga, go to high school. There's no high school in Great Chesterford. The nearest high school is 15 miles away in Bishop's Stortford. You'll travel by train daily with Selma, Cookie and Helga. Since your own school, Spitalfields went back to London, you and Cookie will go to the local high school in Bishop's Stortford, Hertfordshire and Essex High School. Selma and Helga go to Skinner's High School, which didn't return to London and is still evacuated to Bishop's Stortford. The younger children here go to the local Great Chesterford Elementary School. If you need help with homework don't hesitate to come to me. I'll be happy to help you,' Mr Shapiro said.

'That's wonderful. I've needed help for so long. I'm totally lost in Math. Thank you.'

I did not know why my school work, so good before the war, had fallen, but I felt overjoyed with Mr Shapiro's offer to help me. No teacher offered to help girls who fell behind; we either sank or swam. I would so enjoy excelling in school again, as I had before the war.

'Come, I'll show you the big girls' room and introduce you to Selma, Cookie and Helga. They're usually in their rooms before supper,' Mrs Shapiro said, rising.

'I'd better be going to catch my train,' Mummy said, setting her cup down. 'Thank you so much for the tea,' she smiled, in the charming way she had with strangers. She kissed me on the cheek with her violet-scented mouth.

'I'll take you to the door,' Nurse said. I followed.

Just before she turned left at the corner, Mummy turned and waved her white lacy goodbye hanky as she had done so many times before. Her slim body once more disappeared like magic. At least the children of this orphanage, unlike Chingford's, saw that I had a real mother.

Tears rose to my eyes but I was now 14, the oldest girl in the hostel. I mustn't cry.

'Come,' said Mrs Shapiro, and led the way up the curving wooden stairway, its shiny oak banister silky smooth under my left palm. The children on the balcony still hung over it peering at us. Some called through the bars, 'Hallo, what's your name?'

'Gilda, what's yours?' I asked, and they called out, 'Ina,' 'Joey,' 'Eva,' almost all had foreign accents. In the Chingford orphanage I'd been the only child who had parents and the only Jewish child; during evacuation I was always the foster, rather than the natural blonde local country child and the only Jewish child. And here, I was the only British girl and possibly the only one with parents and a family. Once again, I was an outsider. But outsiders observed more.

However, the Shapiros and Mrs Bramson were, like me, British-born and Jewish, although not cockneys. Their British accents seemed to be from North London, a social step above that of East Londoners. Most North and West End London Jews were snobbish toward East Enders. The first question they asked was, 'Where are you from?' If you said Bethnal Green they said, 'Eeeow!' for 'Oh' and looked down their noses. But this staff welcomed me.

Mrs Shapiro led the way upstairs, passing the balcony, where I peeped into open doors seeing rows of small beds in each room. At the top of the main staircase we turned right and started up the second flight of tiny stairs. We came to a landing and a door from behind which pealed girlish laughter.

Mrs Shapiro flung the door open. 'Hallo, girls,' she said. 'This is Gilda. Gilda, this is Selma, Cookie and Helga.'

'Hallo,' the three girls chorused, staring at me.

We entered a sun-flooded room with bare wooden floors. Six narrow army cots with thin mattresses stood lined side by side on one side of the room, every bed showing a dazzling white sheet like a row of white teeth. I recognised the tight 'hospital corner' that I'd learned to make on my sixth birthday at the Chingford orphanage, on the bottom of each bed.

'I'm Selma,' said a tall girl of about 13 who had been lounging on a cot in the corner. She rose lazily, her short brown gym skirt, the Skinner's High School uniform, revealing long, slender legs. A close-fitting red sweater showed full breasts and small waist. Long hair cascaded over her face and shoulders like Veronica Lake's. Although younger than me, she was taller, and had the fully developed body of an 18-year-old woman. Her heavy-lidded eyes, however, stared as though bored and her lashes pointed downward like those of a horse. I would show her how to stroke them upward with Vaseline.

Two other girls sat on the room-wide padded window seat fronted by the clear bay window. Outside, stretched the endless green garden I'd seen from the Shapiro's study.

'I'm Cookie,' said a lanky girl of about 12, with a thick blonde bob, bangs and also with a foreign accent, offering a bony hand. I'd heard Europeans usually shook hands. I shook hers.

'And I'm Helga,' whispered the last girl. Helga, smaller than all of us, her long frizzy hair parted in the middle, her timid eyes and longish nose peeped through her hair. I mentally nicknamed her 'Mouse'.

'Girls, show Gilda where to put her things, right? I'll leave you all to get acquainted. I must help with dinner,' Mrs Shapiro said, leaving us to the fading sound of her feet on the stairs.

Selma looked down at me with laconic brown eyes under heavy, sexy eyelids I'd always envied. But for her mottled skin, bored eyes and drooping eyelashes she would have been beautiful. Perhaps she didn't know where her parents were and felt sad. Or perhaps she thought she looked like Veronica Lake, all the rage.

'You'll be zleeping next to me,' Selma drawled, pointing to her bed in the corner and to mine next to hers. Hearing her guttural English I realised again I was the only British girl here.

'Here's where you hang your clothes. We share this wardrobe.'

Selma opened a creaky old wardrobe, from which hung only a few dresses, and then showed me a squeaky old chest. 'Each girl is allotted half a drawer,' she said.

Since we all wore a school uniform every day, and since clothes were rationed, none of us had much clothing. I supposed the refugees had no money for clothes. While helping me put away my few 'civvies' Helga said, 'What a beautiful cardigan, Jaeger, isn't it?' and stroked the soft wool.

'Yes, Jaeger,' I said. It was one of the best clothiers in London. Mummy had good taste.

'I'll show you round the garden before supper,' Cookie said, in her foreign accent. Cookie was as tall as Selma, but whereas Selma was dark and curvaceous, almost sultry, Cookie was blonde, flat and gangly with long, bony legs. Even her elbows stuck out sharply on both sides, so that I feared she would poke me with them. Her fresh skin was pretty, but a high arched nose and supercilious smile suggested a touch of arrogance.

'Look out for Cookie,' Selma drawled, 'she loves to play pranks on people.'

'Rubbish,' said Cookie, shaking her thick mane of hair, looking down her nose and blinking fast. 'I just hate being bored, so I sometimes liven things up a bit.'

'Where are you from?' I asked the girls.

'I'm from Hagen,' Selma said. I thought it was in Germany, but didn't really know.

'I'm from Berlin,' Cookie said, tossing back blonde hair as if Berlin was superior.

'I was born in Holland,' Helga said, apologetically. 'You're the only English girl here, and the oldest. Don't all English girls live in boarding schools? Have you lived in a boarding school?' Helga asked shyly, as she and Selma helped me put my clothes away.

'Not all English girls go to boarding school,' I laughed, thinking of my East End upbringing with the Lyons girls, the Chingford orphanage, Mrs One-Tit Major, Aunt Ellen, and my 15 or so Christian evacuation foster mothers and fathers. 'I believe boarding school is only for rich Christian girls and boys. I don't think many Jewish girls go to boarding school.'

'I wish we could live in a boarding school; it sounds so wonderful,' Helga said wistfully. 'They have prefects, Head Girls, midnight feasts, and sports. I've read so many books and comics about English boarding schools. I'd love to live in one. Would you be Head Girl here?'

'Just because I'm British doesn't mean I know anything about boarding schools.'

'British? I thought you were English.'

'In England, even if you are born here, if you don't belong to the state church, Church of England, you are called British and not English,' I said. 'Catholics are also called British.'

That's what Mummy had said, and I believed everything she told me.

'Supper time,' called a girl who came running into the room. 'Everybody wash. Oh,' she said, 'are you the new girl?'

'This is Marta Yellinek' Selma said. 'She was in ballet school in Czechoslovakia.'

'Hallo,' Marta said, staring at me.

I stared back at her. She had the most perfect carriage and was the most self-possessed girl I'd ever met. Marta had the composure of a Dègas ballerina figure Daddy had shown me. She was probably only 12, but her face her high, clear forehead and cheekbones, severe large grey eyes and small, perfect nose and mouth fascinated me. Black hair cut in a short bob, the same length all around all exposed a long, shapely, ballerina neck; all her lines were clean, perfect.

Like Daddy, I was a passable artist. Although all my other grades had dropped during evacuation, I still excelled in art class. Daddy had taught me the rudiments of drawing; I decided I must draw Marta, nude if possible. How to ask her?

We all clattered down the wooden stairs, except for Selma, a giraffe among gazelles, who, taller than everyone else drifted down lazily; we big girls joined the crowds of small children streaming downstairs for supper from the balcony floor. The younger children ranged from about five to 11. None of the small boys were older than eight and they all, like Mr Shapiro and Joseph Singer, wore a small kipa on their heads. The girls ranged in age from about six to me, the oldest at 14.

Following others, we all crowded into a kitchen where two sinks and a long table stood.

'Do we eat here? It doesn't look big enough for everyone,' I said.

'No, we just wash in here,' Selma replied. She took a strange metal cup with three handles on it and filling it with water, poured the water over her left hand then over her right.

'I washed before coming; do I have to wash again?' I asked.

'We're already clean. This is for a blessing over bread.'

She dried her hands on a towel and said in English, 'Blessed are you Lord God who has commanded us to wash our hands.' Then she said the blessing, I supposed, in Hebrew. She filled the cup for me and I followed suit except I didn't know the blessing in Hebrew. Each child washed the same way, and then filled the cup with water for the next child. Even the youngest child knew the Hebrew blessing. The older children helped the younger ones. I remembered how only Violet had befriended me at the orphanage and how coldly all the daughters among my goyishe foster parents, had treated me. Here, though we'd barely met, Selma and Helga had immediately befriended me.

'Do we wash like this before every meal?' I asked.

Selma nodded and put her finger to her lips. I followed Selma, Cookie and Helga into the room that stood behind the entrance hall and fire. This dining room was set up with two long tables in an L-shape. Wooden chairs stood all around the tables. Mr and Mrs Shapiro sat at the centre table facing the doors. Selma led the way to the top of the 'L' table facing onto the garden, and pointed to a seat for me at its head. I felt surprised, but pleased to be seated at the head of the table. No one spoke, not even the little children with their small, pointed faces and huge eyes. Mrs Shapiro's child, Stanley had great, brown eyes and tousled hair which appeared just above the table, on which rested his little nose.

Mr Shapiro shook salt onto a piece of bread from the pile in front of him, and like my Zada, said something, perhaps a blessing in Hebrew, and then ate some. The children followed suit then all started to speak.

'What did they say before they ate bread?' I asked Selma.

'Blessed are you Lord our God who brings forth bread from the earth.'

'Why didn't anyone speak until they'd said this blessing?'

'We don't speak between the blessing over washing the hands and the blessing over the bread so that there is no distraction between the two actions. All our actions are holy, so we have blessings for when we eat, arrive safely from a journey, or see a beautiful object.'

I decided to ask Mr Shapiro what Selma meant by, 'all our actions were holy'. He was the first man I felt I could ask any question and he would answer me.

'I'll continue reading to you from Dickens', *Little Druitt*,' Mr Shapiro said, the book propped up in front of him, the way we read at home, only not to each other. As he read, children brought in steaming platters of fried fish, fried potatoes and Brussels sprouts. Each child took food from a platter and passed it to the next child. Children were given extra rations, so there was plenty of food, and we ate from china plates not enamel, as in Chingford's orphanage. No one walked round with a stick hitting us in the back, shouting, 'Sit straight'. In any case we sat on nice chairs, not backless rough benches. I felt wonderfully comfortable. Mr Shapiro stopped reading so he could eat. We could talk while eating like normal children. How much better this Jewish orphanage was than the Chingford orphanage. Unlike the Chingford orphanage, adults ate with us, Mr Shapiro even read to us during the meal. I felt as if I were with the big family I'd always yearned for. And here the adults knew and called each child by name. So not all orphanages were bad! In fact, this one was very good.

I wanted to be home, but if I had to be away from home, this was so far, the best place I'd ever lived in. Did Daddy miss me? After eating, we all chanted a song in Hebrew, which I guessed was a blessing over food. A new set of children cleared the table and carried dishes to the kitchen. We quietly placed our chairs under the table as did all well-bred English children.

'Come on, I'll take you round the garden,' Cookie said.

Cookie danced rather than walked in front of me, her short heavy hair swinging from side to side. We left the house through a side door that led to the back garden. The house from the back was even more beautiful than from the front. Wisps of smoke from the several chimneys curled into the evening sky.

From outside, I peered at the windows and saw children inside cheerfully clearing plates from the dining room tables. Outside the dining room and Mr Shapiro's study, a stone terrace ran along the back of the house on which small children jumped between chalked hopscotch squares. Two boys sat on the terrace played gobs, throwing rough stones in the air, snatching stones off the ground then catching the airborne stones before they fell to the ground. I was good at those games, but wouldn't play with small children.

I imagined that the family that had owned this mansion used to have breakfast on the terrace, the way I'd seen rich families in British films took breakfast on fine days. A maid with a white cap low over her forehead and wearing a white frilly apron would bring breakfast out. I imagined myself in that family, sitting on the terrace, drinking tea, planning a leisurely day.

'Shall we play tennis, drive into London, or visit Aunt Emily, Susan?' I imagined the mother saying to her daughter.

'Oh, what a bore, Mother, let's go shopping at Harrods,' the daughter answered.

Cookie ran ahead, and looking back said like Nurse Harris, 'Come on, don't dawdle.'

As I caught up with her, Cookie snapped several small branches from trees, ripping green leaves off of them, shredding and then scattering the leafy skeletons over the ground.

'How long have you been here?' I asked her.

'I came on the *Kindertransport* just before the war, in 1939, four years ago.'

She stopped and looked far away. 'I was on the last boat out of Germany. England let some children in, but they wouldn't let my parents in. My father put me on the boat and kissed me goodbye. I didn't know if I'd ever see him again.'

'Do you know where he is?'

'He and my mother escaped to Hong Kong. After the war I'll join my parents there,' she said. 'But my parents are divorced.'

I stared at Cookie. Divorce was very, very rare, especially among Jews. My parents often quarrelled; at least Mummy did, but had never once mentioned divorce. 'You must sleep in the bed you make,' Mummy often said. I didn't know anyone who was divorced except for Gertie and Mrs Simpson, and Mrs Simpson was American.

We were walking away from the house over a wide, green lawn where a group of small children were playing Oranges and Lemons. I used to love playing Oranges and Lemons in Shoreditch Churchyard as a child. They were ready for the orange-lemon tug-of-war.

'Heave, heave,' they all cried, and as we passed, the Orange line pulled the Lemon side over the marker and shouted, while falling down in a laughing heap, 'We won, we won.'

Small children ran back and forth across a little bridge over the pond. A little boy threw bread crumbs to fat goldfish that popped heads up, snatched the food and submerged.

'Do Selma and Helga know where their parents are?' I asked, hugging my shoulders. The sun setting, and in spite of my Jaeger cardigan, I had began to shiver.

'Selma doesn't, Helga's parents are in Belsen-Bergen it's a concentration camp,' Cookie said abruptly and ran on a few steps ahead. 'They're allowed to send one postcard through the Red Cross; I think, every two months,' she called back. I caught up with her, passing a wooden bench where two little girls played cat's cradle. Nearby three small boys ran in circles, arms outstretched swooping up and down. 'I'm a Spitfire and I'm going to get you,' shouted one.

'And I'm a Messerschmitt, look out, here I come' shouted the other, circling the first, 'a-a-a-a-a-a-a'. We were still walking. The garden seemed endless.

I turned, walking backward, to look at the White House. Seen in the growing dusk through the trees, its white walls shimmered, and with its brown pointed roof it looked like an enchanted house in a fairy tale. All the windows outlined in brown painted wood, stood clearly against the white house like kindly, wise square eyes. I saw the huge bay-window of our room.

We came to trees behind which stood a wall 'here's the orchard,' Cookie said, dancing ahead of me, her white blouse flashing here and there through dense foliage. Now I saw a small forest of trees, boughs bent low with fruit. It was the first time I'd seen pears and plums growing on trees or anywhere. Since war had began, only essentials were brought from abroad. Vitamin deficiencies had blackened Miss Menzies' nails. Now I could just reach up and, if allowed, like magic, I could pluck an apple, a plum or a pear. Rich green leaves heavy with fruit weighed the branches almost down to my shoulders. I stood under a pear tree, leaning against the cool, solid trunk, my face hidden by thick foliage, then I fitted my eye through a small space between leaves. If we picked a fruit, would the Beast rush out and demand one of us for hostage? Poor, lonely, abandoned Beast. Only a kiss from a kind person had restored him.

Cookie had disappeared. I looked all round for her. 'Coo-ee, can you find me?' I heard her voice. 'I'm up here,' she laughed mockingly, and looking up, I saw her sitting on a branch in a plum thicket, long legs in white socks, swinging. Through the foliage I glimpsed her white teeth glinting. 'Come up? I'll give you a hand,' she said.

I put a hand up to hers, one foot on the tree. She clasped my hand, began to pull me up, my feet were off the ground against the tree when with a raucous laugh she let go of me so that I thumped backward onto the ground. 'Ouch,' I said, rubbing my back. Cookie laughed.

Selma had warned me. I would never trust Cookie again.

Behind the orchard, a high stone wall reared: the end of the hostel grounds. I turned round to look at the house again. Far away I saw figures passing back and forth in the big girls' bay window upstairs, It wasn't quite time for blackout, but as we stood there the sun set and someone drew all the blackout curtains except those of the big girls' room. There was no electricity or gas light in the big girls' room, probably because it had been used by maids, they used candles, so no light, no need for curtains.

The White House windows were now dark, only the mansion gleamed silky under searchlights. The faint boom of gunfire told me the Nazis were still dropping bombs on London. My entire family lived under this nightly bombing. They could be killed at any moment.

The garden, now silent, empty and dark except for searchlights that had followed me to every city and village, London, Newmarket, Ely, and now Great Chesterford, reminded me that even in this hamlet we were at war. Suddenly, British bombers roared overhead on their way to Germany, I hoped, to give them hell as they gave us. 'We shall never surrender,' Churchill said. Though angry with British constant anti-Semitism, I admired British humour and fighting spirit.

By eight o'clock, all the small children had gone in to bed. Cookie and I went in through the back door to the kitchen. Two girls, about 11 were washing dishes, singing *All Through the Night*.

'I can sing a descant to that,' I said to the dark one. One day she'd be beautiful.

'Okay, we'll begin again,' she said.

As we sang together, my voice soared with the descant, hers low with the song. We ended on a hushed note. 'That was beautiful,' I said. I'd never sung in Ely except in music classes with Miss Senior. Now I felt I could sing everything that was in my heart, the way Mummy at home sang so passionately. Selma came into the kitchen, breaking the peaceful mood. 'Tomorrow is the first day of school,' she said. 'On school nights we have to be in bed by nine. But it's only eight. Let's go into the Green Room. It's only for the big girls over 12.'

The Green Room behind the kitchen lived up to its name, its walls painted a harsh apple green. A dozen crooked cabinets with doors hanging off loose hinges made the room look crazy. Still it was exclusive to the Big Girls, our only retreat, especially for our three hour nightly homework. Helga took a sewing basket from the cabinets, and darned her stocking.

'Anyone want a sweet?' Cookie asked, offering some old mangy ones from her cabinet cache. I learned that all food here was kosher. It would be strange, since I liked bacon, though I'd given it up for Moira.

At nine o'clock Helga put away her sewing. Selma had been knitting a khaki scarf; I'd brought some khaki socks I'd been knitting for Tommies. We each wound our wool into a ball; Helga put her two, and I put my five steel needles into the green cabinets.

'I want to ask Mr Shapiro a question,' I said. 'I'll be up soon.'

I knocked. He was sitting in his armchair, a lamp at his side, reading a French book, puffing contentedly on his pipe. I loved the aromatic smell of his pipe.

'I'm sorry to disturb you, but may I ask you a question?'

'Certainly. Come in, sit down.'

'Selma said we were a holy people. What's holy about us? Jews are ordinary people.'

Mr Shapiro smiled. 'The word *kodesh*, holy, has two meanings, holy and separate. The word holy part means emulating God's personality, as near as is possible for men. God is mighty but slow to anger, he's compassionate. We must try to be the same – to Jews and to non-Jews. The Ten Commandments say to worship only one Creator, no idols; these are associated with cruel pagan rituals; we rest on the Sabbath like God, we must not steal, kill, covet our neighbour's wife or property, nor oppress a stranger. We must judge the stranger by the same laws as Jews, not, like the Greeks, the Romans and now the Nazis, by different laws. We must not be prejudiced against people different from us. We must honour our father and mother, and be as good to others as we'd like them to be to us no matter how different they are from us. These laws are about our relations to God and our relations to each other.'

'How does that make us holy?'

'Being as similar to God as possible is one way of becoming holy. Making each of our acts and thoughts in accordance with his wishes makes us holy. That's one meaning of holy. The second meaning of holy is 'separate'. Jews are separate from, and have a different mission than other people.'

'Isn't that exactly what gentiles accuse us of, being separate and different?'

'Many groups of people are separate. Teachers are separate from students. Parents from children, the French from the Germans. Jews are separate because we have a task, a purpose.'

'What's our purpose?' No one I'd lived with so far had seemed to have a purpose.

Mr Shapiro's velvet brown eyes stared into mine, his voice low but intense, he said, 'Our purpose is to teach the world about the Torah. Not by words alone, but by our actions. Every Jew is an example to others. If our actions reflect the rules of the Torah, others will learn it.'

'But people hate us for this. We've had centuries of persecution. The Babylonians, Egyptians, Romans, Greeks, the Crusaders, the Inquisition, and now the Nazis, not to mention our dear old local London Fascists under Mosley all want to kill us.'

'It's true they hate us because we're like a conscience. They hate us for what we don't do. They see that we don't have slaves building gigantic idols and buildings; we don't practice wholesale torture, massacre, forced conversions, murder or exterminate religions that believe differently from us. The nations don't like having a conscience and one coming from such a tiny, insignificant people. We're like the prophets whom even Kings of Israel often wanted to kill. Stop doing evil. Do good. Follow the Torah. We're like unpopular prophets. We don't always want to be a conscience. Like Jonah, we try to run from it, but God or the goyim always remind us of our role. They never let us forget we are Jews. The world always tries to crush this conscience, yet we've outlived nation after nation that has disappeared. The Nazis, too, will fail, but we shall survive.'

'Not without killing millions of men, women and children.'

'True. 'In every generation a new persecutor will arise' but Jews will survive them.'

'It's as if we're the scapegoat for the world.'

'That's a clever way of putting it,' Mr Shapiro said, 'However, don't think we're looking for martyrdom like the Christians. We don't think it's noble to be a martyr. We love life above everything. If there's a conflict between breaking Sabbath or saving a life, we break the Sabbath. If we have to defend ourselves against being killed on Shabbat, we fight. We are not martyrs. The human body is a holy vessel to protect if attacked, and to celebrate joy. We celebrate life: a birth, a wedding, a bar mitzvah, a school exam passed and we celebrate Rosh Hashanah, Passover, Chanukah, Purim, Succoth, and Shavuot, besides Shabbat every single week. We believe in happiness, helping others, and making every act as holy as possible.'

'What did he say? Did he mind you coming to his study so late at night?' Selma whispered. The others slept.

'We had a wonderful talk. He's so clever.'

I undressed in the dark and slid into the single, firm, but comfortable army cot next to Selma. It symbolised the purpose in life Mr Shapiro had just described to me. I admired, and was grateful to him and his wife. They'd welcomed me into a beautiful house, given me a home, a family, friends and a meaning to life.

The only dark spot on my new-found happiness was Cookie.

CHAPTER 20

FIFTEENTH BIRTHDAY: THE ORANGE DIARY

On a January Friday evening after dinner, Selma, Helga, Cookie and I like ladies of the manor strolled arm-in-arm around the immense garden. Ancient oaks towered over us. Patches of white snow still glittered on the ground. But after escaping the blazing fire and warm Shabbat candles of the dining room, I welcomed the cool air on my face. Growing cooler, we pressed closer together. Our closeness in body and mind delighted me.

Although night here was peaceful and quiet, white swathes of searchlights slashing the dark skies reminded us of Nazi warplanes treacherously flying over London: Blitz and death only two train hours away. Millions of calm stars, the gleaming moon reminded us of God's eternity.

Norma Huberman, a giggly 11-year-old girl, ran out of the house and joined us. Tall and slim, with blue eyes, white blonde hair and alabaster skin, Norma could have passed, as did many Jewish girls, as a member of Hitler's supposed 'Aryan master race'. With war finally going our way, evacuees were allowed to visit home. While I was away in London one weekend, Nurse had married a Jewish Brigade soldier in the British Army, the wedding held in the hostel. Norma and Helga, friends with Nurse had been bridesmaids. I felt sorry to have missed the wedding but Norma had given me a photo of Nurse dressed in white, her arm on that of her soldier husband, the two bridesmaids, my friends, next to her. Norma spoke excitedly.

'My brother's coming from London to see me next Sunday, visiting day,' she crowed.

'Really? How old is he?' I asked.

'He's 19.'

'Just in time for your 15th birthday,' Selma said to me.

'Oh, we've never celebrated my birthday at home,' I said.

'You will this time. Cookie has organised a birthday party for you,' Norma said.

'Really? I can't believe Cookie organised it. I thought she didn't like me. She teases me unmercifully. But I've never had a birthday party before. How exciting!!'

'What does your brother do, Norma?' Selma asked.

'He's a diamond cutter. He works in Hatton Garden.'

'Oooh,' we all said, now standing on the bridge of our little pond. The stone seahorse reared gracefully from its centre as if to greet us.

How wonderful it would be to have a birthday party as well as a real young man visit us. What would Norma's brother be like? I imagined anyone who worked in the London diamond centre, Hatton Garden, must be rich. A picture flashed through my mind of Hatton Garden shops encrusted with a million glittering diamonds, people living in diamond houses.

But I only murmured, 'Finally, we'll get to see a man near our own age.'

'Near your age. To me he's an old man,' Cookie said. 'All we see are small hostel boys and Yanks on trains, kids or old men. We'll never meet boys our own age.'

'It must be glamorous working in Hatton Garden,' Anita said, waving her left hand in the air. 'Look at my diamond,' and we pretended to admire a huge diamond on her third left finger.

'It's gorgeous,' I said. 'Was it expensive?'

'It's very rude to ask how much something costs,' Marta snapped.

'When are you getting married, Anita?' Cookie joked.

'Sunday,' Anita said, 'to Norma's brother. We've been writing secretly to each other for six months. And Norma is going to be my new sister-in-law, right?'

We all laughed.

Visiting day arrived, but since most of the children had no relatives, few people came. Although I had many relatives, no one visited me except for Mummy, twice. Probably no one knew it was my birthday. I had disappeared from their lives. Refugee children thought English-born children lucky to have a family. We were certainly luckier than they, but not always as happy as they imagined. Little did they know why a British girl had landed in a refugee hostel. I could have been home. The Blitz had tapered off.

Only three visitors arrived on the afternoon train. One was Mrs Rozenfeld, who was on the Golders Green Hostel Committee that funded the hostel. She came once a month. With her tall, slender figure, her white skin, sparkling dark eyes, aquiline nose, her dresses fitting as if they'd been stitched on to her body yet never tight, she seemed to me the epitome of elegance. As she came in the red front door, we waved and smiled to each other. I was fond of her. She always with genuine concern inquired after my welfare. 'How are you Gilda? How's school?'

The other visitor I noticed was a handsome young man to whom Norma ran and whom she kissed. He had to be her brother. They headed for the kitchen. She was allowed to make him a cup of tea and chat with him there on visiting day. After half an hour, I casually walked through the kitchen to the Green Room. Brother and sister were talking earnestly to each other. I pretended not to see them. 'Gilda, this is my brother, Franz,' Norma called out.

'Oh, Hallo,' I said, feigning surprise.

As he lounged back lazily in his chair, Franz's long, long legs stretched all the way under the table. He unwound himself gracefully and stood, tall and lean, over six feet tall, as elegant as a heron. I admired his immaculate dark suit, white shirt and grey tie. Gold cuff links winked from his shirtsleeves. His wide-brimmed, black velvety hat, worn by religious men, sat aslant his pale blond hair, a lock of which fell into his blue eyes reminding me of 'Bobby Shaftoe tall and fair, combing down his yellow hair, he's my own for ever mair, bonny Bobby Shaftoe.'

'How do you do? I hear it's your 15th birthday today. Many happy returns,' Franz said in a pleasant soft voice with a charming foreign accent like Charles Boyer's.

'Thank you,' I said, feeling my face grow hot, and knowing I was blushing.

'Norma said you're having a birthday party. May I come?' Franz said.

'Of course,' I said, blushing again. 'I'm so excited. I've never had a birthday party.'

Though delighted he was coming, I worried that a man of 19 might feel bored with a hostel party and surrounded by mostly small children.

As a special treat Mrs Bramson had used everyone's flour, margarine and chocolate rations to bake me a huge round chocolate birthday cake. She also made real lemonade, though goodness knows where she ferreted out lemons; citrus fruit was almost impossible to buy. She proudly carried high the cake and lemon juice into the kitchen, deservedly showing off her ingenuity under wartime rationing.

'Thank you, thank you so much,' I said, admiring all that chocolate in one place. 'I've never had a birthday cake before.'

She smiled warmly. Pity she was such a young widow, I thought. Damned Nazis.

After dusting my birthday cake with a fine sprinkling of rationed sugar, Mrs Bramson sat at the kitchen window looking in her mirror, and putting on rouge and lipstick. I wondered if she were expecting a Yank to visit her. Franz frowned.

'What's the matter?' I whispered.

'I hate heavy makeup, it's so false,' he whispered back.

'I do, too,' I said, 'but I'll use a little when I'm older.'

'I hope you don't use it here,' he said, 'Mr Shapiro would be after you.'

Norma smiled but didn't let out my guilty secret. I used Pond's cold cream every night and daytime, a touch of blush and lipstick. Mummy often said, 'You're so pale, use lipstick.'

Franz smiled at me and I smiled back guilelessly with my slightly lipsticked mouth. I left Franz and Norma so they could talk. I had piles of homework waiting.

In the afternoon, sitting on the window seat in the Big Girls' room doing homework, I spied Norma walking in the garden with Franz. Although she hated men, Anita had nagged me all afternoon to go outside. 'Let's walk to the pond, feed the fish,' Anita asked me again.

'Alright, let's go,' I finally conceded.

'Hello,' we said when we passed Norma and Franz, me blushing again.

Norma called to us. 'D'you want to see Franz' new gold cigarette case?'

'Oh, yes indeed,' Anita and I said together.

'Would you like a cigarette?' he asked, producing his gold case.

I was terribly impressed by its glittering slenderness and Franz rose even higher in my estimation. He pressed a tiny button on the side and the lid sprang open. Twelve Turkish gold tipped cigarettes, oval, almost flat, the kind Zada smoked, the kind I loved to smell, lay in a double row, held in place by a gold band across them.

'Do you smoke?' Franz asked.

'Oh no,' I said in horror, eyes wide.

I didn't want him to think I smoked. And if Mr Shapiro saw me smoking he would have a fit. But when I was 12, Mummy had given me a cigarette. 'Try it, see if you like it,' she'd said.

I'd smoked one cigarette with Mummy and didn't see what all the fuss was about. If someone offered me a cigarette, I'd accept it just to be sociable. But I did love the smell of cigarettes, especially the Turkish; I loved watching smoke curl up to the ceiling and the aroma of Mr Shapiro's pipe tobacco. But if Franz didn't like heavy make-up, he wouldn't approve of a woman smoking, so I fibbed. Still, I thought, 'All's fair in love and war.'

The four of us walked back inside the house and sat in the kitchen.

'Excuse me, I'm going to get some more tea for my brother,' Norma said, striking a match for the gas stove, and putting on the kettle. Selma, Franz and I sat silently for a moment.

'I'm hoping to go home to London for the weekend,' I said, to break the silence.

'You must come and visit me,' Franz said immediately.

Dare I visit a man in his house? I'd have liked to invite him to our London house but I felt I couldn't very well if Norma didn't come, too. I'd never heard of her going to London. Did refugee children have any money? But Franz had come here, so either I was wrong or he had permission. I imagined blond Franz and me walking arm in arm. A picture flashed into my mind of Franz and me holding hands, looking enrapt in the windows of Hatton Garden diamond centre for an engagement ring. For the moment I'd forgotten about Joseph Singer and the dark-haired lover from Song of Songs, the poem in the prayer book I peeked at, when bored with prayers.

'When does the birthday party begin?' Franz asked, bringing me back to earth.

'Soon, I hope. Visitors must leave by six and it's five now. What time is your train?'

Before he could answer, Cookie dashed into the kitchen and shouted, 'Everyone into the dining room, the birthday party's about to begin.'

Leaving their tea, Franz lazily unwound his long legs from under the kitchen table again and stood. Helga and Cookie pulled me by my arms like a prisoner, into the dining room. Mrs

Bramson carried in the cake holding it high like a prize, and as if in a parade, Selma followed with the lemonade: and all for me. I almost danced along, Franz following. Everyone began clapping and singing, 'Happy birthday to you,' as shoes clacking on the bare wood floors, now a pleasant sound, we all crowded into the dining room. As we walked, Franz towering over me, he looked Selma up and down once, the way I noticed men did. Then he smiled at me, his lazy, slow smile starting with a crinkle at the corners of his eyes, each corner of his mouth curling up.

Perhaps, after all, he liked girls with dark wavy hair and almond-shaped eyes, I thought.

Piles of hand-made birthday cards and presents from the big girls, in odd, hand-made boxes, tumbled over each other on the dining room table. The small children had nothing with which to make or give a present, but they crowded round the tables gleefully, and in no way envious. This, I never understood. They had so little and gave of their joy so generously.

'Happy Birthday,' the children all shouted at once.

'Thank you,' I said, feeling my face and whole body smile. This was my family.

The entire hostel had gathered: 30 or so girls and boys, Mrs Shapiro, Nurse, Mrs Bramson and Franz came, except Mr Shapiro left to meet with Mrs Rozenfeld in his study.

Franz sat down quite comfortably among the children, long legs stretching under the table, black hat on the back of his head. I thought him terribly sophisticated with his smart clothes and slender cigarette case, yet he smiled indulgently, and stretched his long body, at ease, perhaps having a younger sister helped.

'We have a birthday surprise for you,' Marta said to me.

'Oh, what is it?' I asked. What more could they do for me?

'We've all decided to elect you Head Girl of the White House!' she said.

The Head Girl in a Boarding School was responsible for maintaining school rules and keeping up the girls' morale. She reported to the headmaster, in this case: Mr Shapiro.

'I second the motion,' Selma said.

'All in favour say aye,' Marta shouted.

'Aye,' went up a big roar. The children jumped up and down with excitement.

A dozen friends and children pumped my hand or patted my back. I blushed 10 times.

'What an honour, such a surprise, thank you. I don't know what to say,' I stammered. I knew the older girls liked me, though I wasn't sure about Cookie. Usually, a headmistress appointed a Head Girl or a headmaster appointed a Head Boy, I thought. I was sure Mr Shapiro would agree to this arrangement, but it was good to be elected by popular vote. In either case Head Girl always had the respect and admiration of the girls. Did it matter how she was chosen?

'Hip, hip,' shouted Marta again.

'Hip Hip, Hooray,' everyone roared back three times.

Everyone clapped. Tears trembled on my eyelashes. I was saved from making a speech by Cookie. 'Open your birthday cards,' she commanded.

Hand-drawn or painted, there was a birthday card from each of the big girls, from Selma, Helga, Marta, Cookie, Anita Jacobs and Eva Groner – two new girls – and from Paula and Norma.

'Oh, Cookie's has 15 kisses on it,' I said, counting.

'One must be for me,' Franz teased.

'Go on, give him a kiss,' Cookie said.

'Oh, Cookie,' I said, blushing again, 'don't be daft', and fumbled with the presents.

'Hurry up, open your presents,' Cookie said.

Norma sat, arm linked in her brother's, the two so blonde and blue-eyed, like twins except for the difference in age. How wonderful it must be to have a big brother, or a boyfriend. I peeked at him from under my eyelashes. Was he staring at me? I bent my head to the presents to avoid meeting his blue eyes and to avoid blushing again.

Ripping off brown or newspaper wrappings – there was no fancy paper or string during the war, and gifts were tied with knitting wool, I began opening my presents.

'Oh, a jar of scented bath salts! Beautiful, thank you, Selma,' I said, kissing her cheek.

Helga gave me a pretty lace handkerchief, Marta a little sewing set, and Anita, four new steel knitting needles. I thanked them all, and kissed each on the cheek. Franz watched, smiling.

'Open mine, open mine,' Cookie cried.

'What a lovely orange notebook, thanks Cookie,' I said and kissed her gingerly, barely grazing her lean cheek in case she bit me 'in fun'.

'It's to use as a diary,' Cookie said.

'Just what I wanted. I'll start using it tonight,' I said.

'Let's play Postman's Knock,' Cookie said. 'Go out.'

I went out of the room. 'Come back,' Cookie called out. When I failed her test she said, 'You have to kiss Franz.'

'I couldn't possibly do that, you have to give me something else,' I said, horrified.

Franz sat back, amused. 'I hear you have a good voice will you sing us a song?' Franz said quickly.

I flashed him a grateful smile, stood up and sang:

'When a body meets a body coming through the rye,

If a body kiss a body, need that body cry?

Ilk a laddie ilk a lassie, nane they say, not I,

Yet all the lads they smile at me, when coming through the rye.'

I wasn't sure if the words were right, but refugees wouldn't know the words either. Did they know that 'ilk' meant 'like' and 'nane' meant 'no'? If I couldn't kiss Franz, at least I'd sung a song about kissing. Everyone clapped and cheered.

I cut the birthday cake and gave the staff and all the children a piece: an extra large piece to Franz. Selma poured lemonade for everyone.

'By the way,' Franz said, as we all ate our cake, 'I heard you knew a Joseph Singer.'

'Yes, I did,' I said, my voice trembling a little. 'How do you know him?' I asked.

Did he know about my disastrous letter to Joseph?

'I met him in London.'

'Did he say anything about me?' I asked. Did Joseph ever know about the letter I'd written him saying how much I admired him, and for which 'crime', I'd been sent to Coventry?

Franz was about to answer when Nurse said, 'Visiting hours are over, and visitors must leave in 15 minutes. Cookie, collect money from the visitors to plant trees in Israel.'

'Franz,' I said, as he rose to his feet to leave, 'what did he say?'

'Have to tell you next time,' Franz said, grinning, leaving me dying of curiosity.

'Goodbye,' I said and rushed away, glad that Franz hadn't seen the tears pricking my eyes. Would I ever meet Joseph Singer? What was Franz about to tell me?

Mrs Rozenfeld put her hand on my shoulder. 'Is everything going well, dear?' she asked me. 'Why are you trembling?'

'It's the excitement of my 15th birthday and all the gifts I received,' I lied.

'Your 15th birthday? Well, here's a pound note. Buy something nice for yourself.'

'Many thanks, Mrs Rozenfeld.'

'How are your studies going? Getting ready for Matriculation?'

'I'm trying,' I said, 'but it's hard to concentrate with the hullabaloo going on in the evenings. The younger kids run, slam doors, stamp and jump up and down the stairs. We have three hours of homework a night and there's nowhere quiet to study. If I don't pass the matriculation test I won't be able to apply for college.'

'I'll see what I can do,' she said, wrinkling her brow.

'Thank you, Mrs Rozenfeld.' I squeezed her hand.

I didn't like to tell Mrs Rozenfeld about the recent struggle with Mr Shapiro to get the Green Room which we big girls used to study for our exams. Since he'd begun to work with me, my grades had soared back to A's. But lately, he was irritable and when he was annoyed he took away our Green Room privilege. Why was he being so irrational lately?

The clock struck six.

'Goodbye,' said Franz, 'Happy birthday,' and he leaned down and kissed my cheek. When his warm lips touched me I felt myself blushing again. The girls hugged each other and screamed, 'He kissed her he kissed her!'

I was sure I was scarlet with excitement, pleasure, and embarrassment. Thankfully Mr Shapiro hadn't seen the kiss or he would have closed the Green Room forever.

Franz left quickly, his hat set jauntily on his head. I watched him through the window striding on his daddy longlegs toward the Great Chesterford Station going back to London. That evening I sighed with satisfaction and lay on my cot in the dark. What an exquisite day it had been: I'd had a first, wonderful birthday party, been elected Head Girl, Mrs Rozenfeld had given me a whole pound note and she would get the Green Room back for us. Most important, I'd had my first kiss from a real man.

Strange it was Cookie, my bête noir who gave me what I least expected, a party, and most delightful, a diary. I had already won two literature competition prizes at school. I loved writing.

'A lovely 15th birthday,' I wrote that night in my new orange-covered diary.

I began my diary on my 15th birthday and keep a diary to this day. Cookie's little orange notebook, still in my possession, began my obsession with writing.

For this little orange diary, I am eternally grateful to Cookie.

CHAPTER 21

YANKS ON TRAINS *

As usual Selma, Cookie, Helga and I caught the 8am train to my new high school, Hertfordshire and Essex High School in Bishop's Stortford that was about 15 miles from Great Chesterford. En route, we passed two American Air Force bases, Audley End and Stanford.

The young American airmen who leapt onto the train at these stops, unlike British Tommies, who treated us as children, were friendly. The Yanks liked talking to, and even flirting with us. We preened a little, as to Tommies, our school uniforms relegated us to children. Only Yanks noticed that we were young women. At least, now at 15, I was a young woman.

The four of us walked along the train corridor looking for a good carriage: not too crowded, and one occupied by some Yanks. Suddenly, with a shock I saw a flash of long red hair flying in the wind as Miss Curzon, our new Scottish art teacher leapt onto the train's moving running board, slammed the door behind her, and like a hurricane on three-inch heels, hurtled along the corridor, short skirts flaunting her endlessly long, black-market silk-stockinged legs. How did she get silk stockings? Soon, we saw her benefactor. She strode straight up to a tall Yank officer lolling at the door of a carriage, flung her arms round his neck, pressed her lovely body close to his and kissed him full on the lips. Now I understood the term, 'she threw herself at him'. Was this passionate woman the same curt, unsmiling Miss Curzon, who gave us art lessons as if against her will and who never sang *In Dublin's Fair City* to us during art class, like dear, retired, dandelion-head Miss Lemon?

The officer slowly wrapped his arms round her, smiled, and leisurely, kissed her back.

I pulled the three girls into an empty carriage and pointed down the corridor. 'L-l-look at Miss Curzon,' I said.

When the Yank came up for breath I noticed no bright red lipstick on him and remembered that there was a new rationed lipstick that didn't come off when a lady kissed a man. Miss Curzon was no lady. We all poked our school-hatted heads out of our carriage, and gaped.

'Did you see that?' I said. 'Not only is she kissing a Yank in public, she kissed him first. I can't believe my eyes.'

'And she's wearing shorter skirts and higher heels than any teacher in the school,' Helga said. 'Isn't she afraid of getting found out and reported to the headmistress?'

'She'd be fired, for sure,' Selma said.

'No she wouldn't,' Cookie retorted. 'There's a shortage of teachers, because so many women are in the services.'

'I can't believe she's our art teacher, she's almost unfriendly in class. And she's acting as if she's engaged to him. He's not exactly carried away by her. I'll bet he's married,' I said.

All of our high school teachers were spinsters, forbidden to marry. And they all, but for Miss Brady and now Miss Curzon, wore dull clothes, dreary colours, flat heels and no make-up.

'Can you imagine Miss Atzomer dressed like that?' Helga asked.

'Or someone kissing Miss Stapleton,' I said.

'Who'd want to kiss Miss Stapleton?' Cookie snorted.

We all broke out into our favourite song set to the tune of *By Yonder Green Valley* which exactly fit Miss Stapleton:

My teacher's got a bunion
A face like a pickled onion

A nose like a squashed tomato

And legs like matchsticks.

We collapsed in a heap on top of each other, laughing like the schoolgirls we partly were. After quieting down, we poked our heads out of the carriage door again. Miss Curzon, still locked in the officer's arms, his cap tipped back on his head, the peak gleaming, he now nibbled on her ear. She threw back her head, arching a white neck, which he kissed, and she laughed. She looked like Maureen O'Sullivan.

The train had gathered speed and Miss Curzon and the officer, navels pinned together, swayed to its rhythm. I thought Miss Curzon terribly daring and romantic, but I didn't think I'd ever dare kiss a Yank or any man in public. But I was only 15. If only I could be one year older and as beautiful and as daring as Miss Curzon, I might be allowed to go out with men. Well, I had written to Joseph Singer. Had that been daring or foolish?

'He who hesitates is lost,' and 'Fools step in where angels fear to tread' came to mind.

We sneaked away as if we had misbehaved, found an empty carriage, threw ourselves down on the velvet seats and chattered about Miss Curzon. Cookie's water bottle and our gas masks on the net rack above rocked with the soothing motion of the train, the train wheels chanted, 'Going to school, going to school'.

There was room for about six people on each side. Selma and Helga sat on one side of the carriage, Cookie and I on the other. A cold sun shone through the windows. As the train rattled on we flashed by a Land Girl in jodhpurs and knee-high boots, arm suspended in mid-air throwing hay onto hay stacks with a wicked-looking pitchfork. From the train windows we flashed by sheep and cows, an old man, leg cocked, climbing over a stile between two fields, and a Yank's backside seated on a wobbly bicycle, trying out England. I'd never seen a Yank on a bike. Yanks walked, rode trains or drove jeeps. My eyes snapped a photograph of each scene.

We took Hebrew books from our satchels and began studying our Hebrew homework for Mr Shapiro's night class at the hostel. I was anxious to be well prepared so as to please him. I needed his help to pass upcoming Matriculation exams. Lately, he was so moody. The train squealed to a stop at Audley End.

Two American soldiers or airmen – I couldn't tell the difference – entered our carriage. Selma, Cookie and Helga were used to Americans, since they'd been riding on this train and passing American air bases long before me, but I'd seen only a few Yanks in Ely and on the street where prefects could report us.

Trains were different. No prefects or teachers rode the trains, all students except we four from Great Chesterford were locals, so we could talk to soldiers. Three young Yanks bounced into our carriage. 'Hiya girls,' they exclaimed, with infectious good humour.

'Hallo,' I said cautiously, still unused to speaking to men.

I couldn't help staring at them; compared to Tommies they all looked like film stars with their good teeth, clear skin and well-fitting uniforms.

The train started off again as the stationmaster gravely waved his red flag up and down and blew his whistle. Under the clackety-clack of the wheels I whispered in Selma's ear, 'The Yanks all look so handsome. Their uniforms are much softer and fit much better than Tommies.'

'You can see they have all different size and shape bums. Tommies' trousers are so baggy you can't see the shape of their behinds,' Selma whispered.

She was right. Besides being just tall or short, fat or thin, I realised men, too, had differently shaped behinds, chests and waists. Under my lashes, I stole a look at the Yanks' bodies, exploring new territory. At the next stop, older men boarded, Tommies and Yanks leaped onto the running board of the moving train. A British airman in his light blue uniform entered our compartment. A British officer strode down the platform as the train began to move.

'Ooh, isn't he smart,' Cookie said, pointing at him as the train drew away. His uniform fitted his broad shoulders and slim waist perfectly, more like American uniforms. He was an officer and probably upper class. They could afford, or were allowed hand-tailored uniforms.

'Must have been made in Savile Row,' I said. 'All toffs have their clothes made there.'

'What's the use of that leather band across his chest and that tiny stick in his hand?' Helga said. 'Couldn't kill a fly.'

'It's a swagger stick. Shows he's an officer, I think' I said.

A short Tommie batman with a face like a worried rabbit trotted behind the officer, holding out leather gloves, calling out, 'Captain, Sir, you forgot your gloves.'

People on the platform made way for the officer. He looked neither right nor left nor paused in his stride as his batman ran to catch up with him. I thought it strange a grown man had to have someone look after him. Couldn't he dress himself? The upper class seemed always to have someone to serve them, though now, most servants had been called up. I had mixed feelings about the upper class. My parents stressed that we were working class and that the upper class were snobs. At the same time, I wished I could be one of them. Most were gentiles, though and some, like Mosley and Neville Chamberlain were openly anti-Semitic. But it didn't matter. I'd never be accepted into the upper class anyway. When I said I was born in Bethnal Green, even the Jewish middle-class looked down their noses and said, 'Ohh, reelly?' and walked away.

'Snobby English officers. Never say hello. At least Yanks are friendly,' Cookie said.

Although it was true, I felt disloyal criticising our fighting forces. Tommies had defended us long before Yanks joined in the fight, and only because the Japanese had bombed them. Now young women were going for the more glamorous and generous Yanks. Yanks had good skin, teeth and clothes, cigarettes, gum, chocolate and silk stockings.

The Yanks in our carriage had taken out their Camels and magazines, lounged back, and spread their long legs into the middle of the compartment. In England, it was considered rude for men as well as women to sit with legs spread wide. I watched a Yank's tongue that shoved a revolting wad of pink rubber about in his mouth as he carelessly flicked the pages of a magazine; Betty Grable filled the front page, smiling toothily into the camera, long white legs, in stiletto heels stretched in front of her. 'Woo-hoo,' said the redhead, 'Look at them gams.'

'Ah rayd that her legs are insured for a million dollars,' drawled the blond Yank, his accent stranger than the redhead's.

The blond Yank, who was about 20, leaned toward us. 'Hey kids, lark some chocolate?' He offered me a Hershey bar.

I looked at Selma. She nodded faintly, meaning: 'Okay to accept and it's kosher.'

'Thank you,' we said, as he handed me the chocolate. I caressed the nut bumps through the brown wrapper with my fingertip, already savouring the taste. I hadn't tasted chocolate since my 15th birthday, two months before. Breaking the bar into four pieces, a piece for each of us, I gave each girl her share and put the silver wrapping in my satchel for the war effort and sucked my piece of chocolate, crunching the nuts slowly, trying to make everything last.

An English soldier standing in the corridor muttered to his mate, 'Damned Yanks. Overpaid, over-dressed, oversexed, and over here.'

It was true; a lot of English women went out with Yanks. If I'd been only two years older, I'd have been going for them myself, unless as good a Tommy presented himself. I now had a good figure. I imagined myself in a closefitting blue dress and silk stockings with a square just over the heels and a line up the back of the leg. Many women like Norma, who couldn't get silk stockings, marked a line up the back of their legs with a dark pencil. I saw myself in high-heeled shoes, a darling little hat with a veil, mascara, lipstick, powder and perfume, as glamorous as Aunty Mitzi or Miss Curzon. Yanks and Brits, Canadians, Australians, Free French, and the Jewish Brigade would flock to me- perhaps even Joseph Singer would find me delightful.

As I daydreamed about Joseph Singer, my head rested against the back of the velvet seat, my eyes closed. The Hebrew book of short stories lay in my lap, its heavy square letters sharply outlined against the white page. A Yank next to me suddenly said, 'Hey, I know that language.'

My eyes popped open. 'You do? You can read Hebrew?' I said.

He nodded and laughed, 'You don't think I got barmitzva'd for nothin' do you?'

You're the first Jewish American I've met,' I said. 'I didn't know Jews lived in America.'

'I didn't know they lived in England,' he laughed.

I was so excited to meet an American Jew, I shook his hand. Cookie rolled blue eyes to the ceiling. The redhead smiled happily. He leaned over Selma's Hebrew book to look at it and gently moved back a strand of her hair.

'Don't touch my hair,' she protested, pulling away and he stopped.

'My name's Joey Stern, what's yours?' the Yank next to me said, smiling.

Helga and I told him our names, shyly. Selma ignored any unmarriageable man. This Yank was too old, over 20. Cookie asked, 'Where are you from in the States?'

'I'm from Noo York,' Joey said, 'and my friend here,' he jabbed the blond in the arm, 'is Clint. He's from Mississippi.'

Clint pushed his cap back on his head, looked up from his girlie magazine and said lazily, 'Hiya girls,' then ignored us. Of course, I thought, how could we compete with Betty Grable?

The train chugged on, passing a crossing where six trucks of soldiers behind rail bars waited to cross the tracks. Joey, next to me, his warm breath on my cheek, looked over my shoulder at the Hebrew book. He smelled of a good shaving lotion, like the one Daddy used. The warm, male scent of his body near mine gave my heart a sudden thump. I'd never been this close to a man.

'Say,' he said again, 'So there really are Jews in England?'

'There are not only Jews here, there's even anti-Semitism,' I said.

'Anti-Semitism? You're kidding. The English? Impossible. They're so polite!'

I told him about the Cable Street battle and the British Union of Fascists, how Mosley's hooligans had tried to march through our Jewish East End, smash up shops and people and how Jews, including my own uncle, unionists and communists had come out and beaten them back.

'Ya don't say,' Joey said. I saw he didn't believe me. True, the British had lovely manners. Americans didn't know that British anti-Semitism and good manners could co-exist.

'I hoped that The Cable Street Battle was the end of Fascism but I was mistaken,' I said. 'When I first came to the countryside and we told them we were Jewish, people felt our heads for horns. And there's a horrible local man who tells us Hitler didn't murder enough Jews and he ought to finish the job. My Christian scripture teacher told the whole class right in front of me that all Jews are rich because they're hypocrites, cheats and liars.'

Joey shook his head in bewilderment, 'Unbelievable. You really didn't know there were Jews in America?' Joey said. 'There are Jews in every state.'

The blond Yank, Clint frowned at us but said nothing. Was he anti-Semitic?

The English airman said, 'I've just come back from India and there was a Jewish man I met who knew nine languages without ever having bothered to learn them'.

'He probably escaped across nine countries, and picked them up en route,' I said.

The soldiers all laughed. 'I don't think a hunted man is funny,' I protested. Then to change the subject I said, 'I have a pen pal in America. Last year I saw a letter in *Life* magazine from an American who said he was against segregation of Negroes. I wrote back saying I agreed with him and now we write to each other. His name's Frank Robinson.'

'You mean to tell me some jerk wrote a letter to *Life* magazine saying he was against segregation?' Clint said.

'Yes. I don't believe in segregation, do you?' I said.

'Are you one of them nigger lovers?' Clint said.

'We don't use that word here,' I said. 'Is there really segregation in America?'

'Oh sure, them niggers can't come into our movies, restaurants, stores, bathrooms, or use our water fountains. They get out of line, we lynch 'em.'

'Take it easy, Clint,' Joey said.

The airman said, 'Shut up, pal,' but Clint ignored them.

'I thought America was supposed to be a democracy,' I said angrily. 'Don't African American soldiers fight in the war?'

'Yeah, the Third Regiment. They're segregated from us, too, otherwise I'd kill them before the Nazis got them,' Clint said.

'Oh, how awful,' Selma and I said, together.

'It is a democracy,' Joey said, squirming a little, 'but I have to admit there is segregation. I don't agree with it, but that's America. Maybe things will change after the war.'

Clint jumped up, pretended to stick and twist a knife into someone and shouted, 'I'd like to stick a knife in every nigger's ribs.' His pale face turned red, his eyes were bloodshot, his mouth twisted with hatred. His sudden violence shocked and frightened me. The train thundered along and gave a mournful hoot. I jumped up.

'You're disgusting,' I said, 'I'm calling the conductor then I'm getting out of here.' I raised my arm to pull the emergency brake. Joey gently put a hand on my arm.

'Don't take any notice of him, we're not all like that,' Joey said. 'Please stay.'

'Sorry. We're going to another carriage,' I said, getting up, the girls following me.

'I hope you don't condemn all of us because of him. I was so happy to meet you.'

'Well, we'll stay for you,' I said. 'You shouldn't be punished because of him. Though I wish he'd leave.'

'You're a wonderful girl,' Joey said.

The train hooted again. We girls knew that a long, dark tunnel loomed ahead. Immediately we entered the dark tunnel, I silently slid open the carriage door and stepped into the corridor. We plunged into the pitch black tunnel for two minutes, the train rattling on. As we came out into the light and I slipped back into my seat. Joey said, 'Where did you go? I wanted to kiss you.'

'I know,' I said, and we both laughed.

Clint stood dripping in the aisle screaming, 'I'm soaked, look at me. How did this happen?' Water poured off his head, plopping down his nose and on to his chest. His wet trousers clung to his legs and his wet hair lay flattened to his scalp.

Cookie stared out of the window a little smile on her face, her water bottle on the overhead rack rocking with the train's movement. Clint rushed out to the lavatory, came back, swaying with the train, threw himself on his seat, and fell asleep.

We all breathed a sigh of relief. Cookie winked at me.

'Would you mind opening the window, it's a little smelly in here,' Selma said. Joey pulled hard on a thick leather strap at the bottom of the window and fresh air rushed in. Yanks liked carriages to be hothouses and usually protested anyone opening a window.

'You actually did it!' I said faintly.

Everyone laughed.

At Stansted, the second American air base, the airman and sailor left and four more Yanks entered our carriage. Clint awoke sulkily. The water seemed to have dampened his spirit, but he opened his magazine. I would have left the carriage, but Joey had pleaded with us to stay. He seemed lonely, and I was so glad to meet a Jewish American who read Hebrew.

The new Yanks said, 'Hiyer fellas, hiyer girls.' It was a relief to get back to normal.

'I'm on my way to London,' a tall officer said. 'Hear it's a great city. Got a three-day pass. Boy am I happy, ainchoo?' he asked, poking his long, lean, booted friend in the ribs.

'Wish I could go to London,' I said. 'I love London.'

'Ya don't say. This is our first visit. Dja know what it's like?' asked the captain.

'Do I? I was born there. London is the most wonderful city in the world,' I said.

'I bet you haven't even been to any other countries,' the private said.

'How could I?' I said, 'I'm only 15. The war's been on for almost half my life.'

'Are you from London, too?' the captain asked Selma.

'I'm from Great Chesterford,' Selma lied.

She didn't want to say she'd been born in Germany. Many German Jewish refugees who fled to England were accused of being Nazi spies instead of refugees from Nazism. I found later that a friend's father had arrived in England with his family and the British had interned him in Australia, leaving his wife and children in England alone during the entire six years of the war.

'Where in London do you come from?' the captain asked me.

'From the East End,' I said. 'Yanks never go to the East End. You'll probably only go to the West End, where all the restaurants, theatres, and nightclubs are.'

'Do you know where Piccadilly is?' the private asked me.

'You bet,' I said.

Everyone, even sober Selma, burst out laughing.

'Why is everybody laughing?' I asked, feeling foolish.

Selma whispered into my ear, 'Piccadilly is full of prostitutes.'

I felt myself blushing and shouted indignantly, 'That is definitely not what Piccadilly is known for. It's the centre of West London. None of you knows Piccadilly as I do. Before the war I saw men there wearing tails and silk top hats and women in long dresses and furs with chauffeurs, driving Rolls-Royces. It was the fanciest place in London, where the statue of Eros, the Greek god of love stands, his bow and arrow ready to shoot men in the heart and make them fall in love.'

'Speaking of Eros, I've heard it's a monument to the generosity of your Englishwomen toward us Americans,' the Yank officer said, grinning.

'What do you mean?' I asked.

Selma, Helga and Cookie looked as puzzled as I felt. The men laughed long and loudly.

Joey and Clint got off at the next station. I went to the window to say goodbye to Joey.

From the platform Joey looked up said, 'I'm really sorry about Clint. After the war, I'm sure things will change. But I'm glad we met you girls. Hope we'll meet again. Bye.'

I felt sad to see Joey go and afraid that there were still more people like Clint. Suppose Clint felt toward Jews as he did toward Africans? The idea depressed me. We Jews already had so many enemies. But we also had friends like Joey and a few brave people like Churchill.

As the train moved away from the platform window, I walked through our carriage and looked out the window on the other side of the train. Three dark-haired men wearing one-piece camouflage suits bent over the tracks shovelling stones. They were young, good-looking and seemed healthy. Suddenly one of them looked up and stared at me for a moment, his dark, despairing eyes locked into mine. His hopeless expression shocked me. Shoulders bent, he returned to shovelling stones on the tracks. Letters on his back said: P.O.W.

'What does P.O.W. mean?' I asked Selma.

'Prisoner of War. They're Eyeties, Italians.'

'Surely you've seen P.O.W.s before?' Cookie said.

'No, never,' I said. At first I felt sorry for them, prisoners in a foreign country. Then I thought: these men were followers of Mussolini, fascists like Mosley's thugs, who'd planned a Kristallnacht for Jews in East London in 1936, even before the 1938 German Kristallnacht. Close up, the enemy always looked so human. He could be the boy next door.

I returned to the carriage where the London bound Yanks sat. The Americans talked about their schools, their families and flirted lightly. Perhaps we reminded them of their little sisters or left-behind girlfriends. I realised that like our hostel refugees, they never spoke about the war or what they did during the war. The Yanks behaved like friendly visitors to England, with no responsibilities. But if they lived on the air force base, some of them must have been pilots or bombers who nightly bombed Germany, fought German aircraft, risking their lives.

We girls got off at Bishop's Stortford and said goodbye to them.

'Give my love to London,' I said.

We trudged up the tree-lined street to school.

About a week after the Clint and Joey event, we were on the train going to school. Knitting with the sharp, pointed steel needles Anita had given me for my birthday, I was making a pair of khaki socks for some unknown Tommy. The nine-inch metal needles made tiny clashing noises every time I knitted a stitch. The seats in this particular carriage were arranged in twos, each two behind the others, as on a bus.

Cookie, sitting behind me, kept pulling my hair once, twice, three times.

'Stop,' I said, without turning round.

She pulled my hair harder, for the fourth time.

I turned round furiously to thump her back. As I turned, and lunged forward to hit her, one end of steel needle dug into the back of my seat, the other pointed end pierced my abdomen.

'I'm stabbed,' I screamed, looking down. The glittering needle stuck out of my middle like a sword. Blood oozed out. Selma turned white. Helga screamed.

Two American officers leapt to their feet.

'What's wrong, what happened?' one asked, leaning over me. Although bleeding, I couldn't help noticing that my hero looked like Henry Fonda, handsome, gentlemanly, unhurried and sympathetic. His friend stood behind him peering over his shoulder.

'Does it hurt?' the officer said.

Taught to keep a stiff upper lip like all other English children I answered, 'A bit.' But I was terrified of the glittering steel needle sticking out of me, and stared at it in horrid fascination.

'We'll carry you to school,' the officer said kindly.

'I'm afraid to move, it might go in deeper,' I whimpered.

'I'll move you very gently,' he said.

Cookie just stared out of the window. I hated her all over again. Selma looked anxious, but didn't know what to do and wrung her hands. Helga wept. Cookie slunk away.

When the train pulled into Bishop's Stortford, the handsome officer picked me up in slow motion. He carried me in his soft khaki arms along the tree-lined street, the silver needle sticking straight out of me into the air.

Though it wasn't the romantic entrance on the arm of a handsome Yank I'd dreamed of, I did enjoy an American officer grandly carrying me through the streets to school. Of course, being carried to school by a Yank officer, me with a steel knitting needle sticking out of my middle wasn't exactly as romantic as Miss Curzon with her officer's arms wrapped around her.

The other girls we passed stopped and stared. Although embarrassed at being in this predicament, and furious with Cookie, I pretended the Yank officer was my hero, maybe Clark Gable, and I was Joan Fontaine. Clark Gable had rescued me from the terrible German (Cookie) and was carrying me gently in his arms to hospital. I hoped the needle wouldn't fall out before I got to school. I'd feel a right fool. Curious girls trailed behind me all the way to headmistress's office, where the officer knocked, entered, and gently laid me down on her bench.

Miss Pierce, the new headmistress, sized up the situation immediately. 'Everyone to class,' she said briskly, and the girls slid away whispering to each other, 'What happened, how'd she get a knitting needle stuck in her?'

They should know Cookie, I thought darkly. I hated her as much as I hated Clint.

'Oh, how jolly,' exclaimed Miss Palmer, the gym and First-Aid teacher whom Miss Pierce had summoned. My moment of importance, I knew, was over.

The kind officer and his friend melted away. Without hesitation, Miss Palmer plucked out the needle, which, as I yelped, made a little sucking sound. She pulled up my gym tunic and blouse and I looked down. Blood oozed from the small, black hole in my middle. Miss Palmer wiped a little iodine on the hole and laughed. I thought she ought to be more serious in view of my near fatal accident. Suppose the needle had gone into my heart?

'D'you know something like this once happened to me?' she said.

Shut up, I wanted to say, it's my show.

'I was climbing the wall bars in the gym and my gym teacher came up behind me, put her hands on my bottom and said, 'Push up,' and as she pushed me up, three sharp pencils sticking up in her shirt pocket went into my behind!'

Miss Palmer chortled gleefully. I couldn't have cared less about the pencils in her bum. She should respect my dignity, and not tell jokes about how her gym teacher stabbed her in the behind. Probably she was trying, in her brisk, British, way, to minimise my shock while I wanted to relish the rare attention I was enjoying.

Back in the classroom, the local girls for once eager to speak to me asked, 'How did it happen, who were those divine Yanks who'd carried you to school?'

Very brave and offhand about it all, I felt a mixture of importance and awkwardness. I must have looked both dramatic and silly being carried to school in the arms of a handsome American officer, a steel knitting needle sticking straight up out of me.

I recovered almost instantly and except for my fury with Cookie, by the time school ended, I felt quite well. All the attention didn't hurt, either.

After school Helga, Selma and I got into the train for Great Chesterford. Cookie had disappeared and was staying out of my way, fortunately for her. Though it was an accident, I never forgave her. It was typical of her annoying pranks which this time, could have had serious results. Had the needle entered my heart, and gone in deeply enough, I could have died. Stabbed to death with a knitting needle, I thought. I was too young to die, and not through her.

Although the war was drawing to a close, we were still riding the trains to high school in Bishop's Stortford. The Allies were slowly but surely, winning in Europe. The Arab Mufti and Japan both supported the Nazis and were still at war with the Allies.

One beautiful day in May of 1944, on the way home to the hostel, I treated myself to a bunch of sweet-smelling violets bought from an old lady stood who stood outside Bishop's Stortford station with a basket of the flowers. Violets were Mummy's favourite flower. On the train, I went to the train toilet and changed out of my uniform into my one pretty blue dress. I wanted to celebrate the coming end of the war in Europe by changing from my school uniform to nice 'civvies', as demobbed soldiers would do.

In the compartment, I buried my face in the violets and drank in their sweet scent.

The two Yanks in our carriage – one next to me, a captain, the one opposite, next to Selma, a private – were raucous, cracking jokes and dancing in the aisles of the train, celebrating Allied victories over the Nazis. Yanks never seemed to work, but then we only saw them in the daytime and on trains. Perhaps these same boyish train riders flew the bombers, which passed overhead every day and night, on missions to bomb Germany.

At the stop before Great Chesterford we girls leaned out of the carriage window. The evening breeze riffled our hair across our faces. A group of eight Yanks on the platform below crowded round our window.

'Where you going? Can I have one of your violets?' a tall captain asked me. 'Here,' I said, pulling out a delicate tendril with its heartbreakingly sweet smell and gave it to him. 'Don't forget to water it.'

He laughed. 'Can you come to the dance in Cambridge Tuesday?'

'Our Daddy doesn't let us go dancing with Yanks,' I said, pulling a regretful face.

I would never dare ask Mr Shapiro's permission to go to a dance with Yanks. He was so grumpy lately, and would just expel me. The train began to move away, slowly. The Yanks walked alongside the train until it began to pick up speed. The tall one saluted.

'See you in Tokyo,' the tallest one called after us.

I felt a crushing sense of foreboding. These young men were soon all going to fight the Japanese. Some would be wounded, some taken prisoner, some killed. We'd all been laughing and joking as lightheartedly as if we'd been at a party together and as if they were seeing us off. Playing hooky by leaving school early, I'd seen many war films. I finally realised with a shock that these playful men and boys might be the heroes who ended up missing, wounded or dead.

We'd been seeing them off for the last and possibly greatest battle of the war somewhere in Japan, a place we'd hardly heard of. We'd never seen them serious, taking off in an aeroplane, protecting our lives, defeating Hitler, winning the war.

We children were protected from the terrible fight going on. Only years later reading history, did I realise the daily peril of their daring young lives, how lightly they laughed about it, and how grateful I am to have known, even briefly, these Tommy and Yank ordinary heroes.

CHAPTER 22

UNCLE MAX'S WEDDING

A blue airmail letter from Mummy:
>'122 Vallance Road
>Bethnal Green,
>London E.2
>April, 1943

The bombs have been awful. Hope we make it to the end of the war. Not long, now.
There's been a huge increase in VD since the Yanks got here. As a Lady Almoner, doing essential work for the government, I take down VD patient information when they come in and then they get a yellow bath. The joke is that the British used to supply Yanks with condoms but they were too small. Now they get their condoms from America. Let's hope they fit!
Enclose ten bob for pocket money. Come home for Uncle Max's wedding. Love, Mum

I didn't understand 'the joke is'. I knew what condoms looked like. Fridays nights after a shave, haircut and hot towels the men would say, 'Gimme a Red Letter, Alf'. I had once opened one of the packages and saw it looked like a long, white balloon before you blew it up. One floated like a fish in the chamber pot most mornings. But though Mummy spoke frankly about the body, I still didn't know what condoms were for, or why English condoms were too small for American soldiers. But busy preparing our Purim fancy dress party and play for next week, and excited about Uncle Max's wedding, I forgot about her letter.

I took the train to London for Uncle Max's wedding. Uncle Max was my warmest relative, and the only relative who had remained friendly after Booba banned us from the family.

Uncle Max, Mummy's youngest brother, on leave from Egypt for his wedding, was only 10 years older than me. We'd gone to the Cable Street Battle together, he'd helped Booba in her grocery, and sometimes he helped my father during the Christmas or New Year 'rush' in our shop. He was 25 to my 15, as handsome as Cary Grant, complete with dimple in chin.

Before shipping out to Egypt, Mummy had told me that Uncle Max was stationed at Guilford. I found that Guilford was not far from Great Chesterford. One day I'd skipped school, dressed in civvies and hitchhiked from the hostel to Guilford to surprise him. During the war, it was safe to hitchhike. 'You shouldn't have come,' he said, as soon as I strolled into his barracks, grinning.

'What do you do here?' I'd asked saucily and grown up, as we sat in the Tommie mess.

'I administer intelligence tests to soldiers. Many British soldiers can't read,' he said.

'They can't?' I said surprised, then remembered men in the shop reading only pictures.

'You're going back by train. I'll take you to the station and buy you a ticket,' he said. He sat me on his bike's bar and cycled us both up and down steep hills, wind whistling in my hair, to Guilford's train station. As we flew down hills, he shouted, 'My fiancée, Sylvia, would never ride on my bicycle bar'.

'Oh, pooh,' I said, 'it's nothing.' I was terrified of falling off the bar, but revelled in the fact that I was braver than this Sylvia interloper. I didn't care if he was marrying her. He was my uncle. I knew him long before she did.

Uncle Max bought me a ticket, put me on the train, kissed me and waved goodbye.

'See you at the wedding,' he smiled, as the train pulled out. We'd only been together about an hour, but I felt: 'Mission accomplished.'

A week later, I stood inside cavernous Liverpool Street Station, head thrown back, to gaze up at the familiar high glass, iron-girdered roof as I used to with my friend Joycey Kennel. As usual, I enjoyed going cross-eyed when I looked up at the soaring, now taped, glass roof.

Crowds of soldiers, sailors, blue-uniformed RAF men, and their girlfriends, wives, and mothers rushed back and forth, colliding in hugs and kisses, melting hellos or wrenching, wartime tearful goodbyes. I felt delirious with joy. Although I loved the hostel, I still adored grimy, exciting East London and Liverpool Street Station. They were my paradise.

Saucy East End sparrows perched on the iron roof station's supports, swooping from one girder to another. The grand train station had its own orchestra: birds twittered, monster black trains puffed and shunted, coupling carriages clanged, train doors slammed, engines hooted, steel wheels chugged, the stationmaster's whistle blew shrill and passengers' voices called out, 'Goodbye sweetheart,' or 'Hallo darling,' all echoing against the roof in cacophony.

As usual, and though I had seen neither parent for I forgot how long, no one met me.

I'd brought my bike, left it in the train's luggage compartment. Lonely, I wheeled my girl's bike, suitcase on the bar, toward the station exit. A few uniformed high school children like me milled around. Some evacuees had returned home to London during the 'phony war' in 1939 when no bombs dropped, but never left again. I'd read that about 8,000 children had died in the Blitz. Perhaps those now at the station had come home for the summer holidays, or from evacuation, believing the lull in the bombing meant the Blitz was over, or because the children were unhappy with their foster parents. I heard that Christian children were often happier. The caring Jewish hostel had replaced my family. I'd also read that the last bomb had fallen on Vallance Road and killed 130 victims, mainly Jews.

As soon as I left the station, the welcome tumult of Bishopsgate engulfed me. Buses zoomed, taxis skidded and honked, newspaper 'boys' some old men, in big, floppy caps outside the station shouted, 'Getcha Evenin' News. Raid last night kills 'undreds'. Workers chatted, stinking smoke belched from traffic, and from bombed office buildings, shops and houses.

What if my house had been bombed, the house demolished, my parents killed? I wheeled my bike along the rubble of other still-smoking bombed buildings, flats, some completely shattered and some eyeless without windows. Over a shop with shattered windows, a large sign read, 'Shattered but not shuttered. Sale on damaged goods'. The shop's glass front lay in shards on the street. A one-armed mannequin like a wounded soldier, stood in the shop front, clad in a shrapnel-torn dress and fur coat. Another sign in the window read, 'THE JERRIES CAN'T SHUT US DOWN. STILL OPEN FOR BUSINESS. FIGHT BACK'.

An elegant woman on the street stretched her hand through the glassless window and stroked a fur coat. I imagined her tearing it off the model and running away with it, but she entered the shop through the still intact door, setting its doorbell tinkling like Daddy's shop bell.

'Good morning, Madam,' I heard a cheerful voice sing out. I may have hated British anti-Semites but I admired British guts, especially Churchill's. Others, like Prince Edward, Mrs Simpson, Lord Halifax and Neville Chamberlain would have welcomed Hitler, only Churchill stood firm and declared, 'We shall fight them in the streets…we shall never give up.' He was also the only leader who favoured reviving as of old, the ancient Jewish state of Israel.

I stopped a moment to let a shopkeeper calmly sweep shards of glass from his shattered shop window into the gutter. 'Mornin,' he said cheerfully, as I stepped over broken glass.

'Good morning to you,' I said, feeling like a real Londoner. My heart beat with excitement at the prospect of reaching home, throwing myself into Mummy's arms and getting a rough hug and stubbly kiss from Daddy, dark eyes shining always grinning with a secret joke.

So many houses lay shattered that I feared ours had been bombed and Mummy hadn't told me. Finally, I came to Vallance Road, and saw that the shop and house though shabby, still stood. The old sign 'Alf's Ladies' and Gentlemen's Hairdressing,' now lop-sided from some raid, still hung over the shop window. Our red, white and blue barber pole still twirled lazily overhead. Daddy had nailed plywood over the smashed upstairs windows. Although our shop door was locked and the red shutters were up over the shop windows, the side entrance to the house was, as usual, unlocked. I sighed with relief, ran inside and shouted, 'Hello, I'm home.'

The house was empty and silent. I hadn't been home for at least a year, and no one was there to greet me. Tears sprang to my eyes. I wandered into the kitchen, and peered into the pantry, empty, but for a tin of sardines and half a loaf of bread. I tramped up the bare wooden stairs and pinged listlessly on the piano, pulled open sideboard drawers. I found the old kaleidoscope the brilliant colours and changing patterns of which had thrilled me as a child. I held it up to the boarded window. In the gloom, the scope's brilliant colour formations were a blur. Finally, I heard the front door downstairs slam and ran down, colliding with Daddy. He put down the two heavy carrier bags gave me a quick hello, a hug and a bristly kiss.

'Yer Uncle Sam's seriously ill and Booba asked Mum to come and help her in the shop.'

So Booba was speaking to Mummy again. She treated Mummy with contempt, but Mummy still ran to her gratefully whenever called. With Uncle Max in the army and Uncle Sam in hospital, Booba needed help. Aunty Mitzi would never work in a grocery shop: she was too posh. Now, having married the boss's son, she was part of his family, and still had her old job in Saville Imported Laces. I'd once visited before the war and thrilled to the rainbow colours of exotic laces stacked in bolts from floor to ceiling. Mummy, but never Mitzi, was expected to close her own shop to help Booba. At least my mother was a faithful daughter to her own mother. I understood her yearning after all these years for her mother's love as I yearned for hers. But my mentors and friends at the hostel loved me.

'Want a cuppa?' Dad said.

I nodded and smiled. I wished he wasn't deaf so I could speak to him as other daughters did to their fathers. I began to understand it might be difficult for Mummy to have to shout whenever she wanted to speak to him. Children were trained to speak quietly.

We sat companionably by the fire with our tea and biscuits, neither of us talking, me listening to strains of *Aida* that Mummy and I loved, pouring out of the wireless.

Mummy finally rushed in breathless. We kissed and hugged. Since I'd been at the hostel, Mummy had become warmer. Was it because I was out of her way? Or was it because I was older and could take care of myself?

That night the air-raid siren wailed like a monstrous baby crying.

'Hurry up, get under the stairs,' Mummy said.

We both crouched down on the coal as before. Daddy had gone to bed, he wouldn't hear anything. A terrible thump, like a monster's body falling, the whole house shook, then came a roar and popping sounds as a nearby bomb exploded. Then rumbling like a monster train, buildings collapsed, and glass shattered, tinkling like a piano's top notes. I shivered with fright.

'They're bombing the docks again,' Mummy said.

The bombing relentlessly went on and on, with deafening explosions followed by dread silences. Then came the sharp rattle of ack-ack gunners shooting at German bombers. I was afraid a bomb would drop on us. We would all be killed instantly or worse, our arms, legs, or backs broken. Would the house crumble onto us and we'd be buried alive? No one would find us for days, or until we'd died of thirst. I'd read about a boy of eight buried for seven days under a pub in Paris. When he was finally rescued, he staggered out dead drunk but smiling.

Don't let me lose an arm, I prayed to God, not now. I would look awful at the wedding. 'Should we go to the underground?' I asked, like last time. The same reply.

'No fear. You wouldn't catch me down there sleeping with hundreds of other people on the platforms and tracks. It's bedlam down there. They piss in pails, play music and cards all night, eat and get drunk. I'd rather die in bed.' Mummy said again.

After endless earth-shattering bombing, a thin one-note wail sounded the All Clear.

'Just when we thought they'd stopped bombing London, the Jerries started again,' Mummy grumbled. 'We're so close to winning the war, yet we could be killed by a last bomb.'

We peered outside to see if any houses on our street had been hit. But eastward toward the docks, the whole sky was flaming red, the fire both beautiful and frightening. Almost anything beautiful, I thought, could also be dangerous: fire, ice, the sun and glass, even buildings, if they fell on you. I reminded myself that there would soon be a wedding to enjoy.

In the midst of life there was death, and in the midst of death there was life.

Uncle Max came home for his wedding on seven days' leave. As if I too, served in the army, Mr Shapiro said, 'You can have six days' leave and no more.'

'Why only six days when Mrs Rozenfeld said I could go home for seven days?'

'These children have no family. If you leave to see your family they will be hurt', he said.

'I can't help having a family, and my uncle is getting married,' I answered.

No one knew how important it was for me to come together with my warring family. I'd never told anyone that Mummy and I had been banned from seeing or talking to my family. I had not seen my grandparents, aunts and uncles for years. I would see them all at the wedding.

Booba finally invited Mummy and me to visit her and to see Uncle Max. I ran into my grandfather's arms, and we hugged, but he did not murmur as he used to when I was little, *Bubbele, zeesele, fliegele*, little doll, little sweet, little wing. I was too big to sit in his lap. I kissed my grandmother's cool cheek. We had not seen each other for three years. Aunt Mitzi, now cool and rich, also offered her cheek as she stood with her new, wealthy husband who looked like Claude Raines. I missed her old warm hug and her calling me 'Pussycat'.

Her small son from Adrian, Gabriel, stared at me rudely. His body blocked my entrance to my old favourite haunt: the dining room. My dining room had now become his dining room. It was too humiliating for me to fight with an infant. No one said, 'Let Gilda through,' so I stood silently seething in the shop like the stranger that I now was, usurped by this brat cousin.

The family hugged our young, handsome soldier on leave from fighting Rommel's AfrikaKorps in Egypt. Afrika Corp. His rough Tommy's uniform chafed the skin on my arms.

'You look so handsome, Uncle Max,' I said, admiringly.

'You're not so dusty yourself,' he said. 'Knocking 'em dead?'

'I wish.'

He smiled and kissed me, his dark stubble grazing my cheek. I was so proud of my brave, British, soldier uncle who, when he was 16 and I was six before the war, had taken me to the Cable Street Battle. Now, at 15, I was almost grown up, Yanks flirted with me and now at 25, he was a soldier and an almost husband. Suppose when he married he forgot he had a niece? He was the only one in the family who spoke to Mummy and me after Booba banned us. He must have insisted we be invited to his wedding. In my eyes, he could do no wrong.

Booba finally invited us all into the dining room for tea. Aunt Mitzi picked up her brat and took him in. Throughout tea, he stared at me angrily. When no one was looking, I stuck my tongue out at him, and he cried, but because he couldn't talk, no one knew why, so I grinned.

The next day, Uncle Max, the only one of the family to visit us came to our house for tea. Even though Mummy worked for Booba, Booba still had never visited except to slap Mummy's face over the 'abortion'. I felt angry with Booba, but since infancy Mummy had taught me, and then Mr Shapiro, honour your mother, father and elders, but what if your elders behaved badly? Booba had favoured Aunt Mitzi and excluded Mummy and me. I respected her hard work, but she had never been kind to me or Mummy. Should I honour her?

Mummy and Uncle Max chatted in our kitchen over tea. I had never before seen my mother and her brother talking together. I wished I had a brother or a boyfriend like Uncle Max.

The big day arrived. Mummy wore the same green satin beaded suit with green satin shoes that she'd worn at Aunt Mitzi's first wedding, and I wore a rented white chiffon dress and a circlet of white flowers on my head. Dad wore a smart black suit hired from Moss Bros.

I preened in front of my parents' bedroom wardrobe mirror, admiring my firm breasts, neat waist and good legs and pretty tulle dress. With clothes' rationing, we'd had no pretty clothing since the war began. Mummy had found me black-market silk stockings, and two-inch high-heeled shoes that made me look taller and slimmer. Our wartime diet consisted largely of starchy potatoes and bread, though we worked much of this off with sports. Twirling again before the long bedroom mirror, I thought I looked elegant, even exotic.

The wedding was held at the posh Murray's Club on Beak Street in the West End. In our fine clothes, Mummy, Daddy and I took a bus to Beak Street.

'In peacetime, Uncle Max would have had the ceremony first at the Beehive Lane synagogue, and then gone on to the reception at Murray's Club,' Mummy told me, as the bus bumped along. 'But because of the war, there's no gasoline to take guests from the synagogue to Murray's Club. So they carried the *chuppa* through the streets from the synagogue to Beak Street Club and set it down in the middle of the ballroom. You should have seen weddings before the war,' Mummy said as our red double-decker entered the West End.

As usual, Daddy sat quietly, his dark, humorous eyes, watching everyone, as I did.

'No use any man expecting me to have *nadn*,' I said.

'You're right. Whoever marries you can't expect anything from us. But if you marry one of those religious men, he'll expect a fortune. They all do. And you should be helping me in the shop on Saturday, not going to services.'

I felt terrible. What to do? Please Mummy or break Shabbat? Both were impossible.

'Hello, pussycat,' exclaimed Aunty Mitzi in her old, affectionate way when we entered.

I ran to hug her but she held me by the shoulders keeping me at a distance, put her cheek to mine and kissed the air. 'Mmmmaa!! How grown up you look, quite the young lady!'

Her new husband, Raphael, stood behind her, hair slicked back and parted on one side. He wore a thin moustache, his dark eyes alert. In his perfectly tailored tails, he moved with the ease of the very rich. His ruffled white shirt gleamed, and ruby cufflinks winked at me.

As Mummy said, she always got what she wanted. My aunt seemed happy, her blue eyes dancing, but I missed the old bubbly, saucy Aunt Mitzi and cheeky Adrian. I felt my aunt and Raphael were dancing on his grave.

A pretty young woman in white held Uncle Max's arm. He looked at her adoringly.

'Sylvia, this is my niece, Gilda,' he said to his fiancée, grinning from ear to ear like a schoolboy.

'How do you do?' this Sylvia said, offering me a white, limp hand. My new aunt-to-be. Sylvia wore a real pre-war satin wedding dress, as beautiful as Aunty Mitzi's had been at her first wedding. Sylvia wore a single white rose with a tiny veil on the top of her long, dark curls, a little like Shirley Temple.

It seemed to me that Sylvia's mother had just lifted her veil and given her daughter wine to drink from the silver goblet, when I heard the tinkle of the broken wine glass that Uncle Max had stamped on. Even in joy, we remembered the destruction of the Temple in Jerusalem.

'Mazltov,' everyone shouted.

Uncle Max bent Sylvia back in a dip, his black tails making him look like a black swan leaning over a white swan, and kissed her for so long I was afraid she would suffocate.

My new aunt finally stood up flushed and radiant, and the band struck up *Choson Kallah Mazel tov,* congratulations to the bride and groom. Crowds of people rushed up to the *chuppa* and hugged and kissed Uncle Max and Sylvia, shouting 'Mazltov!!'

I could not manage to call her 'aunt', just kissed my uncle, pecked her velvety cheek and wished them Mazltov. They stared like fools for four minutes into each other's eyes as if they were all alone. I felt a new pang of jealousy. He was my uncle, almost the brother I'd never had. He'd teased me whenever I visited Booba's shop, left his burn mark on my hand; I'd visited his barracks and ridden on the bar of his bicycle. This Sylvia was going to take him away forever and he would never tease me again and he was the only kind person left in the family.

I'd kissed Sylvia's smooth cheek and Uncle Max, smelling his tangy cheek for perhaps the last time. I was due back in Great Chesterford, and he was shortly due back in Egypt to fight Rommel. We had the same leave time of six days. The war was still on.

Booba now pushed Zada, Uncle Max and Sylvia, Uncle Sam, Aunt Mitzi and Raphael into a waiting taxi, and I heard her say to the driver, 'Boris'. Everyone knew Boris, the famous Jewish photographer. I was surprised they hadn't taken Mummy or me with them for photographs; Mummy was Uncle Max's sister and I was bridesmaid. Mummy watched them leave, her eyes brimming with tears. I went to her and held her hand.

'Let's go to the ladies' room,' I said.

Inside she sobbed a little, then powdered her snub nose and freshened lipstick on her full mouth. 'I even have an unfashionable mouth,' she said, peering into the mirror. 'Everyone these days has a thin mouth.'

'I think your mouth is beautiful,' I said, but tears welled in her eyes again. 'My little brother married,' she said, 'and I won't even be in the wedding photos.'

I admired, but didn't like my grandmother. If Booba had been kinder to Mummy, and not favoured Aunt Mitzi so openly, perhaps Mummy would have been kinder to me.

'Why does Booba favour Aunt Mitzi?' I dared ask Mummy, quietly.

'It's simple. Booba loves beautiful things and Aunt Mitzi is beautiful. Booba loves rich people and now Aunt Mitzi is rich. But she made me marry a poor, uneducated man I didn't love so that Mitzi could marry Raphael, and then his family refused her. Only after Adrian died and she received government compensation for his death did Raphael propose. He even adopted Adrian's child. She gets everything she wants; I can't even get into a family photo.'

An hour later, after taking photos I supposed, the family came back for dinner and dancing. Booba acted as if nothing unusual had happened. Mummy pretended to be happy. I myself enjoyed being with my family however cool they were, and the rare, wartime festivities.

The wartime wedding menu was simply soup, fish and chicken, but because Sylvia's father owned a chain of grocery shops, food, though modest, was plentiful.

As Uncle Max and Aunt Sylvia entered the dance floor alone, he held her close but gently, as if she were precious. She put her arm around his neck as if he belonged to her. And he did. They danced cheek to cheek, their bodies pressed as closely together as if they were one. 'And a man shall leave his parents and cleave to his wife,' I remembered reading in the Torah. Everyone clapped as they circled the floor, then other couples slid onto the floor and danced. The band played the latest, at first slow, dreamy waltzes, then a fast, *In the Mood*.

'They're spending the rest of his seven-day leave at the Cumberland Hotel on Park Avenue,' I heard Booba say proudly to a guest.

That must have been a gift from Aunt Sylvia's father. I knew Uncle Max couldn't afford such a fancy hotel. I doubted Booba, notoriously tight-fisted except when it came to Mitzi, would have given them such a gift, even if she could. My favourite person, Zada, was sitting and smoking an after-dinner Turkish cigarette. Looking at his great broad chest made me want to run and nestle in his lap, lean against him and feel him rub his stubble against my skin, as he used to when I was five. But I was now 15, too old for that, a young woman admired by Yanks. Having been away, evacuated for nearly six years, Booba and Zada now treated me as though I were a stranger and daughter of an outcast. It was unfair. I had done nothing wrong. Why should I have been banned because Mummy was?

Each relative did give me a perfunctory kiss and said the traditional, '*Mirtza shem badir*', 'You should also soon find your bridegroom'. No one asked me about my life away from home during the past five years of evacuation. I'd disappeared and they hadn't even missed me. Of course, I thought, they're all wrapped up with the wedding, not you, twerp. Still, I wondered if my new Aunt Sylvia would be friendly to us, or like the rest of the family, exclude my family. Booba probably invited us to the wedding only because Uncle Max insisted on it. As in the Cable Street Battle, he was the one family member who fought for justice.

Just as we left the wedding, I looked back and saw Uncle Max gazing softly into Sylvia's eyes and she into his, and I knew they'd be lovers forever. I'd often wondered if love was important. Yes, love was important. With love, in its spring, you budded, in summer, you blossomed into full flower. Or so I'd read in *Song of Songs*.

Would I ever flower, or always be an unopened bud? Would I ever be able to love, like my uncle and Sylvia? I didn't know if I were able to love or to trust someone else with my love.

Could I ever trust anyone with my love? To love was to be hurt. I trusted no one.

CHAPTER 23

FAREWELL MR SHAPIRO

Back at the hostel, in early March 1945, an outbreak of measles quarantined us all to the White House. We high school girls missed a week of school, a serious loss, because with matriculation exams due shortly, classes and homework had became highly intensive. Failure in this examination doomed a girl or boy for life from even *applying* to college.

Because the hostel was so noisy and homework now so important, I had been moved for weekdays, to a quiet house in Bishop's Stortford where I could study at night undisturbed, I returned to the hostel on Fridays for Shabbat and Sunday. At first, I stayed with two teachers who lived together and close to school. Miss Roberts was tall, fluttery in scarves and frills, her more sober roommate, was also tall, but sharp-tongued and bossy. They did not understand the rules for the kosher food I brought with me, and unused to wine glasses, I accidentally knocked over such a glass served with dinner. When I couldn't get a stain out of the bath, they summarily kicked me out. Somewhere in between them and my next billet, I spent a week in a British government hostel with adult men and women. All I recall is a friendly common room and fire.

I was next billeted with a lovely Jewish couple, the Schenkers. He had a business in London, stayed there weekdays and came home only weekends. Since I left when he arrived on Friday afternoons, I never saw him. Mrs Schenker stayed in Bishop's Stortford, blonde, buxom, very feminine, and agreed to take me in until exams were over. Her house was quiet and calm.

I returned to school with the girls on Monday morning and returned to the Schenkers on Monday after school. There was at least three hours' solid homework every night in English, French, Latin, Math, History, Geography and Art. We continued gym, tennis, hockey, rounders, netball, dance and swimming which, with our starchy diet, probably kept us from becoming fat. Mr Shapiro still helped me. My grades began to climb again.

The year before, aged 15, I'd entered the Hertfordshire and Essex High School Junior Fitzgerald writing contest and won. But I was totally surprised when headmistress announced at morning prayers, that I had won the Senior Literature Contest. When I went up to the stage to receive the prize, all the girls clapped. It did not win me friends, but the local girls for the first time began to greet me. With the hostel outbreak of measles, I thought my entry was impossible.

'We can't send your entry to school; it's contagious,' Mr Shapiro said.

Disappointed, I slapped it onto a shelf in the Green Room and forgot about it.

A week later, Mr Shapiro said, 'You can enter the competition, but to avoid contagion, we have to bake your story.'

'Bake my story?' I laughed, and then said ruefully. 'The deadline's passed.'

Nevertheless, Mrs Bramson heated the oven. 'Slide your story onto the rack,' she said. Gingerly, I slid the ten-page story into the hot oven, sure the pages would burn to a crisp. But they came out whole, warm and crackly, and with little brown bumps on the now cream paper, my story looked like Passover matzot. 'A burnt offering', I laughed and forgot about it. However, burnt or not, on my return to school after quarantine ended, the Hertfordshire and Essex headmistress called me up to the stage to receive my Senior Literature prize. Cookie and I did not sit with the local girls, because their prayers were Christian. We sat upstairs behind a glass partition in *purdah*. When my name was announced as winner, I rushed down the stone steps, paused a moment to catch my breath before entering the hall, entered calmly and mounted the steps to the stage. The girls had waited patiently.

As the girls applauded, I smiled. Due to Mr Shapiro's ingenuity, I had finally achieved some small recognition in the school. But the next day, in late March, Mrs Shapiro told me to go to Mr Shapiro's study. I knocked on the panelled door, heard, 'Enter', went in and sat in the oak-lined room.

'I'm soon going away. Because you are Head Girl, I want you to learn how to give a sermon on Shabbat like me.'

'Leave? Why are you leaving? When?' I asked, dismayed.

He smiled sadly and looked down at his square hands.

'Mr Shapiro, that's impossible. You've studied Torah for years, and I've studied it for only a few months.'

'I have confidence in you. You're a born speaker. You must read through the *Chumash*, the Five Books of Moses to see if there is anything you don't understand. That way you can ask me about it before I leave.'

'I cannot read the entire Five Books of Moses in Hebrew and give your sermon,' I protested. 'No one has your knowledge. I can't possible replace you.'

'Just do as I ask. For me,' he said gently and sorrowfully.

I ran out of his study and to Nurse. 'Why is he leaving us?' I cried.

'I don't know,' she said. 'We'll see in a few weeks. I can tell you this...' she began, but then Cookie came in. 'Just don't say anything to anyone,' Nurse whispered.

'Oh, why all the mystery?' I cried crossly. 'What's happening?'

The next evening, Passover, 30 March would be the first *Seder* in which I'd ever participated. Wearing his white *kittel,* Mr Shapiro sat, leaning on a cushion, the children around him. He now seemed to have reverted to the usual calm, selfless educator persona. 'I'm wearing this white silk coat, a *Kittel* tied with this white belt, to show the seriousness of this ceremony,' he said. 'The *kittel* is worn only on Yom Kippur, during the Passover Seder, for a marriage, or burial. Let's open the *Haggadah*.'

He continued speaking in a low voice. 'I'm leaning on this cushion during the Seder to show we are free men and no longer slaves in Egypt. The word *Seder* means 'order' and we observe Passover rituals in a specific order. This festival is in memory of God delivering us from slavery in Egypt and taking us to the Promised Land; Israel. The story is called and written in the *Haggadah. Haggadah* means, 'Telling a story.' Here, he held up his beautifully illuminated *Haggadah.* Each child had a different *Haggadah.*

Some were reprints from mediaeval times, and showed Jews leaving Egypt dressed in medieval clothing. Israeli Haggadot showed Jews leaving Egypt dressed as modern, Jewish pioneer Zionists wearing shirts, shorts and *kipot.* Although the words were the same, and in the same order in each *Haggadah,* I marveled at the different creative coloured illustrations and that depending on the time printed, the country where the *Haggadah* was printed, that illustrations of Jews leaving Egypt about 3,000 years ago, showed them dressed in clothing at the time of the printing. Mr Shapiro explained the symbolic significance of each item on the table. The youngest in the hostel, four-year-old Stanley Shapiro. now asked The Four Questions. Tiny in his velvet Little Lord Fauntleroy suit, he stood, his curly head and dark eyes just reaching the table, and in his clear, child's voice chanted in Hebrew, 'Why is this night different from all other nights?' Then he sang the answer: 'On all other nights we eat leavened and unleavened bread, on this night only matzo; on all other nights we eat all kinds of greens, on this night, only bitter herbs; on all other nights we don't dip our food even once, on this night, twice; on all other nights we eat either sitting or leaning, on this night we all lean. Leaning shows we are free, and live in luxury, like the Romans at their banquets,' he said.

I thought it strange that we would copy anything from barbaric Romans who crucified thousands of men, or to lean like Greeks who forbade Jews to study Torah. I refused to lean.

All the children clapped Stanley. He smiled shyly, clinging to Mrs Shapiro's skirts. I looked round at the children's shining faces, and under the table, squeezed Selma's hand. She smiled and squeezed my hand back. If any of these orphans had been with their real families on this Passover night, they might have been the youngest child, and would have stood proud to traditionally ask the Four Questions. But at the White House we were one big family of orphans.

Mr Shapiro continued with the ceremony with the ten plagues ending with the death of the firstborn in every Egyptian house. What a terrible outcry there must have been in Egypt as Egyptian fathers and mothers found their oldest child dead. But I also imagined the anguish of Jewish mothers weeping as Egyptians drowned Jewish newborn sons. Even as we spoke, horror rumours were seeping back about Nazis who murdered Jewish children in front of their enslaved mothers. But surely we would win the war, and free Jewish men and women from Nazi slavery.

'And God delivered us...to the Promised Land, Israel,' Mr Shapiro chanted.

I imagined that I entered a *Haggadah* joining thousands of freed Jewish slaves trekking through the wilderness, the Holy Ark in our midst, a pillar of cloud going before us by day and a blazing pillar of fire by night, walking toward the freedom of the Promised Land. I felt a fierce, tribal closeness to everyone at the Seder table. To which of the twelve tribes had my ancestors belonged? Judah the lion would be my tribe. I made a silent promise that one day my children and I would settle in ancient Judah, the way in recent years, many Jews had joined those who since Abraham, had and still lived in Israel. If only the occupying British would let Jewish refugees into Israel, and did not send them back to sure death. They were as cruel as Pharaohs.

Halfway through the Seder, we ate a scrumptious rare wartime meal of soup, roast beef, roast potatoes, peas, and then, cake, rare, served from saved rations and during wartime, only on Shabbat or major Jewish festivals.

'Where did he hide the *afikomen*?' all the little ones asked. Another Greek word. After the Babylonian, Greek and Roman conquests of Israel, conquerors always deported natives to their own countries as slaves and settled their own in conquered lands, which therefore, led to the diversity in Jewish practices. Jews absorb some culture and words from every country they are either exiled to or in which they escape from persecution. Jews have always been escaping persecution, seeking asylum in another country, therefore we are dispersed throughout the world, a most cosmopolitan people. Thus, the *afikomen* was a Greek word, and we lounged in freedom on Passover like Romans. I couldn't see why we used the words or habits of such cruel people.

'Let's find the *Afikomen*,' Mr Shapiro said. 'It is our "desert". We can't finish without it.'

Mr Shapiro had hidden a small piece of matzo at the beginning of the meal. Children scattered, searching the entire three stories of the White House for the *Afikomen*. Little Bertie found it behind a pile of books in the common room.

'What's my reward?' he cheekily asked Mr Shapiro.

'Next week I'll take you to Cambridge to see Little Lord Fauntleroy,' said Mr Shapiro.

'Oooh,' everyone breathed jealously at this wonderful reward.

Finally, we sang '*Chad Gadye*,' 'One Kid' but first Mr Shapiro told us, 'This song represents all the empires that gobbled each other while the littlest nation, Israel, remains.' Being musical, like Mummy, I picked up the tune quickly as we sang in Hebrew very fast barely pausing for breath:

'My father sold a kid for two *zuzim*, then came a cat that ate the kid that my father bought for two *zuzim*; then came the dog that bit the cat, the stick that beat the dog, a fire that burned the stick, water that quenched the fire, the ox that drank the water, the slaughterer who killed the ox, the Angel of Death who killed the slaughterer, and God killed the Angel of Death who killed the slaughterer that killed the ox that drank the water that quenched the fire that burned the stick that beat the dog that bit the cat that ate the kid that my father bought for two *zuzim*.'

Gathering speed as we sang this last part in Hebrew to its end in one breath, we finished and collapsed into each other's arms, laughing. We all sang as a finale, 'Next Year may we be in Jerusalem,' our voices reverberating against rafters. We rose happily, ready for sweet sleep.

But before we could leave, Mr Shapiro said, in a solemn voice, 'Children, there's something I have to tell you. Please sit down.'

I already knew, but did not want to believe what he'd told me.

'Children,' he said in a gentle voice, eyes downcast. 'I will soon have to leave you. I can't tell you how sorry I am. I love studying, learning with you and teaching you, but I cannot stay. God bless you all and good luck in whatever you do.'

Mrs Shapiro, holding Stanley, sat sadly, silent, her eyes also downcast.

There was a total, stunned silence in the dining room except for Bertie, who gulped, sniffled and wiped his nose on his sleeve. We couldn't believe he was leaving us. For some, he'd been their only father; when they were only four, the Nazis had killed their fathers and mothers, sisters and brothers. The only parents they'd known had been the Shapiros. England accepted child refugees between the ages of four to 17. Britain refused entry to parents. Most parents and children not admitted were murdered by the Nazis. Mr Shapiro continued, 'I've been with some of you now for five years. Some of you were only four when you came here, alone and frightened. I've seen you grow up strong, and have daily taught you Hebrew, *Chumash*, and the Torah and we've read to you from Dickens and Shalom Asch. I hope you'll continue studying and make me proud of you when we meet again.'

'I am going to become headmaster of the Menorah Jewish High School in London. Perhaps after the war, I hope some of you will come and see me, or even come to my school.'

He then sat down, head bowed, amid silence except for subdued snuffles.

'Gilda, will you sing for us?' Mr Shapiro finally asked.

I gulped back tears, Selma passed me a handkerchief. What could I sing? I felt so confused. I owed Mr Shapiro everything, not just my education, but also for introducing me to a life of kindness, meaning and significance. I guessed that he had decided the hostel was not the work for him. Perhaps he was lonely stuck out in the country with thirty children, no adults to talk to, and needed a social and intellectual life of his own. He would probably make a wonderful headmaster, have a normal home and social life, evenings alone with his family or with friends. We had probably all driven him mad. That was why he'd been so temperamental, lately. He needed peace and quiet, and the company of educated adults.

I sang the sad, beautiful song Mummy had taught me, *Shuvi nafshi*.

Tears rose to my eyes as I sang. When I finished everyone was silent for a full minute.

As Moses had left behind a close band of dedicated Jews, so Mr Shapiro would leave us. I would miss him, but he'd leave me with the strength, confidence and ability to cope for myself and like him, lead others. I also felt proud to have been among his chosen students.

The children, including Mr and Mrs Shapiro, stood up, held hands, and then we all spontaneously sang in a chorus:

Shalom Aleichem, shalom aleichem, shalom, shalom,

Lehitraot, lehitraot, shalom, shalom.

Hallo and goodbye, may we meet again soon, in peace.

In fact, I did visit him one bitter day in December long after the war. He was sweet and happy.

CHAPTER 24

ROMEO AND JULIET

As if through a revolving door, Mr and Mrs Shapiro left one morning in May before we children even rose, and the same afternoon, new wardens, Rabbi and Mrs Koehler arrived.

The Rabbi and his wife, German Jewish refugees, resembled an illustration of the nursery rhyme, 'Jack Spratt could eat no fat his wife could eat no lean'. The rabbi's bearded face, dark eyes behind thick glasses, allowed a glimpse of a handsome man with Jewish, introspective eyes. He trod the hostel's hallways contemplatively, eyes cast down, hands clasped behind his back, like a German-Jewish gentleman scholar. He'd now been warden for three months.

Contrary to my relationship with Mr Shapiro, no tempestuous love-hate, or any other kind of relationship developed between Rabbi Koehler and me. He was totally unaware of my existence, which meant that although I had less authority neither could I get into trouble. The rabbi and I were just ships passing in the night. We had never spoken one word to each other.

Whereas Mrs Shapiro had been petite, pretty, modern and flirtatious, Mrs Koehler's camel-like bosom preceded her door entries, and her rhinoceros hindquarters hovered after she passed through. As a very religious married woman, she covered her hair according to Jewish laws of modesty - to deter the covetous glances of other men. Her head, wrapped in a tight bandanna, like a small football atop a short neck and massive torso, was deterrent enough. On the other hand, unlike Mrs Shapiro, she personally fussed over every child. '*Ess kindt, ess*,' Eat child, eat, she would croon. The second wife of widowed Rabbi Koehler and stepmother to his two girls, Mrs Koehler was childless.

His older girl, Ruth, was a friendly girl with buck teeth, aged 13; Lili, the younger, was a dimpled girl of 11 with white skin, dark eyes and red lips, looking like fairy-tale Snow White.

The first morning after the Koehler's' arrival, instead of Nurse poking her head in the door at 7am shouting, 'Time to get up,' we heard a scream, '*Aufstehen!*' that we had heard in films about Nazis. It was Mrs Koehler saying, 'Up.'

Horrifyingly she sounded like the films seen when I sneaked into in Bishop's Stortford, skipping class, in which Nazi guards screamed at Jewish prisoners, '*Rausse, rausse, aufstehen.*'

'Does she think we're a German concentration camp?' I grumbled, as we reluctantly tumbled out of our warm army cots. 'How dare she shout at us like a disgusting German?!'

That evening, after supper, Cookie crouched on the window-seat of the big girls' room filing her long, white-tipped fingernails, her one claim to beauty besides her thick, blonde hair. From our third story window we could see the pond, its little bridge and the four-acre garden and tall trees stretching green beyond to the hidden orchard. Summer flowers had died, the wind now skittered red autumn leaves along the veranda outside Mr Shapiro's former study.

I had been sitting on my cot next to Selman writing in the orange diary Cookie had given me for my birthday. I paused. 'He's quite handsome with that great black beard and dark eyes,' I said. 'He reminds me of Theodore Herzl.'

'Who's Theodore Herzl?' Helga asked in her little girl voice. I answered her.

'A famous Zionist. Herzl went to all the kings of Turkey, England, Germany, and Italy and asked them to give Palestine – as the Romans and British insultingly called it to make us seem like Philistines – back to the Jews. Only the Romans and British called Israel Palestine. There never was such a country. Mr Shapiro said the Irgun will get Israel back for us after the war,'

'And just who is the Irgun, Miss Know-it-all?' Cookie asked.

179

'It's a small army of Jewish fighters in Israel trying to get the British out of our country. The British, of course, call the Irgun 'terrorists'. It is the British who are the terrorists. Most Israelis fight for the Allies in the 'British Brigade.' Mr Shapiro told me that the British refuse to integrate The Jews in the 'British Brigade' into the British army. They're a segregated unit. But the Irgun refuses to fight for the British because the Brits turned Jewish refugees from Israel and sent them back to die in concentration camps.'

'I'm sick of talking about war. What do you think of Mrs Koehler?' Anita asked.

'Mrs Koehler is 'the wicked stepmother," Cookie said, crossing her eyes, and looking fiendish. 'She's an old witch to her older stepdaughter, Ruth, and favors beautiful, dimpled Lili.'

'My Booba favors her younger daughter, Mitzi, over my mother. It's caused terrible jealousy between my mother and her sister,' I said. I didn't mention I thought Mummy had constantly sent me away because I resembled her sister. Refugees imagined all British children came from happy homes. I thought that refugee children's parents must have loved them deeply to send them to safety not knowing if they'd ever see them again.

'But Mrs Koehler adores her little dog Schatzi,' Helga said.

'Who doesn't have dogs? We had two Great Danes at home in Berlin,' Cookie said.

'The Koehler are nice people, but he won't help me study for my matriculation exams.'

'Stop biting your nails. You'll pass,' Selma drawled, lying on her bed.

'Someone's knocking on the door,' Helga said.

'Come in,' we all shouted at once.

The Koehler' older daughter, Ruth, slid one foot inside the room and poked her head around the door, showing her red, apple cheeks, merry brown eyes, buckteeth, and sunny smile. 'My stepmother wants you all to come down for dinner,' she said.

A voice came from behind Ruth. 'Can I come in too?'

'Come in, come in,' we all chorused.

Lili edged in slowly. Her lips red against her white skin, her eyes dark.

I said to Ruth, 'Nurse told me that before he came to England, your father had a congregation in Germany.'

'I bet he's still in shock finding himself in charge of a children's hostel,' Cookie said.

'He's used to hostels,' Ruth said, frowning at Cookie. 'He was in charge of a boys' refugee hostel in Birmingham before we came here.'

'A *boys'* hostel?' Marta said. 'Lucky girls. Were they big boys or shrimps like ours?'

'They were aged five to 17,' Ruth said, as we clattered into the kitchen to wash.

'Seventeen! I wish we had big boys here,' I said. I imagined 20 Joseph Singers.

'Phew,' Cookie whistled. 'Why don't we have any big boys?' she pouted, and then we poured water over our hands and said the blessing. Throughout supper, all we could talk about - in low voices of course - were those strange creatures, boys. What were boys like? We were to find out sooner than expected.

Next morning after breakfast Nurse clutched my sleeve. 'I must talk to you.'

'I'm late; I have to catch the train for school.'

'Wait. This is important! Rosh Hashanah, the New Year is coming soon. Rabbi Koehler needs a *minyan,* at least 10 men, or boys over 13 for the New Year services. He's asked five boys from his former boys' hostel, and four Jewish servicemen to come to our hostel.'

'A *minyan?* That means they'll all be over 13. Oh, the girls will be so excited!'

'That's exactly what I mean. As Head Girl, tell the big girls to behave themselves.'

'Being Head Girl seems to mean giving out all the bad news.' I snapped. 'I'll speak to them,' and I dashed out after Selma, Cookie and Helga to catch the train.

'Guess what, girls,' I panted, running along on the gravel road and catching up with them. 'Our wish has come true. Big boys are coming here for Rosh Hashanah.'

As the train pulled in, we leaped in, slammed the door shut, found an empty carriage and flung ourselves onto the velvet seats. 'How many?' Cookie screamed excitedly.

'When are they coming?' Helga asked, fearfully.

'How old?' Selma, practical as ever, only found marriageable boys interesting.

'They have to be at least 13 to be part of a *minyan*. That's all I know,' I said.

Selma said nothing but leaned back into her seat. Even in a year or two, they'd still be too young for husband material.

'Oh dear, I'm afraid of big boys,' Helga said.

'You're such a mouse,' Cookie said.

Cookie grinned mischievously. 'No pranks, Cookie,' I warned. 'You have to behave.'

That night at dinner I announced a meeting of girls 11 and older. There were eight of us including myself. We gathered in the Big Girls' bedroom. 'We're going to host big boys here for Rosh Hashanah,' I announced.

There were screams of delight and a hundred questions.

'Shush. The boys are going to be living right here in the hostel for about a week. We must be friendly but not make fools of ourselves,' I said severely, repeating Nurse's mantra. Anyone would have thought I knew all about boys and girls flirting. I knew nothing. Boys my age, for all I knew about them, could have come from Mars. I had, while living among gentile foster parents, been kissed by one revolting pimply boy who stank of tobacco and beer, and during a summer camp before the hostel, by a divine Jewish refugee, Kurt. But he kissed as I imagined a man would kiss, and frightened me. I was not ready for more than an innocent kiss.

'We promise to behave,' the girls chorused excitedly, all except Cookie, Selma and Anita, suddenly silent. Cookie was planning pranks, Selma didn't care about unmarriageable males, and Anita, because her father abused her mother, hated the entire male race.

Erev Rosh Hashanah – before dark on the evening of the Jewish New Year – October, we big girls stood before the large entrance hall's blazing fire to meet our strange, new guests: Rabbi Koehler's boys. Only Cookie stayed upstairs, biding her time to strike.

Suddenly, the front door burst open, and a howling cold wind blew in five real life boys who tumbled into the White House, hair and ties awry. They came to a dead halt in the entrance hallway and stood clumped together, like the bunch of wild asparagus that I'd discovered growing in the garden.

The shortest boy stood in front of the clump like a little Napoleon, wearing a Chaplinesque check suit with a too short jacket. He stared at me out of enormous black eyes glowing in the whitest eyeballs, two black slashes like paint strokes for eyebrows. His exotic face appeared like one painted on an Egyptian mummy's cask, his skin so smooth and dark, he could have been an Indian rather than a German-Jewish refugee. His checked suit, waistcoat, white shirt, and neat black tie proclaimed him a dandy. The other boys, even the tallest, all stood behind him twitching like the Jewish Free School boys who used to follow us girls round Ely's Woolworths, lunchtime, both groups struck dumb when accidentally coming face to face.

I saw immediately, with disappointment, that these adolescent boys were all too young for me, or I was too mature for them, but I summoned best manners. After all, although the Koehlers didn't know it, I was still Head Girl.

181

'How was your journey?' I asked politely.

'Awful,' Napoleon answered. 'All the straight-through trains from Birmingham were reserved for troops. We had to stand packed in corridors the entire way. We changed at Crewe, Cambridge, and three other places, I'm so tired I can't remember where,' he said, passing a smooth hand over his marble forehead. 'My name is Alex.'

'I am Gilda, Head Girl of the hostel. Welcome to The White House,' I said, and introduced the other girls. I tried to appear calm, but Alex had mesmerised me.

Alex was just over 5ft 2in. He looked to be about 14 years old but stood so straight and sure of himself, spoke so quickly in clipped English with the sardonic tone of an upper class Englishman, with the faintest foreign, and a touch of a Birmingham accent, that he seemed much older than fourteen. I wondered why Rabbi Koehler had left that hostel and come to ours. Alex's extreme self-confidence awed me, but I was damned if I would show it. I wanted to offer the boys a chair and a drink but we girls, save for Norma, had never played hostess. We didn't know how. Another awkward silence followed.

Suddenly, Rabbi Koehler rushed out of his study, enthusiastically pumped all the boys' hands and then spoke to Alex. I'd never before heard him speak.

'Zo, my dear pupil,' he said. 'Alex, you're here at last. Make yourzelves at home, zee you at zervices,' he said, and in his usual absent-minded manner, he patted each boy on the head, then walked off to his study, beard thrust out before him like a flag, hands clasped behind him.

Mrs Koehler appeared down the hallway. 'Bitch!' she screamed, rushing toward Alex, Schatzi under her arm.

Mine and other girls' mouths dropped open. Wasn't he insulted at being called 'Bitch?'

Bad enough to call a woman or even a dog 'bitch' let alone a boy.

She put the dog down and, enfolded in her gigantic hug, Alex disappeared.

'I'm zo pleazed to zee you!' Mrs Koehler exclaimed.

Alex detached himself gently from Mrs Koehler's enormous bosom, kissed her hand, and smiled. His black eyes sparkled with mischief, his white teeth glinted in the coming dusk, his smile wicked, two tiny dimples indented his cheeks.

'How are you, Mrs Koehler? So kind of you to have invited us for Rosh Hashanah,' he said smoothly, eyes laughing. I felt he'd always have a ready answer, always be in control of a situation and always saw sardonic humor in it.

The four other boys looked on, grinning sheepishly, shuffling huge feet in embarrassment and happiness at seeing the motherly Mrs Koehler again. Perhaps she'd taken the place of their own missing mothers. She shook hands with each boy and beamed at them all. Then she babbled to Alex in German. He smiled in a disarming way and answered her in a slightly mocking voice.

Schatzi jumped frantically up at Alex, all four paws off the ground yelping 'Yap, yap, yap.' Alex leaned down and lazily tickled Schatzi's ear. She rolled over and then jumped into his arms and licked his face with her pink tongue, Alex's dark eyes danced.

'Schatzi remembers you. She always loved you!' Mrs Koehler exclaimed.

The other boys stood transfixed, waiting it seemed, for Alex to tell them what to do. The older girls had drawn closer and stood behind me, like the boys behind 'Bitch'. The younger children hung over the banisters and peeped out of the dining room as they had when I arrived.

At last Mrs Koehler said, 'I'm goink to the kitchen to finish cooking for tonight, but I'll have a snack for you in a few minutes,' she said. 'Poor boys. You must be starvink.'

In the silence that followed, Cookie appeared dramatically, at the top of our curving staircase, surveying the boys below like a queen. Jouncing down the grand staircase, she stopped for a fraction of a second, one foot poised over the next step, her eyes fixed on Alex. Alex looked up, his black, locked into her blue eyes. She continued down the stairs, walked straight up to him, held out her hand, and said, 'I'm Cookie. Let me show you the garden.'

I didn't think I had to warn Alex. Surely he'd be immune to Cookie.

But to my chagrin, he followed her. Worse, they left together, staring into each other's eyes, instantly smitten. The other boys, still rooted to the same spot had said not a word.

Tonight, I consoled myself we would all talk with the boys over dinner. We would have a feast for Rosh Hashanah, the New Year. It was also the custom on the New Year to have a new fruit not yet tasted this year; some forbidden fruit?

The tallest boy finally said, 'I'm Ralph, Alex's older brother.'

Although tall and attractive with dark curly hair, dark skin and eyes, and a sensitive mouth, Ralph had none of Alex's verve. He looked to be about 17, but as unsure of himself as Alex was sure. Although older than me, he held no appeal except good manners. 'This is Herman,' Ralph said, introducing a thin, cocky boy of about 15, with a *chutzpernick* face, and a shock of straight sandy hair falling into his eyes. A football lodged under his arm. 'Herman is our sports maniac,' Ralph added. 'This is Joey,' he went on. Joey looked about 14. Joey's shirt hung out of his trousers, he wore scuffed shoes and a too-small donated jacket. With his curly blond hair and blue eyes, he resembled an Aryan cherub flown down from a church ceiling.

'My name is Bernard,' added a tall, angular boy, gaunt, with a big nose and cold green eyes. I guessed Bernard was fifteen and had no sense of humor, his face already worried.

After the introductions, I could contain my curiosity no longer. I asked Ralph,' Why does Mrs Koehler call Alex, "Bitch"?'

'Bitch' is a pet German name from, '*bitschen*', little female doggy. Mrs Koehler adores Schatzi who is a little bitch, and she adores Alex so she calls Alex Bitch as well,' Ralph said.

Now I remembered Mrs Koehler calling her dog, 'Bitschen'.

Without a trace of jealousy, Ralph added, 'My brother was Rabbi Koehler's favorite among the boys, because Alex is such a brilliant Torah and *Gemarah* student. We all call him Bitch.'

All the small children and the big girls – except for Anita – crept closer to inspect the boys. Suddenly, Ruth and Lili Koehler arrived in the hallway. Ruth beamed at the boys, and like a boy, slapped them happily on the back and asked them how they were. Lili hung back but smiled shyly, her red lips soft, her cheeks dimpled. Though they'd all lived together for several years in her father's hostel, Lili, whenever one of the boys looked at her blushed a pretty pink.

'Where's Bitch?' Ruth asked.

'Cookie took him into the garden,' I said.

I hoped Cookie wouldn't pull the same prank on him as she had on me when I first arrived. I couldn't believe that someone as polished as Alex would fall for such a hoyden as Cookie. Perhaps when he found out what she was really like he'd come to his senses. Surely Cookie wouldn't dare torment a boy as self-confident as Alex. I admired him myself. But I knew that no matter how sophisticated he seemed, a14-year-old boy was less mature than a 15-year-old girl. It didn't matter. He was already smitten with my bête noir, Cookie.

Mrs Koehler finally rushed back. 'Come and have somesing to eat, boys. I've got gefilte fish and bread and tea. It'll keep you until after services when we eat. Lili, come kindt.'

She ignored Ruth, her older stepdaughter, who stood staring angrily after Lili and the boys. Ruth's fury reminded me of Mummy's when my grandmother, Booba, so clearly favoured Mummy's younger sister, Mitzi. Lili followed her stepmother and the boys, and Ruth followed the rest of us girls. We went upstairs to the big girls' room and chattered excitedly as in honour of Rosh Hashanah we washed and changed into our best clothes. Cookie returned and joined us.

'What's he like? What did he say? What did you do?' the girls asked.

'Never mind all that. I have a great idea,' Cookie whispered to us, 'why don't we sew up the boys' pajamas at the knee before Rosh Hashanah, so they can't get into them tonight? They're not allowed to tear on *Yom Tov*, so they won't be able to break the stitches,' she laughed. 'Of course, we're not to sew up Bitch's pajamas,' she said, 'just the others.'

'It's not a nice way to greet guests. I asked you not to play pranks on the boys,' I said.

'Oh don't be such a stick-in-the-mud,' Cookie said. 'I even have Nurse's permission.'

'How on earth did you get Nurse's permission?' I asked. Prim and proper Nurse?

Cookie just smirked. Perhaps she'd lied? 'Who's going to help?' she said briskly.

'I'll help,' Marta said, 'but hurry, they're all in the bathroom washing and shaving.'

'Shaving?' the girls chorused.

Shaving was a mystical male rite to girls whose fathers, grandfathers, uncles and brothers had all vanished. But I had often watched Daddy's open, bone-handled razor. glide over a prone man's Adam's apple, worried that Daddy might accidentally cut the man's throat.

'I'm not joining in this childish prank. Besides, it's unkind to guests and the boys will be chilly on such a cold night,' I announced.

But under Cookie's direction, though she forbade anyone to touch Alex's pajamas and against my protests, the girls sabotaged the boys' nightwear. This done, Cookie went to find Alex. From our window we watched Cookie and Alex disappear into the cold garden.

They didn't return until near dusk when it was time to light candles signifying *Yom Tov*, a holyday: the New Year, when God created the world. Both Alex and Cookie looked as if someone had blindfolded them, spun them round three times the way we did the catcher in Blind Man's Bluff and then ripped off the blindfold. I couldn't believe Bitch's infatuation. How could such a self-confident boy be smitten with wicked Cookie?

Perhaps that was *why* he liked her, I thought. They were both devils. It was the first time I'd ever felt a stab of real jealousy. My anger with Cookie over the knitting needle incident returned. In five seconds she'd snapped up the only interesting boy in the group. I felt like a witch that wanted to turn her into a frog.

We held *New Year* services in the common room, setting the seats up in rows, one side for the men and boys, the other for the women and girls, an aisle in between. The five boys, two British airmen and two American soldiers from the Stansted air force base joined Rabbi Koehler to make up the *minyan* of ten men. In the hostel, we couldn't laugh and flirt with the men as we did on the train to and from school. In spite of our bosoms, both Mr Shapiro and Rabbi Koehler still saw us as schoolgirls, both prudish concerning women. Mummy had always spoken openly about sex, though I didn't understand half of what she said. East Enders were bawdy, so I couldn't understand our guardians' failure to recognise that we big girls were young women.

As the boys and men with yarmulkes on their heads prayed devotedly and bowed to God at each blessing, I remembered the first time I'd prayed and fasted on Yom Kippur at the Ely boys' hostel, when I'd fallen for Joseph Singer. If only one of these boys had been someone romantic like him. Of all the girls, why did Alex have to pick my bête noire, Cookie? I was too old for boys my age and too young for Yanks and Tommies!

We ate in the dining room, festive with white cloths, golden challas, braided loaves of white bread reserved for holydays, and wine, and Mrs Koehler's flickering holyday candles. She said the blessing over the candles. Ruth, the eldest, stepped forward to be blessed first, as was her right, but her stepmother put her hands on Lili's head, and blessed the younger girl first, reminding me of Isaac blessing Jacob first, although Esau was his firstborn. I remembered how Jacob favoured Joseph and how bitterly Joseph's brothers punished him for this favoritism; how my grandmother, Booba, favored Aunt Mitzi and how my mother and then I suffered because of this favoritism. When I married and had children, I swore I would never show favouritism.

Rabbi Koehler made the traditional New Year blessing by dipping bread, then a slice of apple in honey and giving each child a piece of each. 'May this year be as good and sweet as this honey,' he said. 'And may we have peace and all be reunited with our loved ones. We pray God that the war ends this year and that we will all be united in Jerusalem.'

Mrs Koehler, batting thyrodic eyes at Rabbi Koehler said to Nurse, 'Mrs Gross, please pass this soup to Rabbi Koehler.'

We knew then that Mrs Koehler was *nide*, impure, that she had her period. During this time, even though she was sitting right next to him, she would not touch him nor directly pass to or receive anything from her husband. Mrs Shapiro had not been that strict, or if she had, had kept it secret. Nurse laughed and so did we, at Mrs Koehler's little flirtatiousness. Nurse took the soup from Mrs Koehler and ostentatiously passed it to the rabbi. Poor Mrs Koehler was still hoping to conceive. But when Sarah, at the age of 100 had given up hope of conceiving, a band of angels in the guise of men had visited, and promised her a child.

What if the visiting boys were a disguised band of angels? What if Mrs Koehler became pregnant, and after their visit, she grew larger than ever? I smiled at the thought. 'Beauty deceives and vanity is worthless,' said King Solomon, 'but a good woman is a jewel.' She was a good woman, except for her favoritism to Lili, and she was good to the hostel orphan-children.

We ended the meal. The rabbi courteously said in Hebrew, 'Gentlemen, shall we say the blessing?'

The men and boys responded in Hebrew, 'Let us do so,' and they courteously rose and bowed to each other, then sat to sing grace. The deep male voices joining our high girlish voices made beautiful music. Having men at the table besides women and children felt as if we were a real family.

'Let's go into the garden,' I said, after the meal. We big girls and the boys went out into the cool night air. Under the moonlit trees the girls hesitatingly asked the boys the usual questions: 'Where were you born? When did you come to England? Did you come alone or with someone? Did you come on the *Kindertransport*?'

I remained silent, uncomfortable. If the boys made the same inquiries about me, they would find out that except for Anita, I was the only British-born girl among thirty or more refugees - an exile among exiles. I felt guilty about not having suffered as much as they had, though I knew little about their sufferings. None of the children in the hostel spoke about their experiences and few, about their families. I believed the Nazis had killed most of their families.

Like Helga's mother and father, Alex and Ralph's parents were in a concentration camp. The Nazis had murdered the other boys' parents. I dared not reveal that I had parents, grandparents, and a full set of relatives. I would never reveal that my relatives didn't, outside of my mother, speak or write to me. I felt ashamed to have a full family when they mostly had none, and ashamed that my family had banished me, along with my mother for her 'crime'. After Uncle Max's wedding, and except for using Mummy to help in the grocery, my family did not communicate with Mummy or with me. This ghost family infuriated me.

Alex and Cookie, both German Jewish refugees, talked, heads close together until bedtime. I tried to draw out Ralph, but he seemed to be listening to a distant, mournful song deep inside himself, his dark, handsome face stricken with some inner turmoil.

'Goodnight, good *Yom Tov*, a good festival,' we all said and drifted out of the garden lit by searchlights, off to our rooms. The boys' assigned room was on the second floor in the left wing of the balcony. We big girls continued up the small stairs on the right to our third floor attic. Once there, we stopped and listened. Sure enough we soon heard the boys' howling.

'Bloody hell. Someone's sewn my pajamas at the knees, I can't get into them.'

We girls, including me, even though I'd refused to sew up their pajamas, had to stifle our giggles, hands over our mouths. But I felt terribly sorry the girls had treated the boys this way.

The next morning at breakfast, we tried to keep straight faces as Alex demanded, 'Which of you girls sewed up our pajamas? It was a rotten trick.' He was half angry, half laughing,

'What us?' Cookie and the girls all feigned innocence.

'Yes, you. Don't play innocent with us. We know you did it,' Alex said.

'We're terrified,' Cookie said, pretending to cringe.

We all giggled knowing there was no way they could chastise us.

A special festival breakfast of yeast cakes with raisins, chocolate chips and hot tea with milk prepared us for the long Rosh Hashanah morning service. The Rabbi honoured Alex by calling him to the *bima*, the lectern in the centre of the common room, to read the special section of the Torah. The scroll, handwritten on white parchment, lay on the high table; its bold black Hebrew letters clear, even from my seat.

Alex chanted from the Torah, a section of which was read every Shabbat. It took skill and training to learn the intricate chant accompanying each phrase of the Hebrew. Only tiny curls, bars and strange marks over or under the Hebrew words – beside the dots and dashes for vowels – denoted the musical phrase for each syllable of the Torah. I'd never heard anyone *trop* or chant as expertly and crisply as did Alex. Everyone silently listened to him while following the Hebrew script in the *Chumash*, the Five Books of Moses as he chanted the ancient words.

I saw Cookie's blue eyes glow with admiration at the confident and clear rise and fall of Alex's deep voice, his quick and perfect musical phrasing, his exacting pronunciation of the Hebrew words. She watched his black curly head bent over the open white scroll, the fringe of his dark lashes on his tawny cheek as he looked down, his huge black eyes moving from right to left, following precisely each Hebrew word as his square hand moved the silver-carved place marker shaped like a pointing finger from right to left. Cookie even watched the rise in his chest when he took a deep breath. I watched Cookie watching Alex's every move, the way I had once watched those of Joseph Singer. Alex finished on a triumphant note and stood straight.

'*Shekoach*, excellent,' Rabbi Koehler said. 'You always were my best student.'

The rabbi grasped Alex's hand and shook it warmly, then hugged him. Alex grinned his wicked white smile. Perhaps the rabbi saw in him the clever son he'd never had.

At the end of the Rosh Hashanah service, the rabbi stood tall and graceful, the white and black-striped prayer shawl draped over his head and beard looking like the classic patriarch. Lifting the *Shofar*, the ram's horn to his mouth, pointing the horn to heaven he blew into it. The strong, unwavering pure sound pouring out flooded through me; closing my eyes, I imagined myself standing high on a hill at the Temple in Jerusalem, wearing white robes that rippled in Jerusalem's breeze. I longed to be in our ancient country: Israel. One day I would go there.

After services, Cookie went to over to Alex, standing so close to him they almost touched. Jealously, I felt the warmth of their bodies flowing into each other's. Neither of them smiled but spoke quietly, looking deeply into each other's eyes as if at a flickering candle flame. Their eyes locked so intensely, they almost stopped breathing. Then Cookie whispered to him and

Alex, her breath tickling his ear, shook himself and smiled his great white, wicked smile. His dark eyes danced as mischievously as hers, and then became once more serious.

They ate breakfast, lunch and dinner together, separating only for services into the men's and women's side, meeting immediately after. At lunch he gallantly pulled the chair out for her and they sat together; also together at afternoon Torah study sessions. Later, they strolled through our gardens like lord and lady of the manor as if they owned the whole estate. The two disappeared into secret nooks emerging with tendrils of leaves in their hair. Once they came out crowned with laurels of leaves and flowers. In the hallways and common room, they talked in intense whispers, oblivious to everyone else - his dark and her blonde head, his black and her blue eyes never leaving the other's like Romeo and Juliet, like the lovers in Song of Songs.

On Sunday, the last day of the festival, Alex appeared at the top of the long staircase, carrying Cookie in his arms. Her arms round his neck, her face unusually serene; she'd won Alex. As he walked slowly down the stairs, her skirt trailed the steps. I'd never seen her so calm.

'Don't they look like Romeo and Juliet?' I whispered to Selma.

'They do. Except they don't belong to warring families.'

'They might after the war. Cookie comes from a wealthy family. Alex's parents coming out of concentration camp, if they survive, will have nothing.'

'How sweet those children are,' Mrs Koehler said, even more naïve than us.

This was not child's play. Alex and Cookie were deadly serious about each other. The war intensified all emotions and made adults out of children in every way except, perhaps, sexually. Women of perhaps seventeen or eighteen sometimes made even that leap when a lover left to fight. 'Lovers' then, meant only romantic men: most women, as far as I knew, were virgins until marriage. Certainly my mother repeatedly said, 'Save yourself for your husband.'

Alex and Cookie were the Romeo and Juliet of the Rosh Hashanah festival, but not the only ones to find romance during the celebration. Marta and Joey drifted by, she with her straight ballerina walk, chin high, white throat stretched long, he a large, bumbling boy, fair hair falling in his face, blue eyes blind with adoration.

Bernard courted Selma who disdainfully consented to go for walks with him but did not, I knew, see him as husband material. She wanted a man, not a boy, and babies to replace the family she'd lost. Herman, a frolicking puppy, chased each girl, but sport came before girls.

On the second evening of the festival, we were all in the garden before dinner. Herman dribbled a ball, tossed it up, hit it with his head a few times, dropped it to the ground and kicked it to Bernard. 'Come and play soccer,' Herman called out to Bernard. Bernard kicked the ball to Joey who, surprisingly fast, kicked it to Ralph. Bitch's brother. Ralph just looked at it. Herman ran hard to get the ball before the others, tripped on a tree root and fell, his hand twisted.

'Oh,' he cried, 'My hand, it's killing me.' He lay still, biting his lip, his face pale.

'Ach, mine poor liddle boy,' Mrs Koehler cried, running out from the kitchen.

Alex squatted and looked at the hand. 'It looks broken. Don't move,' he ordered.

He ran inside and returned with a pillow and blanket; Bitch gently eased the pillow under Herman's head, and covered Herman with the blanket. Herman moaned.

'Alex is going to be a doctor,' Cookie said proudly to everyone.

The new, young and handsome village doctor we'd all been dying to meet, set and bound Herman's hand, and put it in a sling.

'Herman, you look like a glamorous war hero with your arm in a sling,' Cookie teased.

During dinner Rabbi Koehler sat silent, as usual, immersed in his thoughts. I missed listening to Mr Shapiro reading stories to us at the dinner table; I missed his Hebrew lessons, our private discussions and his attention. Now I was almost a nobody. But I didn't get into trouble.

After dinner I went into the cool, dark garden for air. Soon I sensed I wasn't alone. Looking up, I saw Herman sitting in a tree, the glow of his cigarette burning red. Even with one arm in a sling, he slid down agilely, and joined me.

'What do you think of the teenage sweethearts?' Herman said with a laugh.

'It looks serious,' I said quietly.

'It must be. Bitch has never gone for a girl before. But when Bitch wants something, he gets it.'

'I don't see any opposition from Cookie. She's a changed creature; not one prank left.'

'If you say so,' Herman said. 'Please excuse me, I'm going inside. Joey is going to teach me how to play chess.'

I walked further into the garden and sat on a wooden bench near the pond watching the searchlights' and their beautiful and terrible warlights ever swathing dark skies for death on wings.

Ralph appeared and sat next to me. We sat silently for a while staring at the sky. I didn't know what to say to him. He put his head in his hands and caught his breath in a sob.

'What's the matter?' I finally asked.

'I think day and night only of my parents locked away in this hell they call Buchenwald. I made a vow. I swore that if they come out alive, I'd be religious for the rest of my life.'

I kept silent. Jewish religion discouraged vows, because once taken they must be kept. I remembered the terrible story of Jeptha who vowed to sacrifice the first thing he saw on his return from a victory. His daughter came out dancing with shivering timbrels to greet him.

On Yom Kippur, the Day of Atonement, at *Kol Nidre*, our first prayer begged God's release from oaths of conversion to Christianity or Islam that forced Jews to swear to convert under pain of death. Ralph had taken an oath. I was his witness.

'I understand,' I murmured to Ralph, though I didn't completely. We English children didn't know the full horror of the concentration camps, though I'd heard a few terrible stories from refugee cousin Zalman, from the Polish hero Karsky, and others. But I did understand that Ralph could think, helpless to save them, only of his parents' terrible plight. Ralph was then the only refugee I ever heard voluntarily speak of parents. I knew how it felt to long for a family, but could only guess at the torment suffered by European Jews. Ralph seemed so stricken, I wanted to hug and console him but I was far too shy. Religious girls and boys did not touch each other, and I feared to offend him or he might even reject me. He was completely different from Alex. Unable to help, I crept back under criss-crossed searchlights, to the safety of the big girls' room, ashamed for not having suffered enough.

When the festival ended and the boys prepared to leave, Alex and Cookie disappeared behind a great oak in the garden. I walked by out of 'curiosity' and as Head Girl, to see if Cookie was behaving. They were hugging each other lovingly but innocently, like children.

'Promise you'll write twice a week, Wednesday and Sunday,' I overheard him say in that precise, dry voice, now slightly husky. Alex kissed her cheek tenderly.

'I promise, and you'll do the same, right?' Cookie's usually petulant voice was now soft.

'And we'll be back to visit, soon, on *Succoth*. We'll help you build a *succah* here.'

'We'll build a beautiful succah together,' Cookie sighed, staring into his eyes.

Of course we talked far into the night about the boys' visit, but didn't discuss Alex. He was Cookie's private property and only to be discussed if she so decided. We recounted the entire visit, discussed each boy in detail whispering about who had made the greatest impression on us.

For once, the only girl who said nothing was Cookie.

CHAPTER 25
WOUNDED SOLDIERS *

It was now May 1945. The weather was beautiful; The Germans had just surrendered to the Allies in Italy, Mussolini had been killed and then hung by his feet, and Hitler and his bride had committed suicide. We London evacuated high school girls, rejoicing in the end of our six-year exile from London, from countryside boondock billets, and in anticipation of our return to civilization screamed exuberantly. Much as I loved the hostel, I loved London too. Also, many hostel friends would go to live in London. There was a hostel on Cazenove Road for adult, working refugees. I would find friends there.

Soon I could go home to an exciting city life: to my tart grandmother, gentle grandfather, glamorous Aunt, to my teasing uncles, my operatic mother, my silent, bookish and artistic deaf father. But I still had to study hard for Matriculation exams. I couldn't study at the hostel.

The Koehlers had found me the quiet Schenker house to stay at, weekdays. However, between school and the Schenkers – now that I didn't have to catch the 4.30 train back to the hostel, weekdays – I sometimes slipped into a film before supper.

Outside our high school, the small town of Bishop's Stortford was now, in May of 1945, swarming with roughly dressed, rough-talking uniformed British Tommies and smoothly dressed, smooth-talking Yanks. In spite of our horrid uniforms, Yanks in the high street would say, 'Hiya girls, like to go to a movie?'

'We're under 16,' we'd say primly, as taught, and though we still didn't know why, they'd scuttle away. Except for the one glorious weekend when Rabbi Koehler's previous boys' hostel visited us, we had never met boys. In Bishop's Stortford, boys and girls attended separate schools, so there were no boys, uninterested Tommies, and gorgeous Yanks whom sadly, we were too young to date. And suddenly there was a third kind of soldier, never before seen throughout the war, an alien-looking group dressed in brilliant blue cotton suits. These men drifted slowly, packed together, like a school of blue seals on land, out of their element. Some had frightened, some, frightening eyes.

The British wounded had come home.

Every day at four o'clock these blue-clothed wounded soldiers stood shoulder-to-shoulder on the pavement opposite Hertfordshire and Essex High school. Silently, intensely, the wounded watched us uniformed, chattering high school girls pouring out of the red brick buildings, hockey sticks or racquets slung over our shoulders.

The wounded soldiers never crossed the street, nor spoke to us, nor to each other.

Nothing moved except their darting eyes and their blue-cuffed white wounded hands, which simultaneously lifted white cigarettes up and down to their lips, smoke puffing out of their mouths, as if they were orchestrated mechanical dolls.

'Why do they stand and stare at us?' Selma asked.

'Maybe wounded soldiers have a hard time getting dates,' I said.

We became so used to this group of silent blue-clad men that we stopped noticing them.

Once a week Bishop's Stortford held an open-air market in the town square. I was buying a non-rationed suspender belt at a stall when a rare, young civilian, a handsome redheaded English bloke loomed next to me. 'Buying suspenders to keep up your morale?'

'Just to hold up my stockings,' I laughed.

It was far too personal for a man to mention a girl's underwear, but he was so unaffected and boyish I couldn't resist the repartée. Why wasn't he in the services? Demobbed already?

As I was leaving the stall, a wounded soldier in his bright blue cotton suit standing nearby and staring at me, flashed onto the periphery of my eye. I sensed that he would follow me so I walked faster. Suddenly, he was at my side.

'Trying to run away?' he asked calmly. 'Everyone tries to run away from a wounded soldier. Even children won't speak to us. We're outcasts.'

We'd never seen the wounded until the last few weeks. Perhaps earlier, when we were losing the war, the sight of wounded men might have demoralized us. All this time, they'd been hidden somewhere, or were recovering in hospitals. Surely, some with missing limbs, blind or burned were still hidden away. We were seeing only the walking wounded. Now that we had won victory over Germany, we could afford to show our wounds and our wounded.

Tall and slim in his twenties, this wounded soldier's thick blond hair fell into piercing, hurt, blue eyes. Medals hung from his thin chest. Though handsome and glamorous, all I felt was guilt, pity, and panic. I wanted to run. Since he was a war hero, I felt guilty about discouraging him, sorry he was wounded, and terrified in case I liked him or was reported talking to a soldier. Any minute, a teacher or a class prefect in our High Street could spot and report me. I could be expelled, miss the crucial university entrance examination and never see college.

'I've been all over the world, to Europe, Egypt and Africa, and wounded in every limb,' the wounded soldier said.

How did a wound look? Was it bloody, gory, and gruesome? I glanced at him sideways under my lashes, relieved that I couldn't see any. Where were his wounds?

'My name is George Frederick Wrigley. Will you have tea with me?'

'Yes,' I heard a small voice answer. How could I say no to a war hero? I took off my red-banded black velour school hat, though it was against the rules, and crushed it under my coat, reducing the chance of being recognised and reported by a prefect or teacher. I also looked more like an adult without the damned school hat, its red band identifying my school.

I walked with the soldier fast, like an underground spy I'd seen in films, so no one should see us hurrying furtively to Ely's only tea shop Lamb's Tea Room. At four o'clock, tea-time, local Bishop's Stortford schoolgirls and teachers had gone home, and were now gobbling thick slices of toasted white bread, slathered with rationed jam and drinking tea. The streets of Bishop's Stortford were thankfully deserted. It would be a treat to go to a real restaurant. How I missed London restaurants, the lively open markets, my family. I had been away from London for six long war years, with only two visits, both, during frightening bombing.

At Lamb's, the wounded soldier and I sipped strong, steaming tea with milk, and ate ersatz scones. His table manners were good, his hands and nails, clean. Of course they were. The wounded didn't work.

Older women and a few older couples sat in Lamb's, chatting; younger people were in the services. With rationing, there was little choice in food. But I was happy to sip tea like a grown up, though worried that a prefect or teacher might see and report me.

'Why do you wear such bright blue uniforms?' I asked, to distract his adoring eyes.

'The bright blue identifies us as wounded and entitles us to benefits like free train travel.'

He could go to London, travel anywhere, while we civilians were discouraged from travelling so as to leave seating for servicemen. I'd seen fatigued troops packed into train corridors, hunched grey-faced, exhausted, asleep over their duffel bags.

'With these bright uniforms we don't need identification. People can see us from a mile away. If we were in civvies, people couldn't always tell that we're wounded. They'd be handing us white feathers saying we were cowards and asking us why we weren't fighting.'

'I see.'

'I hope you'll meet me again,' he said, his face crumpling. I was terrified he'd cry. He touched my hand, a feather touch as if afraid I'd brush him off. I snatched my hand away in case someone saw. I'd already broken the rules just by being with a man and worse, a soldier. Touching was absolutely forbidden. But his blue eyes pleaded. Here was a man who had fought the Nazis for England and for me. Posters everywhere shouted, 'Support our brave troops.' We knitted, rolled bandages, served in canteens and wrote to soldiers. Girls of 18 went out with them. I was only 16, but Freddy was a hero and I owed it to him; but now that he was wounded, no one wanted him. I too, though ashamed, didn't want a wounded man either. I needed one more like the father I'd barely known. My gentle grandfather had forgotten me, my new cousin had taken my place as only grandchild, and my own deaf father only wrote to me in secret or talked to me outside home. I wanted a man to take care of me. Freddy could not. But how could I hurt a man wounded in every limb and for me?

I'd see him just once, I told myself, and hope that no one saw us.

'I'm seeing *Wuthering Heights* on Monday. Would you like to come?' I whispered.

It would be dark inside so no one would see us, and we wouldn't have to talk during the film. After that I would have done my duty. I would never have to see him again.

'I'd love to,' he said simply. 'Let's meet outside the Phoenix at four.'

I nodded.

'By the way, people call me Freddy,' he said. 'What's your name?'

When I told him Gilda, he said, 'That's a beautiful name.'

Outside the restaurant I said, 'Goodbye, Freddy, see you on Monday.'

He took my strong, tanned hand and stroked it with his pale thin hand, as if mine were precious. I hadn't told him I was Jewish. Some very nice English gentiles were anti-Semitic.

Although wearing the shapeless school uniform, I felt very grown up. He was the first British soldier to approach me. Why did he have to be a wounded British soldier? I quickly looked around to see if anyone from school had seen me with him. I'd already been in trouble for sending that anonymous letter to Joseph Singer. But being seen with a man, especially a soldier, even a wounded one, was an even worse offense than writing to a boy. Suppose they expelled me? I'd never sit for the Matriculation examination and never go to college or become a professor and writer. Even though I felt sorry for Freddy, I *had* to break off with him. But how?

Friday, I ran out of school, heels flying to catch the four-thirty train back to the hostel for the weekend. Suddenly, Freddy stood among the silent crowd of wounded soldiers opposite. He'd never before joined them. To my horror, he began to cross the street, that forbidden road that separated the pale, wounded from us tanned, strong girls.

The local Bishop's Stortford high school girls and their teachers had vanished for Friday four o'clock tea. On Fridays, I met the hostel's other high school girls, Selma, Cookie and Helga at the train station to go back to Great Chesterford. But Mrs Schenker, my weekday foster mother, directly opposite the school might be looking out the window and see me with Freddy. I ran down the hill toward the station and gestured for Freddy to follow.

'I'll get into trouble if I'm seen talking to a soldier,' I whispered. 'Walk behind me.' His eyes crinkled in amusement, but he followed my instructions.

191

Near the station, he caught up with me. 'I *had* to see you,' Freddy said. 'I might be a bit late for the film on Monday because I have a medical exam. I didn't know how else to reach you. Will you come to tea again with me now? Please?'

'I can't. On Fridays I have to catch the 4.30 train to Great Chesterford.'

'I'm going on the train, too. I'll walk with you.'

I thought he wanted to go to tea. But he was coming on the train just to be with me, a 16-year-old schoolgirl whom Tommies ignored. I couldn't help feeling flattered. We walked along the quiet, lush, tree-lined street. A fresh spring breeze ruffled Freddy's blond hair. Walking, forbidden, with a soldier, I again felt terribly grown up.

'I'm 26,' he volunteered, as we walked.

He was old. Ten years older than me. Joseph Singer was only 18.

Freddy walked on the outside, as Daddy did with Mummy; a real gentleman. But apart from his being wounded all over, I knew nothing about him. Anyway, I thought, I won't be seeing him after Monday.

Outside the red brick station, Selma stood waiting for me. When she saw blue-suited Freddy walking beside me, her mouth fell open. None of us from the hostel had ever talked to a wounded soldier. His blue suit was more conspicuous than a Yank's.

The station, but for we girls was deserted. Cookie and Helga were fortunately far down the platform. Cookie would have teased me unmercifully.

'Selma,' I said, 'this is Freddy.' Selma stared at Freddy.

'How do you do,' he said gravely.

I was secretly glad he didn't take her hand as he had mine, even though Selma had a far better figure than I did. I knew, from the night she'd invited me to her bed and said 'Stroke me.'

As our train puffed into Bishop's Stortford Freddy said, 'You know what...?'

'Don't tell me you're going on the same train,' I said.

We all laughed and the tension eased. The train was safe territory. We'd never seen anyone local except Miss Curzon ride on the train. She wouldn't tell.

'I'm going to Cambridge,' Freddy said.

Cambridge was several stops further than Great Chesterford. What a relief. We would get off before him. Freddy and I chatted about school, the war, and films. Selma sat quietly. I was glad he didn't mention we were meeting on Monday. Usually, I told Selma everything, but in this case, I knew she'd disapprove.

As we girls got off at Great Chesterford and the train chugged on, we waved goodbye to Freddy. I knew he had nowhere to go. He'd just come so as to speak to me.

'What do you think of him?' I asked Selma, casually, as we crunched along the stony path from station to hostel. Cookie and Helga had run ahead, hungry for tea.

'He's handsome, but I wouldn't go out with him.'

'Why not?'

'You should only go out with someone you can marry. He's not Jewish. If we all married gentiles, Jews would disappear.'

'But he's wounded,' I said. 'Have *rachmonos*, pity.'

'He'll find other nice girls. Leave him alone.'

'He won't leave *me* alone,' I muttered.

Selma shrugged slim shoulders. Things were clear-cut for her. The Nazis had probably murdered her parents. Her main interest was marrying early and replacing her family. But I was British-born of British-born parents, patriotic, and I owed Freddy for his wounds.

On Monday, Freddy stood bright blue from head to toe outside the Phoenix, his head turning anxiously from right and left, looking for me. Away from home for so long, I enjoyed someone looking for me, waiting for me. I'd changed out of my heavy school uniform, and wore my pale blue frock as if I too were wounded. King George VI said we evacuees also served.

'You look very pretty,' Freddy said, seizing my hand. I snatched it back and looked round for prefects. 'Two balcony seats, please,' Freddy said, bending at the ticket window.

How exciting! I'd never sat in the balcony before. Balcony seats, at two shillings and ninepence, must have been a lot of money for a wounded soldier. Surprisingly, we were alone on the dark balcony but for a Yank and his girl in the last row behind us, wound around each other, and kissing passionately. Who knew the balcony would be so empty? But I realised that at four o'clock the local girls and teachers were at home scarfing tea and toast, men not in the services were at work, and my idol, Laurence Olivier, and Merle Oberon, were blooming onto the screen. I was so rapt with joy, that until he took my hand I'd forgotten Freddy. After about half an hour he slowly raised my hand to his lips, and kissed it. I wondered if my hand was soft and smelled like the face cream stolen from Mrs Schenker's collection left in my room. I'd secretly tried each aromatic cream: also rationed, on my hands.

In the dark, Freddy kissed my palm. This was the exact romantic gesture I had dreamed about, but not with Freddy. I could give him nothing back. He offered me a Craven 'A' cigarette from the red tin box with the smiling black cat on it. I shook my head. Heathcliffe was running away to make his fortune in Australia, because he thought Cathy loved another man. Who wanted to smoke?

'Really, you don't smoke?' he whispered. 'D'you mind if I do?'

'No,' I said, just to shut him up.

'May I put my arm round you?' he asked.

'If you like.' It meant nothing to me. He put his left arm round my shoulder and squeezed it. His left arm was strong. I thought he'd been wounded in every limb.

No grown up man had ever put his arm round me. Freddy pulled me to him and kissed my hot cheek. I felt myself flush in the dark and said, 'Don't.'

Then he said, 'Gilda, I'm sorry, I made a mistake. You're not pretty, you're beautiful. I love you.'

When he tried to kiss my mouth I struggled against him but he pulled me close; his medals pressed into my skin. My heart raced with tension. I felt his beating against mine.

'Don't fight,' he pleaded. 'Let me kiss you, I love you. I'd like to squeeze you to death.'

Squeeze me to death! 'Please, Freddy,' I said, torn between not wanting to hurt him, fear of attracting attention, and fright.

Far behind us, the Yank and his girl wound around each other were kissing, oblivious to anyone else. I suddenly felt like the real, proper schoolgirl I was.

'Stop,' I said angrily, pushing him away.

He fell back into his seat. The struggle had tired him. 'Don't be angry, I'll stop.'

My heart beat furiously. I wished he hadn't said he loved me. I didn't want him, so I couldn't let him kiss me. I'd only been kissed by stinking Bertie in Ely and by a passionate Kurt at a Jewish summer camp Mummy sent me to the summer before the hostel.

Freddy was a real grown-up man. How was I going to break from him? Though I admired him for speaking to me so straightly and honestly, I couldn't be straight and honest with him and confess that I, too, didn't want a wounded man. I'd been away from home and fatherless for six years of war. I wanted someone strong to take care of *me*. Of *my* wounds. How lonely I'd been all through the war. How I needed someone strong to hold and comfort me. But I owed him. He had fought for me.

After the film, we walked through the deserted streets to Mrs Schenker's house. We came to the brown gate in front of the garden. I went through the gate and stood behind it. Freddy, on the other side, made idle conversation. I knew he was thinking about how he could kiss me. He put his arms around me, but though I felt sorry for him I ducked under them, and ran up the crazy stone-flagged path to the Schenker's house. I hoped Mrs Schenker hadn't been watching us through the window. If she had, she might send me away. I needed her quiet place to study for Higher School Certificate. I'd be the first in my family to go to University; I couldn't let everyone down, even if they didn't care about me. I'd show them I was clever.

'Come back,' Freddy called. 'Here's your address. You only went with me out of pity.'

I had to admire his perception, but because he was right, I felt even guiltier.

'You don't want me because I'm crocked up. I'm no good.'

'Don't be ridiculous, you're as good as any man,' I protested, but I ran up the garden path to front door safety. Then I thought, it's true. Freddy was handsome and intelligent. Lots of girls would like him, even if he were wounded. I, too, was war-wounded, lonely for my family and home. No one saw my wounds. I had no blue uniform to identify me as wounded.

I opened the front door and glanced back. Freddy had vanished. Mrs Schenker switched off the wireless. Usually calm, her blonde-haloed face turned on me like a luminous sun, her golden eyelashes blinking rapidly.

'What happened?' I asked.

'Peace has been declared. Victory in Europe, and two days' holiday,' she said.

'Whoopee,' I screamed, like an American. I seized Mrs Schenker round her small waist and danced that plump, dignified lady in a jig round the sofa.

'Don't get carried away, there's still the war in Asia and the Pacific,' she said coolly, detaching herself, a faint spot of pink glowing in her alabaster cheeks.

Mr Schenker loped in jauntily from the garden. 'There's a guy out back for you,' he said. 'I invited him in to celebrate. Champagne!!'

I was astonished to hear Mr Schenker say 'guy' instead of the British, 'bloke', and that he allowed a 'guy' to call for me. Perhaps he was an American who had married Mrs Schenker. Since I left for the hostel weekends, leaving before he came home, I'd seen him only once, and never before heard him speak. Many British women married Yanks.

I ran outside the door to a terrific, joyous din of laughing, cheering and the clanging cacophony of church bells after six years' silence, all ringing all at once. Dazzling gold, green and blue fireworks shot into the sky, soared, and then burst clattering into thousands of golden radiant petals. As I turned joyous eyes up to them, I felt my face light up under their brilliance. The streets were packed with mobs singing and laughing, hugging, kissing and dancing with each other. I rushed down the front path to join the celebration.

Freddy, the war hero stood at our gate, blocking my exit. His back to celebrants, he said quietly, 'I'm sorry for behaving like a fool,' his voice clear in spite of noise.

'We've won the war in Europe,' I shouted over the bells, singing and shouting.

A fresh spurt of fireworks flared into the sky and burst with a bang and clatter into joyous gold smithereens. 'Come inside. We have champagne, let's celebrate.' I shouted.

Freddy wrenched up the blue sleeve of his right arm.

There, lit by the fireworks gleamed a fresh pink, jagged scar shaped like a wide bolt of lightning, that seemed seared like a brand of war into his white skin. The livid scar ran from inside his wrist to the crook of his elbow, three inches wide, and a foot long.

'Celebrate peace? What good does peace do me?' Freddy said bitterly. 'All my muscles are gone. I'll never work again.'

Tears sprang to my eyes, but I could hardly contain my own excitement at visions of freedom, home, a 16-year old girl, back in exciting London. I had been away from home for six long years, as long as Freddy had been a soldier. King George had praised evacuees as having also fought like our soldiers. Bells chimed, people danced and kissed. I longed to be among them. Freddy blocked my way. Peace brought Freddie bitterness, but like the golden, sparkling fireworks shooting into the sky, my joy exploding inside me, I dashed out and dragged and pushed Freddie into the arms of a blonde who kissed him. A British airman seized me, and dancing, I looked over his shoulder to see on Freddy's face, a look of disbelieving joy.

PART 3

POST-WAR ENGLAND
1945–1950

CHAPTER 26
TEA WITH THE EDITOR *

On Friday 3 May I'd come to the White House for the weekend. The arrival of not one, but two letters addressed to me was an added pleasure to the joys of Allied successes in Europe. One, a bright blue airmail letter came from America. I recognised the writing and address of my penpal, Frank Robinson. The other, a thick, creamy envelope on linen-like stationary came from London. I did not recognise the return address, and the elegant handwriting on the envelope mystified me. Who had sent it?

The other children, European, orphaned refugees, or their relatives missing, rarely received letters. The smaller children crowding round me urged, 'Open them, open them!'

Standing in the front hall, where Nurse left letters on a chest, I turned the two missives over in my hands, feeling Frank's flimsy, soft, blue airmail and the pre-war envelope, creamy, thick and firm, each addressed to Miss Gilda Moss, The White House, Great Chesterford, Essex.

'Don't you want to see who they're from?' refugee children asked, pressing warm bodies against mine. Letters, to them, shorn of all outside contacts, were exciting and hopeful.

Selma, Helga and Cookie and I callously abandoned the small children's upturned faces, and we raced up the gracious oak stairway, and then right, up the narrow smaller set of stairs to The Big Girls' Room. Sunlight from our huge bay window flooded the room with golden light. Marta stood straight against the rough barre in the Big Girls' room practicing her plié. Concentrating on her dance movements, she didn't even notice us.

I flung myself on the window-seat and carefully opened Frank's letter, glued shut at the edges by censors. This time, none of Frank's words had been blacked out by censors. As blackbirds and yellow butterflies flew past the bay window, I glanced out over the endless tranquil green with its calm pool, statuary, frolicking children, and at the far end of the garden, hidden from view, I imagined I could hear the deep green orchard leaves rustling, protecting their ripe apples and plums. It was as if there had never been six years of war and endless bombing. Victory in Europe seemed imminent. The one remaining enemy was Japan. We British evacuees and our soldiers were full of hope for an end to war, and eager for return to our beloved London.

'Who's it from, who's it from?' screamed Cookie, trying to snatch the blue letter from my hand. Feeling guilty at being the only girl with a whole family and with two letters, I tried to ignore Cookie's annoying pranks.

'The blue airmail is from my American penpal, Frank Robinson, and the other,' I turned over the creamy, thick envelope, 'is a mystery; certainly not from my mother.'

This writing was even, whereas Mummy's hand-writing had become increasingly spidery during the war and the Blitz.

'Well, what does he say?' Marta asked. Looking like a Dègas, she executed an entrechât. All the big girls in the hostel knew about Frank Robinson.

'So read the letters,' Cookie said, as if it were her business. I'd opened Frank's.

'Dear Gilda,' (I read aloud).

'This is a confession. For a long time I denied that I was Jewish. I kept it a secret but you have made me acknowledge my heritage. I admit that I am Jewish.'

'Girls, girls,' Cookie screamed, 'Frank Robinson is Jewish!'

'I'm amazed, too,' I said. 'We've been writing for months, and he never said so.'

'Now you can marry him,' Selma said, dreamily, lying on her cot, hands behind her head. Selma, at 14, had grown taller, her breasts even more voluptuous, I envied her tiny waist, soft hips, long legs, and shoulder-length hair, even though Yanks on trains had often flirted with me rather than with her. While her figure was gorgeous her expression said 'bored'.

'Let me see the letter,' Cookie shouted, snatching it out of my hand, and holding it in front of her while leaping from cot to cot, while managing to read it, shouted, 'It's true, it's true.' Flinging my letter on the window seat, she cried, 'Read the other letter.'

'This one is from London,' I said, carefully opening the crackly pre-war cream envelope. 'But it's not my mother's handwriting. Who else could have written to me?' Mummy forbade Daddy to write to me. For six years none of my relatives had written one line to me.

I read aloud the single sheet of cream paper, the cream sheet matching the envelope:

Cricklewood
London
May 1, 1945
Dear Miss Moss:

As you no doubt know by now, we forwarded your letter against racism to Frank Robinson's New York address in America.

You sound like a very interesting young lady. My mother and I would like to invite you to tea on May 13th at four in the afternoon. Please let me know by return post if you are able to come.

Yours truly,

Jonathan Goldstein,
Letters' Editor
Life Magazine

'The editor of *Life* has invited you to tea?!' Helga exclaimed. 'What's a Letters' Editor?'

'I'm not sure,' I said.

'Goldstein. That's a Jewish name,' Selma said. 'I bet his mother wants to look you over.'

'Oh, Selma, don't be silly. He's just being kind. I'll wear my new white dress.'

With our clothes ration coupons, Mummy wrote, she had bought me a beautiful new white dress. 'I'm keeping it for you until you come to London.' Now I had *two* dresses. Luxury!

197

'As soon as I'm 16 I'll marry my sweetheart and have babies, like my mother,' Selma said. Secretly, since my family didn't miss me all, I envied her parents' love for each other and for Selma. But I chastised myself for envying her; she had not heard from her parents for six years. However, I was thrilled that the Editor and his mother wanted to meet me.

'Why would the letters' editor of *Life* ask a schoolgirl to tea?' Cookie sniffed.

'I'm 16,' I said. 'I'm a young woman. Besides, he says I sound interesting.'

Cookie flipped a scarce rubber band stingingly at my face making me itch to smack her.

'You *must* write and accept, today,' Helga said, enormous eyes serious.

I wrote immediately to the Letters Editor' to say that I would be delighted to come to tea that Sunday, and would take the next train home to London. Since we had just won the war in Europe, and German bombing had stopped, British evacuees were allowed train travel.

I needed only Nurse's permission to go home for the weekend. I'd stay with my parents, and I'd sleep on the kitchen couch even if Mummy's visitors sat on me and even if the skeletal Polish Free Fighters still rented the spare room. I'd visit my grandparents, Aunt Mitzi, Uncle Sam, (Uncle Max was still a soldier in Egypt now in charge of demobilisation) and the following Sunday, I'd go to tea with the editor.

I boarded the train from Great Chesterford wearing instead of my stodgy daily school uniform, my only 'civvy' dress, the pretty blue wool, a bunch of fresh violets pinned at my throat. Tommies and Yanks, some drunk, crowded into the corridors, singing and cheering. I realised that they, too, like our Tommies, once we finished the war with Japan, were looking forward to returning to their American sweethearts and families.

Outside Liverpool Street Station in London everyone was dancing and singing in the streets, celebrating VE-Day. Although I had written that I was coming home, no one met me. I walked the one or two miles to our East End house. The front door, as always, stood open. 'Hallo,' I called out, entering the kitchen.

Mummy and Daddy sat there drinking tea.

'Oh, I didn't know you were coming,' Mummy said.

'I wrote to tell you I'm going to tea with Mr Goldstein, the editor.'

'I forgot. Dad and I are going to the Fleet Street peace celebration. Coming?'

'Of course.' What a silly question. Of course I wanted to celebrate peace, and with them. No one kissed or hugged me. I had seen Mummy and Daddy only twice in six years.

'Take the camera, Alf,' Mummy shouted to my deaf father.

We three clambered up the winding iron stairs of the red number six bus. I loved riding on the top deck, looking down at everyone scurrying along pavements, and staring through the upstairs windows at those white stone faces of men carved into the first story of buildings en route to Fleet Street. With carved eyes wide, angry, curled beards, frowns, mouths wide open they forever silently shouted epithets at top deck bus riders like me. I didn't mind.

As the bus drove toward Buckingham Palace where the royal family and Churchill would come on to the balcony, the driver called out, 'All off. Can't go any further, too many crowds.'

Some buses stood marooned, empty, and unable to move for the thousands of celebrants blocking exits. Some celebrants were trapped inside buses, exits closed by thick crowds outside. White faces pressed to the windows, limp white hands hanging outside like those of monkeys at the zoo, they watched, trapped, the revelry. My family had found a less crowded street where people moved, eyes dazed, as if sleepwalking, exhausted from six years of nightly bombings and deaths, thousands of demolished houses, anxiety about missing sons and lovers, prisoners of war, depression about wounded and dead soldier relatives, exhausted from past terrors of Nazi invasion, present continued rationing, and still unbelieving of peace, we all drifted, a dreamlike herd, instinctively heading toward Buckingham Palace.

On the way, British flags snapped in the breeze over Nelson's column, the walls pasted with signs read, 'Victory over Germany 1945'. Other signs read '*Annus Mirabilis*' The Year of Miracles', and 'It's all over in the West'. 'Hurray for VE Day, Hurray for Victory in Europe'.

Pockets of people danced in the streets, squeezing aside only to let pass convoys of British and American trucks, into which girls climbed, laughing and kissing dirty, happy soldiers' faces.

Mummy, Daddy and I too, drifted with the massed thousands until we reached the iron railings of Buckingham Palace. The royal family and Churchill stood solemnly on its flag-draped balcony. King George VI and his queen gravely waved, and Churchill, the British Bulldog, gave his famous V for Victory sign. He was my hero, a brave man, and the only Briton in an anti-Semitic country to speak for the establishment of a Jewish Israel that became a reality.

On the royal balcony, draped with British flags and ribbons sat the two Princesses, gracefully still and solemn, as if aware that this day, and their role in it, was historic. The crowd roared and waved thousands of British flags. The royal family, descendants of conquering soldiers, to me were simply decorative. They did not excite me. My real excitement bubbled inside about my invitation to tea with the *Life Magazine* Letters' Editor.

Cricklewood, where the editor lived, was a fancy neighborhood in North London. I imagined the editor and his mother living in a beautiful house with shiny parquet floors, oriental carpets, exquisite white china and a silver teapot. They'd serve watercress and cucumber sandwiches, and if they hadn't used up their sugar ration, little cakes. Suppose they even served crumpets with clotted cream and strawberry jam?

I prepared for the visit by running hot water in our new bath. We'd moved again. Now we lived at 132 Columbia Road, East 2. With restitution money the government gave us for our former bombed out roof and windows, Mummy had halved my new large bedroom and installed in the other half a bathroom with a gas heater. No more going to the palatial Cheshire Street Public Baths with Mummy. I felt a twinge of regret and loss of our rare moments of intimacy.

But I smiled excitedly as I tested our first running hot water, a new post-war luxury. 'The Houses of Parliament', as Mummy called the toilet, noisily flushed by pulling a handle on a chain, newspaper for toilet paper, still stood, smelly in the tiny back yard behind shop and house. We still needed chamber pots at night. But for the first time at home, I had my own bedroom.

Using up our last clothes' ration coupons, Mummy had bought me a beautiful white cotton dress. Wartime dresses – most materials used for uniforms – had been coarse and skimpy. I tried on the new dress and admired myself in my new long bedroom mirror. The gown showed off to perfection my slender throat, the firm rise of my young breasts and my new neat waist and firm legs. The soft whiteness of the dress accentuated my dark curls and green-gold, Tartar eyes. Mr Goldstein would love me in it. When I twisted in it, the whole skirt had whirled round me like a ballerina's. As I laid the white dress on my bed, I stroked the luxurious folds in the skirt: my first really grown-up dress.

After the bath and the sweet shower of talcum powder, I was putting on my brassiere and suspender belt, when Mummy walked into my bedroom. She glanced at the dress; I'd fanned the wide skirt elegantly across my new bed.

'Don't wear that. Wear your school uniform.'

'But Mummy, this dress is beautiful. I want to dress like a young lady.'

'No, wear your school uniform. He'll be an old man and think you darling.'

'I wear that old gym tunic, every day. Meeting an editor at *Life* is a special occasion.'

I didn't say that the uniform hid my new beautiful 16-year-old figure, which Mummy hadn't even noticed. If she had, she'd never mentioned it. The white dress showed me for the ripe young woman I was. The black market silk stockings showed off my good legs, shapely from our school sports and dancing.

'Surely now that I'm 16 I can wear this dress to meet Mr Goldstein,' I said, looking longingly at the pretty white garment that would enhance my new, lovely figure.

'Don't answer back, just do as I say,' Mummy snapped, her face flushing, eyes darkening, her voice ominously lowered. Challenged, Mummy could fly into such a violent rage, that like my father, I avoided all arguments with her. Besides, British children had been trained to obey parents. We were obedient children until 21 and overnight became adults.

Never mind, I thought. The Editor had said I sounded interesting. I would visit him another time wearing the white dress. Slowly, I dressed in the baleful school uniform and school hat, the thick lisle stockings and heavy brogues and boarded the underground to Cricklewood.

I found the house and rang the bell.

The door opened. There stood a tall young man, with curly blond hair, bright blue eyes, as handsome as a fairy-tale prince, wearing a brown tweed suit and brown suede shoes, a joyous smile of welcome on his face until his eyes fell to my school uniform hat, gym tunic and shoes.

'Oh!' he said, his smile fading, face falling as if someone had hit him. I knew immediately he'd expected that other, beautiful girl in the white dress. 'Here, I'm under here,' I wanted to shout. My face burned with anger at Mummy making me wear the uniform, shame that he had spurned me, and chagrin that he so blatantly showed me his disappointment.

'Come in,' he said glumly. I followed, slouching like a criminal behind his tweedy back.

I had hardly entered the house, and tea with the editor was already a disaster.

Inside, the soaring living room I'd expected, the wooden ceiling was so low I feared the editor would hit his head on it, the room windowless and gloomy. On a low couch sat a lady with a mass of auburn ringlets, her eyes dark and passionate as a gypsy's, wearing a décolleté velvet dress that exposed a milk-white throat. Warm amber beads glowed against her white skin.

'This is my mother,' Jonathan Goldstein said in a monotone, not even looking at me.

'What a pleasure to meet you,' she said, extending her white hand like a queen.

I felt she, at least, saw through the uniform to the real me. That didn't help.

'Do come and sit down next to me.' She patted the seat on the couch. 'Excuse the disarray,' she gaily waved at the vast, dark room, empty but for a few sticks of old furniture and dishes. 'We're migrating to America in two weeks. We thought we'd like to meet you before we leave. We are refugees from Hungary who had to leave everything to save our lives and escape. My poor husband was killed.' Her eyes filled with tears. 'We had such a good life there. Every luxury you could want, and now look at us.' She gave a deep, soulful sigh. 'Ah well, we're lucky to get away with our lives, let's be happy.'

Mummy often told me, 'Beware of Hungarians, Romanians and men in suede shoes.' I glanced at Jonathan Goldstein's suede shoes. Then I looked at the room.

Although the day outside sparkled, the room was so shadowed, I could barely see the end of it. Here, in the Goldstein house, the wooden floor tilted downward so much that I felt that at any moment, Jonathan Goldstein, Mrs Goldstein and I, and the thick cheap china piled on the table ready to pack, would likewise all slither to the floor, landing all of us amid smithereens of china.

Beside the tilted couch and huge lopsided table, there was one chair. On that chair sat an old chrome electric toaster looking like a fat cat, its black wire trailing like the cat's tail along the floor and plugged into the wall. So this was what an electric toaster looked like! At home, long tin toasting forks, onto which we stuck thick slices of bread and held over a coal fire, served as our toaster. I'd never before seen an electric toaster.

A few colourful finger puppets lay strewn about the room. 'This is how I earn a little money,' my hostess sighed. 'I make and sell puppets.'

How could they afford to go to America? Probably HIAS, the Hebrew Immigration Aid Society had paid their fare. No doubt the editor, himself a refugee, I now realised, supported his widowed mother. I'd thought Cricklewood was a fancy area. If so, this must be the most austere house in Cricklewood.

The sole pretty item in the room was a gleaming silver toast rack that defiantly shone through the gloom as if symbolizing wartime Jewish survival. Mrs Goldstein rhythmically dropped slices of white bread in the toaster from which like magic, they popped up transformed into brown. As she deftly removed the toast to the silver toast rack, she immediately popped two new slices of white bread into the electric toaster. The second she set toast between the silver bars of the toast rack, Jonathan Goldstein snatched it up, slathered jam on it and wolfed it. The editor was so quick, Mrs Goldstein almost had to pry several pieces away from the rack to offer me before he reached them, and leaning forward, she elegantly offered me slices of toast as if they were sumptuous gateaux instead of heated bread.

Usually, when invited to tea, the hostess served guests with dainty little sandwiches and cakes. Here, there was nothing to eat but toast, jam, and tea. I had travelled a long way, had not eaten before leaving, and had a healthy 16-year-old appetite. Soon, hunger pains began to gnaw at my stomach. So, apparently, did they afflict Jonathan Goldstein, for he rapidly in succession devoured 10 pieces of toast and strawberry jam.

After his cordial letter, I had expected a rousing discussion on racial equality, but since my appearance had so apparently disappointed him, he made absolutely no attempt at conversation. If he didn't like my looks, I thought resentfully, he could at least have tried to talk to me. A curse on my school uniform; I was ready to strip it off and show him my beautiful young body. And what about me being 'an interesting young lady'? What happened to that part of me? He could have tried to explore me. I felt so angry, that all my usual wit that had Yanks on trains laughing hilariously, deserted me.

Jonathan's mother presided over the chipped brown china teapot as if it were chased silver, pouring tea from it with an elegant flick of her wrist. 'Milk? Sugar?' she inquired, staring into my eyes, as if these were crucial questions.

My eyes strayed back to the elegant silver toast rack. In spite of the room's shabbiness, I guessed that this toast rack was one of the few belongings she'd managed to save from her former luxurious Hungarian life.

Jonathan sat silently chewing toast, eyes brooding into space. Perhaps besides being disappointed in me, his home and the sparse tea embarrassed him. Suppose I had worn the beautiful white dress? How would he have been then? All boyish charm, I bet. In his letter he'd said I sounded interesting. Maybe the whole idea had been his mother's and he didn't even want to see me. But his eyes had lit up with joy in that split second between his smiling at me and catching sight of my school uniform and school hat.

Mrs Goldstein chatted incessantly and charmingly about nothing in particular. I thought Selma had been right, that she saw me as a match for her son. Perhaps he'd been going out with a *shiksa*, a gentile girl. I was a respectable, British, Jewish well-educated girl and against racism. To a refugee, whose husband had been murdered because he was Jewish, I may have appealed to her, more than to her son.

How I longed to talk about meeting the racist Yank on the train, about my friends in the hostel, our daily ride to high school, and the fascinating encounters we had with soldiers on the trains; about Frank Robinson, and America. Where were the witty remarks that sprang to my lips on the trains when I rode with Yanks and other foreign servicemen? They always put me at ease. Imprisoned inside my uniform, watching Goldstein wolfing toast and jam, I longed to leave, while at the same time wishing I had worn the white dress, and that he'd liked me.

'You must come and visit us if you come to America.' Mrs Goldstein said, as if I were due to hop over next week. Suddenly I was a schoolgirl, in dress and pocket, totally dependent on my mother and father, without a farthing to my name. How would I ever visit America?

'I'd love to,' I said.

She produced a white parchment card with her name and an American address printed on it in an elegant script. I saw this as a sign to say goodbye.

'Thank you,' I said, taking it, but didn't know how to extricate myself.

As tea with the editor tediously wore on, Jonathan Goldstein seemed, like Whistler's mother, to fade into the wallpaper. My mouth ached from smiling. I was sick of tea and toast. I wanted desperately to go home. When I finally, politely escaped, all Jonathan Goldstein could manage was a faint, dismissive flick of the finger 'goodbye,' as if the effort exhausted him.

'Why did you make me wear that stupid school uniform?' I raged at Mummy when I returned home, risking a slap on my face. Children did not question parents.

'I thought he'd be a fat old fellow and would think you looked a treasure in it,' she answered, for the first time in my life explaining herself.

'He was young and handsome. He wanted to see an elegant young woman and I looked like a stupid shapeless schoolgirl. I *begged* you not to make me wear that uniform. I *begged* you to let me wear the white dress. The whole afternoon was a disaster.'

For the first time in my life I showed Mummy my dramatic side that had won me annual roles in school plays. Only now I was not acting. I waited for Mummy to smack my face for talking back, but she only said, 'Cheer up, the news is good. We've encircled Berlin and caught that anti-Semite, Pétain.'

'Fat lot of good that does me. Tea was a total fiasco. He'll never see me again.'

I promised myself that when I came home for good, after Allied victory over Japan, Mummy would have to stop treating me as a child. And I would go to America; I would meet Frank Robinson and Jonathan Goldstein and his mother. We'd have tea, with their silver toast rack and a perfect china teapot. I'd dress in the white dress, wear silk stockings, high heels like the grown-up I was, and Jonathan Goldstein and Frank Robinson would find me absolutely fascinating. The time to break from Mummy was now.

At that very moment, after telling Mummy Jonathan Goldstein would never see me again, my turning point began. My childhood faded away, and my life as a young woman bloomed.

As Mummy walked out of the room, I whispered, 'Goodbye, Mummy.'

But she had told me that I couldn't legally leave home until I was 21. I was patient, calm, in the face of her steady attempts to break my will to hers. While completing high school and college at the London School of Economics and Political Science, all on scholarships, I secretly arranged for American immigration, applied for and won a post-graduate scholarship to Columbia University. At the age of 21 I could withdraw the money Mummy had saved for me for years to pay the fare to visit America and then go on to settle in Israel. America was to be a stop on the way to visit Editor Goldstein and show him my truly beautiful self, to visit Frank Robinson and my great aunt, Booba's sister, Frieda whose bridegroom Daddy said Booba had stolen. I'd met my sponsor, Danny, in Israel during the summer of 1948 right after the UN voted for Israel's Independence and Israel accepted a two-state Israel-Palestinian division. After the war, Jewish education that mainly stopped in wartime was revived in England, I was recruited for Jewish youth leadership and won a Jewish Youth Leadership scholarship to Israel. There, I met American Danny, while he was visiting relatives. He'd agreed to sponsor my American immigration papers. Being British, I had no trouble obtaining citizenship. I didn't know how long I would stay in America and knew I'd have to work to support myself and, therefore, needed immigration papers. My first stop into the world of freedom would be to set sail for America, visit Jonathan Goldstein and show him the pretty, clever young woman he'd stupidly ignored. Then, I would pursue graduate studies at Columbia University. Finally, I would settle in Israel, the land of my forefathers where the tribe of Judah, the brother who saved Joseph, had lived.

I'd gained the courage to break free from childhood into womanhood because of that disastrous tea with the editor.

I should thank Jonathan Goldstein, but I doubted I would.

CHAPTER 27

RENDEZVOUS

As promised, the four of us, Selma, Helga, Cookie and I, met in London in 1945 after the war. I now lived at home. The other big girls went to the London refugee hostel, Bloomsbury House on Cazenove Road where older, mainly working refugees stayed. Some girls and boys found distant or close relative survivors and joined them.

I called the girls and suggested we meet as planned at the Trocadero in the West End.

The West End was as glamorous as I remembered it during the war, though not as swish as it had been pre-war, and many bombed buildings still stood as reminders of the Blitz. But where for six years it had been as dark as the Fourth Plague, lights now blazed. Whereas the streets had been crowded with glamorous servicemen and women during wartime, few servicemen now appeared in the streets. Some had been demobbed; others appeared on crutches, Uncle Max, still in Egypt, was still demobilising soldiers.

Eager to see the girls after a month's separation, I entered the restaurant.

The Trocadero still had the starched white tablecloths, crystal glasses and roses on each table that I'd glimpsed through its open doorway on the two brief visits home during the war.

The girls were already seated. I took the empty seat. Selma wore a slinky green dress. At 15 she'd become almost beautiful, because her eyes were now alight with joy.

'Look,' she said, holding out her left finger.

I craned to admire her pinprick of a diamond.

'Gorgeous,' I said. 'Magnus, from the Cambridge hostel?'

'The same,' she said, laughing her husky laugh.

At the outbreak of peace, to celebrate, we'd ridden our bikes 15 miles to the Cambridge refugee hostel where she'd met tall, dark magnetic Magnus, also a German Jewish refugee.

The waiter handed us each a long menu. During the war, with limited selections, the menus had all been short. We girls had grown up most of our lives with rationing and short menus; food was still rationed, but the menu had lengthened slightly.

As always Cookie wore a crisp white blouse and skirt. Her thick blonde hair and bangs, though tossed carelessly, looked perfectly arranged, as did her aquiline nose and blue eyes. But she was now more serious, the prankster had left. I remembered that she had given me the orange diary which I still kept daily, and had organised a wonderful 15th birthday party for me. I remembered the knitting needle stabbing me.

'Hallo,' everyone said, greeting me. I smiled at everyone, 'Hallo.'

'What's happening to you?' I asked Cookie.

'I'll soon be joining my mother in Santiago,' Cookie said, soberly.

'Why's your mother in Santiago?' I asked, while Selma and Helga studied their menus.

'She escaped to Chile at the beginning of the war. She has a business there.'

'Is your father well?'

'My father has several factories in Shanghai. I'll visit him after I've seen my mother. '

These were the only divorced people I knew of.

'Is your father rich?' Helga asked Cookie.

Helga, still the smallest and most timid among us, had a child's figure but a sharp brain.

'Very,' Cookie said. 'But I won't have any money, yet.'

Cookie still spoke staccato, in a haughty tone, but since she'd met Alex, she'd become calmer, her voice now held a faint trace of sadness.

'Are you still seeing Bitch?' I asked.

'Only I'm allowed to call him by that name.'

'We all called him Bitch in the hostel,' I argued. 'But, okay, how are you and Alex?'

'We are doing very well, but his mother refuses to meet me. His parents were liberated from Auschwitz, one of the worst concentration camps, and they now live in London. Alex lives with them until he finishes high school.'

'Does she think Alex too young to be serious?'

'His mother asked him where I was born. Bitch told her I was born in Berlin and she said, 'If she says she's from Berlin, she must be Polish. I refuse to meet a Polish Jewish girl. You must marry a German Jewish girl.' She even made Bitch write me a letter swearing never to see me again. But Bitch and I speak on the phone all the time. We always will. We'll never, ever be parted,' she exclaimed.

'After the Germans killed millions of Jews and put her in a concentration camp his mother still admires the Germans?' I asked incredulously.

'Can you believe that some German Jews still think that they're better than Polish Jews? Bitch is so angry he says he's going to marry a *shiksa* just to spite his parents. I think they must have come out of concentration camp crazy. It would be natural after all that starvation and torture, wouldn't it?' Cookie said bitterly. I had never before heard her angry.

'Cookie,' I said, 'I'm so sorry. But when you're both 21 you can marry.'

'Six years is a long time to wait. Bitch still has to finish high school, and then medical school. He'll have no money. My parents also say I'm too young to be serious about anybody and won't give me any money. But they're wrong, they're so wrong,' Cookie cried. 'He's the only one for me, and will be for the rest of my life.'

She was silent a moment, her face somber. 'I have to join my mother in South America, but he'll stay in London. We may never meet again.' For once, Cookie the prankster was sad.

'But you're young. You'll meet someone else and marry,' I said.

'Never,' Cookie retorted.

'Then perhaps you'll wait for each other.'

'Perhaps, each on the other side of the world,' Cookie said, 'with no money.'

'What are your plans, Helga?' I asked, to soften the mood.

'I'm going to join my parents in Amsterdam. They were born in Germany but they refuse to set foot in that disgusting country again. My father is half paralyzed and my mother's heart is bad because in the concentration camp she worked in a steaming laundry 12 hours a day. I'll have to find a job, take a degree in social work at night, and devote the rest of my life to caring for them instead of becoming a sculptor,' she sighed.

'I didn't know you wanted to become a sculptor!' I exclaimed.

'Well, there was no chance for it during the war. And no chance now,' Helga said.

'How long has it been since you saw them?' Selma said.

'Ten years. They sent me away to England when I was four. I barely remember them. We don't even speak the same language. They speak only German and I speak only English. We'll be like strangers,' she cried.

'You're doing a real *mitzvah*, a good deed,' I said, 'by honouring your father and mother.'

'I so wanted to study art and be a sculptress. I'll never have time to practice my art now.'

'Poor Helga,' I said. 'At least your parents are alive.'

'Yes, and they suffered hell while I was safe in England.'

'Would it have been any better if you'd suffered, too?' Cookie said.

'I feel guilty that they suffered and I didn't,' Helga said.

'We all feel guilty for suffering less than our fellow Jews,' I said.

I felt guilty for all the Jews who suffered in concentration camps. I remembered I felt guilty for Freddy's wounds. In war, many suffered pain, and those who didn't, suffered guilt.

The waiter hovered discreetly in the background.

'Good grief, look at these prices,' I said.

'Never mind that. What are you going to do, Gilda?' Selma asked. 'I bet your parents are delighted to have you back.'

They weren't, but a refugee would never understand that. I believed their doomed parents had loved them. Weeping, they had wrenched their children from their breasts, and sent them to England to save their lives, never knowing if they'd ever see them again. For me, going away from home was regular. The war had just extended the time and changed the places to which Mummy sent me. Selma wouldn't understand that. I hardly understood it myself. I felt ashamed of being so unwanted, always a stranger. I felt like a refugee. But they would never believe me. So I never told them the truth. They had their own tragedies, why add to them?

I said instead, 'I plan to finish high school, go to university, study sociology, teach and write. As soon as I'm 21, I'll leave home, visit America and see Mr Goldstein and Frank Robinson, travel a little, and then I'll go to live in Israel.'

I didn't tell them that in washing my hair, Mummy had once deliberately scalded my head, nor that on Yom Kippur, fasting, I had come home to rest between services, and that she had dragged me by the hair to the sink and against my protests, dyed my hair a bright red. I'd cried, tried to cover the red hair with a scarf, but when I returned, ashamed, to evening Yom Kippur services, a religious schoolmate, Sarah Lampel thought I had dyed my hair on Yom Kippur. I didn't tell them that Mummy tried to force me to eat non-kosher food, harangued me to work in the shop on Shabbat, forbade me to see a nice Jewish refugee young man and made me take shorthand lessons with a Jewish convert to Christianity. She forbade me to see a girl friend because the girl was poor. She swore that when I married a religious man I would always have a big belly and be poverty stricken. The night before my matriculation exams she insisted I go out with two young men instead of letting me get a good night's sleep. The next day, exhausted, I passed the examination with honours only in Latin instead of in all subjects as I could have, had I slept the night before. At one time during a fight between my parents, Mummy aimed a plate at my father. My father pulled me in front of him. She hesitated only a fraction of a second then threw it anyway. It hit me hard and left a bruise. I became an insomniac. I never told anyone. As often as possible, I went away to friends and to the *Hachshara* (a simulated kibbutz in Thaxted). This *Hachshara* moved to Israel and became the Israeli kibbutz, Lavee.

The *Bet Din*, or Jewish House of Judgement was located in the East End within walking distance of my house. Rabbi Dayan Jacobovits was head of the *Bet Din*, and his daughter, Shulamit, joined my class at Spitalfieds High School. Her parents often invited me to their home for Shabbat lunch. I revelled in being with a large, Jewish family all educated in both Jewish and secular studies. Shulamit's brother, whom I knew as a skinny young man went on to become Chief Rabbi of Ireland, and eventually was knighted. So in spite of difficulties in my own home, I had good friends in the Jewish community; at school, I was responsible for Jewish girls' separate prayers at Spitalfields, and led a meaningful life outside the house.

It never occurred to me to 'tell' anyone about my mother; I would have felt disloyal. There was no adult I could confide in and telling tales was a crime worse than any other.

When I was 17 and developed insomnia, my mother took me to a fat, single Jewish doctor in his 40s. 'Is anything bothering you?' he asked.

'Nothing,' I lied. I could never have told tales about her. I did not understand for many years that my mother had become emotionally unstable. Perhaps she'd always been. Perhaps she had unconsciously sent me away for my own mental safety.

I looked at Selma. She'd spoken of her wish since she was 13. 'And you, Selma?'

'My plans are simple,' Selma said. 'When I am 16, I'm going to marry Magnus, have a home and children. That's all I've ever wanted.'

'Then you're the luckiest one among us,' Cookie said. 'You'll have your wish.'

'Magnus has an uncle in America who's in the scrap-metal business. Perhaps we'll all meet there,' Selma said.

'You think we're all going to America?' I laughed.

'I hope you'll come to my wedding,' she smiled.

The portly waiter in white shirt and tails approached.

'Ladies,' he said, smiling benignly, 'please let me know when you are ready to order.'

He bowed with a mocking smile and left. We looked at the menu, horrified at the prices.

'How much do you have on you?' I asked the girls.

Each of us furtively, peeked underneath the white tablecloth, consulting our purses. Between us we had one pound and fifty pence. Cookie gave her old raucous laugh. I kicked her.

'We said we'd eat in a fancy restaurant after the war and eat we will,' I said. 'Waiter?'

'Madame is ready to order?' the waiter asked me in mock seriousness.

'We'll have four rolls with butter and four glasses of water,' I said. The water was free.

'Certainly, Madame,' said the waiter, bowing. Smiling indulgently, he returned shortly, carrying high on a silver tray as if it were pheasant, four naked rolls, each on a white plate encircled with gold. Grinning, enjoying his private joke, his other hand clutched the handles of four heavy glasses of water, which years later, I realised were beer mugs.

We all clinked glasses in mid-air.

'Let's meet again in 20 years,' I said.

And we did. And still do.

ACKNOWLEDGEMENTS

Gilda Moss Haber, PhD

Among the many who read *Cockney Girl*, I wish to thank in particular, Elie Wiesel and Sir Martin Gilbert for their letters recommending publication of the entire manuscript. (Many chapters have been published in literary magazines.) I thank Yoma Ullman for her constant support and encouragement. Thanks to Lee Bland, William Pittman, Arleeta Lerner, Ruth Rochel Stokes, Phyllis Fisher, Nancy Goodman, Debbie Rudmann and the Yitzchak Cohen family, the late Rhoda Orlow and Ahuva Newberg and Ahuva's brilliant writer daughters, Rebecca Goldstein and Sarah Stern for support and encouragement.

I thank my late Great Aunt Frieda, sister to formidable Booba, my late father, Abraham Moscovitch and mother, Esther née Goldzummer, who both regaled me with tales of wicked and wise relatives, Uncle Mossie and cousins Gillian and Keith Stella, Geoffrey Robinson, Penina Brander of Alon Shvut, Israel deserve thanks for sharing memories of our British family. I thank my children, in particular, Jonathan, for their interest in our past British Jewish life, I also thank cousin Dolores Schwartz, granddaughter of Great Aunt Frieda, for sharing our American family branch information.

Deep appreciation goes to the Washington Biography Group, in particular Mark Pachter, Chair of the National Portrait Gallery and Pat McNees, WBG Secretary and the WBG group for constructive comments. Holocaust Museum workers win great appreciation, especially Judy Cohen, Michlean Amir, Ness Godin, Dr Herman Taube, Dr Rafael Medoff for archiving parts of *Cockney Girl* and referrals to publishers. Thanks to the London Jewish and Imperial War Museums, the RAF, Tower Hamlets and *The Evacuee* magazine for responding to research requests and to Bishop's Stortford, Newmarket and Ely residents.

Thanks to the Spitalfields girls for the reunion and responding to research requests. Thanks to Bill Shipman for our revisit to the East End together and the Taylors of Golders Green for information on the Rabbi Munk Congregation that sponsored the hostel. Thanks to Nurse, Mrs Wreschner and son Jonathan Wreschner of Efrat, Israel and to Herbert Heinemann and Irene Stein for sharing memories of the hostel.

Of the hostel group, as far as I know, only Alex, Cookie and I survive. We have all returned to the White House to visit, like ghosts of the past, and kindly received. The White House is now amazingly nearly 600 years old, a national monument, though much changed from 1943; the splendid, rambling garden and orchard of 1943–45 have been parceled out, the house divided into two. However, I thank present White House occupants, the Hopewells and Gambles for inviting me to address the Great Chesterford community in 2007 and for their hospitality.

I would love to hear from Sarah Lampel, Shulamit Rappaport, Marta Yellinek, Bessie Lyons and Joycey Kennel families; from Jocelyn Theilkul's, and anyone from Spitalfields Girl's School, London School of Economics: hathaber@gildahaber.com.

Special thanks to editor Laura Brown, and computer guru, Batman to the Rescue, Manasseh Katz. With this terrific imput, I completed *Cockney Girl* though much is omitted. I regret omitting *The Purim Play*, that we girls put on while in the hostel. My final thanks goes to DB Publishing UK, Laura Smith and all the staff for their sterling expertise and the author-friendly publishing journey.

Sometimes I feel like the ghost of Anne Frank, the girl she would have been had she lived. Of course, I thank God I did not endure her experiences and still wonder why so many 'cultured' are ruthlessly cruel. I learned from Mr Shapiro that Jews must judge others by the same rules applied to themselves, and never to discriminate other religions or races. However, her contemporary, and as a teenager who survived, we both concurrently kept a diary: hers called Kitty, mine Toots. We were both innocent, people and boy-fascinated, and we both felt the urge to record our experiences during exciting, traumatic, and for one of us, a deadly time in history. One of us died. Hopefully, her spirit lives on in those of us, refugees or evacuees, who live.